CSR, Sustainability, Ethics & Governance

Series Editors
Samuel O. Idowu, London Metropolitan University, Calcutta House, London, UK

René Schmidpeter, Cologne Business School, Cologne, Germany

In recent years the discussion concerning the relation between business and society has made immense strides. This has in turn led to a broad academic and practical discussion on innovative management concepts, such as Corporate Social Responsibility, Corporate Governance and Sustainability Management. This series offers a comprehensive overview of the latest theoretical and empirical research and provides sound concepts for sustainable business strategies. In order to do so, it combines the insights of leading researchers and thinkers in the fields of management theory and the social sciences – and from all over the world, thus contributing to the interdisciplinary and intercultural discussion on the role of business in society. The underlying intention of this series is to help solve the world's most challenging problems by developing new management concepts that create value for business and society alike. In order to support those managers, researchers and students who are pursuing sustainable business approaches for our common future, the series offers them access to cutting-edge management approaches.

CSR, Sustainability, Ethics & Governance is accepted by the Norwegian Register for Scientific Journals, Series and Publishers, maintained and operated by the Norwegian Social Science Data Services (NSD)

Belén Díaz Díaz • Samuel O. Idowu
René Schmidpeter • Nadia E. Nedzel
Mara Del Baldo • Irene Guia Arraiano
Editors

Building Global Societies Towards an ESG World

A Sustainable Development Goal in the 21st Century

Springer

Editors
Belén Díaz Díaz
Faculty of Economics and Business
University of Cantabria
Santander, Cantabria, Spain

René Schmidpeter
Business School
Bern University of Applied Sciences
Bern, Switzerland

Mara Del Baldo
Department of Economics, Society
and Politics
University of Urbino Carlo Bo
Urbino, Italy

Samuel O. Idowu
Guildhall School of Business and Law
London Metropolitan University
London, UK

Nadia E. Nedzel
Southern University Law Center
Baton Rouge, LA, USA

Irene Guia Arraiano
Polytechnic Institute of Lisbon
Lisbon Accounting and Business School
Lisbon, Portugal

ISSN 2196-7075 ISSN 2196-7083 (electronic)
CSR, Sustainability, Ethics & Governance
ISBN 978-3-031-56618-9 ISBN 978-3-031-56619-6 (eBook)
https://doi.org/10.1007/978-3-031-56619-6

This Springer imprint is published by the registered company Springer Nature Switzerland AG
The registered company address is: Gewerbestrasse 11, 6330 Cham, Switzerland

Dedicated to All Members of the Global Corporate Governance Institute (GCGI) Worldwide

Foreword

Behind the nowadays unprecedented popularity of the word sustainability, we find a significant evolution that seeks to highlight its transformative power, underpinned by the growing awareness of the impact of business activities on the environment, society, and long-term financial stability. Sustainability dominates not only the day-to-day conversations of consumers and individuals, but also the strategic agenda of institutions, regulators, all-sized corporates and, particularly, of the financial sector.

Over the past few years, we have witnessed a remarkable evolution around both the concept of sustainability and the ESG agenda itself, going from a niche concept to a mainstream consideration, from a lifestyle to a global emergency and, ultimately, a common responsibility. Unlike traditional CSR (Corporate Social Responsibility), Corporate Sustainability is the response from the core of the business to the needed balance resulting from the integration into the business practice of the environmental, social, and governance dimensions. The shift is clear: it has changed from looking backwards and trying to compensate negative externalities from a reputational and philanthropic standpoint to a integral long term value generation that meets demands and needs of a much wider range of stakeholders: shareholders, customers, but also employees and the communities in which the company operates. This evolution is very much aligned with the parallel transition from a shareholder capitalism to a stakeholder capitalism that was publicly stated by World Business Round Table. The SDGs (Sustainable Development Goals), 2030 Agenda, IPCC (Intergovernmental Panel on Climate Change) reports, Planet Boundaries, and the updated Global Risks Report from WEF (World Economic Forum) have all contributed to set and define the ESG agenda with a wider and more integrated approach.

There are many quantitative estimates of the investments required for the transition toward a decarbonized, sustainable, and inclusive economy. However, whatever the figure, all of them highlight the need to combine public and private efforts. Hence, the financial industry plays a fundamental role in driving sustainable development and responsible business practices. By financing these transitions, it is in the best position to ensure a more sustainable allocation of resources and a more accurate representation of risks and opportunities, taking into account not only economic but also social or environmental aspects.

Banco Santander advocates that the priorities of climate change and sustainability are an integral part of its strategy. We believe that we can help build a more sustainable and resilient world not only by financing green activity, but also by supporting the transition of others and favoring financial inclusion and showing responsibility with the social challenges of our communities. To this end, we have set specific, measurable, achievable, and ambitious public targets. Moreover, with our *"Santander Way"* culture we align our corporate strategy by doing things the right way.

Santander's aim to promote inclusive and sustainable growth builds on five main pillars: supporting the green transition; promoting financial inclusion and empowerment; providing financial health and education; investing in the community; and supporting higher education, employability, and entrepreneurship. Being the first two directly linked to our day-to-day activity, they merit further elaboration in the context of this foreword.

First, Banco Santander is deeply concerned with the climate emergency and committed with the decarbonization of the economy. Our ambition is to achieve net-zero CO_2 emissions group-wide by 2050 in support of the climate change objectives of the Paris Agreement. On the one hand, we are integrating climate within our governance, strategy, and risk management, defining courses of action and assessing procedures to transition portfolios and industries with the biggest impact on climate toward our net-zero target by 2050. On the other, we are helping our clients transition to a low carbon economy by committing financing (with a public target to mobilize €120bn in green finance by 2025 and €220bn by 2030) and by offering a wide range of products and services that integrate environmental, social, and good governance criteria, from socio-environmental risk policies to specific financing and non-financing offering.

And second, financial inclusion is seen as a key lever to reduce poverty, tackle inequalities, and increase prosperity. Financial inclusion means, for individuals and legal entities, having access to useful and affordable financial products that meet their needs—transactions, payments, savings, credit, and insurance—provided responsibly and sustainably. Every year Banco Santander empowers and helps millions of people through access, finance, or resilience. That is, helping them access financial services, create or develop their businesses, and empower them with the necessary skills to manage their finances through financial education. Under this global strategy, Santander group is committed to financially empower 15 million people between 2019 and 2025. Here in Spain we adapt our financial inclusion strategy to the demographic challenges we face (mainly depopulation and ageing).

Like Santander, most companies are increasingly integrating ESG. One of the primary catalysts for this integration has been the increasing recognition of the interconnectedness between ESG factors and financial performance. Studies have consistently shown that companies with strong ESG practices tend to outperform their peers in the long run. Moreover, in the short term we are witnessing a change in the perception of sustainability toward a competitive value. Sustainability is seen as a business opportunity but also as a unique chance to strengthen its relationship with clients. Responsible, sustainable, and purpose-driven companies generate more loyal customers. The latest published analyses show that the product itself is no longer a differential fact and that customers demand more transformation and more purpose.

Nonetheless, no matter how far along you are on your journey to fully integrate sustainability, we face many hurdles.

Regulatory convergence, smooth implementation, and tackling with new requirements and standards are proving increasingly challenging for companies. As ESG regimes expand, scrutiny increases, and green and social washing becomes a real threat. Simple and clear policy frameworks are needed to unlock demand for sustainable finance. Moreover, the ESG conversation will become more complex by adding to the central focus of climate change other topics such as biodiversity, energy justice, or cost of living crisis.

To overcome these challenges, we can leverage on active and transparent dialogue with internal and external stakeholders and foster cultural change while building organizational capabilities. What distinguishes leaders from laggards is that they place sustainability at the heart of their proposition as a lever of profitability and a powerful tool for good risk management.

Our banks will continue to play a central role in supporting businesses and individuals in the process, but we cannot make this alone. By working together financial institutions, regulators, academics, civil society organizations, and the wider business community we can create a more sustainable and inclusive future, where businesses and finance contribute to the well-being of society and the preservation of our planet.

Responsible Banking and Sustainability Director
at Santander Spain
Madrid, Spain

Marta Aisa Blanco

Preface

This book has selected some of the best papers presented at the 9th International Conference on CSR, Sustainability, Ethics and Governance held in Santander, Spain, in June 2023. The Conference was held under the auspices of the Global Corporate Governance Institute and hosted by Santander Financial Institute (SANFI) and the University of Cantabria. It was the ninth international gathering of this kind after successful events held in London, Nanjing, Cologne, Perth, Santander, Abu Dhabi, Lisbon (virtually), and Baton Rouge in previous years and has been the second hosted in Santander.

It was an excellent platform to deliberate on global themes of Corporate Social Responsibility, Sustainability, Ethics and Governance in all their various dimensions.

This event is one of the largest international conferences focusing on responsible business with delegates from over 18 nations that have presented their latest research and its practical implications for business, society, academia, and politics. 45 papers were presented by academics and business representatives.

This publication collects 16 papers out of those presented at the Conference that have been peer reviewed.

This book explores the current state of Corporate Social Responsibility from an international perspective with the aim to share ideas and visions for a sustainable future and to provide useful tips for academics, practitioners, and policy-makers in the context of the 2030 Agenda for Sustainable Development of the United Nations.

The Editors hope their readers would find the book interesting and that the networks it has created allow all of us to continue generating contributions to build global societies toward an ESG World.

Santander, Spain — Belén Díaz Díaz
London UK — Samuel O. Idowu
Bern, Switzerland — René Schmidpeter
Baton Rouge, LA, USA — Nadia Nedzel
Urbino, Italy — Mara Del Baldo
Lisbon, Portugal — Irene Guia Arraiano
December 2023

Acknowledgments

We are eternally grateful to a number of people who have made the publication of this book on *Building Global Societies Towards an ESG World: A Sustainable Development Goal in the 21st Century* a reality. We express our thanks to all our contributors who have worked tirelessly despite their heavy professional commitments to put together their chapters. We also thank the anonymous peer-reviewers of the chapters. Thank you to everyone.

We would also like to thank our publishing team at Springer headed by the Executive Editor, Christian Rauscher, Barbara Bethke, Anetter Weiss, Sneha Arunagiri and other members who have supported this project and all our other projects.

We are also grateful to our respective families for bearing with us during periods when we should have been with them but chose to spend the time meeting our obligations to completing the book.

Finally, we apologize for any errors or omissions that may appear anywhere in the text, please be assured that no harm was intended to anybody. Causing harm or discomfort to others is simply not the spirit of corporate social responsibility.

Introduction

In the context of the United Nations' 2030 Agenda for Sustainable Development, it is crucial for businesses to collaborate with governments and communities in addressing global challenges such as poverty, inequality, unemployment, and climate change. This collaboration is essential for fostering economic growth and international development.

There is a growing recognition of the necessity to incorporate Environmental, Social, and Governance (ESG) risks into investment valuation. This awareness is driven not only by societal demands for inclusive economic growth for future generations but also by empirical evidence demonstrating a positive correlation between profitability and adherence to ESG criteria.

The research on Corporate Social Responsibility (CSR) and ESG has expanded globally over the past three decades. Despite this evolution, numerous questions remain unanswered, highlighting the need for further research to comprehend the imperative of sustainability in both business and society.

This book aims to explore recent evidence about the significance of ESG for businesses. By gathering experiences from various countries, the primary objective is to contribute to a deeper understanding of the role of ESG in contemporary business practices.

The 16 chapters of the book from around the globe answer pertinent questions relevant to the title of the book—*Building Global Societies Towards an ESG World: A Sustainable Development Goal in the 21st Century.*

This book provides an insight into responsible business practices used by modern corporate entities in Europe, Asia, and North and South America, the continents where contributors of the 16 chapters included in the book are based. The book has been fortunate to join 32 authors from 12 different countries. They are all CSR scholars of repute and have worked in the field of CSR and its related disciplines for a number of years; they are members of the Global Corporate Governance Institute (GCGI) who attended the 9th Conference in Santander, Spain, in June 2023. The views many of them have expressed in their chapters are the results of their research studies on responsible business practices in the relevant countries featured in the book. We hope you will enjoy and find the chapters useful and understandable.

The book has been divided into four parts, each part focusing on issues relating to responsible business practices in the aforementioned continents. Part I—Looks at Ethics and Sustainable Business Models in five chapters. Part II—Focuses on Sustainable Finance in four chapters. Part III—Covers Corporate Governance in two chapters. Part IV—Looks at Global Perspectives and cases in five chapters. Let us now look briefly at each of the 16 chapters.

The very first chapter by Joel Wolff, Esko Hakanen, and Jarno Marttila entitled *Innovation ecosystems as communities of practise: Technologies for incentivising collaboration among competing actors* notes how recent conceptual advancements in the corporate social responsibility literature emphasize the necessity to increase collaboration between corporations and across sectors of society. Such cooperation is argued to produce innovation that better targets contemporary societal challenges and ensures a positive societal impact from business activities. The paper presents a solution based on decentralization technology (i.e., blockchain) offering a novel mechanism for incentivizing coopetition (a combination of cooperation and competition associated with elevated risk due to uncertain returns on the made investments). The authors posit that new digital technologies enable the development of effective mechanisms for incentivizing collaboration among competing actors. They also present a tangible solution for overcoming significant practical barriers to advancing coopetition in (business) ecosystems and argue that effective coopetition enables an accelerated innovation rate to solve the increasingly complex challenges facing societies worldwide.

The second chapter by Rosmel Rodriguez, Rute Abreu, and Armando Dias-da-Fé discusses climate racism in Brazil's favelas. Climate racism is a concept that has gained relevance in recent years, highlighting how certain marginalized populations disproportionately face the impacts of climate change. Usually located in the poorest regions of the planet, far from resources and under careless governments or with few conditions, these vulnerable communities need help to defend themselves from the increasingly constant climatic disasters. The authors' sample is the favelas of Brazil, extremely vulnerable communities composed mostly of Afro-descendants and other marginalized ethnic groups. Rodriguez, Abreu, and Diaz-da-Fé aim to identify and analyze the manifestations of climate racism in these communities, living conditions, exposure to environmental risks and lack of access to basic resources and services, as well as government policies and actions aimed at facing these challenges. The results of this study will contribute to the growing body of literature on climate justice, to a deeper understanding of how climate racism affects these communities, and to the creation of a solid scientific base useful for developing effective strategies.

Keiko Yokoyama and Yukihiro Wakuta, Japanese scholars, in third chapter focus on social entrepreneurship in social businesses created through collaboration. Although there have been some studies on collaboration based on the perspective of social entrepreneurship in recent years, the micro-level process has not been theoretically clarified. Specifically, the authors conducted a case study of a social business that addresses two social issues: solving the problem of discarded clothing and providing employment opportunities for people with disabilities and people who have difficulty in working. They analyzed the case by dividing the period of collaboration into two stages: the collaborative creation stage and the business development stage. As a result, it was found that the three elements of collective social entrepreneurship (framing, convening, and multivocality) and the formation of a platform with improvisation and openness are important in the collaborative creation stage. On the other hand, in the business development stage, social entrepreneurs' legitimization behavior and strategic compromises were observed.

In fourth chapter, Thornberg, Selvam, and Bastons focus on another important issue of CSR. The main purpose of the research is to differentiate the conceptualization of corporate sustainability (CS) from corporate social responsibility (CSR) and corporate solidarity. The objectives are threefold: first, they provide a literature review to show differences in the conceptualizations of the three phenomena and construct a corporate responsibility taxonomy; second, they perform a search of corporations' annual responsibility reports and websites to investigate and analyze their understandings of CS, CSR, and solidarity, and how they apply these terms in business rhetoric; third, based on data collected from 93 different corporations, they investigate the fit between what our taxonomy of corporate responsibility declares and how corporations conceptualize CS, CSR, and solidarity. The results from this study suggest that there is a high degree of ambiguity as to what constitutes corporate responsibility.

In the last chapter of Part I, Anna Napiórkowska, Polish scholar, devotes her chapter to the relationship between Managers' attitudes toward CSR and firm performance. Managers may view CSR activities from a cost or benefit perspective. In the scientific literature there is no compromise on the relationship between managers' motivators and attitudes toward CSR with organization's performance. The ambiguity of the results presented in the literature indicates the need for further research on the leaders' concern for responsibility and sustainability and its relationship with organizationally relevant long-term outcomes. The aim of the research is to identify the impact of managers' attitude toward CSR, their perception of costs and benefits of CSR activities on organization performance, both financial and non-financial. As a research method, a survey on a sample of 241 medium and large companies from fashion, cosmetics and household appliances and consumer electronics industries operating in Poland was conducted. Results show that there is a relation between managers' approach to CSR concept, depending on whether it is perceived in terms of benefits or costs. This relationship is different in the case of financial and non-financial results. The study contributes to the existing CSR literature, in particular on the relation between managers approach to CSR and company performance.

The very first chapter of Part II, which focuses on sustainable finance, is tiled *The Geopolitical Accountability of the Central Banks' Gold Reserve* and has been written by Rute Abreu and Carlos Pinho, two Portuguese scholars. The geopolitical accountability of Central Banks gold reserve is complex, multifaceted and its sustainability plays a significant role. It is important for stakeholders (governments, regulatory bodies, and the gold industry) to work together to ensure that the use of gold reserve is accountable, increase the stability and reduce tensions with the promotion of responsible practices.

In the second chapter of Part II, Francesco Martielli, Antonio Salvi, and Emanuele Doronzo devote the chapter to "Value challenge: the role of sustainability as an open innovation approach." One of the great challenges of our time is to answer the question: how do companies successfully compete in changing markets and environments while contributing to sustainable development? This study aims to find a possible answer to this question by investigating sustainability as an open innovation approach and analyzing its effects on enterprise value. Sustainability is characterized by different scores because an international standard has not yet been identified. Hence, not all sustainability scores can properly evaluate the sustainable strategies implemented by companies. Using a sample of European listed companies, the authors sought to identify which score best represents sustainability as an open innovation approach. In addition, through the implementation of a two-stage regression model, they found a positive effect of sustainability as an open innovation approach on firm value. Overall, their results highlighted that in a changing landscape, open innovation is a successful approach to address sustainability challenges, leading toward value creation.

Elena Sevilla Sanromán and Manuel Fernández López are the authors of the eighth chapter of the book. Their chapter entitled *Analysis of the emerging contribution of the Spanish insurance sector to the development of sustainable finance* explores how insurers themselves and the concept of sustainable finance have an impact on Sustainable Development Goals (SDG), and how they may help to accomplish them. Basing on interviews with experts and reference specialists and on the evaluation of best practices from leading entities, as well as a bibliographical review from institutional sources and monographs, the authors analyze the contribution of the insurance industry to sustainable finance in Spain and how this, in turn, is transforming the insurance industry itself.

The final chapter of Part II entitled *Sustainability in the main Spanish banking entities. A comparative analysis* written by Antonio Baraybar Fernández, Sandro Arrufat Martín, and Cristina González Oñate shows a comparative study of the most important Spanish financial institutions included in the Dow Jones Sustainability Index and identifies their strengths and weaknesses in sustainability. Their findings have allowed general conclusions to be drawn on the management of sustainability in organizations and make specific recommendations on areas for improvement in the companies considered in the sample.

Moving swiftly on to the first chapter of Part III, the tenth chapter of the book by Esko Hakanenç, Joel Wolff, Ville Eloranta, and Claire Shaw focuses on decentralization technologies, such as those based on blockchain, which provides exciting possibilities to coordinate cooperative actions and contributions of independent actors in favor of more sustainable operations. These technologies offer means to operationalize and define rules for the code of conduct for community members and create incentive mechanisms to motivate self-regulation among individuals. However, while such technologies add ways to increase alignment and avoid selfish actions, they are often perceived as technologically complex and challenging to comprehend and rarely utilized in solving collective, practical problems. The authors analyze four practical pilot experiments utilizing novel decentralization technology to engage community members toward more sustainable operations for collective benefits. The four pilots demonstrate how decentralization technology can support highly different communities to better attain their goals. All the pilots have made the solution easy to approach for the intended audience, greatly simplifying the complexity related to the technological protocols. These successes illustrate how translation practices facilitate self-regulation and a shared code of conduct for the community. This chapter illustrates how decentralization technologies can foster sustainable, collective governance for a more prosperous future for partnerships, people, and the planet.

The 11th chapter entitled *Empowering Change: Female External Directors and the Evolution of Corporate Governance in Japan* is authored by Naoe Imura. This chapter explores the significant shift in Japan's corporate governance landscape, emphasizing the integration of gender diversity with a focus on female external directors. By juxtaposing Japan's stakeholder-oriented model with international shareholder-centric practices, this study delves into the institutional and cultural transformations driving this evolution. The study provides a comparative analysis of board composition changes post-2015 and discusses the challenges and progress in enhancing gender diversity. With a focus on the pivotal role of external directors in fostering corporate accountability and performance, the research underscores the need for strategic policy reforms to increase female participation, which is critical for the advancement of corporate governance in Japan.

The final part of the book commences with the 12th chapter of the book entitled *Third Sector's Corporate Social Responsibility* by João de Sousa Assis. It is often perceived that business organizations, in their pursuit for profit, may negatively impact their stakeholders, while not-for-profit organizations do not. But is this always (or ever) the case? In the attempt to shed light on the answer to this question, the duties imposed to not-for-profit organizations' decision-makers are going to be critically reviewed under Portuguese Law. This comparison will allow us to understand if Portuguese law, as a case study, is fit for the purpose of regulating the action of not-for-profit organizations' managers in a way that resonates with the legitimate expectations of the communities where these organizations operate.

Olusegun Ehinfun and Paul R. Sachs authored 13th chapter entitled *An Analyses of the Effects of An Absence of Governance & Community Solutions in Combating Environmental Degradation.* This chapter highlights how the reality of climate action, biodiversity/environmental management, and remediation can be integrated within sustainable social strategies by governments for corporate community relationships. Transforming development policy in least developed countries (LDCs) can, perhaps, achieve sustainable impact, spurring the adoption of joined-up governance, coupled with climate and environmental policies. The participatory governance model being used in India is presented as one promising approach. Effective environmental management requires a coordinated effort between corporations, national stakeholders, and local communities. Such coordination can consider the different information that each party brings, structured in a manner that facilitates clear and complete communication. Using the examples of the Lake Chad and Niger Delta areas, this "model" of coordination is discussed. The successes and failures in those regions and the implications of actions taken are discussed as a guide for future environmental management.

The 14th chapter by Iury Prado Muci de Lima and Diego Fernandes Costa brings a deep and concise analysis of two approaches to incorporating mandatory Human Rights into business ESG frameworks: the recent European Commission directive on Corporate Sustainability Due Diligence; and the Strategic Climate Change Litigation practices in international private law. These new regulatory developments have an imminent influence on private sector activities. The concept of Environmental, Social, and Governance (ESG) has gained significant traction in recent years, with an increasing number of companies voluntarily adopting ESG principles. Often due to a vacuum left by the lack of regulation, companies measure ESG impacts based on financial risks versus the opportunities posed to their business. This approach can limit ESG's positive effect in the real world as companies may prioritize what is easier and what benefits more their brands. Also, there is limited transparency as companies do not disclose the more sensitive and controversial issues in their own operations and their value chain. However, the future of ESG is likely to be shaped by new laws and regulations that may constitute clearer Human Rights obligations to companies.

The 15th chapter by Heejung Yim, Tae Su Kim, Hyunmin Kang, and Seoyoung Kim explores how a company initiates and collaborates with the government and local entrepreneurs to transform its business while minimizing the risk of investment using the case of GS Caltex, a leading petroleum company in Korea. They discuss how their findings contribute to organically create the new mobility ecosystem and increase the sustainability of the community. The challenges in the transformation toward net-zero provide insights that can guide future tools for designing and building new ecosystems.

The final chapter of the book by Paola Martina Pucha Medina, Rebeca García-Ramos, and Belén Díaz Díaz focuses on the importance of internal control in Ecuador's Popular and Solidarity Sector, a cornerstone in the country's economic and social structure. This sector, evolving as a counterweight to conventional financial structures, provides accessible and community-oriented financing alternatives, fostering financial inclusion and community empowerment. Despite excellent microfinance models, traditional management mechanisms prove insufficient, prompting a need for a closer analysis of internal control in the face of evolving challenges. The chapter explores different internal control definitions, perspectives, and applications in financial sector institutions, emphasizing its insertion into microfinance in Ecuador.

The 16 chapters of the book from across the globe in our view have made immense contributions to improving our understanding about ESG and have set up ideas for improving our world and achieving the Sustainable Development Goals.

University of Cantabria
Santander, Spain
Belen Diaz Diaz

London Guildhall School of Business and Law
London, UK
Samuel O. Idowu

Contents

About the Editors

Belén Díaz Díaz holds Ph.D. in Finance. She is Associate Professor of Finance at the University of Cantabria (Spain) and Academic Director at Santander Financial Institute (SANFI). Previously, she has been Vice-Dean of the Faculty of Economics and Business Administration and Director of Campus and Social Development at the University of Cantabria. She has been visiting researcher at the University of California in Berkeley, the London School of Economics, the University of Technology in Sydney, and at different universities in Mexico, Chile, Brazil, Argentina, and Morocco. Professor Díaz is author of several papers about CSR, Corporate Governance, banking and corporate finance in academic journals and books. The quality of her research was recognized with the "Sanchis Alcover Award," awarded by the Scientific Association of Economy and Management in 2006. Since 1996, she has written several reports and developed more than 50 R&D projects about different financial and economic issues commissioned by different public and private entities.

Samuel O. Idowu is a Senior Lecturer in Accounting and Corporate Social Responsibility at London Guildhall School of Business & Law, London Metropolitan University, UK. He researches in the fields of Corporate Social Responsibility (CSR), Corporate Governance, Business Ethics and Accounting and has published in both professional and academic journals since 1989. He is a freeman of the City of London and a Liveryman of the Worshipful Company of Chartered Secretaries and Administrators. Samuel is the President of the Global Corporate Governance Institute (GCGI). He has led several edited books in CSR and he is the Editor-in-Chief of three Springer's reference books—the Encyclopedia of Corporate Social Responsibility, the Dictionary of Corporate Social Responsibility and an Editor-in-Chief of the International Journal of Corporate Social Responsibility and the Encyclopaedia of Sustainable Management. He is also a Series Editor for Springer's books on CSR, Sustainability, Ethics and Governance. One of his edited books won the most Outstanding Business Reference book Award of the American Library Association (ALA) in 2016 and another was ranked 18th in the 2010 Top 40 Sustainability Books by *Cambridge University, Sustainability Leadership*

Programme. He is on the Editorial Boards of the International Journal of Business Administration, Canada and Amfiteatru Economic Journal, Romania. Samuel has delivered a number of Keynote Speeches at national and international conferences and workshops on CSR and has on two occasions 2008 and 2014 won Emerald's Highly Commended Literati Network Awards for Excellence. To date, Samuel has edited several books in the field of CSR, Sustainability and Governance and has written seven forewords to books. Samuel has served as an external examiner to a number of UK Universities and has examined PhD theses in the UK, South Africa, Australia, the Netherlands, and New Zealand.

René Schmidpeter is professor for sustainable management at the IU—International University in Munich and Research Professor at the BFH in Bern. He is visiting professor at ISM in Vilnius as well as guest professor at various universities worldwide. He is a series editor for Springer's *CSR, Sustainability, Ethics and Governance* books, editor of the *Encyclopedia of Sustainable Management* (ESM), and an editor of the *Dictionary of Corporate Social Responsibility* (DCSR). His research and teaching activities focus on the management of Corporate Social Responsibility, international perspectives on CSR, Social Innovation and Sustainable Entrepreneurship as well as the relationship between business and society. He has published widely and is the editor of the German *management series on Corporate Social Responsibility* at Springer Gabler and is member of various think-tanks, sustainability initiatives, and advisory boards in Europe and abroad. He has conducted research for the Federal Ministry of Education and Research, the European Union, the Bavarian Ministry of Social Affairs, the Anglo-German Foundation, the Bertelsmann Foundation as well as the Deutsche Forschungsgesellschaft (DFG). He works closely with chambers of commerce and businesses in Europe to develop innovative strategies and entrepreneurial solutions for the sustainable transformation of business and society.

Nadia Nadzel In addition to her roles with the GCGI, Nadia E. Nedzel, J.D., LL.M. is a Professor of Law Emerita at Southern University Law Center in Baton Rouge. The focus of her research is on the interaction among the "*Rule of Law, Economic Development, and Corporate Governance*," which is also the title of her recent book (Edward Elgar 2020). Her most recent publication is *Fuller, Dworkin, Scientism, and. Liberty: The Dichotomy between Continental and Common Law Traditions and their Consequences,* Laws Journal: Special Issue (Zurich University-MDPI. Pub. Beijing): https://www.mdpi.com/2075-471X/12/3/37. She is an attorney licensed to practice in Louisiana. Professor Nedzel received her BA from Northwestern University in English, French, Spanish, and Russian; her J.D. Magna Cum Laude is from Loyola (New Orleans), and her LL.M. (with Honors) is from Northwestern School of Law in Chicago. She teaches Common Law Contracts, Civil Law Obligations, Civil Law Sales and Lease and both International Law and International Business Transactions. In addition to teaching law, she clerked for a U.S. 5th Circuit judge, practiced International Trade and Admiralty, and lectured around the world—including discussing the Rule of Law with the justices of the Russian Constitutional Court.

Mara Del Baldo is Associate Professor (recognized as Full Professor by the Italian National Agency—ANVUR) of Business Administration; Economics of Sustainability and Accountability at the University of Urbino (Italy), Department of Economics, Society and Politics. She has extensive experience in collaborative research, in conjunction with universities and private industry. She visited several European Universities, i.e. the University of Vigo (Spain), the New Bulgarian University of Sofia (Bulgaria), the Corvinus University in Budapest (Hungary), and the University of Craiova (Romania). She is a member of the European Council for Small Business, the Center for Social and Environmental Accounting Research (St. Andrews), the SPES Institute, and the European Business Ethics Network (EBEN) Italia, as well of different Italian scientific associations. Mara is also a member of the academic advisory committee in the Global Corporate Governance Institute (USA). She is part of the editorial board and she serves as a reviewer of several scientific journals, including the Springer's International Journal of Corporate Social Responsibility. Among her main research interests are: entrepreneurship and SMEs; Corporate Social Responsibility; entrepreneurial leadership and business ethics; social accountability; integrated and sustainability reporting and accounting and gender. She published in several Italian and foreign journals as well as in national and international conferences proceedings and books, including the Springer Series CSR, Sustainability, Ethics & Governance.

Irene Guia Arraiano PhD in Financial Economics and Accounting, is a Professor in Lisbon Accounting and Business School, Lisbon Polytechnic Institute (ISCAL), Lisbon, Portugal. She wrote her PhD-thesis about "Analysis of Socially Responsible Investing in European Stock Markets." She earned both Bachelor and Master's in Applied Mathematics Statistics and Operational Research at the Faculty of Sciences at Lisbon's University. Irene Arraiano is a Professor in the Mathematics Department and currently teaches Operational Research. She is a mobility coordinator in the Erasmus + Program for the Business course. She is a member of the Research Centre of Évora University (CEFAGE) and the main research interests predominantly focus on the interaction between Finance, Mathematics, Corporate Social Responsibility and Investing. Irene Arraiano has actively participated in the organization of National and International scientific events as the Chair of the Scientific and Organizational Committees. She participates in National and International Conferences as well as publishes in International academic journals. Throughout her academic career, Irene Arraiano has taken part of various scientific and management bodies of ISCAL, such as Scientific, Directive, Pedagogical Councils and Assembly of ISCAL representatives.

Part I
Ethics and Sustainable Business Models

Innovation Ecosystems as Communities of Practise: Technologies for Incentivising Collaboration Amongst Competing Actors

Joel Wolff, Esko Hakanen, and Jarno Marttila

1 Introduction

Climate change is popularly considered the most urgent problem calling for coordinated actions, but it is only one amongst several problems challenging the welfare potential of future generations. For instance, Rockström et al. (2009) introduced planetary boundaries as risks facing Earth's entire ecosystem, and the United Nations launched both the Millennium Development Goals and the subsequent Sustainable Development Goals to frame wide-arching challenges that the nations of the world should collectively aim to mitigate (United Nations, 2015). Challenges such as these are often referred to in the sustainability literature by the term wicked problems, a concept lacking a clear common definition but widely used to describe challenges lacking simple solutions or even unsolvable challenges (Lönngren & van Poeck 2021). In the management literature, such challenges have collectively been

J. Wolff (✉)
Department of Industrial Engineering and Management, School of Science, Aalto University, Espoo, Finland
e-mail: joel.wolff@aalto.fi

E. Hakanen
Department of Industrial Engineering and Management, School of Science, Aalto University, Espoo, Finland

Strategic Management, School of Management, University of Vaasa, Vaasa, Finland
e-mail: esko.hakanen@aalto.fi

J. Marttila
Department of Industrial Engineering and Management, School of Science, Aalto University, Espoo, Finland

Streamr Network, Zug, Switzerland
e-mail: jarno.marttila@aalto.fi

B. Díaz Díaz et al. (eds.), *Building Global Societies Towards an ESG World*, CSR, Sustainability, Ethics & Governance,
https://doi.org/10.1007/978-3-031-56619-6_1

called *societal grand challenges*, which "by their very nature, require coordinated and sustained effort from multiple and diverse stakeholders toward a clearly articulated problem or goal" (George et al., 2016, p. 1881).

The request for multiple stakeholders to coordinate actions in support of sustainable development has been echoed for over a decade (Kemp et al., 2005; Elkington, 2018), but how to best manage such coordination remains to be seen. Partly in response to such calls, the concept of corporate social responsibility (CSR) has been reformed during the last decades. Concepts such as the new generation of CSR, embedded CSR, and CSR 4.0 all emphasise the necessity to increase cross-sectoral collaboration that would enable businesses to innovate solutions which ensure a positive impact from their activities (Aguinis & Glavas, 2013; Munro, 2020; Stohl et al., 2009). Such collaboration implies a need for an ecosystem of actors which can coordinate collective innovation activities by producing shared system-level outputs (Wolff & Hakanen, 2021; Wolff et al., 2023).

In this work, we introduce a technological solution for coordinating stakeholder activities that could address societal grand challenges. While this solution is based on a relatively well-known "blockchain" technology, the presented implementation of the solution differs significantly from the prevalent approaches in utilising such technologies (Hakanen et al., 2022). Put differently, the suggested solution does not assimilate the most common applications of the technology, such as Bitcoins or stock exchanges, for trading them or other cryptocurrencies, but utilises a similar decentralisation technology to create a system for incentivising collaboration among competing actors within a community. In the following, after briefly introducing the literature on ecosystems (Autio & Thomas, 2021) and communities (Hawley, 1950), we reflect both against the concept of communities of practice (Wenger, 1998). After a short note on research design, we present key insights on the "Streamr Community Awards" case, an effort to coordinate open-source software development in a new way. Last, after summarising our main implications, we conclude by discussing the applicability of such an approach to other complex issues facing societies worldwide.

2 Background

2.1 On Ecosystems, Coopetition, and Incentives

In short, management research generally considers *ecosystems* "a set of actors that contribute to the focal offer's user value proposition" (Kapoor, 2018). In simpler terms, the ecosystem refers to a situation where multiple participants (e.g., firms and organisations) voluntarily invest their resources (including money, work, or other assets) in producing a collective output that is often considered more valuable than the sum of its parts. This stream of literature was initiated by Moore's seminal paper that described ecosystems as "a new ecology of competition" and argued that "only truly sustainable advantage comes from out-innovating the competition" as "companies co-evolve capabilities around a new innovation" (Moore, 1993, pp. 75–76). While the ecosystem concept has been investigated from multiple complementary perspectives in the management context (Autio & Thomas, 2021), two main views stand out. First, *business ecosystems* have typically been defined as a set of actors connected by their shared part in enabling the production of a specific value proposition (Autio & Thomas, 2021). Second, *innovation ecosystems* focus on collaborative innovation and the production of knowledge (Granstrand & Holgersson, 2020).

Both streams of the ecosystem literature exhibit, at least implicitly, coordinated innovation activities carried out between a diverse set of interdependent actors (Autio & Thomas, 2021) that depend on "coopetition" (Bacon et al., 2020). Drawing from the principles of game theory, coopetition is a derivative of "competition and cooperation" (Brandenburger & Nalebuff, 1997). It is defined as "cooperating with a competitor to achieve a common goal or get ahead" (Brandenburger & Nalebuff, 2021). Accordingly, coopetition is associated with elevated risk and uncertain incentives (Gernsheimer et al., 2021) and is likely to demotivate investments in enabling technologies that are difficult to monetise but are necessary for realising the intended focal value proposition (Teece, 2018). Yet, our technologies and economic models are poorly suited for tracking contributions beyond their monetary value. Such uncompromising focus on economic aspects is firmly against the ideas of a triple bottom line and sustainability (Elkington, 2018).

While ecosystems are often perceived as a potential solution for coordinating collective contributions (Adner, 2017; Kapoor, 2018; Wolff et al., 2023), past research shows how coordinating activities without social bonds is challenging (Ghosh, 1998; Hakanen et al., 2022). New approaches may be needed to provide incentives to overcome coopetition obstacles to support more sustainable ecosystems (Lovett & Thomas, 2021). As the literature describes, ecosystems may rely on members and stakeholders who act voluntarily, remain unknown, or operate without hierarchical coordination.

In other words, the boundaries of an ecosystem are not clearly defined and may include authorities, businesses, and end-users, all influencing the ecosystem's outcome (Adner, 2017; Wolff et al., 2023). Ecosystems' boundary conditions are often defined vaguely or rely on subjective interpretations (Wolff et al., 2023). Accordingly, Kœnig (2012) criticises Moore for having defined the concept of the business ecosystem so vaguely that it has confused how to determine the ecosystem boundaries. Since system boundaries are a central aspect of any systems analysis (Brown, 1966), such criticism of loosely defined boundaries is well-founded. In their review, Granstrand and Holgersson (2020) stress that the interrelations amongst actors are crucial for innovation ecosystems. Still, the outer boundaries remain undefined, except for in the regionally defined innovation ecosystem (Oh et al., 2016). The importance of system boundaries, therefore, deserves future attention.

More recently, Hakanen et al. (2022) extended such critique to the context of decentralised systems, which can, indeed, help to coordinate collective efforts but are likely to aggravate the confusion regarding the participants of the ecosystem, its boundaries or even the overall goal of different interactions. In such a context, a more appropriate term might not be an ecosystem but a more profound notion of a "community." For example, open-source software development has long been considered a community guided by alternative incentive mechanisms. Sometimes, such work has been referred to as a new form of "gift economy" (Barbrook, 1998) that exemplifies the "trade" of free goods and services within the community (Ghosh, 1998). The success of such collective outputs illustrates the force of communities.

2.2 Communities and Their Impact on the Ecosystems

The *community* concept has been studied in several scientific disciplines for at least a few centuries, but a standard and precise definition has yet to be discovered. Instead, the only common characteristic is that a community is a collection of people, while the defining aspects of this collection, such as the community boundaries, have remained context-dependent (Jewkes & Murcott, 1996). Hawley (1950) ties his analysis of communities to a foundational human ecology by showing how societal structures can be logically derived from the axiomatic interrelationships between organisms and their environment.

Hawley's (1950) conceptualisation of a community is not too dissimilar to the method that Moore (1993) applied in his seminal paper on business ecosystems, comparing innovative businesses to natural ecosystems of species. However, Moore does not outright explain the conceptual relationship between the business ecosystem and the community (or provide any definition for a community) while constantly implying that a business ecosystem is a community. Most often, communities refer to groups of individuals, and ecosystems refer to organisational actors, but this distinction is far from obvious.

Based on such conclusions, we can infer that business ecosystems and communities are a group of actors (actors which can be both individuals or groups in themselves), varyingly depending on the surrounding society or environment. Similarly, in his work on communities, Hawley argues that from "the standpoint of the actual business of living … the individual is a unit but in an atomistic sense … [and] has no existence apart from a larger whole" (Hawley, 1950, p. 207). Hence, a human being is a collection of organisms, such as single cells, bacteria, and fungi, all working in a coordinated manner to support the individual human. Additionally, a human is only a small part of a larger community which, according to Hawley, itself constitutes but a part of a larger society. From that notion, we can infer that the unit of a community, although typically defined as a human being, does not limit the conceptual model of a community. Yet, we concur that the legitimacy of drawing on natural organisms' behaviours and functional systems should be approached cautiously.

The distinction is simply in the units that make up the group and how the group interrelates with other parts of the larger society. According to Hawley, the measure of dependency is an essential aspect of communities, where an independent community is highly self-sufficient and "produces most of the goods and services it consumes" (Hawley, 1950, p. 223), while a dependent community cannot survive in isolation because it "obtains its sustenance materials through exchange with other communities" (Hawley, 1950, p. 225). These shared characteristics support our notion that similar incentive mechanisms may serve ecosystems and communities.

Based on Hawley's (1950) theory on community structure, we argue that ecosystems can be described as communities, showing varying degrees of dependency on external systems. Yet, such a claim long predates our work. For instance, drawing from Hawley's ideas, Hannan and Freeman (1977) argued that each organisational form is a direct consequence of its surrounding environment shaping its development. Moreover, since humans constitute a part of a natural ecosystem, the artificial societies we create are by extension natural in the same sense as we are. Therefore, ecosystems of human communities share the characteristics of any community, only at a different level of inquiry.

2.3 Learning in Communities and Ecosystems: Communities of Practice

We have now established the link between communities and ecosystems, but the scope changes when exploring the community of practice. Strongly linked to communities and ecosystems, *communities of practice* have been defined as a "relatively informal, intra-organizational group specifically facilitated … to increase learning or creativity" (Cox, 2005, p. 538). The original works elaborating on this concept highlight how social practices affect and construct the identities of the active participants (Wenger, 1998). However, these communities are in various, partially conflicting, discussions assigned the traits of sharing a common purpose, developing an identity, and solving problems (Cox, 2005).

The community of practice evolves over time, and because it is defined by a shared sense of purpose or identity, it cannot, strictly speaking, be formed by design, only enabled by actions leading to its formation in time (Wenger, 1998). Such a view poses a stark contrast to the ecosystem literature: the works on management have often portrayed the ecosystem as a relatively static and predictable construct in which the participation is primarily determined by technological or operational interdependencies (e.g., Adner, 2017; Jacobides et al., 2018; Kapoor, 2018). Hence, unlike the business or innovation ecosystem (Moore, 1993; Granstrand & Holgersson, 2020), a community of practice is far from static. Consequentially, a member of such a community may not necessarily be aware of being part of the community (Roberts, 2006).

Such an aspect of unknown or unintended membership in an ecosystem has not garnered attention in the management literature—perhaps due to challenging the inherent notion of "management" of operations and actions. Despite some more recent works, especially ones focusing on ecosystems facilitated by decentralised systems (e.g., Hakanen et al., 2022; Mindel et al., 2018), have begun to explore such questions, it remains uncertain whether an actor in an ecosystem always knows about their role as part of it and how that affects the boundary conditions. The prevalent view in the management literature still considers ecosystems and their boundaries (including key partners, followers, and other stakeholders) a matter to be resolved with a concise analysis of the industry, the potential participants, and the technological complementarities amongst them (e.g., Adner, 2022; Jacobides et al., 2018; Teece, 2018). In turn, the works on the innovation ecosystem have a different reason for assuming a clear definition of ecosystem boundaries, as its actors are often defined as all parties relevant to a specific innovation activity (Granstrand & Holgersson, 2020). Thus, one of the contentions raised by, for instance, Oh et al. (2016), is the notion that innovation ecosystems are artificial, and therefore designed, which starkly contrasts slowly emerging and developing natural ecosystems.

Next, to bridge the reviewed literature and address the challenge of coordinating stakeholder activities for societal challenges, we focus on decentralisation technologies. In particular, we will present evidence from a pilot experiment on aligning and incentivising community members in their efforts to develop open-source software. Hence, we connect to the long tradition of investigating the role of communities and incentives in such work (e.g., Barbrook, 1998; Ghosh, 1998) and extend this legacy with more recent examples exploring novel technologies in providing distributed governance mechanisms and non-monetary incentives (Elo et al., 2023; Hakanen et al., 2022; Mindel et al., 2018). After briefly describing our research design and the pilot case, we provide evidence on how digital technologies enable incentive mechanisms to drive coopetition within an ecosystem.

3 Research Design and Case Description

Our evidence is based on a pilot experiment conducted as part of the EU-funded project ATARCA (Accounting Technologies for Anti-Rival Coordination and Allocation, https://atarca.eu). The project was designed to test the effectiveness of non-monetary incentivisation and accounting mechanisms in guiding communal work. The Streamr Community pilot focused on open-source software development and was "intended to motivate and coordinate ecosystem stakeholders' activities toward the ecosystems' goals" (Hakanen et al., 2023, p. 146). The ATARCA consortium has compiled reports that provide both qualitative and quantitative evidence on the observed impact of these experiments. Our insights are the result of abductive analysis.

According to Ketokivi and Choi (2014), abduction is particularly useful when elaborating on theory and showing its practical implications for explaining a specific phenomenon. In the process, we connect previously unrelated concepts. By elaborating on the potential offered by a pilot case in a particular community, we infer that there is a high likelihood for a derivative of the technology to incentivise ecosystems as well. In this work, OpenAI's large language model service ChatGPT3.5 was utilised, although only to a limited degree. It was used in two stages of the writing of this chapter: first, as a conversational partner to explore concepts, ideas, and challenges, and second, during the initial drafting stage of the section discussing the pilot case, for recommending a suitable and intelligible form for presenting an otherwise unreasonably challenging section filled with technical jargon.

The pilot's primary focus was exploring alternative incentivisation mechanisms to guide the work towards the Streamr project. Streamr is a blockchain project dedicated to developing a decentralised peer-to-peer data-sharing network. Developing the core technology and building decentralised platforms and other supporting services rely on the collaborative efforts of Streamr community members. Hence, blockchain projects provide a fitting context for investigating the mechanisms for coordinating joint innovation activities (Bacon et al., 2020) that showcase coopetition. The Streamr community comprises diverse participants and stakeholders worldwide, all working towards a shared mission of successfully constructing and operating infrastructure for decentralised real-time data transport. Members' efforts aim towards a common goal while simultaneously competing with other participants for the best or most suitable solution for a specific purpose (Brandenburger & Nalebuff, 2021). Hence, the pilot sought to enhance the Streamr platform and cultivate a more engaged community by incentivising high-quality community contributions while increasing the alignment of member contributions.

The pilot addressed such challenges by searching for means to incentivise the community members in non-monetary ways while providing fair recognition to the contributing members and aligning the collective efforts more effectively. In the Streamr Community pilot, the existing Streamr platform was enhanced with "anti-rival tokens" (i.e., tokens that gain value in use and have little to no exchange value) through the development of a new standard for shareable non-fungible tokens (sNFTs; see Hakanen et al., 2023) which was launched as an EIP-5023 token standard (Marttila & Moravek, 2022). The resulting system provided a means to account for "anti-rival" value to assess, both qualitatively and quantitatively, the impact of a new type of non-monetary token-based incentive mechanism on the Streamr community members (Hakanen et al., 2023).

4 Targeting Contributions in a Community of Practice

Within the Streamr ecosystem, community members assume various roles and responsibilities. They actively participate in the system's governance by submitting improvement proposals, voting on such proposals, engaging in discussions, and sharing their knowledge and ideas. Additionally, many community members contribute to the technical infrastructure of the peer-to-peer network by providing bandwidth and hardware for data transport. As such, the Streamr ecosystem fits the broader definition of a community of practice (Cox, 2005).

The pilot implemented three types of tokens to incentivise such activities: Streamr Community Award tokens, Like tokens, and Endorse tokens. Streamr

Community Award tokens represent contributions evaluated, verified, and awarded by Streamr project staff. Recipients of these tokens can further share them with other community members to recognise their participation in the awarded community contribution by minting a copy of the received Community Award token to another community member. Each token will have an accompanying description of the member contribution. For instance, for the shared Community Awards, this appending metadata will detail how the recipients have assisted the original contributor. In addition, Like and Endorse tokens are associated with specific Streamr Award tokens and enable community members to express their preferences for certain contributions. Like tokens can be minted by anyone within or outside the Streamr community, whereas Endorse tokens can only be minted by community members who have received a Streamr Award token. Minters of Endorse tokens also have the option to leave short messages of appreciation or encouragement to the owners of Streamr Award tokens through the pilot platform. Such an approach appreciates the community as comprised of interdependent populations (Hawley, 1950) that are shaped and impacted by their environment (Hannan & Freeman, 1977).

Accordingly, the designed reward system carefully addressed the motivational factors for attracting cooperation among community members (Brandenburger & Nalebuff, 2021; Gernsheimer et al., 2021). The Streamr Award tokens recognised contributions and served as a registry or history of significant contributions to the Streamr community. They also give examples for the community, providing insights into the types of efforts and contributions previously acknowledged. The community members can compare, sort, and filter the recognised community contributions based on their perceived significance by applying likes and endorsements to awarded contributions.

The pilot's results were evaluated through both quantitative analysis and community surveys. Observed changes in community size, messaging frequency, awarded contribution tokens, and the minting of like and shared award tokens were measured quantitatively in the platform. The results showed that the community members were active in minting and sharing tokens. This outcome indicated improved efficiency in allocating members' resources based on their preferences, helping the community attain collective goals (Elo et al., 2023; Hakanen et al., 2023). The survey responses highlighted that Streamr Awards positively impacted the Streamr community. The survey respondents agreed that distributing Streamr Awards benefited the entire community. Participants reported spending more time contributing to the Streamr project due to the incentives provided by Streamr Awards. Additionally, metadata associated with Streamr Awards helped respondents identify potential collaborators within the community. These findings indicate that Streamr Awards increased the overall allocative efficiency within the community by guiding contributions and aligning conducted work (Elo et al., 2023).

In summary, the results of the Streamr pilot experiment on tokenised incentives demonstrated that it is possible to increase community engagement and motivate individuals to contribute more effectively (Hakanen et al., 2022). Part of this increased motivation was related to establishing more engaging and egalitarian governance practices (Kemp et al., 2005) that helped support a community of practice

(Cox, 2005). Although the tokenised incentives in this experiment have been centrally managed to this stage to streamline the adoption of the new service, the Community Award tokens could easily be decentrally managed in the future. The pilot experiment, which introduced tokenised incentives through Streamr Awards, increased community members' activity levels on the Streamr Network. This suggests that the incentives motivated individuals to participate actively in the community. While the incentive mechanisms were designed to support and reward cooperative actions within the network (Brandenburger & Nalebuff, 2021), they added coopetition within the community by increasing transparency on the actions other community members found valuable or not (Elo et al., 2023; Hakanen et al., 2022). The pilot experiment also positively impacted community members' engagement and activity levels, as reflected in the increase in active users and message volume on the Discord platform during the pilot period compared to the pre-pilot period.

5 Implications for Incentivising Coopetition in Ecosystems

Moore (1993) was specific about the notion that business ecosystems work cooperatively and competitively (i.e., businesses are in coopetition). Concerning ecology, this reflects how organisms within a natural ecosystem compete for the resources they all share while exchanging, directly or indirectly, those they do not. In the community setting, Hawley calls this a "symbiotic-commensalistic phenomenon" (Hawley, 1950, p. 209). It is easy to understand why such a combination has led to positive results for the end-users, as they can enjoy the additional value created by complementarities between different products while knowing that prices are kept low thanks to rivalling providers (Brandenburger & Nalebuff, 2021). Thus, coopetition can enable offerings that derive from the more efficient combination of existing resources and opportunities.

The possibility of integrating several competing offerings in a user-friendly manner can challenge conventional value chains and make them more diversified (Kapoor, 2018). For example, there is a dedicated movement to decentralise the governance of traditional transportation through concepts such as open Mobility as a Service (Wolff & Hakanen, 2021). As argued by the authors, such approaches attempt to "optimize efficiency from a user perspective, thus promoting modularity, fragmentation, and complementary market offerings in an open ecosystem" (ibid., p. 22). Such possibilities directly connect to the premises of coopetition, as the increased openness and modularity allow for cooperative solutions to serve the users better. At the same time, the fragmentation of the offerings leads to intensified competition amongst the providers.

Hence, there is an apparent demand for solutions that create additional incentives for coopetition and more diversified offerings, such as ones based on distributed ledgers (Elo et al., 2023; Hakanen et al., 2023). We can elaborate on this claim with the previous example on mobility; while the technology required to restructure mobility service systems is simple enough, it remains to be seen who will reap the benefits from the restructuring. A thriving ecosystem largely depends on shared enabling technologies (Granstrand & Holgersson, 2020; Teece, 2018), as their quality and possibilities largely define those of all market offerings. In the case of mobility, the enabling technologies are open application programming interfaces that allow for interoperability between all other functions (Wolff & Hakanen, 2021). But while the utility of such a technology is universal, the incumbents are disincentivised to contribute, as they fear losing market shares from the disruption. We argue that such incentive mechanisms are required for realising ecosystems and, for instance, the user-centric value propositions associated with new mobility systems (Wolff & Hakanen, 2021). A similar conclusion can be derived from various other industries.

In response, a crucial avenue for further exploration is the concept of "decentralised autonomous organisation" (DAO), which is said to facilitate governance models for a more sustainable society (Atzori, 2015; Lovett & Thomas, 2021). While the Streamr community pilot offered promising indications of developing more substantial incentives for coopetition in ecosystems, the system relies on centralised governance mechanisms to a large extent, posing questions about whether an ecosystem approach is applicable (Elo et al., 2023; Wolff et al., 2023). In the pilot, a preselected small group of managers maintain the power to mint the original tokens. As such, the technology does not yet support a fully decentralised or collective management of community goals. The presented Streamr Community pilot did not have suitable management and governance practices but relied on the leading team (i.e., Streamr employees) to make the first judgement on contributions to reward. Since past research has emphasised that more participatory governance can facilitate sustainable development (Kemp et al., 2005; Lovett & Thomas, 2021), we argue that the designed reward system, and the distributed ledger technology in general, can support decentralised and collective management practices that are suited for developing solutions that are "best for the world" (Elkington, 2018) by more effectively organising distributed activities (Swan, 2015).

Thus, it is essential to understand who leads the development and who has the power to decide in an ecosystem. Accordingly, ecosystems rely on functional governing rules and mechanisms that allow collective management and rewarding incentives for the conducted work. As a concept, the ecosystem draws from a compelling idea of organisms working in harmony with symbiotic relationships for mutual benefits. However, in the management context, a more accurate description is instead the survival of the fittest (Moore, 1993) in an environment shaped by coopetition, which can be motivated by mutual benefits or a shared fear of being outrun by mutual rivals (Brandenburger & Nalebuff, 2021).

Finally, our work concurs with the previous calls that the management literature should better acknowledge the ecological and "biological" roots of the ecosystem metaphor. The accuracy of the connection between business or innovation ecosystems and ecology has been criticised on multiple occasions, either as excessive and poorly founded (Oh et al., 2016) or based on faulty premises (Kœnig, 2012). The connection can be made more accurate, though. For instance, Ritala and Almpanopoulou (2017) point out that artificial ecosystems also grow, transform, and end in the process of adapting to their environment. Hakanen et al. (2022) further such argumentation, stressing that the artificial ecosystems facilitated by the decentralised systems fit poorly to the deterministic, managerial definitions of an ecosystem (cf. Jacobides et al., 2018; Kapoor, 2018) but more aptly to the interaction patterns found in natural ecosystems.

6 Conclusion

In this study, we illuminate the similarities between communities and ecosystems, connecting both discourses to the concept of communities of practice. We presented a pilot study, Streamr Community Awards, where a novel accounting technology was tested successfully. Similar collectively managed accounting technologies may produce effective incentive mechanisms for aligning collaboration amongst competing actors. The technology offers a tangible solution for overcoming some of the significant practical barriers to developing sustainable practices based on coopetition in ecosystems, which should enable an accelerated innovation rate to solve the increasingly complex issues facing societies worldwide.

Acknowledgements The authors of this chapter received funding from the European Union's Horizon 2020 research and innovation programme under grant agreement No 964678.

References

Adner, R. (2017). Ecosystem as structure: An actionable construct for strategy. *Journal of Management, 43*(1), 39–58. https://doi.org/10.1177/0149206316678451

Adner, R. (2022). Sharing value for ecosystem success. *MIT Sloan Management Review, 63*(2), 85–90.

Aguinis, H., & Glavas, A. (2013). Embedded versus peripheral corporate social responsibility: Psychological foundations. *Industrial and Organizational Psychology: Perspectives on Science and Practice, 6*(4), 314–332. https://doi-org.libproxy.aalto.fi/10.1111/iops.12059

Atzori, M. (2015). Blockchain technology and decentralized governance: Is the state still necessary? Available at *SSRN 2709713*, 1–37.

Autio, E., & Thomas, L. D. W. (2021). Researching ecosystems in innovation contexts. *Innovation & Management Review, 19*(1), 12–25. https://doi.org/10.1108/INMR-08-2021-0151

Bacon, E., Williams, M., & Davies, G. (2020). Coopetition in innovation ecosystems: A comparative analysis of knowledge transfer configurations. *Journal of Business Research, 115*, 307–316. https://doi.org/10.1016/j.jbusres.2019.11.005

Barbrook, R. (1998). The hi-tech gift economy. *First Monday, 3*(12).

Brandenburger, A. M., & Nalebuff, B. J. (1997). *Co-opetition (Paperback)*. Doubleday.

Brandenburger, A., & Nalebuff, B. (2021). The rules of co-opetition. *Harvard Business Review, 99*(1), 48–57.

Brown, W. B. (1966). Systems, Boundaries, and Information Flow. *The Academy of Management Journal, 9*(4), 318–327. https://www.jstor.org/stable/254950

Cox, A. (2005). What are communities of practice? A comparative review of four seminal works. *Journal of Information Science, 31*(6), 527–540. https://doi.org/10.1177/0165551505057016

Elkington, J. (2018). 25 years ago I coined the phrase "triple bottom line." Here's why it's time to rethink it. *Harvard Business Review, 25*, 2–5. https://hbr.org/2018/06/25-years-ago-i-coined-the-phrase-triple-bottom-line-heres-why-im-giving-up-on-it

Elo, T. M., Marttila, J., Cutillas, S., & Hakanen, E. (2023). Elements of antirival accounting with sNFT. In *International Conference on Computational Science*.

George, G., Howard-Grenville, J., Joshi, A., & Tihanyi, L. (2016). Understanding and tackling societal grand challenges through management research. *Academy of Management Journal, 59*(6), 1880–1895. https://doi.org/10.5465/amj.2016.40

Gernsheimer, O., Kanbach, D., & Gast, J. (2021). Coopetition research : A systematic literature review on recent accomplishments and trajectories. *Industrial Marketing Management, 96*, 113–134. https://doi.org/10.1016/j.indmarman.2021.05.001

Ghosh, R. A. (1998). Cooking pot markets: An economic model for the trade in free goods and services on the internet. *First Monday, 3*(3).

Granstrand, O., & Holgersson, M. (2020). Innovation ecosystems: A conceptual review and a new definition. *Technovation, 90–91*, 102098. https://doi.org/10.1016/j.technovation.2019.102098

Hakanen, E., Eloranta, V., Marttila, J., & Amadae, S. M. (2023). Digital protocols as accounting and incentivization mechanisms in anti-rival systems – Developing a shareable non-fungible token (sNFT). In T. Seppälä, T. Mucha, & J. Marttila (Eds.), *The fifth wave: BRIE-ETLA collection of articles* (pp. 139–160). Taloustieto Oy.

Hakanen, E., Eloranta, V., & Shaw, C. (2022). Forming digital commons: The role of signaling and sociology of translation in decentralized systems. *Academy of Management Proceedings, 2022*, 11067.

Hannan, M. T., & Freeman, J. (1977). The population ecology of organizations. *American Journal of Sociology, 82*(5), 929–964.

Hawley, A. (1950). *Human ecology: A theory of community structure*. The Ronald Press Company.

Jacobides, M. G., Cennamo, C., & Gawer, A. (2018). Towards a theory of ecosystems. *Strategic Management Journal, 39*(8), 2255–2276. https://doi.org/10.1002/smj.2904

Jewkes, R., & Murcott, A. (1996). Meanings of community. *Social Science & Medicine, 43*(4), 555–563. https://doi.org/10.1016/0277-9536(95)00439-4

Kapoor, R. (2018). Ecosystems: Broadening the locus of value creation. *Journal of Organization Design, 7*(12). https://doi.org/10.1186/s41469-018-0035-4

Kemp, R., Parto, S., & Gibson, R. B. (2005). Governance for sustainable development: moving from theory to practice. *International Journal of Sustainable Development, 8*(1–2), 12–30. https://doi-org.libproxy.aalto.fi/10.1504/IJSD.2005.007372

Ketokivi, M., & Choi, T. (2014). Renaissance of case research as a scientific method. *Journal of Operations Management, 32*(5), 232–240. https://doi.org/10.1016/j.jom.2014.03.004

Kœnig, G. (2012). Le concept d'écosystème d'affaires revisité. *M@n@gement, 15*(2), 208–224.

Lönngren, J., & van Poeck, K. (2021). Wicked problems: A mapping review of the literature. *International Journal of Sustainable Development & World Ecology, 28*(6), 481–502. https://doi.org/10.1080/13504509.2020.1859415

Lovett, M., & Thomas, L. (2021). A fork in the road: Perspectives on sustainability and decentralised governance in digital institutions. *First Monday, 26*(11).

Marttila, J., & Moravek, M. (2022). *ERC-5023: Shareable non-fungible token – An interface for creating value-holding tokens shareable by multiple owners*. Ethereum Improvement Proposals. https://eips.ethereum.org/EIPS/eip-5023

Mindel, V., Mathiassen, L., & Rai, A. (2018). The sustainability of polycentric information commons. *MIS Quarterly, 42*(2), 607–631. https://doi.org/10.25300/MISQ/2018/14015

Moore, J. F. (1993). Predators and prey: A new ecology of competition. *Harvard Business Review, 71*(3), 75–83.

Munro, V. (2020). The future of CSR and the new ecosystem for CSR 4.0. In V. Munro (Ed.), *CSR for purpose, shared value and deep transformation* (pp. 203–229). Emerald. https://doi.org/10.1108/978-1-80043-035-820200009

Oh, D.-S., Phillips, F., Park, S., & Lee, E. (2016). Innovation ecosystems: A critical examination. *Technovation, 54*, 1–6. https://doi.org/10.1016/j.technovation.2016.02.004

Ritala, P., & Almpanopoulou, A. (2017). In defense of 'eco' in innovation ecosystem. *Technovation, 60–61*, 39–42. https://doi.org/10.1016/j.technovation.2017.01.004
Roberts, J. (2006). Limits to communities of practice. *Journal of Management Studies, 43*(3).
Rockström, J., Steffen, W., Noone, K., Persson, Å., Chapin, F. S., Lambin, E. F., et al. (2009). A safe operating space for humanity. *Nature, 461*(7263), 472–475. https://doi.org/10.1038/461472a
Stohl, C., Stohl, M., & Popova, L. A. (2009). New generation of corporate codes of ethics. *Journal of Business Ethics, 90*, 607–622. https://doi-org.libproxy.aalto.fi/10.1007/s10551-009-0064-6
Swan, M. (2015). *Blockchain–Blueprint for a new economy*. O'Reilly Media.
Teece, D. J. (2018). Profiting from innovation in the digital economy: Enabling technologies, standards, and licensing models in the wireless world. *Research Policy, 47*, 1367–1387. https://doi.org/10.1016/j.respol.2017.01.015
United Nations. (2015). *Transforming our world: The 2030 agenda for sustainable development*. United Nations. https://sdgs.un.org/sites/default/files/publications/21252030%20Agenda%20for%20Sustainable%20Development%20web.pdf
Wenger, E. (1998). Communities of practice: Learning as a social system. *Systems Thinker*. https://participativelearning.org/pluginfile.php/636/mod_resource/content/3/Learningasasocialsystem.pdf
Wolff, J., & Hakanen, E. (2021). Managing the disruption of mobility services: How to align the value propositions of key ecosystem players. *Technology Innovation Management Review, 11*(4), 13–25. https://doi.org/10.22215/timreview/1433
Wolff, J., Jakubik, M., Siltaloppi, J., Wolff, L.-A., & Hakanen, E. (2023). Sustainability transitions by ecosystem innovation. In S. Idowu & Z. Liangroung (Eds.), *The Elgar companion to corporate social responsibility and the sustainable development goals* (pp. 48–67). Edward Elgar.

Joel Wolff, MA in Arts & Design, is a doctoral candidate at Aalto University School of Science's Department of Industrial Engineering and Management. His research focuses on business ecosystems, particularly their potential to foster sustainable innovation, with a special emphasis on stakeholder dynamics. His broader research interests encompass sustainability transformation, socio-technical systems, and transdisciplinary innovation, with a particular emphasis on mobility services and cross-sectoral collaboration. Wolff is a representative member of the MaaS Alliance, reflecting his research involvement in Mobility as a Service. His background in strategic service design and sustainability studies equips him with co-creative design skills to facilitate sense-making and strategic development in complex environments. Wolff applied these skills as a Coordinator for the recent EU-funded interdisciplinary innovation project, ATARCA.

Esko Hakanen, is a postdoctoral researcher in the areas of digitalization, platforms, and ecosystems. He is employed by two Finnish institutions: Aalto University and University of Vaasa. His work builds on an interdisciplinary background that combines operations management with contextual knowledge of the manufacturing industry and is particularly interested in elaborating how emerging technological practices map against the theoretical models in the academic literature. In addition to his research activities, he has had various organizational responsibilities. He served as the Project Manager of the H2020-funded ATARCA project, which explored the means for a more efficient digital economy by leveraging the prospect of anti-rivalry (i.e., replicability and value amplifying properties) of digital goods. He is the Research Manager for his research group on Service Engineering and Management. He has also acted as the Academic Coordinator for the Department of Industrial Engineering and Management at Aalto University.

Jarno Marttila, is a DevRel Engineer at Streamr with 10+ years of experience in Web 2/3 technologies and software development. He is an author of EIP-5023 standard for shareable NFTs and holds master's degrees in computer science from Tampere University of Technology and in economics from University of Vaasa. He is pursuing a doctoral degree at Aalto University, School of Science. He is passionate about delivering value and bridging the gap between novel technologies and their practical applications.

Climate Racism in Brazil's Favelas: A Sustainable Discussion

Armando Dias-da-Fé, Rosmel Rodríguez-Barroso, and Rute Abreu

1 Introduction

This research deals with poverty and inequality as the two major socio-economic issues in the global south (UN, 2019a). The lack of access to economic opportunities, decent employment and basic services, such as education, health and sanitation perpetuate poverty. Discrimination and social exclusion (Castañeda et al., 2018), income inequality (Alvaredo et al., 2018) and the concentration of wealth (Piketty, 2014) generate social tensions and conflicts (Stiglitz, 2012). Climate change exacerbates these conditions, disproportionately affecting the most vulnerable populations (Hallegatte et al., 2015), posing greater challenges to improving their quality of life in a context of increasing socio-economic and environmental pressures.

This chapter focus on the socio-economic context and the urbanization in the global south to engender new ideas (WEF, 2020) and sustainable discussion fighting the "*persistence of its conceptual opacity*" (Cobbinah et al., 2015: 2) and the vulnerability of the built environment (Mileti, 1999).

However, urbanization in the global south has been predominantly disorderly and unsustainable, creating challenges and vulnerabilities for communities in marginalized areas and favelas (Davis, 2006). These challenges include infrastructure

A. Dias-da-Fé
Instituto Politécnico da Guarda, CICF-IPCA, Guarda, Portugal
e-mail: armando.jr@ipg.pt

R. Rodríguez-Barroso
CES-Universidade de Coimbra, Coimbra, Portugal

R. Abreu (✉)
Instituto Politécnico da Guarda, CICF-IPCA, CISeD-IPV, CiTUR, Guarda, Portugal
e-mail: ra@ipg.pt

B. Díaz Díaz et al. (eds.), *Building Global Societies Towards an ESG World*,
CSR, Sustainability, Ethics & Governance,
https://doi.org/10.1007/978-3-031-56619-6_2

problems, limited access to basic services, and difficulties in planning and regulating urban growth, which negatively affects the quality of life of its inhabitants.

The global south has experienced an accelerated process of rural exodus in recent decades, which has resulted in an increasing concentration of the population in urban areas (UN, 2019b). Several factors such as population growth, industrialization (Rodrik, 2011), globalization and its economic effects (Satterthwaite et al., 2020) and the search for better economic opportunities (Lucas, 2004) have driven this phenomenon.

Migration, both national and international, influences the dynamics of urbanization in the global south (UN, 2019a). Indeed, rural–urban migration (Lucas, 2004) in search of employment and basic services contributes to the growth of urban areas, generating challenges in infrastructure (Cohen, 2006), housing and public services (McGranahan et al., 2016) that facilitate the emergence of disorderly megacities, for example, the case study of Favelas in Brazil.

As an explanation of the case study, migrants settling in slums face considerable challenges in improving their living conditions and achieving greater socio-economic stability. These informal settlements tend to lack adequate urban planning and infrastructure investment, leading to limited access to basic services such as sanitation, clean water, health care and education (Ezeh et al., 2017).

In addition, the lack of access to formal and well-paid jobs in these urban areas can lead to an increase in labour informality, crime and the perpetuation of the cycle of poverty. Consequently, the inhabitants of these informal settlements can be trapped in a situation of precariousness and social exclusion, increasing their vulnerability to extreme weather events and natural disasters (Corburn & Sverdlik, 2017).

This chapter is divided into four parts, starting with the introduction to address the problem under research which is the climate racism (Snyder, 2019) as a sustainable discussion. Followed by the methodology that presents the detailed process to generate knowledge and deals with data scarcity that is an opportunity to upgrade social assessment impact. The third section is a comprehensive literature review on the topic under analysis, followed by an approach to the various schemes used in financial statements. Next, it provides an analysis of concepts and functionalities of financial statements and the application of the checklist as a method of analysing fraud. Finally, conclusions and recommendations are presented.

2 Methodology

In this chapter, the authors have set out to examine whether people living in poverty and on the margins of society (Alves & Rocha, 2020) are facing increased environmental dangers, either because of the high levels of production and consumption in more affluent countries or due to their own actions, neglect or lack of resources. By conducting a thorough review of existing literature (Birkmann et al., 2022), the authors have aimed to explore these issues on a large scale, including topics such as Climate Racism and climate change (Dessai et al., 2004). When focusing on specific cases, our analysis allows for a deeper understanding of how these issues interact with other factors.

While the results from these specific cases studies (Yin, 2022) may not be easily generalized, they provide valuable theoretical insights and offer a solid foundation for future research (Eisenhardt, 1989) and public policies aimed at reducing the environmental risks faced by vulnerable populations (Cutter, 1996). Regarding the literature review, it is important to note that the authors are dealing with case studies, and also image analysis in histology that demands objectivity (Gonzalez & Woods, 2002; Tadrous, 2010). Despite consulting different sources, the authors focus is solely on the favelas of Brazil. It is essential to differentiate this type of review from a literature analysis, as they serve different purposes. In this context, the literature review has been dedicated to deeply understanding and analysing the environmental issues specifically affecting these vulnerable communities in Brazil (Silva Lopes, 2023). The depth of the literature review provides a strong foundation for future research (Snyder, 2019) and the development of public policies aimed at reducing the environmental risks faced by this population.

It is crucial to emphasize the importance of properly contextualizing the results obtained, while acknowledging the limitations inherent to focusing solely on Brazilian favelas. While this approach provides a detailed understanding of the reality experienced by these communities, it should not be seen as a complete reflection of all marginalized and impoverished communities worldwide. Each region and community has its own unique characteristics, challenges and dynamics, highlighting the need for tailored and contextualized approaches and solutions.

Additionally, it is important to consider the power dynamics and socio-economic structures that perpetuate marginalization and increase the vulnerability of these communities to environmental risks. While our review has identified patterns and trends, it has also highlighted the need to move beyond simply recognizing problems and actively working towards sustainable and equitable solutions.

Therefore, this work not only aims to provide a comprehensive description of the specific environmental challenges faced by the favelas in Brazil but also seeks to inspire change and encourage academics, policymakers and social actors to proactively engage in addressing environmental injustices. Ultimately, our goal is to contribute to the well-being and resilience of these communities, ensuring that their right to a safe and healthy environment is fully recognized and protected.

Case studies are analysed from multiple perspectives (Yin, 2022). For Tellis (1997), this means that the researcher considers not only the voice and perspective of actors but also the relevant groups of actors and the interaction between them. This aspect is a salient point in the characteristic that case studies have. The problem in case studies is to establish the meaning instead of the location.

Also, case studies involve in-depth location-based research that focuses on a specific exposure unit. As Ford et al. (2010, 375) point out, work on climate change:

> that uses case studies and analogues can help develop an understanding of the determinants of vulnerability and how they interact and identify opportunities to reduce vulnerability and increase adaptive capacity to risks current and future climatic conditions.

The case study "*focuses on holistic description and explanation*" (Merriam, 1998: 29), described as particularistic, heuristic or descriptive. A heuristic case study can shed light on the phenomenon, allowing the reader to extend their experience, discover new meaning or confirm what is known. It

Also, according to these authors, the findings and information collected and systematized can help policy makers to develop adaptation plans and integrate adaptation to climate change into other decision-making processes and policies. In case studies, this multiplicity of sources and the possibility of deeper analysis and from different perspectives, something that can be done using several data sources (Yin, 2022), allows inferring less generalist answers.

3 Literature Review

Poverty is present across the planet, however, unevenly and in different dimensions. Goal number 1 of the UN 2030 Agenda, consolidated in the Sustainable Development Goals (SDG) is: "End poverty in all its forms, everywhere". Goal 1.1 says: "By 2030, eradicate extreme poverty for all people everywhere, currently measured as people living on less than US$1.25 a day". However, in 2021, multidimensional poverty affected 1300 million people (Alves, 2021), with the majority in the 5563 million people in Sub-Saharan Africa, 5317 million people in South Asia, 1112 million people in East Asia and the Pacific, 49.6 million people in Arab States, 37.4 million people in Latin American and the Caribbean and 1.1 million people in Europe and Central Asia.

For Declaration of Pretoria related with Habitat III (UN, 2016a: 1), the concept of informal settlements are residential areas where:

1) inhabitants have no security of tenure vis-à-vis the land or dwellings they inhabit, with modalities ranging from squatting to informal rental housing;
2) the neighbourhoods usually lack, or are cut off from, basic services and city infrastructure; and
3) the housing may not comply with current planning and building regulations and is often situated in geographically and environmentally hazardous areas. In addition, informal settlements can be a form of real estate speculation for all income levels of urban residents, affluent and poor.

However, to this date (2022), the research (2020 census) had not yet been concluded due to several problems in data collection and only with the help of entities such as Data Favela and *Central Única das Favelas* (CUFA) to conclude. Also, Declaration of Pretoria related with Habitat III (UN, 2016a: 1), the concept of slums are:

> the most deprived and excluded form of informal settlements characterized by poverty and large agglomerations of dilapidated housing often located in the most hazardous urban land. In addition to tenure insecurity, slum dwellers lack formal supply of basic infrastructure and services, public space and green areas, and are constantly exposed to eviction, disease and violence.

The definition of a favela, according to the official definition of the Brazilian Institute of Geography and Statistics (IBGE, 2020), is marked by its vulnerabilities, by what it does not have, as follows:

> Subnorm al agglomeration is a form of irregular occupation of land owned by others—public or private—for housing purposes in urban areas and, in general, characterized by an irregular urban pattern, lack of essential public services and location in areas with restricted occupation.

In other words, a favela is a group of households with at least 51 housing units, which occupy, in a disorderly and dense manner, land owned by others (public or private) and which do not have access to essential public services. For Meirelles, founder of the Data Favela Institute and responsible for the census in favelas defines (Meirelles & Athayde, 2014: 5):

> the favela is the demographic expression of social inequalities

Lack of adequate urban planning and insufficient investment in infrastructure and basic services are crucial factors in creating vulnerabilities in slums. The lack of sanitation networks, access to drinking water (Bain et al., 2014), electricity supply, efficient public transport (Edwing and Cervero, 2010) and quality medical care, amongst other aspects, compromise the health, quality of life and safety of the inhabitants of these communities (WHO, 2018). For example, until December 2019, according to an IBGE survey (IBGE, 2020), there were 13,151 Subnormal Agglomerates (favelas) in Brazil, located in 734 Municipalities, representing 5,127,747 households and a total around of 16 million inhabitants.

Climate change further exacerbates these deficiencies, causing extreme events such as floods (Jongman et al., 2012), droughts (Wilhite & Pulwarty, 2017) and heat waves (Mora et al., 2017), which intensify adverse living conditions in these settlements (Revi et al., 2014). These extreme events can cause forced displacement, loss of property and livelihoods, and increase exposure to disease and other health risks (IBGE, 2020).

The challenges associated with lack of urban planning and insufficient investment in infrastructure and basic services in marginal areas and slums require the implementation of integrated policies and strategies that promote sustainable and climate-resilient urban development, ensuring the equitable provision of essential services such as sanitation, drinking water, energy and public transport, as well as access to quality health care and education for all inhabitants of these communities (UN, 2016b).

In this sense, it is vital to develop and implement climate change adaptation and mitigation measures specifically designed for these settlements, which reduce the exposure and vulnerability of their inhabitants to extreme weather events (Agyeman et al., 2003) and improve their capacity to face the challenges associated with climate change (Hallegatte et al., 2015).

Lack of access to decent and affordable housing is a major challenge for slum communities. The precariousness of housing (Gilbert, 2007), land, the absence of legal and secure property titles (Payne et al., 2009) and informality in construction processes (Roy, 2005) increase the vulnerability of these areas to extreme weather events and natural disasters (Bull-Kamanga et al., 2003).

The lack of regulation and control in urban planning favours the expansion of informal settlements in high-risk areas unsuitable for urbanization, such as unstable hillsides prone to landslides (van Westen et al., 2006) or areas susceptible to flooding, especially for riverside communities (Douglas et al., 2008). This situation increases the exposure of communities to the adverse effects of climate change (Revi et al., 2014) and potentially has devastating consequences for the lives and well-being of their inhabitants.

To mitigate these problems, it is necessary to implement policies and strategies that facilitate access to decent and affordable housing in slums and favelas. These policies should include actions to improve housing quality and security, ensure secure land tenure and promote the formalization of construction, all under an integrated and participatory approach involving local communities and other relevant actors (UN, 2016b).

In addition, it is essential to strengthen regulation and control in urban planning to prevent the expansion of informal settlements, both in areas of environmental preservation and water resources and in areas of risk, to mitigate the impacts of climate change (Revi et al., 2014). This also involves developing resilient infrastructure and promoting adaptation measures and reducing exposure to climate change impacts specific to these settlements, thus ensuring greater protection and well-being for their inhabitants in the context of a changing climate (Hallegatte et al., 2015).

Communities in marginalized areas face a range of environmental and social risks that increase their susceptibility to disasters (Bull-Kamanga et al., 2003). These risks include environmental degradation, deforestation (Bradshaw et al., 2009), air pollution (Künzli et al., 2001), water pollution (Bain et al., 2014), and soil degradation (Lal, 2001), soil sealing and erosion, all of which contribute to deteriorating living conditions in these areas and worsening the effects of climate change. Thus, exposure to natural disasters such as floods (Jongman et al., 2012), landslides (van Westen et al., 2006), fires and earthquakes is exacerbated by the lack of preventive and preparedness measures (Twigg, 2004), as well as by the fragility of emergency response and recovery systems (Oliver-Smith, 1996) as the case study of *São Gonçalo*, where residents look the loss of their house after a landslide.

This situation is aggravated by the lack of financial and technical resources to implement adequate solutions (Birkmann et al., 2013), by the low participation of the population in decision-making (Fung, 2006) and by the lack of coordination between the different levels of government and the institutions responsible for risk management (Cohen & Werker, 2008). The social and economic inequalities that affect these communities (Pelling & Wisner, 2009) also influence, generating conditions of vulnerability that are amplified in the context of natural disasters and extreme climatic events.

3.1 Climate Change and Its Effects on Slums in the Global South

It is widely acknowledged that the Global South will bear the brunt of the effects of climate change, with extreme weather events and shifts in temperature and precipitation patterns posing a significant threat to the survival and well-being of communities in these regions (Diffenbaugh & Giorgi, 2012). A range of phenomena, such as prolonged droughts (Wilhite & Pulwarty, 2017), increasingly frequent and severe floods (Hirabayashi et al., 2013), tropical storms (Knutson et al., 2010) and sea level rise (Church et al., 2013), are particularly vulnerable to the impacts of climate change due to their environmental and socio-economic conditions (Revi et al., 2014).

In addition to natural disasters, the unregulated growth and lack of state regulation in these areas exacerbate the risks faced by residents. Climate change can also be attributed to unchecked production and consumption practices on a global scale, further contributing to the environmental dangers faced by vulnerable populations.

The consequences of climate change have far-reaching effects on public health and food safety (Wheeler & von Braun, 2013) in the Global South. Residents of these communities are at increased risk of vector-borne diseases (Ermert et al., 2012), respiratory and cardiovascular illnesses (Brook et al., 2010), and food insecurity due to the impacts of climate variability and extreme events (Mora et al., 2017). Climate variability and extreme events can also affect agricultural production and food availability (Lobell et al., 2011), which in turn can result in food insecurity and malnutrition in these communities (Lloyd et al., 2011).

The limited availability of resources and uncertain funding for climate change initiatives further hinders the ability of these communities to implement long-term solutions (Leichenko & Silva, 2014). The lack of coordination and governance mechanisms within public institutions, as well as the absence of technical and scientific capacity pose significant obstacles to addressing climate change in these areas (Béné et al., 2012).

The unequal distribution of risks and damages caused by extreme events and climate change is evident in marginalized communities such as Brazil's favelas (Moss et al., 2010). These communities, predominantly inhabited by racialized and marginalized populations, are often situated in high-risk areas with poor infrastructure, making them particularly susceptible to the impacts of climate change (Adger et al., 2005).

In their efforts to adapt to climate change and increase resilience, communities in the Global South are confronted with various challenges, including limited economic resources (Leichenko & Silva, 2014), weak institutional structures (Béné et al., 2012), and a lack of technical and scientific expertise. These factors hinder the implementation of policies and measures to adapt to and mitigate the impacts of climate change. The intricate and uncertain nature of climate change impacts (Moss et al., 2010), as well as the interactions between social, economic and environmental factors (Adger et al., 2005), further complicate planning and decision-making processes.

The current resources available to address climate change in the Global South are inadequate and uncertain, restricting communities' ability to implement long-term solutions (Ayers & Huq, 2009). This situation is exacerbated by the fragility of public institutions, which often lack efficient coordination and governance mechanisms (Pelling & High, 2005). Similarly, the lack of technical and scientific capacity in the Global South poses a significant obstacle to addressing climate change, as communities often lack access to relevant information and knowledge (Muttarak & Lutz, 2014). This context makes it challenging to identify and prioritize appropriate adaptation and mitigation measures (Eakin & Lemos, 2006).

Uncertainty regarding the impacts of climate change and the complex interactions between social, economic and environmental factors present additional challenges in planning and decision-making (Dessai et al., 2004). Addressing these challenges requires integrated and participatory approaches involving multiple actors and sectors (Few et al., 2007).

In Brazil's favelas, manifestations of climate injustice are evident in the unequal distribution of risks and damages caused by extreme events and climate change. These communities, predominantly inhabited by marginalized populations, are often situated in high-risk areas such as unstable hillsides, riverbanks, flood-prone areas and areas with inadequate infrastructure (Baker, 2012). Additionally, favelas frequently lack access to essential services such as clean water and sanitation, exacerbating their vulnerability to the effects of climate change (Bullard, 1990).

The issue of favelas in Brazil is significant: there are 11,403 communities classified as favelas, with a total of 6.6 million "residences" housing 16 million people, according to official data from the Brazilian Institute of Geography and Statistics (IBGE, 2020). However, obtaining an accurate count is challenging due to residents' reluctance to participate in the census (UOL Economia, 2023). For example, the city of Bethlehem has the highest percentage of its population living in favelas at 55.4%, while Manaus, Amazonas, has 53.3% of its population living in these precarious conditions (Casado, 2023).

The population without access to adequate housing seeks out uninhabited land or buildings to occupy and construct their homes using low-quality, flammable and entirely irregular materials that do not meet housing standards. These properties are typically private, with owners seeking state intervention. This leads to a process of expropriation or eviction, which depends on lengthy legal proceedings that can take decades or remain unresolved, leaving both owners and residents in legal limbo and preventing them from accessing public services (Gotham, 2010).

This situation arises from the lack of resources or public initiatives that promote unplanned urban growth. In the favelas, the population feels discriminated against reducing their trust in the state. Because of this absence of state intervention, non-state groups coordinated by criminal elements emerge and take advantage of this neglect (Gehl, 2013).

The absence of the state in these areas creates a challenging situation, where legal uncertainty leaves both residents and property owners in limbo. This lack of intervention from the state has led to the emergence of non-state groups, often associated with criminal elements, who take advantage of the neglect in these communities (Phansalkar, 2017).

In both scenarios, the state struggles to fulfil its obligations in ensuring the right to housing and protecting private property. In some cases, reappropriation processes involve violent actions by law enforcement or non-state groups (Kreiger, 2020). These groups exert their influence through environmental discrimination, controlling territory and its resources, exploiting them from a purely discretionary perspective, engaging in armed conflict over land and natural resources, and intimidating the population in the use of these spaces (Peluso & Watts, 2001).

Discrimination and social marginalization are evident in urban policies and practices that limit these communities' ability to improve their living conditions and environment. Their exclusion from decision-making processes perpetuates their vulnerability and restricts their capacity to adapt (Rolnik & Klink, 2011). Additionally, the historical accumulation of socio-economic disadvantages and lack of access to resources and opportunities further expose favelas to climate and environmental risks (Marengo et al., 2017).

Addressing climate justice in Brazil's favelas requires an approach that tackles the underlying socio-environmental inequalities. This approach should aim for equity not only in the distribution of climate change impacts but also in the responsibilities and capacities for adaptation and mitigation (Schlosberg, 2013).

This requires policies and actions that recognize and address discrimination and social exclusion as factors that increase vulnerability to climate. It is essential to empower these communities by providing them with the resources and capacities needed to adapt to and mitigate the impacts of climate change in a sustainable manner (Adger et al., 2005). Finally, climate justice also involves the active and meaningful participation of these communities in decision-making related to climate and the environment.

This participation is essential to design and implement strategies that consider their specific needs and capacities and that contribute to sustainable and equitable development. Additionally, the voices and experiences of these communities is essential to promote climate justice (Roberts & Parks, 2007) and improve their resilience to the challenges posed by climate change (Nelson & Gubesic, 2018).

3.2 Manifestations of Climate Racism in the Favelas

The concept of climate racism, although not yet widely disseminated in the academic literature, has emerged as a fundamental prism to unravel socio-environmental inequalities (Bullard, 1990). The authors agree with Bullard (1990), explaining that the effects of climate change tend to disproportionately affect marginalized communities, often those with predominantly black populations.

In the case of Brazil, this reality manifests itself particularly acutely. Brazil's favelas, which are home to some 13.6 million people, or 6.5% of the country's total population (IBGE, 2020), are mostly inhabited by Afro-Brazilian communities and are amongst the most vulnerable to the impacts of climate change (Marengo et al., 2017). These impacts include extreme weather events such as floods and landslides, which are exacerbated by poor housing conditions and insufficient infrastructure in these communities (EM-DAT, 2022).

This vulnerability is compounded by existing socio-economic disparities. Favelas are often neglected in terms of investment in basic infrastructure and public services, including those that could mitigate the impacts of climate change, such as adequate drainage systems and flood-resistant housing (Fernandes, 2011). In this sense, climate racism in Brazil is a product of both historical inequalities and structural factors that perpetuate and aggravate these disparities.

Therefore, understanding and addressing climate racism in Brazil's favelas requires a recognition of the intersections between race, social class, geographic space, infrastructure and climate change, as well as a critical analysis of the policies and practices that contribute to these inequalities (Agyeman et al., 2003; Florida, 2017).

The manifestations of climate racism in Brazil's favelas are diverse and multifaceted (Carey, 2014; Phansalkar, 2017). A significant example is that of floods and landslides. Due to their geographical location and lack of adequate infrastructure, favelas are particularly vulnerable to these phenomena.

Cunha (2023) states that Brazilian cities are not prepared for the effects of climate change, using the number of occurrences, intensity and permanence to corroborate his statement. Disasters resulting from heavy rain have increased year by year and the number of fatalities has been greater each year. Report that brings together the main tragedies with fatal victims in the last 10 years (Gomes, 2023). This highlights the number of deaths and people at risk of natural disasters, where 2011 recorded 918 deaths in just one land flood in *Petrópolis* in *Rio de Janeiro* (Brazil).

According to data from EM-DAT (2022), Rio de Janeiro's favelas, for example, are regularly affected by severe flooding and landslides during the rainy season, resulting in loss of life and significant material damage. Afro-Brazilian families, who make up most of these communities, are the most affected (Bulkeley, 2013; Gomes, 2018) as the case study of Petropólis, in February of 2022, with and emission caused by torrential rains hitting.

In addition, the lack of access to basic services, such as clean water and adequate sanitation, often because of insufficient or discriminatory public policies, increases the vulnerability of favelas to climate change. For example, during periods of drought, which are becoming more frequent and severe due to climate change (Marengo et al., 2017), many favelas face severe water shortages, affecting the health and well-being of their inhabitants.

These manifestations of climate racism reflect and amplify existing socio-economic inequalities, contributing to a cycle of marginalization and vulnerability. It is therefore crucial that climate change mitigation policies and strategies consider these inequalities and strive to promote climate justice. Therefore, the focus must not only be on adapting to and mitigating the physical impacts of climate change but also on building fairer and more equitable societies (Rosenzweig, 2011).

In a thorough analysis of the situation in Brazil's favelas, it is imperative to highlight the intrinsic relationship between the devastating effects of climate change and climate racism. This connection is not merely coincidental but results from decades of neglect, discrimination and structural inequalities. The Afro-Brazilian communities, predominantly residing in these favelas, face a dual threat: historical discrimination and the increasing risks associated with climate change. It is essential that, in addressing the climate crisis, the deep-rooted causes of climate racism are also confronted and combated, thereby ensuring a more just and resilient future for all inhabitants of Brazil.

3.3 Policies and Actions to Address Socio-environmental Inequalities in Brazil's Favelas

From the approach of climate justice and sustainability as a tool for social emancipation, the best way to build the ecological subject (Moura, 2004) as a nucleus of socio-environmental equity in the favelas of Brazil. This transition goes through three areas of development: natural space, economic sustainability and environmental governance as a focus on overcoming inequalities (UN, 1987). Talking about the natural space, it is about building a model of coexistence between the physical space that the human being designs for his subsistence and the natural environment that surrounds him (Gehl, 2013). It goes from the rediscovery of the architectural sense of the favela, from a sustainable and resilient perspective for the population, oriented from the rediscovery of alternative technologies that focus on the projection of energy sources, durable materials and feasible structures for the subsistence of the populations (Braungart & McDonough, 2009).

There have been models of community equipment made by waste material, purified water supply system, and solar and wind energy system for the use of spaces, as well as the renovation of the environment with styles and mechanisms that respect the environment (Gehl, 2013). On economic sustainability, it refers to the creation and adaptation of new models and practices of economic sustainability, based on the digital migration of productive practice in favour of the environment. They are referred to as a priority, the creation of sustainable models to the environment and respectful of the economic sense of the subsistence of the human being. Productive models such as the circular economy and models of promotion and impulse of transport mechanisms with alternative energy are added, as a sign of the impulse and innovation of the popular sectors (UN, 1987).

It is about the promotion of modernization of the practices of the work process in sustainable and digital techniques that allow the development of the environment and the satisfaction of needs of the individual from a perspective of climate justice and social inclusion from the instructional, educational and training aspects to potentiate the capacities in function of the development of goods and services that can enhance the economy (Agyeman et al., 2003). It is important to clarify the concept of "glocal" and a neologism resulting from the fusion of two global and local thermos. In the aspect of environmental governance, it is about generating models of participation, institutionality and social impact in local spaces and "glocal" vocation, to promote equitable models for the development of an environmental citizenship that renews the innovation of the socio-political, from the awareness of the strengthening of nature as a synergy of development (Obando & Portilla, 2009).

The construction of the ecological subject goes through a communion with nature and a respectful use of the environment, with economic dynamics that empower the members of the favelas from the formula of new development models, culminating with the construction of models of sustainable citizen political institutionality to become familiar with a harmonious model between the person and his natural context (Agyeman et al., 2003).

According to Gupta, Leeuw and Moel (2008, 144), GHG emissions are essentially local in nature, but it is their cumulative concentration level that is a critical factor in causing climate change. These authors also highlight that although emissions are issued locally, they are often the result of local to global processes and policies and that these policies are usually being taken from the global to the local level and that local communities are encouraged to develop possible options, policies "Where national governments are reluctant to act, provincial and local governments have stepped in to develop policy."

4 Conclusions and Recommendations

The conclusions of this chapter identify two groups of intensifiers of the consequences of climate change. The first group, at a local level, presents a vicious circle given by the absence of legal and secure property titles stands out (Payne et al., 2009) and the precariousness of employment relationships that make access to financing difficult, which reinforces the precariousness of housing (Gilbert, 2007), land and informality in construction processes (Roy, 2005), which end up limiting people, inhibiting access to basic living conditions and education, increasing the vulnerability of these areas to extreme weather events (Bull-Kamanga et al., 2003).

If in the first group the economic and social system promotes exclusion, and the political system consolidates these exclusions, in the second, the responsibility is more personal, it falls on our actions. However, usually those who pollute the most, theoretically, suffer the least consequences. In both cases, a global plan to keep the planet in balance, where each country contributes with the resources they have, whether financial, is something to discuss. For a long-term plan, breaking the vicious cycle with the creation of formal, quality jobs can open doors to bank credit and the construction of houses that are more adapted to climate change. Sometimes this change can only occur with professional qualifications and formal education, acquired in schools and preparatory courses.

The second group is due to decisions made by people around the planet. Climate change is usually seen because of excessive consumption, inefficient modes of production and pollution. Personal decisions that affect everyone, but disproportionately for those who are least able to defend themselves. Regarding environmental aspects, the local effects of decisions taken, and the use of certain resources can have global effects, and these effects can provide different consequences in each location, depending on local development characteristics and available physical, technological or financial resources.

This chapter wishes to answer to the research question: How does climate change exacerbate urban inequality in Brazil's favelas? Undeniably, the chapter identifies three channels through which the inequality-aggravating effect of climate change materializes, namely (a) increase in the exposure of the disadvantaged groups to the adverse effects of climate change; (b) increase in their susceptibility to damage caused by climate change; and (c) decrease in their ability to cope and recover from the damage suffered.

Also, the chapter aims to answer another research question: How does Climate Racism manifest itself in areas of urban poverty? Therefore, the favela is mostly perceived only as a space of exclusion, violence and poverty. This stereotype helps local governments to continue excluding these urban clusters from public priorities, as if these communities did not belong to the city. The view remains that the favelas are a world apart. This vision limits investments in the organization of favela space, such as urban cleaning, leisure spaces, electricity, asphalt and transport (Ribeiro, 2023).

Truly, the data indicate that deaths and losses due to natural disasters mainly affected slums and residences in areas of risk or with poor infrastructure. The state has reduced the budget for disaster prevention and cannot even apply the budgeted resources due to lack of project (and communication, perhaps). The Brazilian Institute of Statistics (IBGE, 2020) concluded that 75.2% of the poorest 10% in Brazil are black or brown. The rain was astounding, above average, but the deaths and tragedies are the result of the rain meeting precarious socioeconomic conditions, with the denial of rights, poverty, misery and structural racism. The rain is "natural"; death is not.

Furthermore, the chapter's answer to additional research question: What alternatives can climate justice and sustainable development offer as a mechanism for overcoming inequalities and poverty? Thus, lack of access to decent and affordable housing is a major challenge for slum communities. The precariousness of housing (Gilbert, 2007), land, the absence of legal and secure property titles (Payne et al., 2009) and informality in construction processes (Roy, 2005) increase the vulnerability of these areas to extreme weather events and natural disasters (Bull-Kamanga et al., 2003).

Promoting climate justice in Brazil's favelas requires a focus that addresses the roots of these inequalities. In this sense, climate justice implies not just equity in the distribution of risks and impacts of climate change but also equity in responsibilities and capacities for adaptation and mitigation (Schlosberg, 2013).

The gap of social inequalities that surround the case of the Brazilian favelas involves understanding the term climate racism, as the remnant of social policies and services lacking quality to offer solutions to this population. It was demonstrated that the victims of inequality also entail a correlate, discrimination and segmentation by hegemonic patterns and characterizations of modes of production, governance and environmental relationship of predatory mechanism.

The vulnerabilities of the sectors and their context were shown, which offered a balance between the impact of the problems of the favelas and the environmental responsibility that implies unsatisfied basic needs, as well as their failure to maintain the oppressive dynamics of action for the general transformation of the environment. The favelas are a sign of climate racism, suffering first-hand the sufferings of natural disasters in their infrastructures in addition to suffering the consequences derived in health, economy and habitat issues. This is part of the impact that surrounds climate change on popular sectors and their living conditions.

It is worth highlighting derivative analyses, such as the realization of sustainability analyses in popular sectors and non-urban environments, not to describe the impact of climate change that it could generate, but to offer spaces for empowerment and sustainable development as a mechanism for equity and satisfaction of the basic needs of the population. Combining sustainable logic, through the 2030 agenda and linking with the culture of the popular sectors and their indagated stigmas, involves invigorating the communities, individuals and institutions of these environments as integral empowered subjects to strengthen the capacities of the environment, for the benefit of their overcoming.

To end this chapter, the relevance of the sustainable discussion demands new ways and new proposals that break with the chains of climate racism and assume themselves as a subject of law with recognized capacities to integrate into society. While the authors hope that from a sense of recognition of their culture and in order to identity towards the perspective of sustainability as a tool for visibility and strengthening of those communities that are being overshadowed by narratives imposed by contexts of power.

Acknowledgments The authors aim to thank anonymous reviewers for the improvements made in earlier versions of this paper. The third author would like to acknowledge that this work is financed by national funds through FCT—Foundation for Science and Technology, I.P., within the scope of multi-annual funding UIDB/04043/2020.

References

Adger, W. N., Arnell, N. W., & Tompkins, E. L. (2005). Successful adaptation to climate change across scales. *Global Environmental Change, 15*(2), 77–86.

Agyeman, J., Bullard, R., & Evans, B. (2003). *Just sustainabilities. Development in an unequal world*. Routledge.

Alvaredo, F., Chancel, L., Piketty, T., Saez, E. & Zucman, G. (2018). *Informe Mundial sobre la Desigualdad 2018*. Laboratorio Mundial de Desigualdad.

Alves, J. E. D. (2021). Mapa da pobreza extrema em suas várias formas. *OutrasMidias*. Available at https://outraspalavras.net/outrasmidias/mapa-da-pobreza-em-suas-varias-formas/

Alves, H. P. F., & Rocha, H. S. (2020). Análise intraurbana da vulnerabilidade socioambiental no município de Guarulhos no contexto das mudanças climáticas. *Novos Cadernos NAEA, 23*(1).

Ayers, J. M., & Huq, S. (2009). Supporting adaptation to climate change: What role for official development assistance? *Development Policy Review, 27*(6), 675–692.

Bain, R., Cronk, R., Hossain, R., Bonjour, S., Onda, K., Wright, J., Yang, H., & Slaymaker, T. (2014). Global assessment of exposure to fecal contamination through drinking water based on a systematic review. *Tropical Medicine and International Health, 19*(8), 917–927.

Baker, J. L. (2012). *Climate change, disaster risk, and the urban poor: Cities building resilience for a changing world.* World Bank Publications.

Béné, C., Wood, R. G., Newsham, A., & Davies, M. (2012). Resilience: New utopia or new tyranny? Reflection about the potentials and limits of the concept of resilience in relation to vulnerability reduction programmes. *IDS Working Papers, 2012*(405), 1–61.

Birkmann, J., Cardona, O. D., Carreño, M. L., Barbat, A. H., Pelling, M., Schneiderbauer, S., & Welle, T. (2013). Framing vulnerability, risk and societal responses: The MOVE framework. *Natural Hazards, 67*, 193–211.

Birkmann, J., Liwenga, E., Pandey, R., Boyd, E., Djalante, R., Gemenne, F., Filho, W. L., Pinho, P. F., Stringer, L., & Wrathall, D. (2022). Poverty, livelihoods and sustainable development. In H.-O. Pörtner, D. C. Roberts, M. Tignor, E. S. Poloczanska, K. Mintenbeck, A. Alegría, M. Craig, S. Langsdorf, S. Löschke, V. Möller, A. Okem, & B. Rama (Eds.), *Climate change 2022: Impacts, adaptation and vulnerability. Contribution of working group II to the sixth assessment report of the intergovernmental panel on climate change* (pp. 1171–1274). Cambridge University Press.

Bradshaw, C. J., Sodhi, N. S., Peh, K. S.-H., & Brook, B. W. (2009). Global evidence that deforestation amplifies the risk and severity of flooding in the developing world. *Biology of Global Change, 15*(11), 1–9.

Braungart, M., & McDonough, W. (2009). *Cradle to cradle*. Vintage Books.

Brook, R. D., Rajagopalan, S., Pope, C. A., III, Brook, J. R., Bhatnagar, A., Diez-Roux, A. V., & Kaufman, J. D. (2010). Particulate matter air pollution and cardiovascular disease: An update to the scientific statement from the American Heart Association. *Circulation, 121*(21), 2331–2378.

Bulkeley, H. (2013). *Climate change in cities: Innovations in multi-level governance*. Routledge.

Bullard, R. D. (1990). *Dumped in Dixie: Race, class, and environmental quality*. Westview Press.

Bull-Kamanga, L., Diagne, K., Lavell, A., Leon, E., Lerise, F., MacGregor, H., Maskrey, A., Meshack, M., Pelling, M., Reid, H., Satterthwaite, D., Songsore, J., Westgate, K., & Yitambe, A. (2003). From everyday dangers to disasters: The accumulation of risks in urban areas. *Environment and Urbanization, 15*(1), 193–204.

Carey, M. B. (2014). Climate change and vulnerability in the southern tropical Andes. *Proceedings of the National Academy of Sciences*, 7336–7341.

Casado, J. (2023). *As maiores capitais da Amazônia estão virando grandes favelas*. Available at https://veja.abril.com.br/coluna/jose-casado/as-maiores-capitais-da-amazonia-estao-virando-grandes-favelas#:~:text=Bel%C3

Castañeda, A., Doan, D., Newhouse, D., Nguyen, M., Uematsu, H., & Azevedo, J. P. (2018). Un nuevo perfil de los pobres del mundo. *Desarrollo mundial, 101*, 250–267.

Church, J. A., Clark, P. U., Cazenave, A., Gregory, J. M., Jevrejeva, S., Levermann, A., Merrifield, M. A., Milne, G. A., Nerem, R. S., Nunn, P. D., Payne, A. J., Pfeffer, W. T., Stammer, D., & Unnikrishnan, A. S. (2013). Sea level change. In *Climate change 2013: The basis of physical science. Contribution of working group I to the fifth assessment report of the intergovernmental panel on climate change* (pp. 1137–1306). Cambridge University Press.

Cobbinah, P. B., Erdiaw-Kwasie, M. O., & Amoateng, P. (2015). Rethinking sustainable development within the framework of poverty and urbanisation in developing countries. *Environmental Development, 13*, 18–32.

Cohen, B. (2006). Urbanization in developing countries: Current trends, future projections, and key challenges for sustainability. *Technology in Society, 28*(1–2), 63–80.

Cohen, C., & Werker, E. D. (2008). The political economy of "natural" disasters. *Journal of Conflict Resolution, 52*(6), 795–819.

Corburn, J., & Sverdlik, A. (2017). Slum upgrading and health equity. *International Journal of Environmental Research and Public Health, 14*(4), 342.

Cunha, A. D. S. (2023). *A Gestão de risco para redução de desastres naturais e a construção de cidades resilientes.*

Cutter, S. L. (1996). Vulnerability to environmental hazards. *Progress in Human Geography, 20*(4), 529–539.

Davis, M. (2006). *Planet cities misery: Urbanization and marginality in the 21st century.* Economic Culture Fund.

Dessai, S., Adger, W. N., Hulme, M., Turnpenny, J., Köhler, J., & Warren, R. (2004). Defining and experiencing dangerous climate change: An editorial essay. *Climate Change, 64*(1–2), 11–25.

Diffenbaugh, N. S., & Giorgi, F. (2012). Climate change hotspots in the CMIP5 global climate model ensemble. *Climate Change, 114*(3–4), 813–822.

Douglas, I., Alam, K., Maghenda, M., Mcdonnell, Y., Mclean, L., & Campbell, J. (2008). Unjust waters: Climate change, flooding, and the urban poor in Africa. *Environment and Urbanization, 20*(1), 187–205.

Eakin, H., & Lemos, M. C. (2006). Adaptation and the state: Latin America and the challenge of capacity-building under globalization. *Global Environmental Change, 16*(1), 7–18.

Edwing, R. and Cervero, R. (2010). Travel and the built environment: A meta-analysis. *Journal of the American Planning Association*, 76(3), 265–294

Eisenhardt, K. M. (1989). Building theories from case study research. *The Academy of Management Review, 14*(4), 532–550.

EM-DAT. (2022). *The international disaster database*. Center for Research on the Epidemiology of Disasters (CRED). https://www.emdat.be/publications/

Ermert, V., Fink, A. H., Morse, A. P., & Paeth, H. (2012). The impact of regional climate change on malaria risk due to greenhouse forcing and land-use changes in tropical Africa. *Environmental Health Perspectives, 120*(1), 77–84.

Ezeh, A., Oyebode, O., Satterthwaite, D., Chen, Y. F., Ndugwa, R., Sartori, J., & Lilford, R. J. (2017). The history, geography, and sociology of slums and the health problems of people who live in slums. *The Lancet, 389*(10068), 547–558.

Fernandes, E. (2011). *Regularization of informal settlements in Latin America.* Lincoln Institute of Land Policy.

Few, R., Brown, K., & Tompkins, E. L. (2007). Climate change and coastal management decisions: Insights from Christchurch Bay, UK. *Coastal Management, 35*(2–3), 255–270.

Florida, R. (2017). *The new urban crisis: How our cities are increasing inequality, deepening segregation, and failing the middle class—And what we can do about it.* Basic Books.

Ford, J. D., Keskitalo, E. C. H., Smith, T., Pearce, T., Berrang-Ford, L., Duerden, F., & Smit, B. (2010). Case study and analogue methodologies in climate change vulnerability research. *Wiley Interdisciplinary Reviews: Climate Change, 1*(3), 374–392.

Fung, A. (2006). Varieties of participation in complex governance. *Public Administration Review, 66*, 66–75.

Gehl, J. (2013). *Cities for people*. Island Press.

Gilbert, A. (2007). The return of the slum: Does language matter? *International Journal of Urban and Regional Research, 31*(4), 697–713.

Gomes, P. C. (2018). Climate change impacts on the water resources of the Rio Carioca basin, Rio de Janeiro, Brazil. *Water*, 700.

Gomes, R. (2023). *Relembre tragédias causadas pela chuva no país na última década.* Available at https://www1.folha.uol.com.br/cotidiano/2023/09/relembre-as-principais-tragedias-causadas-pela-chuva-no-pais-na-ultima-decada.shtml

Gonzalez, R. C., & Woods, R. E. (2002). *Digital image processing*. Prentice-Hall.

Gotham, K. F. (2010). Race, place, and environmental justice after hurricane Katrina: Struggles to reclaim, rebuild, and revitalize New Orleans and the Gulf coast. *Contemporary Sociology: A Journal of Reviews, 39*, 25–26.

Gupta, J., Van Der Leeuw, K., & De Moel, H. (2008). Climate change: A 'glocal' problem requiring 'glocal' action. *Environmental Sciences, 4*(3), 139–148.
Hallegatte S., Bangalore, B., Bonzanigo, L., Fay, M., Kane, T., Narloch, U., Rozenberg, J., Treguer, D., & Vogt-Schilb, A. (2015). *Shock waves: Managing the impacts of climate change on poverty. Climate Change and Development Series*. The World Bank.
Hirabayashi, Y., Mahendran, R., Koirala, S., Konoshima, L., Yamazaki, D., Watanabe, S., Kim, H., & Kanae, S. (2013). Global flood risk under climate change. *Nature Climate Change, 3*(9), 816–821.
Instituto Brasileiro de Geografia e Estatística (IBGE). (2020). *Synthesis of social indicators: An analysis of the living conditions of the Brazilian population*. IBGE.
Jongman, B., Ward, P. J., & Aerts, J. C. (2012). Global exposure to river and coastal flooding: Long term trends and changes. *Global Environmental Change, 22*(4), 823–835.
Knutson, T. R., McBride, J. L., Chan, J., Emanuel, K., Holland, G., Landsea, C., Held, I., Kossin, J. P., Srivastava, A. K., & Sugi, M. (2010). Tropical cyclones and climate change. *Nature Geoscience, 3*(3), 157–163.
Kreiger, T. P. (2020). *Environmental conflicts, migration and governance*. Bristol University Press.
Künzli, N., Medina, S., Kaiser, R., Quenel, P., Horak, F., Jr., & Studnicka, M. (2001). Assessment of deaths attributable to air pollution: Should we use risk estimates based on time series or on cohort studies? *American Journal of Epidemiology, 153*(11), 1050–1055.
Lal, R. (2001). Soil degradation by erosion. *Land Degradation & Development, 12*(6), 519–539.
Leichenko, R., & Silva, J. A. (2014). Climate change and poverty: Vulnerability, impacts, and alleviation strategies. *Wiley Interdisciplinary Reviews: Climate Change, 5*(4), 539–556.
Lloyd, S. J., Kovats, R. S., & Chalabi, Z. (2011). Climate change, crop yields, and undernutrition: Development of a model to quantify the impact of climate scenarios on child undernutrition. *Environmental Health Perspectives, 119*(12), 1817–1823.
Lobell, D. B., Schlenker, W., & Costa-Roberts, J. (2011). Climate trends and global crop production since 1980. *Science, 333*(6042), 616–620.
Lucas, R. E., Jr. (2004). Life earnings and rural-urban migration. *Journal of Political Economy, 112*(S1), S29–S59.
Marengo, J. A., Torres, R. R., & Alves, L. M. (2017). Drought in Northeast Brazil—Past, present, and future. *Theoretical and Applied Climatology, 129*, 1189–1200.
McGranahan, G., Schensul, D., & Singh, G. (2016). Inclusive urbanization: Can the 2030 agenda be delivered without it? *Environment and Urbanization, 28*(1), 13–34.
Meirelles, R., & Athayde, C. (2014). *Um País chamado Favela*. Editora Gente.
Merriam, S. B. (1998). *Qualitative research and case study applications in education*. Jossey-Bass.
Mileti, D. (1999). *Disasters by design: A reassessment of natural hazards in the United States*. Joseph Henry Press.
Mora, C., Dousset, B., Caldwell, I. R., Powell, F. E., Geronimo, R. C., Bielecki, C. R., Counsell, C. W., Dietrich, B. S., Johnston, E. T., Louis, L. V., Lucas, M. P., McKenzie, M. M., Shea, A. G., Tseng, H., Giambelluca, T. W., Leon, L. R., Hawkins, E., & Trauernicht, C. (2017). Global risk of deadly heat. *Nature Climate Change, 7*(7), 501–506.
Moss, R. H., Edmonds, J. A., Hibbard, K. A., Manning, M. R., Rose, S. K., van Vuuren, D. P., Carter, T., Emori, S., Kainuma, M., Kram, T., Meehl, G., Mitchell, J., Nakicenovic, N., Riahi, K., Smith, S., Stouffer, R., Thomson, A., Weyant, J., & Wilbanks, T. J. (2010). The next generation of scenarios for climate change research and assessment. *Nature, 463*(7282), 747–756.
Moura, I. (2004). *Ambientalismo e juventude: o sujeito ecológico e o horizonte da ação política contemporânea. apud R. e. Novaes, Juventude e Sociedade; trabalho, educação, cultura e participação*. Fundação Perseu Abramo e Instituto da Cidadania.
Muttarak, R., & Lutz, W. (2014). Is education a key to reducing vulnerability to natural disasters and hence unavoidable climate change? *Ecology and Society, 19*(1), 42.
Nelson, J. R., & Grubesic, T. (2018). Environmental justice: A panoptic overview using Scientometrics. *Sustainability, 10*(4), 1–18.

Obando, L. A., & Portilla, M. (2009). *The Glocality and its importance to recognize the microhistory and configure the regional identity through Environmental Education*. Narino.
Oliver-Smith, A. (1996). Anthropological research on hazards and disasters. *Anthropology Annual Review, 25*(1), 303–328.
Payne, G., Durand-Lasserve, A., & Rakodi, D. C. (2009). The limits of land titling and home ownership. *Environment and Urbanization, 21*(2), 443–462.
Pelling, M., & High, C. (2005). Understanding adaptation: What can social capital offer to adaptive capacity assessments? *Global Environmental Change, 15*(4), 308–319.
Pelling, M., & Wisner, B. (Eds.). (2009). *Disaster risk reduction: Cases from Urban Africa*. Earthscan.
Peluso, N. L., & Watts, M. (2001). *Violent environments*. Cornell University Press.
Phansalkar, A. R. (2017). Climate change, urban vulnerability, and poverty reduction: A study of informal settlements in Mumbai, India. *Habitat International*, 91–100.
Piketty, T. (2014). *Capital in the 21st century*. Harvard University Press.
Revi, A., Satterthwaite, D. E., Aragon-Durand, F., Corfee-Morlot, J., Kiunsi, R. B., Pelling, M., Roberts, D. C., & Solecki, W. (2014). Urban areas. In *Climate Change 2014: Impacts, Adaptation and Vulnerability. Part A: Global and sectoral aspects. Contribution of Working Group II to the Fifth Assessment Report of the Intergovernmental Panel on Climate Change* (pp. 535–612). Cambridge University Press.
Ribeiro, A. (2023). *Contrastes nas favelas*. Brasil Escola. Available at https://brasilescola.uol.com.br/brasil/contrastes-nas-favelas.htm
Roberts, J. T., & Parks, B. C. (2007). *A climate of injustice: Global inequality, north–south politics, and climate policy*. The MIT Press.
Rodrik, D. (2011). *The future of economic convergence*. National Bureau of Economic Research Working Paper No. 17400.
Rolnik, R., & Klink, J. (2011). Crescimento econômico e desenvolvimento urbano: por que nossas cidades continuam tão precárias? *Novos estudos CEBRAP*, 89–109.
Rosenzweig, C. S. (2011). *Climate change and cities: First assessment report of the urban climate change research network*. Cambridge University Press.
Roy, A. (2005). Urban informality: Towards an epistemology of planning. *Journal of the American Planning Association, 71*(2), 147–158.
Satterthwaite, D., Archer, D., Colenbrander, S., Dodman, D., Hardoy, J., Mitlin, D., & Patel, S. (2020). Building resilience to climate change in informal settlements. *One Earth, 2*(2), 143–156.
Schlosberg, D. (2013). Theorising environmental justice: The expanding sphere of a discourse. *Environmental Politics, 22*(1), 37–55.
Silva Lopes, J. L. (2023). *Arena pública, colonialidade e resistência em um território amazônico: o Fórum de Desenvolvimento Sustentável das Ilhas de Belém-PA*. Editora Dialética.
Snyder, H. (2019). Literature review as a research methodology: An overview and guidelines. *Journal of Business Research, 104*, 333–339.
Stiglitz, J. E. (2012). *The price of inequality: How today's divided society endangers*. W. W. Norton & Company.
Tadrous, P. J. (2010). On the concept of objectivity in digital image analysis in pathology. *Pathology, 42*(3), 207–211.
Tellis, W. (1997). Introduction to case study. *The Qualitative Report, 3*(2), 1–14.
Twigg, J. (2004). *Disaster risk reduction: Mitigation and preparedness in development and emergency programming*. Humanitarian Practice Network: Overseas Development Institute.
United Nations. (1987). *World commission on environment and development: Our common future*. United Nations.
United Nations (UN). (2016a). *Pretoria Declaration: Outcome document of the Habitat III thematic meeting on informal settlements*. Pretoria. UN.
United Nations (UN). (2016b). *World cities report 2016: Urbanization and development - Emerging futures*. United Nations Human Settlements Program. UN-HABITAT.

United Nations (UN). (2019a). *Human development report 2019: Beyond income, beyond averages, beyond today: Inequalities in human development in the 21st century*. United Nations Development Program.
United Nations (UN). (2019b). *World urbanization prospects: The 2018 revision*. Department of Economic and Social Affairs New York: United Nations.
UOL Economia. (2023). *IBGE: Brasil tem 11.403 favelas*. Available at https://economia.uol.com.br/noticias/estadao-conteudo/2023/03/17/ibge-brasil-tem-11403-favelas-onde-vivem-cerca-de-16-milhoes-de-pessoas.htm?cmpid=copiaecola
van Westen, C. J., van Asch, T. W., & Soeters, R. (2006). Danger of landslides and risk zoning: Why is it still so difficult? *Engineering Geology and Environment Newsletter, 65*(2), 167–184.
Wheeler, T., & von Braun, J. (2013). Impacts of climate change on world food security. *Science, 341*(6145), 508–513.
Wilhite, D. A., & Pulwarty, R. S. (2017). *Drought and the water crisis: Integrating science, management, and policy*. Press CRC.
World Economic Forum (WEF). (2020). *Toward common metrics and consistent reporting of sustainable value creation*. WEF.
World Health Organization (WHO). (2018). *Health in the urban environment*. Informational page. Taken from https://www.who.int/heli/risks/urban/en/
Yin, R. (2022). *Case study research: Design and methods*. Sage Publishing.

Armando Dias-da-Fé is a professor at the Guarda Polytechnic Institute. He has a degree and master's degree in Accounting from the University of São Paulo (USP), a doctorate from the Universities of Aveiro and Minho, and an MBA in Biofuels (UESC-Petrobras). He worked in the financial market through Banco Nossa Caixa and Caixa Economia Federal. He is currently a business consultant. He has dedicated himself to the environment and labor relations with a patent on a biodiesel plant and a virtualized time clock. As a hobby, he enjoys teaching mathematics and financial literacy.

Rosmel Rodríguez-Barroso is a Venezuelan political scientist with an MBA from EUDE Business School in collaboration with Universidad Camilo José Cela in Madrid. He pursued postgraduate studies in sustainable development management at the University of Cambridge and policy analysis at the London School of Economics. Currently, he is pursuing his PhD in Democracy at the University of Coimbra in Portugal. In addition to his academic pursuits, he currently serves as the European Climate Pact Ambassador and works as a lecturer at the Central University of Venezuela, specializing in the field of political ecology. His academic research and work focus on youth participation in climate action and climate justice.

Rute Abreu is Coordinator Professor, with tenure, of Accounting and Finance at the *Instituto Politécnico da Guarda* (Portugal), Department of Management and Economy. Rute teaches financial analysis, corporate finance, schedule and appraisal investment, auditing, financial accounting, taxation, firm valuation, quality, and social responsibility management. Actually, Rute is the Accounting Degree Director and the Integrated Management System master's degree Director. Rute holds a master's degree in industrial engineering at the *Universidade Nova de Lisboa* (Portugal) and PhD in Accounting and Finance at the Universidad de Salamanca (Spain). Their scientific research is based as an integrated researcher at the Center for Research in Accounting and Taxation of the Cávado and Ave Polytechnic Institute, Portugal and as collaborate researcher at the Center for Research in Digital Services. Rute, also, collaborates with MackPesquisa of Universidade Presbiteriana Mackenzie, Brasil. Rute develops scientific activities with Social Responsibility Research Network and Global Corporate Governance Institute and her research focuses on CSR, corporate governance, accounting and firm valuation and it has been published in several journals and participates in the organization, all over the world, of conferences, seminars, and meetings. Also, Rute participates in the blind review process for several journals and helps as

Associate Editor on The Social Responsibility Journal and Accounting and Management Review of Ordem dos Contabilistas Certificados (Portugal). Particularly, Rute is involved in projects with higher impact on social reintegration on Higher Education on Accounting. Very relevant as public servant always promotes the transfer of knowledge to the society related to Agriculture Sustainability (Olive oil in Portugal and autochthonous race (Burro-de-Miranda-AEPGA)), Accounting Education (Accountant 5.0), Tax and Auditing Citizenship, Management Quality Systems in Social Economy and Accounting Firms, and Performance Analysis at Beauty Firms.

Social Entrepreneurship Through Collaboration: A Case Study on Sustainable and Inclusive Social Business Development in Japan

Keiko Yokoyama and Yukihiro Wakuta

1 Introduction

Collaboration plays a significant role in social entrepreneurship, but the discussion on why, when, and in what form collaboration is developed has not been sufficiently conducted and is considered an unexplored topic (de Bruin et al., 2017). In addition, research on cross-sectoral heterogeneous collaboration among organizations as collaboration to solve social problems has been conducted mainly in discussions at the organizational level (e.g., Austin, 2010). On the other hand, there have been few studies that have closely followed the micro movements of the people and leaders of the organizations involved in the cross-sector, and how these movements led to the creation of new value has rarely been analyzed from the perspective of entrepreneurship (Huxham & Vangen, 2000; Waddock & Post, 1995; de Bruin et al., 2017). In other words, there have not been sufficient discussions of social entrepreneurship, which functions in collaborative settings for solving social problems.

Based on the above issues, we clarify social entrepreneurship in collaboration to solve social problems. Specifically, we will analyze a case study of social business creation in which for-profit companies play a central role and collaborate to solve multiple social issues.

K. Yokoyama (✉)
Kansai Universit, Suita, Osaka, Japan
e-mail: yokokei@kansai-u.ac.jp

Y. Wakuta
Nagoya University, Nagoya, Aichi, Japan
e-mail: wakuta@info.human.nagoya-u.ac.jp

B. Díaz Díaz et al. (eds.), *Building Global Societies Towards an ESG World*, CSR, Sustainability, Ethics & Governance,
https://doi.org/10.1007/978-3-031-56619-6_3

2 A Brief Review of Previous Studies

2.1 *Social Entrepreneurship (SE)*

Social entrepreneurship (hereafter SE) is considered a difficult concept to grasp and define (Choi & Majumdar, 2014). However, the common perception is that it is a movement that places social value creation above individual and shareholder interests as its priority (Austin et al., 2006) and is understood as a process of combining resources in new ways to create value (Short et al., 2009). Martin and Osberg (2007) state that "the social entrepreneur aims for value in the form of large-scale, transformational benefit that accrues either to a significant segment of society or to society at large" (pp. 34–35). Saebi et al. (2019), after an extensive review that includes the above, states that most definitions emphasize the hybrid nature of combining social mission and entrepreneurial activity, a concept in which organizational purpose converges with the primacy of social value creation.

This study investigates the SE phenomenon through collaboration through examples of social businesses created in collaboration with many organizations.

2.2 *SE in Collaborative Research*

Collaboration is essential in solving social problems (Austin, 2010). Discussions on cross-sectoral collaboration in solving social problems have emerged in various forms. They consist of social partnerships (Waddock, 1991), cross-sector collaboration (Logsdon, 1991; Bryson et al., 2006), cross-sector partnerships (Googins & Rochlin, 2000), cross-sector socially oriented partnerships (Selsky & Parker, 2005), and collective impact (Kania & Kramer, 2011).

Selsky and Parker (2005) point out that cross-sectoral collaboration to solve social problems is a diverse phenomenon and difficult to grasp because it varies in scale, scope, and purpose. In other words, there are various forms of collaboration, ranging from dyadic (one-to-one) two-sector to multi-sector (three or more sectors) collaboration, from local to global level, and from short-term to long-term. Therefore, Selsky and Parker (2005) typify cross-sectoral collaborations by their objectives and the circumstances in which they emerge and examine each of them by phase of collaboration. Bryson et al. (2006) consider various aspects of cross-sectoral collaboration: assumptions and initial conditions, processes, structures and governance, facilitators and constraints, outcomes and accountability. They then review several prior research and derive propositions for cross-sectoral collaboration.

However, most researchers have only discussed this at the organizational level. Few theoretical studies have examined the leadership required at the intersectoral interface (Huxham & Vangen, 2000; Waddock & Post, 1995; Selsky & Parker, 2005).

2.3 Collaborative in SE Research

Very few researchers have focused on actors of collaboration such as social entrepreneurs (de Bruin et al., 2017). For example, Pret and Carter (2017) discuss why local moral obligations induce social value creation and collaboration; Kwong et al. (2017) examine the relationship between collaboration and resource mobilization, organizational relationships, and mission drift in SE; and Huybrechts et al. (2017) examine the types of collaboration in SEs.

Although there are a growing number of papers on SE and collaboration, how practitioners can initiate, coordinate, and evolve collaborations that create social value, in other words, research on entrepreneurial behaviors and practices for collaboration is scarce (de Bruin et al., 2017). Collaboration research is important for social enterprises because collaborative arrangements and partnerships improve access to resources and funding, and enhance legitimacy of social enterprises and also provide a means for the exchange of tacit knowledge (de Bruin et al., 2017).

Kosmynin (2022) conducted a systematic literature review (SLR) of academic articles on collaboration in social entrepreneurship organizations (SEOs). The SLR used the Scopus and Web of Science databases and ultimately yielded 40 scholarly articles. After a close review of these articles, Kosmynin (2022) points out that collaborative SEO, while increasingly recognized as an important entrepreneurial process, has not been adequately studied, and there is a dearth of research on entrepreneurial "actions" (practices) for collaboration. How are collaborations for solving social issues generated and linked to the creation of social business? What functions do SEs, which are responsible for collaboration, fulfill in this process? This study clarifies this question through a case study considering the issues raised by previous studies.

3 Case

3.1 Reason for Case Selection

In this study, we conducted a case study on collaborative social entrepreneurship. A case study is a research strategy that focuses on observing relationships among factors and their changes in individual situations and is used for a variety of purposes, including description, theory testing, and theory generation (Eisenhardt, 1989). Since the purpose of this study is to gain new perspectives for theory development by observing the dynamics of collaboration, the case study method was deemed appropriate.

This study examines a case in which a for-profit company developed sustainable and inclusive social business in collaboration with diverse organizations. The case study to be taken up is the development of a new brand of "compost" by Urban Research Corporation (UR). UR is an apparel company founded in 1974 in Osaka,

Japan, with the following corporate philosophy: "We make an unusual effort to discover something valuable that has both quality and originality from all over the world in order to share those with our customers." This case is representative because the "compost" development project was a collaborative effort between UR, a for-profit company, and various actors, including NPOs (Pettigrew, 1990; Yin, 1994).

The data source was a survey of interviews with key stakeholders regarding this development project. We conducted a total of nine interviews with seven key stakeholders: Mr. A, Mr. B, Mr. C, Mr. D, Ms. E, Mr. F, Ms. G. The average interview duration was approximately 1.5 h. All interview data were recorded and transcribed into written form within 24 h. To complement the interview data, we also collected publicly available documents and newspaper articles related to this case study. By analyzing these multiple datasets, we approach the following research questions. How and why was a for-profit company able to collaborate with multiple organizations to build its social business? What function does the SE perform in this collaborative process?

3.2 Overview of a Case

UR, an apparel company, in collaboration with the Colour Recycle Network research team of the Kyoto Institute of Technology Graduate School (CRN research team) and the non-profit organization Kitashiba (Kitashiba), has created a new sustainable brand called "compost," which is made by upcycling discarded clothing. The compost business is a social business that addresses two social issues: solving the problem of discarded clothing and providing employment opportunities for people with disabilities and others who have difficulty working.

Compost's first product, the Multi-purpose Bag, is a water-repellent bag that can be used for a variety of purposes, including plant pot cover, laundry bag, trash can, stationery storage, kitchen storage, and camping gear storage.

Specifically, the CRN research team at the Kyoto Institute of Technology Graduate School has developed a new color-based fiber recycling technology called the "Colour Recycle System." The system makes it possible to recycle waste fibers, which are difficult to sort by material, into value-added materials by separating them by color. Using this technology, a new material, WFRP sheet (Waste Fibre Reinforced Plastic Sheet, hereafter referred to as fibre sheet), was developed from UR's dead stock (clothing that could not be sold and had to be discarded due to scratches and dirt). The new fibre sheet material was created using the "colour of the company's products," which is an essential part of the fashion identity.

UR spent time with Kitashiba exchanging ideas on design and sewing methods to plan a product using this new fibre sheet material. As a result, the MULTI-purpose Bag was selected as the first sustainable product under the Compost brand. By outsourcing the sewing and finishing of the product to Kitashiba, UR has created work opportunities for people who do not fit into the work style of being employed somewhere and working set hours (e.g., women with small children, elderly people who are not very physically fit, people with disabilities, etc.). This story has been told to the shop assistants and sales have been good.

The life cycle of this Multi-purpose Bag is as follows (see Fig. 1).

① Sorted by color from UR's dead stock.
② CRN's research team (now colourloop inc.) creates a new fiber sheet by breaking up fibers and compositing them with resin.
③ Kitashiba produces the product.
④ UR sells the products.
⑤ UR collects unused products from customers at its stores.

3.3 *Collaboration Creation Stage*

The Universal Work Study Group (UWSG), this is where the collaboration began. The UWSG was a study group to solve the social issues that UR had been facing. The social issues were reducing waste clothing and increasing the employment rate of people with disabilities. At the time, UR's business performance was expanding, and the number of employees was increasing due to the expansion of the store network through new store openings, and accordingly, there was a need to increase the employment of people with disabilities in order to meet the legally mandated employment rate. At the same time, the company was aware of the need to address the problem of disposing of dead stock, a common issue in the apparel industry.

To solve the social issues of UR, Mr. A, an executive officer of UR, and Mr. B, a staff member, consulted with Mr. C and Mr. D of GDP, a non-profit organization that works with partner companies to create systems for the proper treatment and recycling of feather products. As UR was a member organization of GDP, Mr. C and Mr. D decided that as part of GDP's commitment to member services, they would

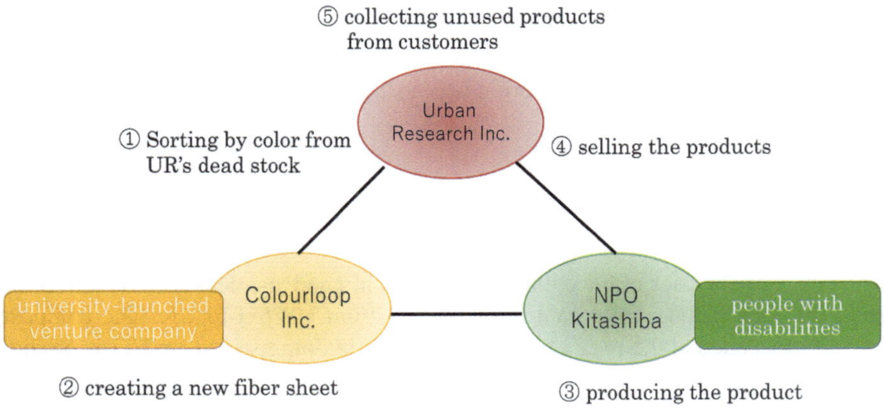

Fig. 1 Business development stage

first organize a study group, the UWSG, to help UR solve its social problems. The UWSG was formed in 2017 with various members led by Mr. A, Mr. B, Mr. C, and Mr. D.

The study group lasted for 2 years. The meeting was organized in two parts, with the first part being a topic presentation and the second part being a discussion toward practice, which took more than 3 h each time.

The first meeting was held in April 2017 with the participation of three commercial companies involved in the welfare of persons with disabilities. Here, the topic "The significance of disabled people's work and the role of companies" was presented and discussed to understand the difficulties that disabled companies face in their lives as well as their strengths. Subsequently, the employees of the UR participated in 'communication training with persons with disabilities' by the company that provided the topic. Thus, each time, experts and practitioners related to the social issues were invited there, and Mr. A and Mr. B established beneficial networks on this occasion.

The impetus was an encounter with Ms. E of the CRN research team, who had completed her doctoral thesis on the production of new materials by separating waste clothing by color at the Kyoto Institute of Technology Graduate School and had created a new upcycling material from waste clothing. Herein, an idea of upcycling UR waste clothing using the CRN research team's technology was born.

Next, Mr. F and Ms. G of Kitashiba joined the UWSG through Mr. D. Kitashiba was engaged in job creation as a support for the unemployed. Here, UR, the CRN research team, and Kitashiba were connected, and the compost project (production of the Multi-purpose bags) was developed.

This study group, UWSG, included a study tour, where participants learned about the employment of people with disabilities in various ways. In particular, they learned about the creation of places where everyone can participate while placing the focus on care and the possibility of balancing social welfare business and economic activities.

The structure of the first half of the collaboration up to this point can be summarized as shown in Fig. 2. UR, Kitashiba, and the CRN research team sat at the same table and sought to collaborate by bringing their respective themes and strengths. They also learned about social issues and reconciled their philosophies, objectives, and awareness. This period was a stage for creating collaboration.

3.4 Business Development Stage

Once the three entities of the collaboration were aligned and decided to create compost, the role of the core organization shifted from UWSG to UR. The compost project proceeded at the pace of the business, but in doing so, the emphasis on dialog remained in place.

The production of the multipurpose bags was based on intense communication and interaction. First, to establish a process for sorting and recycling discarded

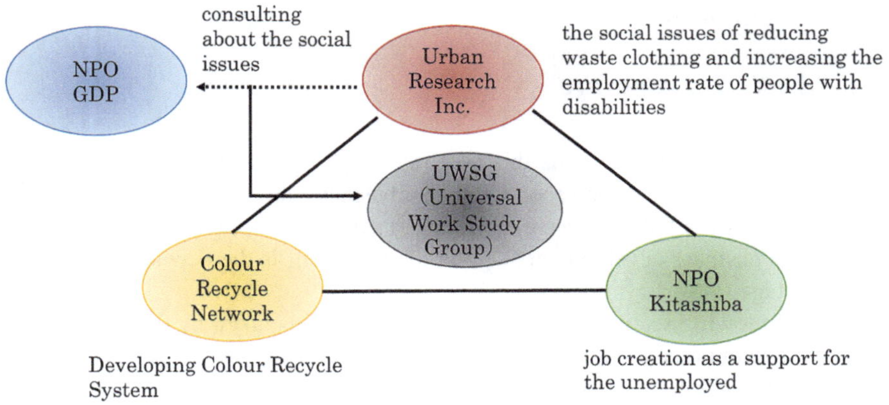

Fig. 2 Collaboration creation stage

clothing, Ms. E visited UR's warehouse many times to discuss sorting methods with people with disabilities. In the prototype stage, members of the Kitashiba team came to offer various ideas and created the production process through close communication. Kitashiba, which is responsible for the production of the multipurpose bags, checks the fiber sheets, produces the multipurpose bags, and delivers the bags to UR's warehouse.

The production process of multipurpose backs is based on a detailed division of labor. The unit labor cost was determined for each stage of the process: drafting (line drawing) on the fiber sheet, sewing with a sewing machine, shaping, and attaching price tags. UR and Kitashiba decided on the unit labor cost by converting it to an hourly wage, and UR took a "not forcing excessive work to people with disabilities" stance toward Kitashiba's manufacturing site, and both parties worked together to set a sustainable unit labor cost. This was because production was handled by a diverse group of people, including people with disabilities and housewives with child care. Kitashiba wanted to adhere to a style in which this diverse group of people could "come when they want and engage in production when they want." UR fully understood this policy through meetings and in-depth communication, and worked to improve the production process.

As shown in Fig. 1, the Multi-purpose bags made by the division of labor among the three organizations were launched in mid-November 2018. Although Kitashiba produces 300 bags each month, it is the first time to make that many bags, and Kitashiba made various detailed adjustments while consulting with UR.

In this way, UR led the latter half of the collaboration that developed into the main businesses of UR, the CRN research team, and Kitashiba. This period is called the business development stage (see Fig. 1).

When UR launched the Multi-purpose bags in stores and online on November 2018, they sold them so much that production soon could not keep up.

4 Case Analysis

4.1 Analysis Procedure

As we have seen, we can divide this case into the first half, the collaboration creation stage (Fig. 2), and the second half, the business development stage (Fig. 1). The first half, the collaboration creation stage, forms a place or platform for collaboration. The business development stage in the latter half is the new social business creation stage.

In the following section, we will organize the actions taken by the various collaborative actors (social entrepreneurs), A-G, in each stage and analysis the functions of these action processes.

4.2 Collective SE in the Collaboration Creation Stage

We interpret the behavioral characteristics of collaborative actors in the collaboration creation stage with the strategic activities of the collective SE of Montgomery et al. (2012). They called for the need to analyze the collective activities of actors working together to solve social problems rather than from the standpoint of a narrative in which individuals who solve social problems are the heroes (Dacin et al., 2011) and proposed the concept of collective SE. They define collective SE as "collaboration amongst similar as well as diverse actors for the purpose of applying business principles to solving social problems" (p. 376).

Montgomery et al. (2012) identified three interrelated strategic activities needed to facilitate and enhance collective SE activities; (1) framing, (2) convening, and (3) multivocality. (1) Framing refers to the creation and translation of ideas and meanings among diverse actors to promote mutual understanding of issues and to negotiate consensus. (2) Convening refers to convening a wide range of diverse actors to share their understanding of an issue and to utilize collective knowledge. (3) Multivocality refers to the ability to speak to an audience by combining multiple voices and lenses of view and requires an understanding of diverse interpretations and lenses, as well as a forum for exchanging ideas and opinions.

In the following section, we examine whether the behavioral patterns corresponding to (1), (2), and (3) are observed in the interpretation of the case study.

At UR, Mr. A and Mr. B took the lead in identifying the company's social issues of waste clothing and employment of people with disabilities and consulted with external actors, Mr. C and Mr. D, to solve these issues. Meanwhile, Mr. C and Mr. D's NPO was also looking for ways to collaborate with member companies to create employment for people with disabilities. They took the lead in organizing a study group called UWSG. In particular, Mr. C and Mr. D brought together a diverse range of outside experts and practitioners in the UWSG.

What this move means is that Mr. A and Mr. B of UR took the lead in setting the agenda (1), while at the same time, Mr. C and Mr. D convened various heterogeneous participants (2).

Mr. C has adopted a method that emphasizes collaboration and dialog, believing that it is important to share values. As a result, the "UWSG," a place established in the collaboration creation stage, promotes understanding from various lenses, including the welfare perspective of employment of people with disabilities, the business perspective of business creation, the SDGs perspective of ethical product development, the perspective of a team of researchers, and the NPO perspective (3). In addition, since it was not just a study session but was oriented toward business creation, it also served the function of a meeting place for social entrepreneurs for this purpose (2).

In summary, we found that (1) framing, (2) convening, and (3) multivocality, the strategic activities of collective SE described by Montgomery et al. (2012), functioned in the SE of the collaborative actors.

4.3 Legitimacy in the Business Development Stage

Once the specific product development direction was determined, the UWSG activities came to an end and the business development stage began, in which the product was to be established as a business.

In the start-up phase of a new business, its visibility is low, and legitimacy needs to be widely promoted both internally and externally. The social recognition required for resource mobilization, or so-called legitimacy, has been discussed in various contexts (Suchman, 1995). Legitimacy is defined as generalized perception or assumption that the actions of an entity are desirable, proper, or appropriate (Suchman, 1995, p. 574). Here, we examine the case in terms of three routes of creative legitimacy process behavior of Takeuchi et al. (2012).

The first route is the route of gaining supporters through above-average effort and ingenuity in order to increase the number of supporters; it is an action that develops a route beyond the scope of routine interactions into a specific domain. The second route is to broaden the supporters by diversifying and expanding the interpretation of the meaning of the reasons for resource mobilization. The third route is to acquire supporters who are capable of exceptionally strong resource mobilization, not only through direct methods such as gaining the support of top management but also through indirect methods such as increasing influence on top management through enhanced external evaluation. In the following section, we will analyze the acquisition of legitimacy in the organization by using the expansion of supporters as route L (1), the expansion of reasons as route L (2), and the development of strong resource providers as route L (3).

After the move to collaborate with UR, Kitashiba, and the CRN research team to develop a product, Mr. A explained this new project move at the weekly management meeting at UR. When the prototype was ready, he brought it to the management meeting to explain it, but the executives and the sales side questioned the product's commercial potential and said, "It may not sell." In response, he focused on the fact that the product's value came from collaborative efforts and that it would contribute to solving the problem of discarded clothing and employment of people with disabilities (L (2)), persuaded people internally to cooperate (L (1)) and overcame opposition and launched the product. Mr. A convinced that UR could become a frontier if it made a full-fledged genuine effort to tackle the SDGs now.

The initial release was only experimental in number. As a result of the sales, there was a growing awareness within the company that times were changing and a project team led by Mr. A was created to address SDGs and sustainability on a company-wide basis (The team was named SDR; Sustainable Development Research). In other words, the fact that the company had established a track record through experimental sales on a small scale was instrumental in gaining legitimacy (L (3)). In the spring of 2019, UR Terrace Inc. was established as a subsidiary company. This company was specially designed to employ people with disabilities.

As described above, we found L (1), (2), and (3) as behavioral characteristics within one organization.

On the other hand, a peculiar strategy was also observed in the collaborative process in which heterogeneous actors were convened. During the product development period, Kitashiba discussed with UR the maximum number of units to be produced as a non-negotiable point. As a result of the discussions, it was decided to settle on the current production limit of 300 pieces per month, as there was a priority to maintain a work style that did not bind people with disabilities with quotas.

Mitzinneck and Besharov (2019) presented three compromise strategies as legitimacy mechanisms for decision making in cross-organizational collaboration. These are the temporary compromise strategy, in which value priorities change over time; the structural compromise strategy, which offers a variety of options and freedom of choice; and the collaborative compromise strategy, in which common standards are jointly developed to maintain value. In this case, the participants in the collaboration shared the values of "not forcing excessive work to people with disabilities" and "come when they want and engage in production when they want," and the production process of the products was created based on these values. This fact represents the collaborative compromise strategy (Mitzinneck & Besharov, 2019). This collaborative compromise allowed Kitashiba to demonstrate a new model for working.

The CRN research team in charge of developing new materials commercialized the technology, leading to the establishment of colourloop, Inc. in August 2019. Ms. E could obtain the need to establish a university-launched venture by participating in UWSG.

5 Discussion and Conclusion

This study identified the following points.

In the first half of the collaborative creation stage, a platform called UWSG was established. In this stage, strategic activities of collective SE such as framing, convening, and multivocality were developed. At this stage, there was no conspicuous legitimizing behavior. The UWSG platform functioned as a meeting place where the openness and diversity of values were tolerated and where mutual understanding was fostered. This made it possible to attract different collaborative actors.

On the other hand, in the business development stage, UR is at the core. We found its internal and external legitimization behavior at this stage. Internally, creative legitimization was demonstrated, and externally, cooperative compromise strategies were seen as interorganizational justification activities.

Figure 3 illustrates this relationship.

In creating social business in collaboration to solve social issues, it is necessary to create a platform for social entrepreneurs. This is the function (framing)(convening)(multivocality) of collective SE as expressed by Montgomery et al. (2012).

In this stage, legitimacy activities are not required. Openness and freedom are required. SEs can participate in this stage with a relatively casual stance. Therefore, the importance of this type of entrepreneurship is sometimes forgotten, but value sharing through the demonstration of entrepreneurship in this stage has a significant impact on legitimizing behavior in the next stage.

During business development, each cooperative actor will develop legitimizing behavior within and outside the organization. Sometimes, heterogeneous logics of legitimation struggle among organizations, but if the collective SE functions well in the platform at the preliminary stage, a compromise strategy can be found.

Finally, this case study revealed that different types of entrepreneurs formed a collective SE. Tracey and Stott (2016) categorize entrepreneurial activities for social innovation into social entrepreneurship, social intrapreneurship, and social extrapreneurship. Social entrepreneurship is the most well-known of the categories in their typology. They think of social entrepreneurship as the process of creating and growing a venture, either for-profit or non-profit, where the motivation of the

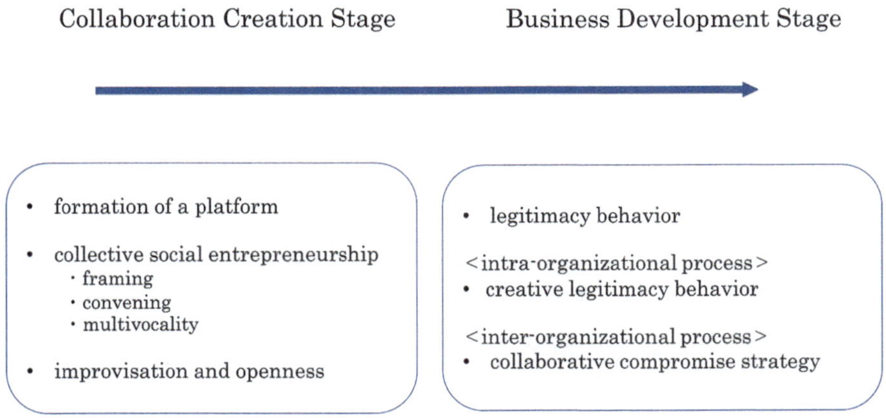

Fig. 3 Social entrepreneurship through collaboration

entrepreneur is to address a particular social challenge or set of challenges. Social intrapreneurship is characterized by the process of addressing social issues from within an existing organization. Social extrapreneurship, on the other hand, is " the process of inter-organizational action that facilitates alternative combinations of ideas, people, places and resources to address social challenges and make social change" and "can be characterized as working in and between organizations and networks, not only to create apparently novel solutions, but also to develop a range of support mechanisms for the 'ecosystems' and 'platforms' that shape social change" (Tracey & Stott, 2016, p. 55).

In this study, GDP Representative Directors Mr. C and Mr. D, who created and operated the UWSG platform, are considered social extrapreneurs. The social intrapreneurs are Mr. A and Mr. B of UR and Mr. F and Ms. G of Kitashiba, while the social entrepreneur is Ms. E of the CRN research team. Although the discussion of collective SE emphasizes multivocality among various types of actors, the development project of "Compost" was a collaboration among social extrapreneurs who created and operated the platform, social intrapreneurs who used the internal resources of the company, and social entrepreneurs who brought technology and ideas.

Tracey and Stott (2016) consider the three types of entrepreneurial activity (social entrepreneurship, social intrapreneurship, and social entrepreneurship) as independent concepts, but do not consider collaboration between different types of entrepreneurial activity. However, in this case study, we were able to see how the three types of entrepreneurial activity collaborated to create a single project. Figure 3 illustrates the processes and functions of Social Entrepreneurship through Collaboration. This figure can be said to illustrate the collective knowledge of different entrepreneurial activities.

The challenge of this study is that it is a single case study and lacks robustness to generalization. However, this study could derive the process and function of SE through collaboration. In the future, we would like to elaborate on arguments based on multiple case studies and quantitative analysis.

References

Austin, J. E. (2010). *The collaboration challenge: How nonprofits and businesses succeed through strategic alliances* (Vol. 109). Wiley.

Austin, J. S., Stevenson, H., & Wei-Skillern, J. (2006). Social and commercial entrepreneurship: Same, different, or both. *Entrepreneurship Theory and Practice, 30*(1), 1–22.

Bryson, J. M., Crosby, B. C., & Stone, M. M. (2006). The design and implementation of cross-sector collaborations: Propositions from the literature. *Public Administration Review, 66*, 44–55.

Choi, N., & Majumdar, S. (2014). Social entrepreneurship as an essentially contested concept: Opening a new avenue for systematic future research. *Journal of Business Venturing, 29*(3), 363–376.

Dacin, M. T., Dacin, P. A., & Tracey, P. (2011). Social entrepreneurship: A critique and future directions. *Organization Science, 22*(5), 1203–1213.

de Bruin, A., Shaw, E., & Lewis, K. V. (2017). The collaborative dynamic in social entrepreneurship. *Entrepreneurship & Regional Development, 29*(7–8), 575–585.
Eisenhardt, K. M. (1989). Building theories from case study research. *Academy of Management Review, 14*(4), 532–550.
Googins, B. K., & Rochlin, S. A. (2000). Creating the partnership society: Understanding the rhetoric and reality of cross-sectoral partnerships. *Business & Society Review, 105*(1), 127–144.
Huxham, C., & Vangen, S. (2000). Leadership in the shaping and implementation of collaboration agendas: How things happen in a (not quite) joined-up world. *Academy of Management Journal, 43*(6), 1159–1175.
Huybrechts, B., Nicholls, A., & Edinger, K. (2017). Sacred alliance or pact with the devil? How and why social enterprises collaborate with mainstream businesses in the fair trade sector. *Entrepreneurship & Regional Development, 29*(7–8), 586–608.
Kania, J., & Kramer, M. (2011). Collective impact, Stanford. *Social Innovation Review* (Winter), 36–41.
Kosmynin, M. (2022). Social entrepreneurship organisations and collaboration: Taking stock and looking forward. *International Journal of Entrepreneurial Behavior & Research, 28*(2), 441–470.
Kwong, C., Tasavori, M., & Wun-mei Cheung, C. (2017). Bricolage, collaboration and mission drift in social enterprises. *Entrepreneurship & Regional Development, 29*(7–8), 609–638.
Logsdon, J. M. (1991). Interests and interdependence in the formation of social problem-solving collaboration. *Journal of Applied Behavioral Science, 27*(1), 23–37.
Martin, R. L., & Osberg, S. (2007). Social entrepreneurship: The case for definition. *Stanford Social Innovation Review*, 2007, 29–39.
Mitzinneck, B. C., & Besharov, M. L. (2019). Managing value tensions in collective social entrepreneurship: The role of temporal, structural, and collaborative compromise. *Journal of Business Ethics, 159*(2), 381–400.
Montgomery, A. W., Dacin, P. A., & Dacin, M. T. (2012). Collective social entrepreneurship: Collaboratively shaping social good. *Journal of Business Ethics, 111*(3), 375–388.
Pettigrew, A. M. (1990). Longitudinal field research on change: Theory and practice. *Organization Science, 1*, 267–292.
Pret, T., & Carter, S. (2017). The importance of 'fitting in': Collaboration and social value creation in response to community norms and expectations. *Entrepreneurship & Regional Development, 29*(7–8), 639–667.
Saebi, T., Foss, N. J., & Linder, S. (2019). Social entrepreneurship research: Past achievements and future promises. *Journal of Management, 45*(1), 70–95.
Selsky, J. W., & Parker, B. (2005). Cross-sector partnerships to address social issues: Challenges to theory and practice. *Journal of Management, 31*(6), 849–873.
Short, J. C., Moss, T. W., & Lumpkin, G. T. (2009). Research in social entrepreneurship: Past contributions and future opportunities. *Strategic Entrepreneurship Journal, 3*(2), 161–194.
Suchman, M. C. (1995). Managing legitimacy: Strategic and institutional approaches. *Academy of Management Review, 20*(3), 571–610.
Takeuchi, A., Aoshima, Y., & Karube, M. (2012). *Reasons for innovation*. Yuhikaku.
Tracey, P., & Stott, N. (2016). Social innovation: A window on alternative ways of organizing and innovating. *Innovation, Organization & Management, 19*(1), 51–60.
Waddock, S. A. (1991). A typology of social partnership organizations. *Administration & Society, 22*(4), 480–515.
Waddock, S. A., & Post, J. E. (1995). Catalytic alliances for social problem solving. *Human Relations, 48*(8), 951–973.
Yin, R. K. (1994). *Case study research: Design and methods* (2nd ed.). Sage Publications.

Keiko Yokoyama , Professor, Faculty of Business and Commerce, Kansai University. Representative Director of Sobakuri Labo, a general incorporated association. Completed the

Graduate School of Economics, Hokkaido University. Ph.D. in Business Administration. While working in the field of research, she came into contact with people who were boldly working to create new value by breaking out of the existing framework and became fascinated by the way of life of entrepreneurship. She has edited several books, including *Corporate Social Strategy and NPOs, Ethical Entrepreneurship* and *Collective Impact in Japan.*

Yukihiro Wakuta, Associate Professor in the Graduate School of Environmental Studies at Nagoya University. He received his master's degree from Keio University. He is currently vice president of the Japan Society for Information and Management. His research interests include institutional theory and sustainable entrepreneurship. His recent paper is "How digital platform leaders can foster dynamic capabilities through innovation processes: The case of taobao" (*Technology Analysis & Strategic Management*, 09 Mar 2022, DOI: 10.1080/09537325.2022.2050690).

Corporate Responsibility: Understanding (and Misunderstanding) of Corporate Social Responsibility, Sustainability, and Solidarity

Emma Ann Thornberg, Rejina Mary Selvam, and Miquel Bastons

1 Introduction

There has been growing pressure in recent years on corporations to address their role in environmental, economic, and social problems (Matten & Moon, 2008; Sharma & Henriques, 2005; Starik & Marcus, 2000). Corporations face an increasing responsibility to go beyond the scope of traditional, single bottom-line entities. Considering this, many corporations have responded by publishing annual reports of their involvement in responsible and sustainable actions (Xie & Hayase, 2007). Such escalating pressure has also motivated scholars to study corporations' involvement in environmentally, economically, and socially responsible actions (Andersson & Bateman, 2000; Howard-Grenville, 2006; Sharma, 2000). A problem has emerged, however, in both practice and academia as the number of corporations publishing corporate responsibility reports increases, and fundamental constructs of corporate responsibility proliferate (Bansal, 2005; Carroll, 1999; Kolk & Perego, 2014). There appears to be a certain overlap and some misunderstanding amongst corporate sustainability, corporate social responsibility, and corporate solidarity in both research and practice (Dahlsrud, 2008; Montiel, 2008; Rim et al., 2016).

CS, CSR, and corporate solidarity were historically distinct from one another. CS fell within the environmental responsibility realm of business (Sharma & Henriques, 2005; Shrivastava, 1995). Meanwhile, CSR addressed socially and economically responsible practices (Montiel, 2008), and supposed acts of solidarity

E. A. Thornberg (✉) · M. Bastons
International University of Catalunya, Catalunya, Spain
e-mail: ethornberg@uic.es; bastons@uic.es

R. M. Selvam
Serra Hunter Fellow, University of Barcelona, Barcelona, Spain
e-mail: rselvam@ub.edu

B. Díaz Díaz et al. (eds.), *Building Global Societies Towards an ESG World*, CSR, Sustainability, Ethics & Governance,
https://doi.org/10.1007/978-3-031-56619-6_4

were viewed as purely altruistic actions (Lantos, 2002; Sprinkle & Maines, 2010). The demarcation between environmental, social, economic, and altruistic actions made CS, CSR and corporate solidarity more easily distinguishable. In recent decades, however, conceptualizations of CS, CSR and corporate solidarity have begun to dovetail, blurring the line between the three terms (Melissen et al., 2018). A lack of consensus has resulted in a critical plight putting business executives in cumbersome situations and academics in significant ambiguity. Our aim is to provide a literature review that helps distinguish CS, CSR, and corporate solidarity from one another. We will then examine the fit between what our taxonomy of corporate responsibility declares and what managers understand.

This chapter is structured as follows. The next section reviews existing literature on corporate social responsibility, corporate sustainability, and corporate solidarity. The subsequent section presents the development of the taxonomy and the research question. The penultimate section presents the research methodology followed by the results of this study. Finally, the implications, limitations, and concluding remarks of this study are presented.

2 Corporate Social Responsibility

Corporate social responsibility is the "serious attempt to solve social problems caused wholly or in part by the corporation" (Fitch, 1976, p. 38). According to Lu and Liu (2014), "CSR was merely a theoretical and ethical concept 40 years ago" (p. 125), but CSR evolved over the years as corporations faced new demands to be socially responsible (Pinkston & Carroll, 1996). CSR became a medium for corporations to address their responsibility to maximize their profits and, at the same time, contribute to the improvement of their stakeholders' welfare (Hediger, 2010; Melissen et al., 2018).

CSR took its first step in addressing stakeholder needs by taking on social issues and economic responsibilities (Pinkston & Carroll, 1996). Historically, CSR underrepresented environmental issues (Bansal & DesJardine, 2014; Dewangga et al., 2008). This changed in the 2000s, however, as CSR grew to be associated with the triple bottom line (Moon, 2007). CSR has broadened its scope to include an environmental dimension of responsibility in addition to social and economic responsibility (e.g., Pan et al., 2021). In fact, in an analysis of 37 definitions of CSR, at least 24 of the definitions alluded to some aspect of environmental responsibility (Dahlsrud, 2008).

Maclagan (1999) argues that CSR can be defined "in terms of the social and environmental impact of systemic organizational activity" (p. 43). A corporation's responsibility to identify, measure, and report its impacts on society, the environment, and its economic welfare is the basis upon which CSR is operationalized (Ashrafi et al., 2020). In adopting CSR, corporations consider the ethicality of their actions and the effects their decisions have on stakeholders (Hopkins, 2004). Fitch (1976) argues that for a corporation to achieve social responsibility, it must "attempt to identify and solve those social problems in which they are intimately involved" (p. 45).

At its core, CSR is when a corporation takes active responsibility for consequences it has caused, regardless of whether the consequence was intentional or unintentional (Mishra & Sarkar, 2017). In Table 1, we will be able to see a summary of Corporate Social Responsibility.

Table 1 Corporate social responsibility definitions

Definition source	Definition
Davis and Blomstrom (1971), as cited in Gavin and Maynard (1975)	The substance of CSR arises from the institution's ethical obligation to evaluate the effects of its decisions and actions on the whole social system
Fitch (1976)	Corporate social responsibility is defined as the serious attempt to solve social problems caused wholly or in part by the corporation
Fitch (1976)	The socially responsible corporation places a high priority on solving those social problems in which the corporation's productions or services are a contributing factor. An example would be provided by a distillery which chooses to attack the social problems of alcoholism
Fitch (1976)	Corporations can achieve social responsibility if they attempt to identify and solve those social problems in which they are intimately involved
Reder (1994)	An all-encompassing notion [corporate] social responsibility refers to both the way a company conducts its internal operations, including the way it treats its workforce, and its impact on the world around it
Maclagan (1999)	CSR can be defined in terms of the social and environmental impact of systemic organisational activity
Ethics in Action Awards (2003), as cited in Dahlsrud (2008)	Socially responsible companies consider the full scope of their impact on communities and the environment when making decisions, balancing the needs of stakeholders with their need to make a profit
Ethical Performance (2003), as cited in Dahlsrud (2008)	At its best, CSR is defined as the responsibility of a company for the totality of its impact, with a need to embed society's values into its core operations, as well as into its treatment of its social and physical environment. Responsibility is accepted as encompassing a spectrum—from the running of a profitable business to the health and safety of staff and the impact on the societies in which a company operates
IndianNGOs.com (2003), as cited in Low (2016)	CSR is a business process wherein the institution and the individuals within are sensitive and careful about the direct and indirect effect of their work on internal and external communities, nature, and the outside world
Roberts (2003)	The adoption within the firm of new forms of measurement and incentives to motivate increased attention to the ethical, social, and environmental impacts
Steurer et al. (2005)	CSR is about meeting current stakeholder needs
Greller and Valentine (2019)	Corporate social responsibility (CSR) addresses the purpose, responsibilities, and impact of an organization
Carroll (2021)	Factoring stakeholders into decisions is at the heart-and-soul of CSR
Foster (2023)	An example of an activity by a CSR-aware company is offering children at local schools or in local colleges the chance to get work experience at the company's expense
Foster (2023)	In order to define CSR, we start by noting that we construe 'social responsibility' to be the responsibility that an individual or organization has to the wider society within which they reside. Hence, 'CSR' is that social responsibility or duty that relates to a corporation or firm
Mitnick et al. (2023)	Corporate social responsibility (CSR) is about the moral purpose of business and its proper relationship to society
Rodrigues and Kurnaz (2023)	Corporate social responsibility (CSR) is an expression used by companies to show that they are aware that their role in society or in the community in which they operate is not just to seek profit

3 Corporate Sustainability

Corporate sustainability became a popularized term in the early 1990s after sustainable development was first defined in the Brundtland Report, Our Common Future, in 1987 (Montiel, 2008). The report defined sustainable development as "development which meets the needs of current generations without compromising the ability of future generations to meet their own needs" (Brundtland, 1987, p. 54). The definition of CS is therefore adopted from sustainable development. When transposing sustainability into the business realm, Dyllick and Hockerts (2002) define CS as "meeting the needs of a firm's direct and indirect stakeholders, without compromising its ability to meet the needs of future stakeholders as well" (p. 131).

A fundamental aspect of CS is a corporation's responsibility for the effects it causes through its decisions and operations, even if such effects are unintentional (Bastons & Armengou, 2017). Bastons and Armengou (2017) write that "sustainability goes far beyond the purely environmental aspects related to minimizing resource consumption and pollutant emissions throughout the life cycle of a technical process" (p. 971). Most modern definitions of CS include environmental, social, and economic lines (Choi & Ng, 2011; Elkington, 1998; Sheth et al., 2011).

Key aspects of economic CS include working towards value creation, enhanced financial performance, economic prosperity, and considering the impact of actions on future generations (Bansal, 2005; van Marrewijk, 2008; Martínez & Rodríguez del Bosque, 2014). Meanwhile, social CS addresses the impact corporations have on social equity between generations (Bansal, 2005). Social sustainability ensures that a corporation's business decisions and use of resources "do not lead to diminished quality of life due either to losses in future economic opportunities or to adverse impacts on social condition" (Hutchins & Sutherland, 2008, p. 1688). Environmentally sustainable corporations consider earth's limited regenerative capability (Shaw & Cosbey, 1995).

CS is like CSR, in that it is when a corporation takes active responsibility for consequences it has caused, regardless of whether the consequences were intentional or unintentional. However, CS differs from CSR in its temporal scope, as it adopts a long-term perspective (Bansal & DesJardine, 2014).

Held (2001) wrote that "sustainable development is inherently a temporal concept that includes future generations and their needs" (p. 351) and stated the relevance of 'timescape' for understanding whether different corporate activities are sustainable or unsustainable. Meanwhile, most CSR definitions do not include temporal aspects for evaluating corporate activities (Dahlsrud, 2008; Montiel, 2008; Sarkar & Searcy, 2016). Ashrafi et al. (2020) maintains that CS consists of a temporal focus that comprises both short-term and long-term considerations which is not found within the notion of CSR.

Even scholars who consider CSR to have a temporal scope consider it a short-term concept. Steurer et al. (2005) writes, "the management approach of CSR is more or less implicitly about meeting the demands of (primary or key) stakeholders today in order to secure resources, which are vital for the company's performance in the near future" (p. 274). Therefore, CS can be considered an 'extension' of CSR. It takes corporate actions one step further by approaching decisions and business operations with a long-term outlook and sustainable mind-set. In Table 2, we will be able to see a summary of Corporate Sustainability Definitions.

Table 2 Corporate sustainability definitions

Definition source	Definition
Brundtland (1987)	Sustainable development is development that meets the needs of the present without compromising the ability of future generations to meet their own needs
Dyllick and Hockerts (2002)	Ecologically sustainable companies use only natural resources that are consumed at a rate below the natural reproduction, or at a rate below the development of substitutes. They do not cause emissions that accumulate in the environment at a rate beyond the capacity of the natural system to absorb and assimilate these emissions. Finally, they do not engage in activity that degrades eco-system services
Dyllick and Hockerts (2002)	Economically sustainable companies guarantee at any time cash flow sufficient to ensure liquidity while producing a persistent above average return to their shareholders
Bansal (2005)	Describes the economic dimension of CS as economic prosperity through value creation: "Firms create value through goods and services they produce. Therefore, firms increase the value created by improving the effectiveness of those goods and services efficiently"
Steurer et al. (2005)	CS is a corporate guiding model, addressing the short- and long-term economic, social, and environmental performance of corporations
Sheth et al. (2011)	The economic dimension of CS relates to the impact of corporate consumption on economic well-being of consumers
Bastons and Armengou (2017)	CS is a corporation's ethical responsibility for the effects it causes through its decisions and operations, even if such effects are unintentional
Carroll (2021)	Businesses have been picking up on the true meaning of sustainability and likely will be focusing more vigorously on their current and long-term impacts on society and stakeholders
Araújo et al. (2023)	Corporate sustainability explains how the performance of economic, social, and environmental practices ensures the long-term functioning of companies
Kavadis and Thomsen (2023)	Business behaviour that meets the needs of current stakeholders, above and beyond the financial interests of current shareholders, and without compromising the ability of future generations to meet their own needs

Table 3 Corporate solidarity definitions

Definition source	Definition
Kanungo and Conger (1993)	Altruistic behaviour in organizations is any work-related behaviour that benefits others regardless of the beneficial effects of such behaviour for the benefactor
Cima and Schubeck (2001)	Benevolence refers to a free-will offering that is optional in the non-obligatory sense
Villadsen (2011)	There are some specific connections and parallels between nineteenth-century philanthropy and social work
Prainsack and Buyx (2013)	Solidarity involves the voluntary commitment to accept burdens for the sake of others
Bastons and Armengou (2017)	Solidarity is an act of responsibility aimed at alleviating problems one has not caused
Bastons and Armengou (2017)	An act of solidarity is not necessarily of sustainability. It must be noted that solidarity can be exercised to solve problems caused by others, but without assuming responsibility for what we have caused ourselves

4 Corporate Solidarity

Corporate solidarity is a form of corporate responsibility in which a corporation acts to alleviate problems it has not caused (Bastons & Armengou, 2017). It is important not to confuse CSR and CS with solidarity. CSR and CS are when a corporation takes responsibility for impacts it causes; in contrast, solidarity is when a corporation assumes responsibility for impacts it did not cause. Solidarity "involves the voluntary commitment to accept burdens for the sake of others" (Prainsack & Buyx, 2013, p. 4). Solidary is a discretionary act of "adopted" responsibility that refers to a "free-will offering that is optional in the non-obligatory sense" (Cima & Schubeck, 2001, p. 218) and must be understood as a form of philanthropy (Villadsen, 2011), altruism (Kanungo & Conger, 1993), beneficence, or charity.

This "adopted" responsibility is what makes corporate solidarity fundamentally different from CSR and CS. Bastons and Armengou (2017) differentiate between solidarity and other forms of corporate responsibility by stating, "Sometimes social responsibility may be directed at alleviating problems one has not caused (famine in Africa); it is an act of solidarity, not necessarily of sustainability. It must be noted that solidarity can be exercised to solve problems caused by others, but without assuming responsibility for what we have caused ourselves" (p. 974). According to corporate solidarity, the corporation itself did not cause the wrong, yet still adopts responsibility to alleviate the wrong. In Table 3, we summarize Corporate Solidarity Definitions.

5 Strategy-Based Motives

It is important to note that not all corporate actions can be categorized as CS, CSR, or Corporate Solidarity. Corporations also engage in strategy-based actions for their personal benefit (Schaltegger & Burritt, 2018). Strategy-based motives are geared towards the corporation's own interests, such as improving corporate image (Lozano, 2015) and increasing profitability (Piedra-Muñoz et al., 2016). Bearing in mind that corporations engage in actions that are targeted towards maximizing business performance (Hofmann & Reiner, 2006), we decided to include strategy-based items in our multi-item questionnaire.

6 Identifying Misconceptions

The literature review and a review of different corporations' annual responsibility reports and websites (if available) have helped us as part of the methodology process to identify the existence of the misconception of corporate responsibility. We chose to review annual responsibility reports because they are "the most widely distributed of all public documents produced by a company" and they "can be accepted as an appropriate source of a company's attitudes towards social reporting" (Campbell, 2000, pp. 84–85). Adams et al. (1998) wrote that "the single most important source of information on corporate activities is in most, if not all cases, the annual report" (p. 5).

7 Misconceptions in Practice

Through our evaluation, we found that many corporations had misconceptions of CS, CSR, and corporate solidarity. For example, Sanofi Group Russia reported in their 2011 CSR Report that they offer a CSR training that consists of three modules to increase employee awareness of CSR issues (Sanofi, 2011). The first module of their CSR training, however, is about sustainable development. Hasbro, a toy company, stated in their 2016 CSR report, "Our deep commitment to corporate social responsibility (CSR) reflects our desire to help build a safer, more sustainable world for future generations" (Hasbro, 2016).

The results of our investigation of annual responsibility reports and websites supported the claim from Hartman et al. (2007) that many EU firms rely heavily on sustainability terms to communicate their CSR message. For example, we found that Inditex wrote that their CSR policy is based upon sustainability and defined sustainability as "the offer of a range of fashion products that strictly observe Human and Social Rights throughout the production line and that meet the most exacting environmental and health and safety standards, all of which is based upon transparency and continuous dialogue with the Company's stakeholders" (Industria De Diseño Textil, 2015). This definition that Inditex claims as sustainability, however, does not meet sustainability standards because it does not address short- nor long-term economic, social, or environmental impacts. By the same token, CaixaBank published its 2020 Corporate Responsibility report with the title, "Principles of the Corporate Sustainability/ Corporate Social Responsibility Policy," and made no distinction between the two terms (CaixaBank, 2020), suggesting that CaixaBank does not consider the two terms different from one another.

Van den Brink and van der Woerd (2004) acknowledged that corporations demonstrate a misunderstanding of CSR and CS when they attempt to implement these concepts into business engagements. Panapanaan et al. (2003) commented that "the overlaps of environmental and social issues make it easy for many companies to assume that their sustainable development agenda covers CSR already along with environmental management. However, such an assumption is unclear and a grey area for discussion" (p.139). The confusion between CSR and CS is clearly shown in the Global Reporting Initiative's database of sustainability reports (Global Reporting Initiative, 2020). There is a plethora of terminologies corporations use to refer to their social and environmental reports, including "Corporate Citizenship Report," "Corporate Responsibility Report," "Annual Activity and Responsibility Report," "Sustainability Report," and "Environmental Impact Report." This mixture of sustainability jargon shows that the distinction between the three forms of corporate responsibility is not well understood by corporations.

8 Misconceptions in Research

Misconceptions are not only visible in practice but also in research. Consistent with the aforementioned corporations, some researchers have resorted to joining the terms together as CSR sustainability, implying they do not recognize the difference between reporting on CSR and reporting on CS (Ferns et al., 2008; Quaak et al., 2007). Moreover, other researchers have come to use the terms CSR and CS interchangeably, making no clear distinction between the two dimensions (Dyllick & Hockerts, 2002; van Marrewijk, 2008; van Marrewijk & Werre, 2003). For example, Szegedi et al. (2023, p. 3) acknowledged, "In our study, we use the concepts of CSR and corporate sustainability as synonyms." Such confusion has real consequences in research. For example, in a table for CSR models, Kaman (2015) cited two models that measure corporate sustainability: Aras and Crowther (2009)'s Model of Sustainable Development and Delai and Takahashi (2011)'s Sustainability Measurement System.

Misunderstandings of what differentiates corporate solidarity from CSR can be seen in academia (Melissen et al., 2018). Though it is true that some researchers may assert that a clear difference exists between corporate solidarity and CSR, they do not offer sound supporting arguments because it is difficult to disentangle altruistic intentions from profit-seeking aspirations. Their argument would be that corporate solidarity cannot be an act of CSR because solidarity is an act of altruism (i.e., no expectation of an external reward) and organizations engage in CSR for self-serving reasons (Lantos, 2002; Sprinkle & Maines, 2010). Opponents, however, would argue that it is impossible to tell if an act is purely altruistic because corporations engage in corporate responsibility to placate pressure groups (such as non-governmental organizations), improve public image, comply with laws, recruit skilled employees, and increase retention rates (Idowu & Papasolomou, 2007). This raises significant doubts as to whether it is possible for corporations to engage in responsible practices without any expectations of external rewards. So where does this leave corporate solidarity? With such contradiction, it is no wonder as to why organizations and researchers would have trouble differentiating between forms of corporate responsibility.

We can also see misunderstandings between the three dimensions in measuring instruments. For example, the DJSI EURO STOXX Index is claimed to be a measurement tool for CS (Consolandi et al., 2009). Yet, there are items on the index that align with CSR and corporate solidarity rather than CS (Hartman et al., 2007). This has led researchers to misuse the DJSI EURO STOXX Index to measure CSR. We can observe further misunderstandings with the FTSE4-Good Index Series; it is designed to measure CSR performance, but the first item of the index series states, "working toward environmental sustainability," which suggests a measurement of CS rather than CSR.

As ambiguous conceptualizations of CSR, CS, and corporate solidarity remain (Montiel, 2008), uncertainty in approaches to corporate responsibility and miscommunication of corporate responsibility activities persists (Hartman et al., 2007). Therefore, it is crucial for corporations and researchers to understand what constitutes corporate responsibility. Such examples of the misconceptions of CSR, CS, and corporate solidarity helped to justify the development of our study's research question.

9 Taxonomy of Corporate Responsibility

As stated by Porter and Derry (2012), our traditional toolkits for problem-solving are ill-equipped to capture and respond to sustainability issues. Sustainability tests our decision-making systems. More specifically, sustainability forces companies to reflect on the direct and indirect effects of their decisions, due to an increasing "awareness of the consequences" of their actions (Hörisch et al., 2020).

The evaluation of the consequences is at the root of the current debate on responsibility. Social corporate responsibility, sustainability, and solidarity can be seen as three ways of becoming aware of the consequences of our decisions and exercising responsibility. Thus, a taxonomy conceptualizing CSR, CS, and corporate solidarity can be drawn up according to which agent causes the consequences and its temporal scope (Fig. 1). Corporate social responsibility is when a corporation attempts to rectify the consequences it is responsible for inflicting to current stakeholders. Corporate sustainability is when a corporation takes active responsibility for consequences it is responsible for inflicting to future stakeholders. Corporate solidarity is when a corporation responds to consequences that it did not cause; it is an "adopted" responsibility.

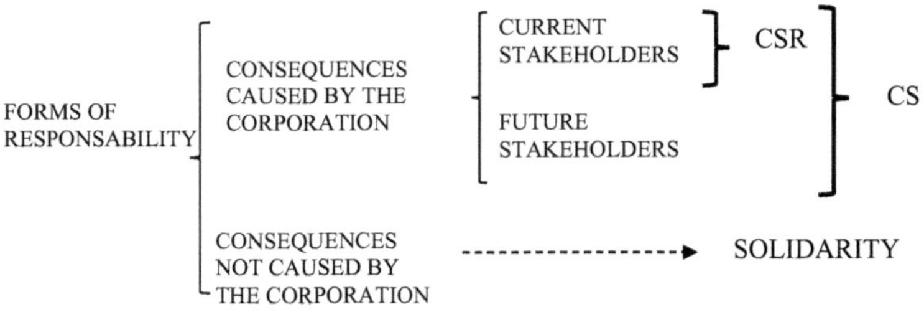

Fig. 1 Taxonomy of forms of corporate responsibility: Differentiating CSR, CS, and SOLIDARITY, according to the type consequences caused or not caused by the corporation

10 Research Question

Though it has been shown throughout this chapter that the three forms of corporate responsibility are distinct from one another, they are closely related. This leads us to wonder if managers of sustainability in corporations have misconceptions of CSR, CS, and solidarity. Based on the literature presented, we have drawn up the central research question of this study: Is there a misfit between what the taxonomy of corporate responsibility declares and what managers in corporations understand?

In the following sections, we performed empirical data analysis using a field study collected from 93 companies' sustainability managers to demonstrate the misunderstanding on the taxonomies and in practice how the implementation of these responsibilities discussed above are also used for strategy-based actions. Furthermore, we analysed if investments on these responsibilities were perceived to be satisfactory by managers with the sustainability results obtained.

11 Methodology

11.1 Instrument and Data Collection

For data collection, a survey instrument was designed to capture the agreement of managers with respect to sustainability investments and actions in their corporation, based on each of the three types of corporate responsibility: CS, CSR, and corporate solidarity. The questionnaire was distributed via email to managers who have a leadership role in sustainability actions of their corporations.

The corporations were chosen from different sectors such as energy, telecommunications, retail, and banks and came from either the United States or Spain. Furthermore, we emailed the questionnaire to B Corps, which are a "hybrid organization exemplar, blending traditionally for-profit practices with traditionally non-profit practices to address social and/or environmental issues" (Moratis et al., 2018, p. 63). We chose B Corps because they adopt a framework that "considers social, economic and other effects on employees, customers, suppliers, the environment the community and the society, in addition to profit" (Wilburn & Wilburn, 2015, p. 265). The sample consisted of responses from 93 managers from 93 corporations that was completed and duly returned, out of the 500 questionnaires sent. The average age of respondents ranged between 36 and 50 years, 40 per cent were female, and the average work experience as sustainability manager ranged between 5 and 10 years.

12 Measures

Identifying misconceptions through the extensive literature review and investigation of corporations' annual responsibility reports and websites, dimensions of the study, as well as our taxonomy of corporate responsibility, the scales and items were formulated (see Tables 4 and 5 for multiple literature sources, on constructs with items used in the survey instrument, which comprised of standard validated statistical measures).

Table 4 The highest percentage of our sustainability actions and investments

CS items	CSR items	Solidarity items	Strategy-based items
Practices that improve the future state of the environment (Bocken et al., 2014; Sanchez-Planelles et al., 2021)	The current welfare of employees (Gharleghi et al., 2018)	Social equality in underdeveloped countries (Bastons & Armengou, 2017)	Supply chain management (Hofmann & Reiner, 2006)
Waste reduction (Bocken et al., 2014; Nunhes et al., 2020; Sanchez-Planelles et al., 2021)	Education opportunities for the local community and/ or employees (Gharleghi et al., 2018; Silberhorn & Warren, 2007)	Solidarity with underdeveloped countries for the betterment of the community and education (Bastons & Armengou, 2017)	Business and consumers (Hofmann & Reiner, 2006)
Green technologies and business model innovations (Bansal, 2005; Bocken et al., 2014; Nunhes et al., 2020)	Employee personal development (Gharleghi et al., 2018)	Humanitarian aid (Kanungo & Conger, 1993)	
	Socially responsible policies (Gharleghi et al., 2018; Kolk et al., 2010; Silberhorn & Warren, 2007)	Voluntary giving, irrespective of whether the firm will reap financial benefits or not (Cima & Schubeck, 2001)	
	Volunteering in the community (Basil & Erlandson, 2008; Gharleghi et al., 2018)		

Table 5 Reflect on your level of agreement on the results obtained by the organization from its sustainability investments made during previous years?

CS items	CSR items	Solidarity items	Strategy-based items
Improved future health and safety of employees and/or local community (Bansal, 2005)	Increased employee satisfaction (Gharleghi et al., 2018)	Underdeveloped countries have benefited (Bastons & Armengou, 2017)	Increased productivity (Schaltegger & Burritt, 2018)
We have answered many environmental concerns (Sanchez-Planelles et al., 2021)		Poverty has decreased in underdeveloped countries (Bastons & Armengou, 2017)	The general image of the company has improved (Sen & Korschun, 2006)
Reduction of harmful environmental impacts (e.g., reduction in greenhouse gas emissions) (Bansal, 2005; Nunhes et al., 2020)		Welfare of citizens in communities where the organization does not conduct business operations has improved (Kanungo & Conger, 1993)	Profitability has increased (Marín et al., 2016)
Increased opportunities for employees to meet future personal goals (Nunhes et al., 2020)		Allocation of resources to underdeveloped countries has increased (Bastons & Armengou, 2017)	
Increase in long-term benefits for the organization and local community (Bansal, 2005)			

In addition to items that pertained to either CSR, CS, or corporate solidarity, we included items that aligned with strategy-based motives to identify whether there was confusion between sustainability and motives for the personal benefit of the corporation. Each question clearly asked about corporate sustainability. The items following each question were mixed to detect any misconceptions of corporate responsibility. Finally, for criterion related validity, we included a separate variable measuring satisfaction of managers on sustainability investments (Cronbach $\alpha = 0.84$). All variables were measured on a 5-point Likert scale (ranging from 1 (strongly disagree) to 5 (strongly agree)). The measures were revised and validated through a pilot study by five experts in sustainability field to ensure managers understood them. The pilot study helped to verify the instrument on clarity, face validity of the measurement items.

Table 4 displays the items seen in Table 6, which were provided to respondents in the questionnaire following the statement: "The highest percentage of our sustainability actions and investments corresponds to."

To determine the dimensions or the latent constructs amongst the measurement items, a factor analysis was conducted using principal component analysis to explore their natural dimensions. The next section shows that the exploratory analysis yielded three dimensions. Consequently, the dimensionality of each of the three dimensions, reliability of the constructs and the divergent validity were analysed. Once all the dimensions showed the correct psychometric properties, a confirmatory factor analysis (CFA) was performed.

Table 6 Matrix of three components extracted for sustainability-oriented investment and actions

	CSR	Solidarity	Strategy-based
Practices that improve the future state of the environment		0.799	
The current welfare of employees			0.651
Supply chain management		0.479	0.628
Shareholder benefits			0.381
Voluntary giving, irrespective of whether the firm will reap financial benefits or not	0.378	0.689	
Social equality in underdeveloped countries	0.416	0.610	
Solidarity with underdeveloped countries for the betterment of the community and education	0.419	0.655	
Waste reduction		0.801	
Business and consumers			0.767
Green technologies and business model innovations		0.540	0.495
Future market ventures			0.626
Education opportunities for the local community and/or employees	0.551		0.510
Humanitarian aid	0.532	0.550	
Employee personal development	0.754		
Socially responsible policies	0.740		
Volunteering in the community	0.806		

Note: Only loadings >0.35 are shown

Table 5 displays the items seen in Table 9, which were provided to the respondents in the questionnaire following the question: "Reflect on your level of agreement on the results obtained by the organization from its sustainability investments made during previous years?"

13 Results

This section is composed of two subsections with exploratory factor analysis, reliability, and validity assessment for each of the responsibility dimensions based on investments and actions and strategy separately.

Responsibility dimensions based on investments and actions:

13.1 Exploratory Factor Analysis

The 16 items of sustainability actions and investments corresponding to the three dimensions (Table 6 shows factor loadings), stated a Kaiser–Meier–Olkin statistic of 0.65 and a Barlett test with ×2 = 816.93 and p-value = 0.000. These results confirmed a linear dependence between the variables supporting that the results were sound. Three factors emerged with eigenvalues >1, accounting for 60.10 per cent of the variance in the sample. The scale was analysed with strict criteria that the items load at 0.40 or more on a factor; do not load at more than 0.50 on two factors; and have an item to total correlation of more than 0.40 (Bernardo et al., 2012).

The first factor accounting for 33.81 per cent of the variance corresponded to CSR, with four items loading over 0.50 stated as sustainability by the respondents. The second factor accounting for 47.84 per cent of the variance corresponded to solidarity, with seven items loading over 0.53 stated as sustainability by the respondents. Finally, the third factor accounting for 59.11 per cent of the variance corresponded to strategy-based investments, with five items loading over 0.38 stated as sustainable actions and investments by the respondents. Except for one item (very close to the threshold), every other item loaded above 0.60.

13.2 Reliability and Validity Analyses

Composite reliability in every case exceeded the threshold value of 0.7 showing internal consistency (Table 7). The variance extracted for each factor was very close to the threshold of 0.5, except for strategy-based dimension. The Cronbach's α values do not improve when any of the items were removed from the scales of each dimension. The correlations between each item and the total corrected scales were >0.35. Overall, convergent validity was confirmed for all factors as all items showed significant loads ($t > 2.58$).

For the confirmatory factor analysis, model fit was evaluated using the sample variance-covariance matrix of the 16 items as input and a maximum likelihood solution. For the three-factor model, the overall chi-square was statistically significant ($\chi 2 = 185.33$, $df = 54$, $p < 0.01$), the Comparative Fit Index was 0.98, the Tucker–Lewis Index was 0.96, and the standardized root mean square residual was 0.03.

Discriminant validity was analysed using linear correlations or standardized covariances between latent factors by examining whether the inter-factor correlations were less than the square root of the average variance extracted (AVE). As square roots of each AVE were greater than the off-diagonal elements, discriminant validity was confirmed (Table 8).

Responsibility dimensions based on results:

Table 7 Reliability statistics

	CSR	Solidarity	Strategy-based
Range of correlations between items	0.41–0.67	0.40–0.80	0.35–0.50
Cronbach's α if one item is removed	0.74–0.81	0.79–0.84	0.60–0.72
Cronbach's α	0.81	0.85	0.69
Composite reliability	0.73	0.78	0.71
Average variance extracted	0.47	0.48	0.39

Table 8 Correlation matrix of latent factors

Variables	1	2	3
Sustainability—CSR	0.69		
Sustainability—Solidarity	0.55	0.69	
Sustainability—Strategy	0.24	0.39	0.62

Note: Diagonal elements are the square roots of the average variance extracted (AVE)

Table 9 Matrix of four components extracted for sustainability-oriented investments results

	Solidarity	Strategy-based CSR	Sustainability
Improved future health and safety of employees and/or local community		0.810	0.391
Increased productivity		0.841	
Increased employee satisfaction		0.785	
We have answered many environmental concerns	0.360		0.728
The general image of the company has improved		0.806	
Underdeveloped countries have benefited	0.841		
Profitability has increased		0.729	
Poverty has decreased in underdeveloped countries	0.796		
Welfare of citizens in communities where the organization does not conduct business operations has improved	0.693		0.367
Allocation of resources to underdeveloped countries has increased	0.897		
Reduction of harmful environmental impacts (e.g., reduction in greenhouse gas emissions)			0.904
Increased opportunities for employees to meet future personal goals		0.367	0.555
Increase in long-term benefits for the organization and local community		0.820	

Note: Only loadings >0.35 are shown

To ensure dimension definitions, we set forth to form the responsibility dimensions based on the results achieved from investments and actions implemented as sustainable responsibility in organizations.

13.2.1 Exploratory Factor Analysis

The results obtained through sustainable actions and investments corresponding to the dimensions of the three responsibilities (Table 9 shows factor loadings), stated a Kaiser–Meier–Olkin statistic of 0.68 and a Barlett test with ×2 = 758.61 and p-value = 0.000. These results confirmed a linear dependence between the variables and supported our view that the results were sound. Three factors emerged with eigenvalues >1, accounting for 77.18 per cent of the variance in the sample.

All 13 items corresponded to a mix of strategy-based CSR, solidarity, and sustainability dimensions, initially meant to be measured as only sustainability results. The factor Solidarity, accounting for 36.35 per cent of the variance, loaded with four items over 0.69. The items of CSR and strategy-based results grouped into one factor, accounted for 66.70 per cent of the variance, loaded with six items over 0.73. Finally, the factor sustainability accounted for 77.18 per cent of the variance, loaded with three items over 0.55.

13.2.2 Reliability and Validity Analyses

Composite reliability in every case exceeded the threshold value of 0.7 showing internal consistency (Table 10). The variance extracted for each factor was >0.50. The Cronbach's α values do not improve when any of the items were removed from the scales of each dimension. The correlations between each item and the total corrected scales were >0.35. Overall, convergent validity was confirmed for all factors, as all items showed significant loads ($t > 2.58$).

For the confirmatory factor analysis, model fit was evaluated using the sample variance-covariance matrix of the 13 items as input and a maximum likelihood solution. For the three-factor model, the overall chi-square was statistically significant ($\chi2 = 245.33$, $df = 77$, $p < 0.01$), the Comparative Fit Index was 0.97, the Tucker–Lewis Index was 0.96, and the standardized root mean square residual was 0.04.

Discriminant validity was analysed using linear correlations or standardized covariances between latent factors by examining whether the inter-factor correlations were less than the square root of the average variance extracted (AVE). Discriminant validity was confirmed as square roots of each AVE were greater than the off-diagonal elements (Table 11).

Finally, to detect criterion-related validity, we analysed correlations between measures of corporate responsibility results and satisfaction of managers on the sustainability investments. The correlations showed a significant ($p < 0.001$) positive relationship for all variables (Strategy-based CSR, 0.35; Solidarity, 0.35; Sustainability, 0.48). We also conducted regression analyses to determine if the subscales added any explanatory variance on the satisfaction of sustainability investment variable. We found significant results (R2 = 0.27, F = 2.73, p = 0.02) for sustainability ($\beta = 0.34$, $p < 0.05$) and solidarity ($\beta = 0.20$, $p < 0.05$) variables and not for Strategy-based CSR ($\beta = 0.12$, ns).

Table 10 Reliability statistics

	Solidarity	Strategy-based CSR	Sustainability
Range of correlations between items	0.43–0.69	0.35–0.65	0.48–0.65
Cronbach's α if one item is removed	0.75–0.84	0.74–0.78	0.65–0.79
Cronbach's α	0.84	0.81	0.79
Composite reliability	0.88	0.88	0.78
Average variance extracted	0.65	0.66	0.55

Table 11 Correlation matrix of latent factors

Variables	1	2	3
Solidarity	0.81		
Strategy-based CSR	0.27	0.81	
Sustainability	0.36	0.55	0.74

Note. Diagonal elements are the square roots of the average variance extracted (AVE)

14 Discussion

The ability to agree on a universal definition for each of the forms of corporate responsibility in this study has been somewhat challenging for the field. We have learned from the review of pertinent scientific literature that a multitude of interpretations of the different forms of corporate responsibility exist in both practice and research. Our investigation of corporations' annual responsibility reports and websites provided meaningful insight into how corporations perceive corporate responsibility. In this study, we use our extensive review of the literature to construct a taxonomy that helps to define CS, CSR, and corporate solidarity more clearly. This enabled us to effectively formulate a questionnaire to test our research question.

Our empirical finding supports our assumption: There is a misfit between what our taxonomy of corporate responsibility declares and what managers of sustainability departments understand. In our data collection, all our questions were clearly asked based on sustainability. We included items, however, that pertain to other forms of corporate responsibility to detect whether respondents mistook CS for CSR, corporate solidarity, or strategy-based motives.

Our analysis showed that the respondents answered to items that related to CSR, corporate solidarity, and strategy-based motives when asked about sustainability investments and actions. There was a clear misfit between sustainability and solidarity. When asked about the highest percentage of sustainability investments in the corporation, respondents indicated that they invested in solidarity with underdeveloped countries for the betterment of the community and education; social equality in underdeveloped countries; and voluntary giving irrespective of whether the firm would reap financial benefits or not. The respondents also wrote that their sustainability investments were related to items that pertained to CSR, such as employee personal development and education opportunities for the local community and/or employees. Lastly, the analysis revealed a misunderstanding between sustainability and strategy-based motives. Respondents indicated that their sustainability investments corresponded to shareholder benefits, future market ventures, and business and consumers. These strategy-based items relate to benefits for the corporation, not sustainability. A possible explanation for this result could be that corporations utilize strategy-based actions and market them as sustainability. Using sustainability marketing helps corporations enhance their performance (Taoketao et al., 2018). In fact, research shows that corporations that market their actions as sustainable see an improvement in their profitability (Piedra-Muñoz et al., 2016), customer loyalty (Chen, 2015; Endiana et al., 2020), and corporate image (Lozano, 2015). This could serve as a reason for why a corporation would use CS as the terminology to refer to what is a strategy-based action.

When asked about the results achieved from investments and actions implemented as sustainable responsibility in corporations, there was misunderstanding between sustainability and the other forms of corporate responsibility. For example, respondents showed confusion between results generated by sustainability investments and results generated by CSR and strategy-based investments. When asked about the results the corporation achieved from sustainability investments, the respondents answered with items that pertain to CSR and strategy-based results: increased productivity, increased employee satisfaction, improved company image, and increased profitability. Improving the company image, for example, is not a result associated with sustainability investment, but rather a CSR and strategy-based investment. Surprisingly results also suggest that respondents associated the current welfare of employees with other items that related to strategy-based responsibility. One possible explanation for this could be that there is a relationship between the welfare of employees and profitability (Singh et al., 2015).

Respondents also showed confusion between sustainability and solidarity. Respondents indicated that their corporation's sustainability investments corresponded to items that were representative of solidarity: welfare of citizens in communicates where the corporation does not conduct business operations; the benefit of underdeveloped countries; decreased poverty in underdeveloped countries; and increased allocation of resources to underdeveloped countries.

Finally, it should be noted that managers' satisfaction on the sustainability investments were explained by sustainability and solidarity results obtained, but not from strategy-based CSR results. This implies that future research is needed to understand if the relationship is linear or non-linear, and it would be interesting to consider the reason behind managers' satisfaction and sustainability, as it could be because of the organizational models (i.e., mechanistic, humanistic, and organic). It would also be interesting to find dispersion in patterns of managers' satisfaction and long-term commitment to the sustainability actions and investments for the different types of organizational models.

Our research is not without limitations. The first limitation to note was that the corporations selected for this study came from the United States and Spain. It is acknowledged that cultural differences may affect the way people conceptualize corporate responsibility. We believe our study provides a good steppingstone for future studies to include multiple geographical locations. Future researchers may want to consider studying a larger sample of corporations from different countries for more generalizable results. Second, the study is mainly based on quantitative methods which have limited use in exposing misconceptions; therefore, the results must be interpreted with caution. Though we performed a detailed search of corporations' annual responsibility reports and websites, future researchers may wish to conduct additional qualitative research to establish a more precise understanding of how managers conceptualize corporate responsibility. Finally, we suggest that future research considers exploring the various interpretations of CSR within the countries under examination, as cultural factors may lead to divergent understandings.

The present study has several implications. First, no prior study, to our knowledge, has offered a taxonomy that differentiates between the three forms of corporate responsibility. The definitions proposed in this study can be used by managers to properly establish CSR, CS, and corporate solidarity goals for their corporation. This will also allow managers to measure with greater accuracy their success in accomplishing CSR, CS, and corporate solidarity objectives. Furthermore, our findings may assist corporations in making financial investments that concern corporate responsibility with more precision. Lastly, existing literature demonstrates, if not an absolute vacuum, at least a considerable paucity as to what constitutes CSR, CS, and corporate solidarity. Therefore, this study may assist researchers in using these terms more accurately and applying instruments to measure with more veracity.

15 Conclusion

Corporations and researchers have shown a lack of consensus around what defines each of the three forms of corporate responsibility. It is critical for corporations to discern what constitutes corporate responsibility to be able to financially invest with more accuracy in CSR, CS, and corporate solidarity. We offered insight into how corporations understand these concepts by searching corporations' annual responsibility reports and websites. The literature review was used to construct a taxonomy that differentiates the conceptualization between the three forms of corporate responsibility. Our quantitative analysis investigated the understanding of corporate responsibility in corporations in the United States and Spain. The results of this study show a misfit between what the taxonomy of corporate responsibility declares and what sustainability managers in corporations understand. More specifically, the findings show that managers have an imprecise conception of CSR, corporate solidarity, and strategy-based motives regarding sustainability investments and actions. The findings also highlight that in some cases managers misjudge the results of their sustainability investments with the results of their CSR and strategy-based investments. The literature review, the search of annual responsibility reports and websites, and our quantitative analysis suggest that there is a high degree of ambiguity as to what constitutes CSR, CS, and corporate solidarity.

References

Adams, C. A., Hill, W. Y., & Roberts, C. B. (1998). Corporate social reporting practices in western europe: Legitimating corporate behaviour? *British Accounting Review, 30*(1), 1–21. https://doi.org/10.1006/bare.1997.0060

Andersson, L. M., & Bateman, T. S. (2000). Individual environmental initiative: Championing natural environmental issues in U.S. business organizations. *Academy of Management Journal, 43*(4), 548–570. https://doi.org/10.5465/1556355

Aras, G., & Crowther, D. (2009). Making sustainable development sustainable. *Management Decision, 47*(6), 975–988. https://doi.org/10.1108/00251740910966686

Araújo, D. J. C., Araújo, S. A. G., & de Barros Câmara, R. P. (2023). Corporate sustainability in small and medium enterprises (SMEs) of Brazil. In *Handbook of research on acceleration programs for SMEs* (pp. 387–400). IGI Global.
Ashrafi, M., Magnan, G. M., Adams, M., & Walker, T. R. (2020). Understanding the conceptual evolutionary path and theoretical underpinnings of corporate social responsibility and corporate sustainability. *Sustainability (Switzerland), 12*(3). https://doi.org/10.3390/su12030760
Bansal, P. (2005). Evolving sustainably: A longitudinal study of corporate sustainable development. *Strategic Management Journal, 26*(3), 197–218. https://doi.org/10.1002/smj.441
Bansal, P., & DesJardine, M. (2014). Business sustainability: It is about time. *Strategic Organization, 12*(1), 70–78. https://doi.org/10.1177/1476127013520265
Basil, D. Z., & Erlandson, J. (2008). Corporate social responsibility website representations: A longitudinal study of internal and external self-presentations. *Journal of Marketing Communications, 14*(2), 125–137. https://doi.org/10.1080/13527260701858497
Bastons, M., & Armengou, J. (2017). Realism and impartiality: Making sustainability effective in decision-making. *Science and Engineering Ethics, 23*(4), 969–987. https://doi.org/10.1007/s11948-016-9850-6
Bernardo, M., Marimon, F., & Alonso-Almeida, M. (2012). Functional quality and hedonic quality: A study of the dimensions of e-service quality in online travel agencies. *Information and Management, 49*(7–8), 342–347.
Bocken, N. M. P., Short, S. W., Rana, P., & Evans, S. (2014). A literature and practice review to develop sustainable business model archetypes. *Journal of Cleaner Production, 65*, 42–56. https://doi.org/10.1016/j.jclepro.2013.11.039
Brundtland, G. H. (1987). Report of the world commission on environment and development: Our common future.
CaixaBank. (2020). Principles of the corporate sustainability/corporate social responsibility policy. Retrieved May 4, 2022, from https://www.microbank.com/deployedfiles/microbank/Estaticos/PDF/ENG_Politica-corporativa-de-Sostenibilidad_RSC.pdf.
Campbell, D. J. (2000). Legitimacy theory or managerial reality construction? Corporate social disclosure in Marks and Spencer Plc Corporate Reports, 1969-1997. *Accounting Forum, 24*(1), 80–100. https://doi.org/10.1111/1467-6303.00030
Carroll, A. B. (1999). Evolution of a definitional construct. *Business & Society, 38*(3), 268–295.
Carroll, A. B. (2021). Corporate social responsibility: Perspectives on the CSR construct's development and future. *Business & Society, 60*(6), 1258–1278. https://doi.org/10.1177/00076503211001765
Chen, R. J. C. (2015). From sustainability to customer loyalty: A case of full service hotels' guests. *Journal of Retailing and Consumer Services, 22*, 261–265. https://doi.org/10.1016/j.jretconser.2014.08.007
Choi, S., & Ng, A. (2011). Environmental and economic dimensions of sustainability and price effects on consumer responses. *Journal of Business Ethics, 104*(2), 269–282. https://doi.org/10.1007/s10551-011-0908-8
Cima, L. R., & Schubeck, T. L. (2001). Self-interest, love, and economic justice: A dialogue between classical economic liberalism and catholic social teaching. *Journal of Business Ethics, 30*(3), 213–231.
Consolandi, C., Jaiswal-Dale, A., Poggiani, E., & Vercelli, A. (2009). Global standards and ethical stock indexes: The case of the dow jones sustainability stoxx index. *Journal of Business Ethics, 87*(Suppl 1), 185–197. https://doi.org/10.1007/s10551-008-9793-1
Dahlsrud, A. (2008). How corporate social responsibility is defined: An analysis of 37 definitions. *13*, 1–13.
Davis, K., & Blomstrom, R. L. (1971). Business, society, and environment: Social power and social response. In *Business, society, and environment: Social power and social response* (2nd ed.). McGraw-Hill.
Delai, I., & Takahashi, S. (2011). Sustainability measurement system: A reference model proposal. *Social Responsibility Journal, 7*(3), 438–471. https://doi.org/10.1108/17471111111154563

Dewangga, A., Goldsmith, S., & Pegram, N. (2008). Social responsibility guideline and sustainable development: Integrating a common goal of a sustainable society. 1–32.

Dyllick, T., & Hockerts, K. (2002). Beyond the business case for corporate sustainability. *Corporate Environmental Responsibility*, 213–224. https://doi.org/10.4324/9781315259277-7

Elkington, J. (1998). Accounting for the triple bottom line. *Measuring Business Excellence, 2*(3), 18–22.

Endiana, I. D. M., Dicriyani, N. L. G. M., Adiyadnya, M. S. P., & Putra, I. P. M. J. S. (2020). The effect of green accounting on corporate sustainability and financial performance. *Journal of Asian Finance, Economics and Business, 7*(12), 731–738. https://doi.org/10.13106/jafeb.2020.vol7.no12.731

Ethical Performance. (2003). Introduction: Defining corporate social responsibility. http://www.ethicalperformance.com/bestpractice/archive/1001/introduction.html.

Ethics in Action Awards. (2003). What is corporate social responsibility? http://www.ethicsinaction.com/whatiscsr/qanda.html.

Ferns, B., Emelianova, O., & Sethi, S. P. (2008). In his own words: The effectiveness of CEO as spokesperson on CSR-sustainability issues—analysis of data from the Sethi CSR Monitor©. *Corporate Reputation Review, 11*(2), 116–129. https://doi.org/10.1057/crr.2008.11

Fitch, H. G. (1976). Achieving corporate social responsibility. *Academy of Management Review, 1*(1), 38–46. https://doi.org/10.5465/amr.1976.4408754

Foster, M. J. (2023). An enhanced role for CSR in corporate governance. *BOHR International Journal of Business Ethics and Corporate Governance, 2*(1), 1–11.

Gavin, J. F., & Maynard, W. S. (1975). Perceptions of corporate social responsibility. *Personnel Psychology, 28*(3), 377–387. https://doi.org/10.1111/j.1744-6570.1975.tb01545.x

Gharleghi, B., Jahanshahi, A. A., & Nawaser, K. (2018). The outcomes of corporate social responsibility to employees: Empirical evidence from a developing country. *Sustainability (Switzerland), 10*(3). https://doi.org/10.3390/su10030698

Global Reporting Initiative. (2020). GRI sustainability disclosure database. https://database.globalreporting.org/.

Greller, M. M., & Valentine, S. R. (2019). A leasehold approach to corporate social responsibility. *Employee Responsibilities and Rights Journal, 31*, 71–97.

Hartman, L. P., Rubin, R. S., & Dhanda, K. K. (2007). The communication of corporate social responsibility: United States and European union multinational corporations. *Journal of Business Ethics, 74*(4), 373–389. https://doi.org/10.1007/s10551-007-9513-2

Hasbro. (2016). Playing with purpose: 2016 corporate social responsibility report. https://csr.hasbro.com/downloads/CSR_2016_Report.pdf.

Hediger, W. (2010). Welfare and capital-theoretic foundations of corporate social responsibility and corporate sustainability. *Journal of Socio-Economics, 39*(4), 518–526. https://doi.org/10.1016/j.socec.2010.02.001

Held, M. (2001). Sustainable development from a temporal perspective. *Time and Society, 10*(2–3), 351–366. https://doi.org/10.1177/0961463X01010002011

Hofmann, P., & Reiner, G. (2006). Drivers for improving supply chain performance: An empirical study. *International Journal of Integrated Supply Management, 2*(3), 214–230. https://doi.org/10.1504/IJISM.2006.008594

Hopkins, M. (2004). Corporate social responsibility: An issues paper. In international labour office working paper (issue 27).

Hörisch, J., Wulfsberg, I., & Schaltegger, S. (2020). The influence of feedback and awareness of consequences on the development of corporate sustainability action over time. *Business Strategy and the Environment, 29*(2), 638–650. https://doi.org/10.1002/bse.2394

Howard-Grenville, J. A. (2006). Inside the "black box": How organizational culture and subcultures inform interpretations and actions on environmental issues. *Organization and Environment, 19*(1), 46–73. https://doi.org/10.1177/1086026605285739

Hutchins, M. J., & Sutherland, J. W. (2008). An exploration of measures of social sustainability and their application to supply chain decisions. *Journal of Cleaner Production, 16*(15), 1688–1698. https://doi.org/10.1016/j.jclepro.2008.06.001

Idowu, S. O., & Papasolomou, I. (2007). Are the corporate social responsibility matters based on good intentions or false pretences? An empirical study of the motivations behind the issuing of CSR reports by UK companies. *Corporate Governance, 7*(2), 136–147. https://doi.org/10.1108/14720700710739787

Industria De Diseño Textil. (2015). Inditex corporate social responsibility policy. https://www.inditex.com/documents/10279/240918/Inditex+Corporate+Social+Responsibility+Policy/b7441b41-e378-4f90-95a3-1bc6cc542fc3.

Kaman, Z. (2015). Corporate social responsibility (CSR) models: An approach to environmental perspective. *International Research Journal of Engineering and Technology, 23*(2), 151–167. https://www.researchgate.net/profile/Zeittey_Karmilla/publication/299451891_Corporate_Social_Responsibility_CSR_Models_An_Approach_to_Environmental_Perspective/links/56f8b28008ae81582bf3a41b/Corporate-Social-Responsibility-CSR-Models-An-Approach-to-Enviro

Kanungo, R. N., & Conger, J. A. (1993). Promoting altruism as a corporate goal. *Academy of Management Executive, 7*(3), 37–48.

Kavadis, N., & Thomsen, S. (2023). Sustainable corporate governance: A review of research on long-term corporate ownership and sustainability. *Corporate Governance: An International Review, 31*(1), 198–226.

Kolk, A., Hong, P., & van Dolen, W. (2010). Corporate social responsibility in China: An analysis of domestic and foreign retailers' sustainability. *Dimensions, 303*, 289–303.

Kolk, A., & Perego, P. (2014). Sustainable bonuses: Sign of corporate responsibility or window dressing? *Journal of Business Ethics, 119*(1), 1–15.

Lantos, G. P. (2002). The ethicality of altruistic corporate social responsibility. *Journal of Consumer Marketing, 19*(3), 205–232. https://doi.org/10.1108/07363760210426049

Lu, L. Y., & Liu, J. S. (2014). The knowledge diffusion paths of corporate social responsibility–from 1970 to 2011. *Corporate Social Responsibility and Environmental Management, 21*(2), 113–128.

Low, M. P. (2016). Asian journal of social sciences and management studies corporate social responsibility and the evolution of internal corporate social responsibility in 21st century. *Asian Journal of Social Sciences and Management Studies, 3*(1), 56–74. http://www.asianonlinejournals.com/index.php/AJSSMS56

Lozano, R. (2015). A holistic perspective on corporate sustainability drivers. *Corporate Social Responsibility and Environmental Management, 22*(1), 32–44. https://doi.org/10.1002/csr.1325

Maclagan, P. (1999). Corporate social responsibility as a participative process. *Business Ethics: A European Review, 8*(1), 43–49. https://doi.org/10.1007/s11846-021-00472-x

Marín, L., Cuestas, P. J., & Román, S. (2016). Determinants of consumer attributions of corporate social responsibility. *Journal of Business Ethics, 138*(2), 247–260. https://doi.org/10.1007/s10551-015-2578-4

van Marrewijk, M. (2008). A typology of institutional frameworks supporting corporate sustainability. *Development, 2002*, 1–16.

van Marrewijk, M., & Werre, M. (2003). Multiple levels of corporate sustainability. *Journal of Business Ethics, 44*(2), 107–119. https://doi.org/10.1023/A:1023383229086

Martínez, P., & Rodríguez del Bosque, I. (2014). Sustainability dimensions: A source to enhance corporate reputation. *Corporate Reputation Review, 17*(4), 239–253. https://doi.org/10.1057/crr.2014.13

Matten, D., & Moon, J. (2008). "Implicit" and "explicit" CSR: A conceptual framework for a comparative understanding of corporate social responsibility. *Academy of Management Review, 33*(2), 404–424. https://doi.org/10.5465/AMR.2008.31193458

Melissen, F., Mzembe, A. N., Idemudia, U., & Novakovic, Y. (2018). Institutional antecedents of the corporate social responsibility narrative in the developing world context: Implications for sustainable development. *Business Strategy and the Environment, 27*(6), 657–676. https://doi.org/10.1002/bse.2023

Mishra, R. K., & Sarkar, S. (2017). Addressing social and environmental risks through CSR—an Indian perspective. *IPE Journal of Management, 7*(1), 149–158. https://www.ipeindia.org/microsites/data/IPE-JoM-(Vol-7-No-1-Jan-Jun-2017)-Final.pdf#page=5

Mitnick, B. M., Windsor, D., & Wood, D. J. (2023). Moral CSR. *Business & Society, 62*(1), 192–220.

Montiel, I. (2008). Corporate social responsibility and corporate sustainability: Separate pasts, common futures. *Organization and Environment, 21*(3), 245–269. https://doi.org/10.1177/1086026608321329

Moon, J. (2007). The contribution of corporate social responsibility to sustainable development. *Sustainable Development, 15*(5), 296–306. https://doi.org/10.1002/sd.346

Moratis, L., Melissen, F., & Idowu, S. O. (2018). Sustainable business models principles, promise, and practice.

Nunhes, T. V., Bernardo, M., & José de Oliveira, O. (2020). Rethinking the way of doing business: A reframe of management structures for developing corporate sustainability. *Sustainability (Switzerland), 12*(3), 1–32. https://doi.org/10.3390/su12031177

Pan, X., Sinha, P., & Chen, X. (2021). Corporate social responsibility and eco-innovation: The triple bottom line perspective. *Corporate Social Responsibility and Environmental Management, 28*(1), 214–228.

Panapanaan, V. M., Karvonen, M., & Phan, V. T. (2003). *Roadmapping Corporate Social Responsibility, 44*, 133–148.

Piedra-Muñoz, L., Galdeano-Gómez, E., & Pérez-Mesa, J. C. (2016). Is sustainability compatible with profitability? An empirical analysis on family farming activity. *Sustainability (Switzerland), 8*(9). https://doi.org/10.3390/su8090893

Pinkston, T. S., & Carroll, A. B. (1996). A retrospective examination of CSR orientations: Have they changed? *Journal of Business Ethics, 15*(2), 199–206. https://doi.org/10.1007/BF00705587

Porter, T., & Derry, R. (2012). Sustainability and business in a complex world. *Business and Society Review, 117*(1), 33–53. https://doi.org/10.1111/j.1467-8594.2012.00398.x

Prainsack, B., & Buyx, A. (2013). Solidarity. Reflections on an emerging concept in bioethics. Summary. *Jahrbuch Für Wissenschaft Und Ethik, 17*(1). https://doi.org/10.1515/jfwe.2012.17.1.331

Quaak, L., Aalbers, T., & Goedee, J. (2007). Transparency of corporate social responsibility in Dutch breweries. *Journal of Business Ethics, 76*(3), 293–308. https://doi.org/10.1007/s10551-006-9282-3

Reder, A. (1994). *In pursuit of principle and profit: Business success through social responsibility*. G. P. Putnam's Sons.

Rim, H., Yang, S. U., & Lee, J. (2016). Strategic partnerships with nonprofits in corporate social responsibility (CSR): The mediating role of perceived altruism and organizational identification. *Journal of Business Research, 69*(9), 3213–3219. https://doi.org/10.1016/j.jbusres.2016.02.035

Roberts, J. (2003). The manufacture of corporate social responsibility: Constructing corporate sensibility. *Organization, 10*(2), 249–265. https://doi.org/10.1177/1350508403010002004

Rodrigues, A. A. B., & Kurnaz, S. (2023). Challenges for corporate social responsibility practices. *Revista de Gestão e Secretariado, 14*(1), 737–749.

Sanchez-Planelles, J., Segarra-Oña, M., & Peiro-Signes, A. (2021). Building a theoretical framework for corporate sustainability. *Sustainability (Switzerland), 13*(1), 1–21. https://doi.org/10.3390/su13010273

Sanofi. (2011). *Corporate social responsibility reporting*, 2011. https://www.sanofi.com/-/media/Project/One-Sanofi-Web/Websites/Global/Sanofi-COM/Home/en/publications/33109_CSR_reporting_2011.pdf

Sarkar, S., & Searcy, C. (2016). Zeitgeist or chameleon? A quantitative analysis of CSR definitions. *Journal of Cleaner Production, 135*, 1423–1435. https://doi.org/10.1016/j.jclepro.2016.06.157

Schaltegger, S., & Burritt, R. (2018). Business cases and corporate engagement with sustainability: Differentiating ethical motivations. *Journal of Business Ethics, 147*(2), 241–259. https://doi.org/10.1007/s10551-015-2938-0

Sen, S., & Korschun, D. (2006). The role of corporate social responsibility in strengthening multiple stakeholder relationships: A field experiment. March. https://doi.org/10.1177/0092070305284978.

Sharma, S. (2000). Managerial interpretations and organizational context as predictors of corporate choice of environmental strategy. *Academy of Management Journal, 43*(4), 681–697. https://doi.org/10.2307/1556361

Sharma, S., & Henriques, I. (2005). Stakeholder influences on sustainability practices in the Canadian forest products industry. *Strategic Management Journal, 26*(2), 159–180. https://doi.org/10.1002/smj.439

Shaw, N., & Cosbey, A. (1995). GATT, the WTO and sustainable development: Positioning the work program on trade and environment.

Sheth, J. N., Sethia, N. K., & Srinivas, S. (2011). Mindful consumption: A customer-centric approach to sustainability. *Journal of the Academy of Marketing Science, 39*(1), 21–39. https://doi.org/10.1007/s11747-010-0216-3

Shrivastava, P. (1995). The role of corporations in achieving ecological sustainability. *Academy of Management Review, 20*(4), 936–960. https://doi.org/10.5465/amr.1995.9512280026

Silberhorn, D., & Warren, R. C. (2007). Defining corporate social responsibility: A view from big companies in Germany and the UK. *European Business Review, 19*(5), 352–372. https://doi.org/10.1108/09555340710818950

Singh, H., Saufi, R. A., Tasnim, R., & Hussin, M. (2015). The relationship between employee job satisfaction, perceived customer satisfaction, service quality, and profitability in luxury Hotels in Kuala Lumpur. *Advanced Science Letters, 21*(5), 1538–1541.

Sprinkle, G. B., & Maines, L. A. (2010). The benefits and costs of corporate social responsibility. *Business Horizons, 53*(5), 445–453. https://doi.org/10.1016/j.bushor.2010.05.006

Starik, M., & Marcus, A. A. (2000). Introduction to the special research forum on the management of organizations in the natural environment: A field emerging from multiple paths, with many challenges ahead. *Academy of Management Journal, 43*(4), 539–547. https://doi.org/10.2307/1556354

Steurer, R., Langer, M. E., Konrad, A., & Martinuzzi, A. (2005). Corporations, stakeholders and sustainable development I: A theoretical exploration of business-society relations. *Journal of Business Ethics, 61*(3), 263–281. https://doi.org/10.1007/s10551-005-7054-0

Szegedi, K., Németh, T., & Körtvési, D. (2023). Employer branding in the fashion industry: CSR actions by fashion SMEs. *Sustainability, 15*(3), 1827.

Taoketao, E., Feng, T., Song, Y., & Nie, Y. (2018). Does sustainability marketing strategy achieve payback profits? A signaling theory perspective. *Corporate Social Responsibility and Environmental Management, 25*(6), 1039–1049. https://doi.org/10.1002/csr.1518

Van den Brink, T. W. M., & van der Woerd, F. (2004). Industry specific sustainability benchmarks: An ECSF pilot bridging corporate sustainability with social responsible investments. *Journal of Business Ethics, 55*(2), 187–203. https://doi.org/10.1007/s10551-004-1901-2

Villadsen, K. (2011). Modern welfare and 'Good Old' philanthropy. *Public Management Review, 13*(8), 1057–1075. https://doi.org/10.1080/14719037.2011.622675

Wilburn, R., & Wilburn, K. (2015). Evaluating CSR accomplishments of founding certified B corps. *The Eletronic Library, 6*(2), 2041–2568.

Xie, S., & Hayase, K. (2007). Corporate environmental performance evaluation: A measurement model and a new concept. *Business Strategy and the Environment, 16*(2), 148–168. https://doi.org/10.1002/bse.493

Emma Ann Thornberg, a dedicated Ph.D. researcher, holds a Bachelor of Science in Psychology from Virginia Tech. Building upon her passion, she pursued a Master's in Work, Organizational, and Personnel Psychology at the University of Barcelona, gaining expertise in the intricacies of sustainability within organizational settings. Currently a second-year Ph.D. student at the International University of Catalunya, Emma's research focuses on the intersection of economics and corporate sustainability.

Rejina Mary Selvam is a Lecturer Serra Hunter Fellow in Work and Organizational Psychology at the University of Barcelona. She has a Ph.D. in Human Resources Psychology, from the Department of Social Psychology and Quantitative Psychology (methods for behavioral sciences), from the University of Barcelona. She has been a visiting research scholar at the University of Pennsylvania State, University of Stirling, and University of West London and has participated in national and international research projects. She has participated in various competitive projects from the Ministry of Spain and Generalitat de Catalunya, including the Santander Universities research projects. Her previous employments were at the Universitat Internacional de Catalunya and IESE Business School (University of Navarra). Her research interests are in Purpose Mission, Sustainable decision making, Internal and Institutional communication (CSR), and Measurement of organizational behavior (Leader-subordinate relationships, team performances). Her research studies from these lines of investigations have been published in scientific journals and books such as International Journal of Production Economics, Human Review, and Routledge Publications.

Miquel Bastons holds Ph.D. in Philosophy and Ph.D. in Management. He has been teacher at three universities and currently he is Associate Professor of Decision Analysis and Ethics at the School of Economics and Social Sciences of the International University of Catalonia (Spain), where he has been vice-rector for Academic Organization and Teaching Staff, and Dean of School of Economics and Social Sciences. His research focuses on organizational decision-making and business ethics. He has published in the Journal of Business Ethics, Journal of Management & Organization, Journal of Agricultural and Environmental Ethics, Science and Engineering Ethics, and Long Range Planning. He has been Section Editor of the Handbook of Virtue Ethics in Business and Management (Springer) and editor of the book Purpose-driven Organizations: Management Ideas for a Better World; and he is reviewer of the Journal of Business Ethics, Journal of Management & Organization, Journal of Academic Ethics, Habitat International, Journal of Agricultural and Environmental Ethics, and European Management Journal.

Managers' Approach to CSR and Its Relation with Firm Performance

Anna Napiórkowska

1 Introduction

The concept of corporate social responsibility (CSR) is widely described in the literature, but despite its rather long history, there is still no consensus on its precise definition or identification of barriers and incentives that affect it (Fabrizi et al., 2014). While there is a rich theoretical and empirical literature examining the determinants of CSR, researchers agree that a better understanding of the effective drivers for CSR engagement and the barriers that hinder it is needed (Agudo-Valiente et al., 2017). In the literature on CSR, there are two important elements that motivate organizations to apply CSR practices. These are moral motivators related to the ethics and values of managers, followed by strategic motivators in the form of increasing profits, improving reputation and meeting stakeholder demands (Graafland & van de Ven, 2006).

Managers play a key role in the company's commitment to CSR. Their values and attitude towards CSR influence the extent to which their companies are involved in practices related to this concept (e.g., Aguilera et al., 2007). Mishra and Schmidt (2018) indicate that in the academic literature, leadership attitudes and cultural diversity are the two dominant barriers to CSR. According to Hung (2011), companies where managers show greater concern for stakeholder issues seem to see the

The article is a result of research conducted at the Collegium of World Economy of the SGH Warsaw School of Economics, financed by subsidies from the Ministry of Science and Higher Education.

A. Napiórkowska (✉)
Department of International Business, SGH Warsaw School of Economics, Collegium of World Economy, Warsaw, Poland
e-mail: anna.napiorkowska@sgh.waw.pl

B. Díaz Díaz et al. (eds.), *Building Global Societies Towards an ESG World*, CSR, Sustainability, Ethics & Governance,
https://doi.org/10.1007/978-3-031-56619-6_5

need for effective CSR more often. Managers who have an integral, responsible and effective view of CSR tend to develop it in their companies (Hung, 2011). If managers do not perceive CSR as a priority, then they do not allocate and mobilize the necessary resources to implement this concept (Tefera et al., 2019).

In recent years, the concepts of ethical leadership and CSR play a key role for the competitiveness of both manufacturing and service companies (Roeck & Farooq, 2018; Saha et al., 2020). On the other hand, the COVID-19 pandemic resulted in a high level of CSR initiatives, mainly in the field of philanthropic activities and volunteering for the benefit of society. Many entrepreneurs showed solidarity with society and tried to help solve the most acute problems caused by the pandemic (e.g., García-Sánchez & García-Sánchez, 2020). There has also been an increased research interest in the relationship between ethical leadership, CSR and corporate performance (Saha et al., 2020). The manager's subjective perception of the relationship between CSR and the company's performance takes into account ethical, moral and philanthropic issues. On the other hand, from an objective point of view, CSR has an instrumental application (Agudo-Valiente et al., 2017). From this perspective, CSR influences performance and provides a mechanism by which it responds to institutional pressure to ensure long-term benefits and gain a competitive advantage resulting in above-average profit (Husted & Allen, 2006; Lattemann et al., 2009; Agudo-Valiente et al., 2017). Saha et al. (2020) in their literature review on the relationship between ethical leadership, CSR and companies' performance, point to the influence of managers' personal values on CSR practices and the direct and indirect impact of these values on the performance of enterprises. The study of the above mentioned researchers shows that the biggest barrier to the implementation of CSR practices is the financial factor. Studies on the impact of ethical leadership on financial performance are visible in the literature (e.g., Tuan, 2012; Aslan & Sendogdu, 2012), but as indicated by Du et al. (2013) and Saha et al. (2020) there is no consensus on the strength of this impact.

Therefore, the chapter aims to examine the managers' CSR perception in terms of costs and benefits and its influence on firms' performance. The author tries to answer the question: How does managers' perception of the benefits and costs of CSR affect the firm's financial and non-financial performance? By answering this question, the chapter will add to filling the knowledge gaps of CSR and to the theory of antecedents of CSR and its relation with firm financial and non-financial performance.

This chapter is divided into five parts. The first part contains an introduction to the study. The second part provides a brief overview of relevant theoretical and empirical research in this field. The third part discusses the research methodology used in the study. The fourth part presents the research results and discussion. The fifth part summarizes the main findings of the study and indicates future research directions.

2 Literature Review

2.1 Managers' Attitudes Towards CSR

Based on the analysis of the scientific literature on drivers/barriers of CSR, Agudo-Valiente et al. (2017) identified two types of drivers/barriers: subjective and objective. The authors point to subjective factors as those related to the personal values and beliefs of managers, while objective factors are linked to outcome-oriented position (profit or costs). The authors indicate that companies perceive not only barriers generating net costs related to the implementation of CSR but also opportunities generating net benefits, but all this is conditioned by the subjective interpretation of CSR by managers.

Also Gowindasamy and Suresh (2017) indicate two main types of factors that affect CSR visible in the literature: the moral driven (holistic interpretation) and the profit driven (instrumental interpretation). In accordance with this division, the authors suggest that some of the factors conducive to the development of CSR are related to ethical theories, according to which involvement in CSR is determined by voluntary commitment to the public good. Morality, charity, honesty and moral beliefs of managers are just some of the factors that justify such an interpretation of CSR. From this perspective, companies have a duty to be socially responsible because it is morally correct to do so, even if it comes at a cost (Hemingway & Maclagan, 2004). This kind of perception of CSR is sometimes referred to as the 'wide approach to CSR' (Quazi & O'Brien, 2000), which entails a wider range of economic, legal, ethical, moral and philanthropic responsibilities. The perception of CSR in a broad way refers to the support of ethical management, transparency towards stakeholders, treating company as a citizen focusing on the common good (Freeman et al., 2010).

Other factors conducive to the development of CSR are based on the instrumental stakeholder theory, where CSR is perceived as a strategic tool for achieving economic goals through social activities and creating competitive advantage strategies (Garriga & Melé, 2004). Long-term benefits can be achieved by improving relations with stakeholders, improving the company's reputation, increasing customer loyalty or cost savings. Adoption of CSR practices may also entail additional costs, which in turn may reduce the company's cash reserves, cause deterioration of the economic situation and competitiveness. The cost of the project is a key factor influencing the company's level of commitment to CSR. The high costs of CSR projects can make them difficult to implement (Aupperle et al., 1985). Agudo-Valiente et al. (2017) reported the cost of CSR as an objective barrier that affects the degree of CSR development in the company.

As indicated by Arevalo and Aravind (2011), the barriers hindering the development of CSR in companies are related to the maximization of value for shareholders, an assumption corresponding to the classical capitalism of Friedman (1970), who perceives CSR as a utopia, a passing fashion, an image strategy or pure philanthropy and focuses his attention to the institutional function of the organization, ownership rights and maximizing shareholder value from the instrumental stakeholder theory. This approach to the concept of corporate responsibility is often called the "narrow approach to social responsibility" (Quazi & O'Brien, 2000) and is closely related to the classical perspective, which suggests that the main function of business is to provide goods and services leading to the maximization of profit within the requirements of legal rules (Friedman, 1970). Managers with this approach have a narrow concept of corporate responsibility and are sceptical about CSR because they believe it is contrary to good company practice as it undermines profit maximization (Agudo-Valiente et al., 2017).

The narrow and wide understanding of the approach to CSR is evident in Quazi and O'Brian's two-dimensional CSR model, which divides CSR activities along horizontal and vertical axes (Quazi & O'Brian, 2000). The horizontal axis presents the concept of corporate social responsibility with two extremes and focuses on the so-called "wide" long-term and "narrow" short-term liability. On the other hand, the vertical axis shows the expected results of this social involvement, and the two ends of the axis are: benefits and costs of social responsibility. In this model, the firm is ultimately located in one of the four quadrants formed by the two axes. The four created quadrants describe the modern view and the social-economic view, as the two elements that are considered to benefit from CSR, and the philanthropic view and the classic view, rather linked to costs of CSR (Quazi & O'Brien, 2000).

Due to society's increasing awareness about the importance of sustainable development, an increasing number of firms invest in corporate social responsibility (Cantele & Zardini, 2018). The existing literature presents mixed findings on the impact of external and internal CSR on performance outcomes (Sardana et al., 2020). There are many studies in the literature on CSR that emphasize the importance of this concept for financial performance (e.g., Osmanagić et al., 2013; Kim et al., 2015), but there is still no consensus on whether the effect of CSR on firm's performance is positive, negative or neutral (e.g., Youn et al., 2015). Firms may invest in CSR activities that benefit external stakeholders (e.g., business partners and the local community) or internal stakeholders (e.g., employees) (Cao et al., 2023). Also, companies often invest in CSR to improve their profitability rather than social and environmental goals, making financial impact often more important than social performance (Saha et al., 2020).

An extensive body of literature argues that managerial values and attitudes towards CSR in a given institutional context are likely to have a strong influence on the outcomes of CSR initiatives (Hemingway & Maclagan, 2004; Roeck & Farooq, 2018). As part of research on the relationship between CSR and performance, an innovative leadership style, often associated with empathetic and ethical leadership, is increasingly associated with company effectiveness (Lee & Roh, 2012) and has been significantly related to financial performance (Carpenter et al., 2004). Common benefits of ethical leadership and financial performance are employee satisfaction, employee morale and productivity, and firm's goodwill. Meanwhile, the irresponsible actions of firms may affect the stakeholders' confidence and become a source of conflicts (Saha et al., 2020). Brown et al. (2005) claimed that ethical leadership influences the employee outcomes as ethical leader is considered as credible and legitimate role model. Russell (2000) argued that personal values not merely influence the leader behaviour but also encourage paramount organizational performance.

Taking into account the conclusions of the literature review, the following research hypotheses were formulated:

Hypothesis 1. The more managers perceive CSR as a cost, the worse their non-financial performance.
Hypothesis 2. The more managers perceive CSR as a cost, the worse their financial performance.
Hypothesis 3. The more managers perceive CSR as a benefit, the better their non-financial performance.
Hypothesis 4. The more managers perceive CSR as a benefit, the better their financial performance.

3 Research Concept and Method

In connection with the research gap identified as a result of the literature review, the subject of this empirical study is to determine the relationship between managers' CSR perception and its influence on financial and non-financial firm performance.

In the empirical study, the following factors as managers' CSR perception were taken into account:

1. managers' perception of CSR in terms of costs.
2. managers' perception of CSR in terms of benefits.

Company performance was analysed taking into account the following indicators:

1. financial (net profit, operating margin, revenue on sales—ROS, sales value),
2. non-financial (market share in terms of value, the number of customers who make purchases on a regular basis, customer loss rate, number of new clients, awareness of the key brand amongst customers, company/key brand image, the perceived quality of company brands/products).

Data on financial and non-financial results were collected on the basis of the respondents' assessment of changes in the aforementioned companies' results in 2021 compared to the end of the year 2019 (before the COVID-19 pandemic).

The conceptual model of the relationship between the variables included in the study is presented in Fig. 1.

In order to verify research hypotheses, the author applied quantitative research using the CAWI/CATI survey on 241 medium (50–249 employees) and large (250 and more employees) companies operating in Poland from fashion, cosmetics and household appliances/consumer electronics industries. Researched companies were operating on the B2C market and were manufacturers or trade intermediaries. The sampling frame for the aforementioned sample was Bisnode base (previous

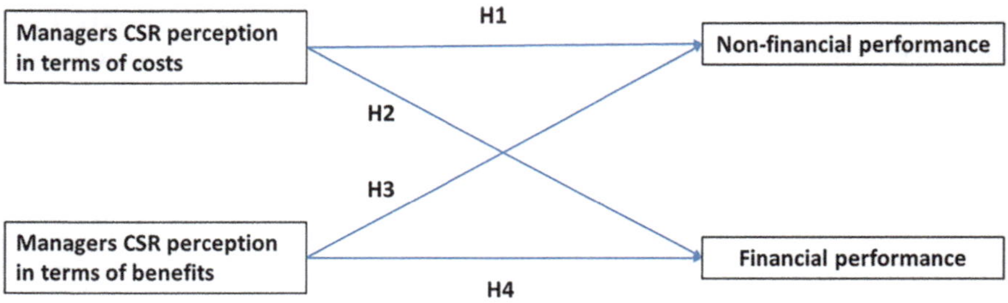

Fig. 1 Conceptual model of the relationship between the variables included in the study. *Source*: Own elaboration

Hoppensted & Bonnier, HBI). This base includes data on more than 7 million companies, of which 4.6 million are active companies whose data is constantly updated (database updated on a daily basis). Respondents to the survey were owners of the surveyed companies, senior managers responsible for marketing, including CSR.

The questionnaire consisted of closed questions with a 7-point Likert scale (statements about managers' CSR perception) and a 5-point Likert scale (statements about companies' performance). The study was conducted in July–August 2021 and was preceded by a pilot study on 10 companies. On its basis, it was confirmed that the questionnaire form is a properly prepared tool, in particular, that the questions included in it are unambiguous and understandable for the respondents. Finally, the sample from the pilot study was included in the target quantitative survey. Amongst the companies surveyed, the cosmetics industry represents the largest number of firms—89 (36.9%), followed by the household appliances/consumer electronics—78 (32.4%) and fashion industries—74 (30.7%). This means that similar numbers of companies represent all three industries included in the study.

For data analysis was used the PLS-SEM method using the Smart PLS 3 software, which is gaining importance in research used for exploratory or theory development purposes (Hair et al., 2017). PLS-SEM gives the possibility of extracting hidden variables and estimating the regression coefficients of the relationship between the variables. In order to estimate the distribution of estimation errors and to determine the statistical significance of the regression paths, PLS-SEM uses the bootstrapping procedure (Hair et al., 2014).

4 Research Results

4.1 Structural Model Analysis

Separated on the basis of literature, two determinants (i.e., managers' CSR perception in terms of costs and managers' CSR perception in terms of benefits) were introduced to the structural model using the PLS-SEM method.

The model consists of two main conceptual components:

1. Managers' perception of CSR, which consist of two exogenous reflective constructs:
   - managers' perception of CSR in terms of costs (CSRCT),
   - managers' perception of CSR in terms of benefits (CSRBE),
2. surveyed companies performance, which consists of two endogenous formative constructs:
   - non-financial results (PNFI).
   - financial results (PFI).

Variables concerning companies' financial and non-financial results have been summed up for the purposes of the model, i.e., creating the dependent variable indices of financial and non-financial results.

Reflective constructs assume that the cause is the construct itself, and its manifestations are observable variables (as strongly correlated indicators). In the case of formative constructs, measurable variables form a construct for which pointers are the cause, so these constructs are indexes for which a change in the value of the index translates into a change in the value of the construct.

Figure 2 shows the structural model of the relationship between managers' CSR perception and the performance of the surveyed companies. The factor loadings for the variables measurable in the model are listed in Table 1.

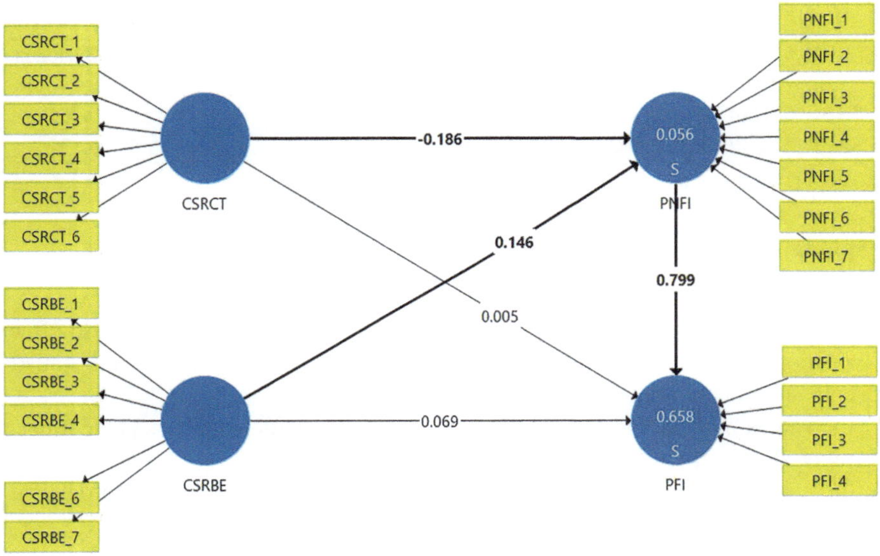

Fig. 2 Structural model of the relationship between managers' CSR perception and the company's performance of the surveyed companies estimated using the PLS-SEM method ($N = 241$). *Source*: own elaboration with the use of SmartPLS software

Table 1 Managers' CSR perception

Indicators	Statements	Source	Factor loadings
Managers' CSR perception in terms of costs (CSRCT)			
CSRCT_1	A company that ignores social responsibility may have a cost advantage over the one that respects it.	Quazi and O'Brien (2000)	0.850
CSRCT_2	Enterprises are primarily economic actors and are most socially responsible when they focus on their economic goals.		0.835
CSRCT_3	Business should only deal with those social problems that arise as a result of its own actions.		0.452
CSRCT_4	Social involvement can be detrimental to a smaller enterprise, as it can be excluded from the market due to the high costs associated with it.		0.609
CSRCT_5	It is unwise to require a company to solve social problems created by others that will not bring it any potential profit.		0.777
CSRCT_6	Business has a lot to do anyway and should not take any extra responsibility.		0.875
Managers' CSR perception in terms of benefits (CSRBE)			
CSRBE_1	CSR is an effective tool for competing on the market.	Quazi and O'Brien (2000)	0.684
CSRBE_2	CSR programmes help create a favourable image of enterprises.		0.772
CSRBE_3	Contributing to the resolution of social problems can be profitable for business.		0.736
CSRBE_4	CSR programmes introduced in the company may encourage investors to start cooperation.	Osmanagić et al. (2013)	0.651
CSRBE_5	CSR can strengthen the ability to attract, motivate and retain employees.		Excluded
CSRBE_6	CSR can increase sales and market share.		0.764
CSRBE_7	CSR can increase customer loyalty.		0.804

Source: Own elaboration

Explanations

- circles represent hidden variables,
- arrows (regression paths) between hidden variables indicate their cause-effect relationships resulting from theoretical assumptions (bold lines indicate statistically significant relationships),
- the values indicated in the arrows represent path coefficients (i.e., standardized regression coefficients),
- the values given inside the hidden variables indicate the coefficients of determination R^2.
- squares -measurable variables (indices of hidden variables).

The sample size for the structural model estimated in PLS-SEM meets the requirement of the so-called "10 times rule", i.e., the number of observations should be greater than 10 times the largest number of paths leading to one of the variables hidden in the model (Hair et al., 2014).

The evaluation of the model began with the determination of the parameters of the measurement (external) part. For this purpose, factor loadings were determined, the applied reflective measurement model has the direction of the relationship from the hidden variable to its indicators (Hair et al., 2014:92). Indicators with very low loadings (below 0.4) have been removed (Hair et al., 2011). The reflective indicators of the constructs related to managers' CSR perception that met the requirements of the measurement model assessment are presented in Table 1.

Table 2 Model quality criteria: Composite Reliability (CR), Average Variance Extracted (AVE), Co-efficient of determination (R^2)

	Cronbach's Alpha	CR	AVE	R^2
CSRBE	0.852	0.876	0.543	
CSRCT	0.844	0.880	0.561	
PFI				0.056
PNFI				0.658

Source: own elaboration with the use of SmartPLS software

Another model quality criterion is Composite Reliability (CR) and Average Variance Extracted (AVE). In the presented model, all constructs present the AVE value greater than the required minimum level of 50% (Hair et al., 2014). This means that all reflective constructs of the model present a high level of convergent validity. The most frequently used measure to assess the structural model is the coefficient of determination (R^2), calculated for each endogenous construct (Hair et al., 2011). The values of R^2 for endogenous variables in the structural model are presented in Table 2.

The model meets the discriminant validity criterion as well (Table 3). To assess this quality criterion, the Fornell–Larcker criterion was used as recommended by Hair et al. (2014).

The next step in the analysis was to test the research hypotheses, i.e., the analysis of the structural (internal) model. The estimation of the structural model started with checking the collinearity (Hair et al., 2014). All constructs of the presented structural model present the VIF (Variance Inflation Factor) below 5.00 (Hair et al., 2014), which indicates the lack of collinearity between the constructs.

Based on the estimated path coefficients and their statistical significance, it was determined whether the research hypotheses of the conceptual model are empirically confirmed (Table 4).

The results of the structural model allow to determine that the "managers' CSR perception in terms of costs (CSRCT)" has statistically significant and negative relationship with company non-financial performance (−0.186, significance = 0.001). Therefore, the **Hypothesis 1: The more managers perceive CSR as a cost, the worse their non-financial performance** can be confirmed.

The "managers' CSR perception in terms of costs (CSRCT)" has no statistically significant relationship with company financial performance. Therefore, the **Hypothesis 2: The more managers perceive CSR as a cost, the worse their financial performance** cannot be confirmed.

Table 3 Discriminant validity: Fornell–Larcker criterion ($N = 241$)

	CSRBE	CSRCT	PFI	PNFI
CSRBE	0.737			
CSRCT	−0.001	0.749		
PFI	0.185	−0.143		
PNFI	0.146	−0.186	0.808	

Source: own elaboration with the use of SmartPLS software

Table 4 Path coefficients and significance of relations between constructs ($N = 241$)

Hypothesis	Path coefficients	Original sample	*P* values
H1-confirmed	CSRCT - > PNFI	−0.186	**0.001**
H2-rejected	CSRCT - > PFI	0.005	0.895
H3-confirmed	CSRBE - > PNFI	0.146	**0.011**
H4-rejected	CSRBE - > PFI	0.069	0.115
	PNFI - > PFI	0.799	**0.000**

Source: own elaboration with the use of SmartPLS software

The "managers' CSR perception in terms of benefits (CSRBE)" positively correlates with company non-financial performance (0.146, significance = 0.011). Therefore, the **Hypothesis 3: The more managers perceive CSR as a benefit, the better their non-financial performance** can be confirmed.

The "managers CSR perception in terms of benefits (CSRCT)" has no statistically significant relationship with company financial performance. Therefore, the **Hypothesis 4: The more managers perceive CSR as a benefit, the better their financial performance** cannot be confirmed.

5 Conclusions

The processes underlying the relationship between the degree of CSR development in companies and the drivers/barriers determining this development are still at the center of an intense debate (Agudo-Valiente et al., 2017). In order to reap the potential benefits of CSR, leaders need to change their behaviour from reactive to proactive, and thus understand that the short-term costs associated with CSR projects would multiply their profitability in the long run (Saha et al., 2020). Managers are considered the main source in the organization that determines the values and environment based on ethics (Mishra & Schmidt, 2018).

This study contributes to the literature related to CSR drivers and barriers, in particular managers' CSR perception and its influence on company's performance. This research also answers the call for studies that can build connections between managers' motivations to engage in CSR and achieving competitive advantage and better financial results (e.g., Agudo-Valiente et al., 2017).

The results of the survey on a sample of 241 medium and large companies operating in Poland from the fashion, cosmetics, and household appliances/consumer electronics industries indicate that managers' CSR perception has a significant relation with company's non-financial performance. When managers take a broad approach to CSR and perceive this concept in terms of benefits, then the relationship with non-financial results is positive. When managers take a narrow approach to CSR and see the concept in terms of costs, then the relationship with non-financial results is negative.

The results presented are consistent with previous studies (e.g., Graafland & van de Ven, 2006) that have shown that leaders who see the benefits from implementing CSR activities take the long-term approach to these initiatives and more willingly build honest and responsible relations with their stakeholders, which in turn has a positive impact on corporate reputation, brand image, or customer loyalty. CSR requires short-term costs and generates profit only in the long-term, which is very often an entry barrier to the adoption of CSR practices (Saha et al., 2020). Managers who perceive CSR only in terms of costs are less likely to take actions related to this concept, because they present a narrow concept of corporate responsibility and are sceptical about CSR.

This study has some limitations as well. One of them is limiting the research to three industries: fashion, cosmetics, and household appliances/consumer electronics. The research can be extended by comparing the results amongst big and medium companies, by comparing analysed three industries or by including other industries, e.g., FMCG. The study is also limited to one market, i.e. Poland. An interesting approach would be to compare results between different foreign markets. Future research can also consider taking into account a wider range of CSR determinants. A possible solution would be taking into account, in a broader perspective, managers' values and ethics in their daily work.

References

Agudo-Valiente, J. M., Garcés-Ayerbe, C., & Salvador-Figueras, M. (2017). Corporate social responsibility drivers and barriers according to managers' perception: Evidence from Spanish firms. *Sustainability, 9*(10), 1–24.

Aguilera, R., Rupp, D., Williams, C., & Ganapathi, J. (2007). Putting the S back in corporate social responsibility: A multilevel theory of social change in organizations. *Academy of Management Review, 32*(3), 836–863. https://doi.org/10.5465/AMR.2007.25275678

Arevalo, J. A., & Aravind, D. (2011). Corporate social responsibility practices in India: Approach, drivers, and barriers. *Corporate Governance: International Journal of Business in Society, 11*, 399–414.

Aslan, S., & Sendogdu, A. (2012). The mediating role of corporate social responsibility in ethical leader's effect on corporate ethical values and behavior. *Procedia: Social and Behavioral Sciences, 58*, 693–702. https://doi.org/10.1016/j.sbspro.2012.09.1047

Aupperle, K. E., Carroll, A. B., & Hatfield, J. (1985). An empirical examina-tion of the relationship between corporate social responsibility andprofitability. *Academy of Management Journal, 28*(2), 446–463.

Brown, M. E., Treviño, L. K., & Harrison, D. A. (2005). Ethical leadership: Asocial learning perspective for construct development and testing. *Organizational Behavior and Human DecisionProcesses, 97*, 117–134.

Cantele, S., & Zardini, A. (2018). Is sustainability a competitive advantage for small businesses? An empirical analysis of possible mediators in the sustainability–financial performance relationship. *Journal of Cleaner Production, 182*, 166–176.

Cao, S., Yao, H., & Zhang, M. (2023). CSR gap and firm performance: An organizational justice perspective. *Journal of Business Research, 158*, 113692. https://doi.org/10.1016/j.jbusres.2023.113692

Carpenter, M. A., Geletkanycz, M. A., & Sanders, W. G. (2004). Upper echelons research revisited: Antecedents, elements, and consequences of top management team composition. *Journal of Management, 30*(6), 749–778.

Du, S., Swaen, V., Lindgreen, A., & Sen, S. (2013). The roles of leadership styles in corporate social responsibility. *Journal of Business Ethics, 114*(1), 155–169. https://doi.org/10.1007/s10551-012-1333-3

Fabrizi, M., Mallin, C., & Michelon, G. (2014). The role of CEO's personal incentives in driving corporate social responsibility. *Journal of Business Ethics, 124*, 311–326.

Freeman, R. E., Harrison, J. S., Wicks, A. C., Parmar, B., & de Colle, S. (2010). *Stakeholder theory: The state of the art*. Cambridge University Press.

Friedman, M. (1970). The social responsibility of business is to increase its profits. *The New York Times*. 13 September.

García-Sánchez, I. M., & García-Sánchez, A. (2020). Corporate social responsibility during COVID-19 pandemic. *Journal of Open Innovation: Technology, Market, and Complexity, 6*(4), 1–21.

Garriga, E., & Melé, D. (2004). Corporate social responsibility theories: Mapping the territory. *Journal of Business Ethics, 53*, 51–71.

Govindasamy, V., & Suresh, K. (2017). Exploring approaches to drivers and barriers of corporate social responsibility implementation in academic literature. *EDP Sciences, 33*, 1–8.

Graafland, J., & van de Ven, B. (2006). Strategic and moral motivation for corporate social responsibility. *Journal of Corporate Citizenship, 22*, 111–123.

Hair, J. F., Jr., Matthews, L. M., Matthews, R. L., & Sarstedt, M. (2017). PLS-SEM or CB-SEEM: Updated guidelines on which method to use. *International Journal of Multivariate Data Analysis, 1*(2), 107–121.

Hair, J. F., Ringle, C. M., & Sarstedt, M. (2011). PLS-SEM: Indeed a silver bullet. *Journal of Marketing Theory and Practice, 19*, 139–151.

Hair, J. F., Hult, G. T., Ringle, C. M., & Sarstedt, M. (2014). *A primer on partial least squares structural equation modeling (PLS–SEM)* (1st ed.). SAGE Publications, Inc..

Hemingway, C. A., & Maclagan, P. W. (2004). Managers' personal values as drivers of corporate social responsibility. *Journal of Business Ethics, 50*, 33–44.

Hung, H. (2011). Directors' roles in corporate social responsibility: A stakeholder perspective. *Journal of Business Ethics, 103*, 385–402.

Husted, B. W., & Allen, D. A. (2006). Corporate social responsibility in the multinational enterprise: Strategic and institutional approaches. *Journal of International Business Studies, 37*, 838–849.

Kim, K., Kim, M., & Qian, C. (2015). Effects of corporate social responsibility on corporate financial performance: A competitive-action perspective. *Journal of Management, 20*(10), 1–22.

Lattemann, C., Fetscherin, M., Alon, I., Li, S. M., & Schneider, A. M. (2009). CSR communication intensity in Chinese and Indian multinational companies. *Corporate Governance: International Review, 17*, 426–442.

Lee, J., & Roh, J. J. (2012). Revisiting corporate reputation and firm performance link. *Benchmarking: An International Journal, 19*(4/5), 649–664. https://doi.org/10.1108/14635771211258061

Mishra, P., & Schmidt, G. B. (2018). How can leaders of multinational organizations be ethical by contributing to corporate social responsibility initiatives? Guidelines and pitfalls for leaders trying to do good. *Business Horizons, 61*(6), 833–843. https://doi.org/10.1016/j.bushor.2018.07.011

Osmanagić, N. B., Fafaliou, I., Porada-Rochon, M., Rausch, A., & Labas, D. (2013). Corporate social responsibility and company performance—Evidence from four European countries. *The Holistic Approach to Environment, 3*(3), 153–173.

Quazi, A. M., & O'Brien, D. (2000). An empirical test of a cross–national model of corporate social responsibility. *Journal of Business Ethics, 25*, 33–51.

Russell, R. F. (2000). The role of values in servant leadership. *Leadership and Organization Development Journal, 22*(2), 76–84.

Roeck, K. D., & Farooq, O. (2018). Corporate social responsibility and ethical leadership: Investigating their interactive effect on employees' socially responsible behaviors. *Journal of Business Ethics, 151*, 923–939. https://doi.org/10.1007/s10551-017-3656-6

Saha, R., Shashi, C., & R., Singh, R., Dahiya, R. (2020). Effect of ethical leadership and corporate social responsibility on firm performance: A systematic review. *Corporate Social Responsibility and Environmental Management, 27*, 409–429. https://doi.org/10.1002/csr.1824

Sardana, D., Gupta, N., Kumar, V., & Terziovski, M. (2020). CSR 'sustainability' practices and firm performance in an emerging economy. *Journal of Cleaner Production, 258*, 120766.

Tefera, M. A., Yuanqiong, H., & Luming, L. (2019). A link between top managers' perception and corporate social responsibility: Transformational leadership as a moderator. *International Journal of Research in Business and Social Science (2147-4478), 9*(1), 01–14. https://doi.org/10.20525/ijrbs.v9i1.605

Tuan, L. T. (2012). Corporate social responsibility, ethics, and corporate governance. *Social Responsibility Journal, 8*(4), 547–560. https://doi.org/10.1108/17471111211272110

Youn, H., Hua, N., & Lee, S. (2015). Does size matter? Corporate social responsibility and firm performance in the restaurant industry. *International Journal of Hospitality Management, 51*, 127–134. https://doi.org/10.1016/j.ijhm.2015.09.008

Anna Napiórkowska, Ph.D., Assistant Professor at the Department of International Business in the Collegium of World Economy at the SGH Warsaw School of Economics, Warsaw, Poland. Author or co-author of publications in the field of corporate social responsibility, ethical leadership, CSR legalization, retail chains' CSR strategies in peer-reviewed journals and scientific books.

Part II
Sustainable Finance

The Geopolitical Accountability of the Central Banks' Gold Reserve

Rute Abreu and Carlos Pinho

1 Introduction

This research aims to discuss the geopolitical accountability of central banks' gold reserve that can be controversial for several reasons (Samano, 2022; Baur, 2013). One of the relevant reasons is the publicly available report that must be disclosed annually by central banks to reaffirm their commitment to provide "effective and informed support to the design of public policies and acting as a guide for economic agents" (BP, 2023). Other reason is the need for stability on the financial system since central banks have regulatory and supervisor activities (Sinclair, 2005). The third important reason that has been pointed by Borio (2014, p. 19) concludes "there is a risk that central banks will lose their credibility as the body politic and public at large lose confidence in their ability to fulfil their mission." That is not to deny that there are externalities that must take in account that arise, for example, as Obstfeld and Taylor (2017, p. 3) remember due to "the gold standard of the late nineteenth and early twentieth centuries implied fixed exchange rates because all gold-standard central banks fixed their currencies 'values in terms of gold." But, for a while, the monetary and financial systems deliver stability to the economy (Widdowson & Hailwood, 2007). The reality changes every day, and central banks can reinforce the role of supervisor of bank credit (Borio & Lowe, 2002).

One of the most frequent discussions about investment (Sherman, 1986) considers gold as a commodity (Levin & Wright, 2006), despite the risks (Aggarwal &

R. Abreu (✉)
Instituto Politécnico da Guarda, CICF-IPCA, CISeD-IPV, CiTUR, Guarda, Portugal
e-mail: ra@ipg.pt

C. Pinho
Universidade de Aveiro, GOVCOPP; DEGEIT, Aveiro, Portugal
e-mail: cpinho@ua.pt

B. Díaz Díaz et al. (eds.), *Building Global Societies Towards an ESG World*,
CSR, Sustainability, Ethics & Governance,
https://doi.org/10.1007/978-3-031-56619-6_6

Lucey, 2007) and uncertainties it carries (Borio & Disyatat, 2015; Cassis, 2011). As a result of the market price mechanism, gold price changes in the space (i.e., markets of supply or demand), time (i.e., volatility of the market itself), and also in different proposals of use (i.e., jewels, informatics or businesses itself (Harmston, 1998). Traditionally, citizens invest in jewellery, because gold as an asset (Michaud et al., 2006) has become a long-term demand (Batchelor & Gulley, 1995).

In several economies, the gold price is volatile (Aggarwal, 1992) and investors' expectations grow to fight against tendencies (Shafiee & Topal, 2010). Indeed, the best interests of investors are expressed on the gold market security (Bordo, 1981). Furthermore, this research is centered on the central bank's gold reserve as a critical asset (Lawrence, 2003) on the international relations (Ariovich, 1983) that ensure the accountability in their decision-making process (Borio & Disyatat, 2015).

This research is based on the perspective that Beckmann and Czudaj (2013) defend that "gold is no longer a central cornerstone of the international monetary system since the breakdown of Bretton Woods, it still attracts considerable interest from both investors and researchers." In addition, Worthington and Pahlavani (2007) argue that "gold sets itself apart from other commodities by its being durable, relatively transportable, universally acceptable, and easily authenticated." Indeed, as Aizenman and Inoue (2012) defend "central banks also still keep maintaining passive stocks of gold, independently of the patterns of the real price of gold."

Furthermore, the Chalu (2021, p. 578) preserve that the "monetary policies depend on the accounting information generated by the accounting system and accounting policies of the CBs, among other factors." This research deals with multifaceted research, because as Bindseil (2004) explains the role of the three main instruments (open market operations, standing facilities, and reserve requirements) and reviews their use in the twentieth century used by US Central Bank.

This chapter is structured into five further sections. In addition to this introduction presented in Sect. 1, Sect. 2 explores the theoretical analysis based on the patterns (price and quantity) of the gold as an asset on the balance sheet of central banks. Section 3 establishes the methodology of the research and establishes the research question, present the materials and the methods. Section 4 presents the empirical analysis of the Gold Price, Gold Production and Gold Reserves, especially related with the central banks. Finally, Section 5 presents the chapter's conclusions and explores limitations and suggestions for future research.

2 Theoretical Analysis

The gold reserve of central banks has been characterized "by a relatively high degree of international integration, freedom and stability" on the period of the classical gold standard (1880–1913) (Hoffmann, 2013, p. 2). In addition, European Union and Euro system generates the introduction and the promotion of the Euro. It is important to understand that "while countries on the gold standard held on to their domestic currencies, joining the euro area meant to abandon them" (Hoffmann, 2013, p. 4).

Indeed, this demand to defend that gold standard, despite the economic and financial arguments, promotes less risks and "benefits from lower transaction costs and a reduction of uncertainty in finance and trade" (De Grauwe, 2009, p. 14). But at the same point, Morris and Shin (1999) detail that "create conditions for a critical mass of speculators that converts a vulnerable currency into a crisis victim, if the authorities are believed to view currency defence as too expensive."

The authors defend the concern of Kirshner (1995) that confirms "States can use international monetary systems—and the leading role of their national currencies—as an instrument of power." But, unfortunately, more than a decade, monetary policy in the euro area was highly accommodative (BP, 2023).

Many difficulties rise for the monetary system with consequences to the financial system (Blose 2010). As Borio and Lowe (2002) argue, "the reason is that the lag between the build-up of systemic risks and the emergence of financial distress is considerably longer than the lag associated with keeping inflation under control." Also relevant is the perspective of Reynard (2023) that justifies "balance sheet expansions have however been followed by drastically different inflation outcomes." Traditionally, on the European Union countries, inflation is not a concern, but nowadays it is a macroeconomic indicator essential to economic and financial markets (Kolluri 1981; Ghosh et al. 2004). These changes have geopolitical consequences on the finance of firms and citizens (Adrangi et al. 2003; Bampinas & Panagiotidis 2016).

The central banks, concerned with welfare of firms and citizens, reinforce their decision-making power to supervise markets. "Consequently, the likelihood is that global support for international economic integration will remain as strong, if not be strengthened, in the coming years" (Posen & Juluis, 2012, p. 4). It is also becoming important to the private and public investors to focus on the profitability of investments and to mitigate risks. As an alternative, it depends on the decline of smaller and losses in investment on gold market (Baur & Lucey 2010, Baur & McDermott 2010). Nevertheless, central banks' gold reserves are crucial as they are assets of the balance sheet, which is crucial to assess the financial position of the central bank.

3 Methodology of the Research

The methodology of the research is subdivided on the theoretical analysis supported on the literature review of the accounting information system of central banks, and also reports, documents and statistics published by different entities. Additionally, the geopolitical accountability justifies the conceptual framework under discussion (Oxford Analytica, 2020). The empirical analysis is based on the case study methodology that highlights through visual analysis (i.e. graphs with visual mapping) and content analysis (i.e. reports and statistics with econometric studies) different strategic approaches (Krippendorff, 2019) to recognize the responsibility in the implementation of sustainable policies and accountability strategies of central banks. Indeed, it will be used "graphs as data structures capturing relationships between entities" (von Landesberger et al., 2011, p. 1739) that it has been proposed by Tukey (1977, p. 24) in order to "looking at data to see what is seems to say."

Research can also be supported on the theoretical basis through graphs and figures (Rose, 2013). Indeed, Gliner et al. (2009) detailed that the research problem is stated for an understanding of research design and data analysis using design approach to provide relations between variables about the causes of the research. Due to the specificity of this data research, Tracy (2020) proposes the use of visuals to immerse on the research itself and requires a holist examination of data. Thus, this implication as Heywood and Sandywell (2012) explain allows to improve the understanding of the effects of visual materials.

The method used to develop the research is focus on the annual report of central banks and therefore it demands to be a deductive approach support on the content analysis (Carduff, 2022; Krippendorff, 2019; Parker, 2005). White and Marsh (2006) argue that it is highly flexible and is related with research objectives and more important is a systematic and rigorous approach to analyse annual reports. The authors follow the procedure of the quantitative content analysis proposed by White and Marsh (2006, p. 30). So, the research process starts on the first step, after the literature review, by establishing the research question:

Is there geopolitical accountability in relation with the central bank gold reserve?

In the second step, it is mandatory to investigate the appropriate data from databases and websites with publicly available annual reports (Tower, 1993). The hypothesis inherent to the research question demands research about gold reserves in the central banks all over the world as Table 1 presents.

In the fourth step is the draw of the sample. It presents several difficulties to obtain the full data from the world population of central banks (Ashton et al., 1989), for this reason that it starts to appear omissions of the public disclosure and this demands to make the selection of central banks that will belong to the sample (Table 2).

The voluntary disclosures tend to be smaller, despite the technological progress, there is developments justifying the increase of transparency and the detail of the disclosure of information published by central banks due to their public interest in the information published and to garner support in their legitimacy to capture aspects of the human decision-making process (Gorry & Morton, 1971).

The fifth step details patterns, informations, and interactions amongst accounts on the annual report and then allow the authors to summarize the findings based on the data from the annual report of the central banks (White & Marsh, 2006, p. 34). In this process, of research, the authors must face the contextual nature of literacy and highlights the view that "the more complex the society, the more complex the notion of literacy becomes" (Jackson, 1993). The countries where the financial literacy is promoted tend to be more transparent, and the annual reports of central banks increasingly present more accountability in compliance with monetary and financial systems. The citizen gets more protection for these entities and the stability of the systems gives more trust to the society. It is also clear that the culture of each country defines the international accounting models (Hofstede, 1980), which are Anglo-Saxon, Continental, Latin American, Mixed markets, and Islamic and then as Gray (1988) defines their characteristics: secrecy versus transparency; conservatism versus optimism; uniformity versus flexibility.

Table 1 World population of central banks

Central Banks			
Afghanistan	Denmark	Lao PDR	Romania
Albania	Dominican Republic	Latvia	Russian Federation
Algeria	Ecuador	Lebanon	Saudi Arabia
Argentina	Egypt	Libya	Serbia
Armenia	El Salvador	Lithuania	Singapore
Aruba	Eritrea	Luxembourg	Slovakia
Australia	Estonia	Malawi	Slovenia
Austria	Fiji	Malaysia	South Africa
Azerbaijan	Finland	Malta	South Korea
Bahrain	France	Mauritania	Spain
Bangladesh	Gabon	Mauritius	Sri Lanka
Belarus	Germany	Mexico	Suriname
Belgium	Ghana	Mongolia	Sweden
Bolivia	Greece	Morocco	Switzerland
Bosnia and Herzegovina	Guatemala	Mozambique	Syrian Arab Republic
Brazil	Haiti	Myanmar	Taiwan (POC)
Bulgaria	Honduras	Nepal	Tajikistan
Burundi	Hong Kong SAR	Netherlands	Thailand
Cambodia	Hungary	Nicaragua	Trinidad and Tobago
Cameroon	Iceland	Nigeria	Tunisia
Canada	India	North Macedonia	Turkey
Chad	Indonesia	Norway	Turkmenistan
Chile	Iraq	Oman	Ukraine
China	Ireland	Pakistan	United Arab Emirates
Colombia	Italy	Papua New Guinea	United Kingdom
Comoros	Japan	Paraguay	United States of America
Congo	Jordan	Peru	Uruguay
Costa Rica	Kazakhstan	Philippines	Uzbekistan
Croatia	Kenya	Poland	Venezuela
Cyprus	Kuwait	Portugal	Yemen
Czech Republic	Kyrgyzstan	Qatar	

Source: World Gold Council (2023)

The sixth step details the discussion of the results from the theoretical and empirical analysis. The monetary system remains indisputably dominated by the United States (Fantacci & Gobbi, 2023). However, this apparent consensus is strongly affected by economic ascent of the Popular Republic of China and other major emerging markets that are fighting to get higher place on globalization centered on their own interests (Posen & Juluis, 2012).

All this questions allow the authors to agree with Bazot et al. (2016, p. 87), when they defend that "first, central banks should raise their discount rate when their gold reserves decrease; Second, they should not sterilize gold flows." In these

Table 2 Sample of international central banks

Central Banks			
Argentina	Cyprus	Ireland	Portugal
Australia	Czech Republic	Italy	Romania
Austria	Estonia	Latvia	Slovakia
Belgium	Finland	Lithuania	South Africa
Brazil	France	Luxembourg	Sweden
Bulgaria	Germany	Malta	Switzerland
Canada	Greece	Netherlands	United Kingdom
Croatia	Hungary	Poland	United States of America

Source: World Gold Council (2023)

circumstances, the authors present concerns about the geopolitical accountability of central banks gold reserves related to necessary equilibrium of the monetary system.

4 Empirical Analysis

Before starting the empirical analysis, it is important to detail one of the databases that has been used to research, that is, the World Gold Council (2023) which argues: "The gold market is broad and complex, so producing statistics on demand and supply is challenging. But having such statistics is crucial to understanding the fundamentals of the market."

Table 3 presents the distribution of gold production by geographic region, from 1980 to 2022 (in tonne).

Table 3 presents the distribution of gold production by geographic region, from 1980 to 2022 (in Tonne), knowing that Western Europe produces the lowest rate of gold with an average of 28.95 tonne and standard deviation of 16.94 tonne and Middle East and Africa is the biggest producer gold with an average of 649.33 tonne and standard deviation of 81.04 tonne.

All over the world, the production has registered a maximum of 3482.60 tonne in 2018 and minimum of 961.10 tonne in 1980. In these 22 years of analysis, the increase of gold production has reached 231.4% and all the geographic regions with exception of the Middle East and Africa only produce 37.4%, so the Middle East and Africa are very important in the production of gold. But this tendency changes in 1988 and since then, until the year 2009 and 2010 with 422.4% and 417.0%, respectively. Other relevant conclusion is the increase in the Asia Pacific, the North America and the Australiasia region with steep increase of 871.8%, 946.3% and 1586.7%, respectively.

It is notable to mention that, despite the small dimension, the Eastern Europe has increased the production of gold to 13.506%, it is true that in 1980 only 2 tonne was produced and increased to 271.2 tonne in 2022. Another important change happened in Asia Pacific region where there was a leap from 88.30 tonne in 1980 to

Table 3 Distribution of gold production by geographic region, from 1980 to 2022 (in tonne)

Geography region	1980	2022	Max	Min	Average	Standard deviation
World	961,10	3.184,80	3.482,60	961,10	2.294,71	758,29
Asia Pacific	88,30	769,80	959,50	88,30	521,67	269,07
Middle East and Africa	699,60	758,00	789,10	462,50	649,33	81,04
Latin America	62,20	588,60	675,70	62,20	366,53	197,76
North America	84,10	419,40	533,70	84,10	360,53	126,95
Australasia	19,60	311,00	334,50	17,30	219,20	111,47
Eastern Europe	2,00	271,20	334,30	2,00	148,48	106,50
Western Europe	5,30	66,90	67,30	5,30	28,95	16,94
China	45,00	309,80	453,50	45,00	220,62	133,58
Indonesia	0,20	100,30	162,60	0,20	70,77	49,44
Papua New Guinea	14,70	26,40	135,10	14,70	53,62	21,83
Kazakhstan	–	117,90	117,90	12,50	43,94	34,60
Uzbekistan	–	109,50	109,50	65,00	85,73	10,53
Philippines	20,00	27,10	40,80	15,80	28,57	6,78
Kyrgyzstan	–	16,20	31,00	1,20	16,57	8,09
Mongolia	–	20,20	24,10	0,80	11,99	7,22
South Korea	1,30	0,20	20,80	0,00	3,50	5,74
Japan	3,20	6,20	10,30	3,10	7,32	1,86
North Korea	–	10,00	10,00	2,00	5,79	3,03
Tajikistan	–	8,50	8,80	0,40	3,25	2,46
Laos	–	2,90	7,10	2,90	5,37	1,25
Armenia	–	2,50	5,90	0,20	2,05	1,59
Thailand	–	2,30	5,60	0,10	3,25	1,67
Fiji	0,80	1,10	4,70	0,70	2,43	1,34
Malaysia	0,20	1,30	4,70	0,20	3,14	0,96
Azerbaijan	–	3,30	3,70	0,40	2,48	1,04
India	2,50	0,80	3,70	0,80	2,15	0,65
Solomon Islands	–	–	3,50	0,00	0,51	0,89
Taiwan	0,40	0,00	2,20	0,00	0,56	0,67
Myanmar	–	1,10	1,70	0,10	0,51	0,52
Vietnam	–	0,70	1,70	0,00	0,40	0,46
Pakistan	–	1,60	1,60	1,60	1,60	0,00

Source: Euromonitor International (2023)

806.2 tonne in 2022, and in the year 2018, it reached a maximum value of 959.5 tonne.

Table 4 presents the distribution of the gold production by 24 countries, from 1980 till 2022 (in tonne). This table only includes countries that formally produce gold; the maximum was registered by Popular Republic of China with 453.5 tonne in 2016 and minimum was registered by some countries and few countries that did not produce any gold at all from 1980 till 2022.

The Popular Republic of China produced the highest value with 453.50 tonne in 2016 and the lowest value with 45 tonne in 1980, but the tendency of decreased in

Table 4 Distribution of gold production from 1980 to 2022 (in tonne)

Geography region	1980	2022	Max	Min	Average	Standard deviation
China	45,00	309,80	453,50	45,00	220,62	133,58
Indonesia	0,20	100,30	162,60	0,20	70,77	49,44
Papua New Guinea	14,70	26,40	135,10	14,70	53,62	21,83
Kazakhstan	–	117,90	117,90	12,50	43,94	34,60
Uzbekistan	–	109,50	109,50	65,00	85,73	10,53
Philippines	20,00	27,10	40,80	15,80	28,57	6,78
Kyrgyzstan	–	16,20	31,00	1,20	16,57	8,09
Mongolia	–	20,20	24,10	0,80	11,99	7,22
South Korea	1,30	0,20	20,80	0,00	3,50	5,74
Japan	3,20	6,20	10,30	3,10	7,32	1,86
North Korea	–	10,00	10,00	2,00	5,79	3,03
Tajikistan	–	8,50	8,80	0,40	3,25	2,46
Laos	–	2,90	7,10	2,90	5,37	1,25
Armenia	–	2,50	5,90	0,20	2,05	1,59
Thailand	–	2,30	5,60	0,10	3,25	1,67
Fiji	0,80	1,10	4,70	0,70	2,43	1,34
Malaysia	0,20	1,30	4,70	0,20	3,14	0,96
Azerbaijan	–	3,30	3,70	0,40	2,48	1,04
India	2,50	0,80	3,70	0,80	2,15	0,65
Solomon Islands	–	–	3,50	0,00	0,51	0,89
Taiwan	0,40	0,00	2,20	0,00	0,56	0,67
Myanmar	–	1,10	1,70	0,10	0,51	0,52
Vietnam	–	0,70	1,70	0,00	0,40	0,46
Pakistan	–	1,60	1,60	1,60	1,60	0,00

Source: Euromonitor International (2023)

2016 until 2022 with 309.8 tonne or 588.4%. The representation of China gold production on the world is 9.73% in the first place, Kazakhstan gets 3.70% in the second place, Uzbekistan register 3.44% in the third place, and Indonesia gets 3.15% on the fourth place.

Interesting is the case study of the Papua New Guinea with an increase from 0.2 tonne in 1980 to 26.4 tonne in 2022, but in 2018, production increased to a maximum of 135.1 tonne. Another relevant case study is Solomon Islands that almost does not produce gold, but despite this conclusion it has a maximum increase in 1999 with 3.5 tonne and also pertinent is the gold production by periods, for example from the year 1998 (1.6 tonne) till 2000 (0.3 tonne) and year 2007 (0.1 tonne) till 2013 (0.6 tonne).

Furthermore, the case study of Japan deserves to be noted because as smaller gold production registered 10.6 tonne in 1986 and minimum register of 3.1 tonne in 1981, 1983, but the gold production does not have stability which is the reason to register 6.2 tonne in 2022.

Figure 1 presents the distribution of the difference between production and selling reserves of gold by total countries, from 1980 to 2022 (in tonnes).

Fig. 1 presents the difference between the value in tonne of the production and the selling gold reserves by total countries, from 1980 to 2022. It is very relevant to note that gold production increased in 1991, 2008 and 2017, thus the investment growth, and the decrease of the production in 2018, 2019, 2007, 2015, 2013 and 2022, hence with a strong reduction in the investment. This figure presents several movements of the production and selling of gold reserves, but without a tendency, what could be related with volatility of the markets and the increase of the price level that generates strong movements to reduce investment or to increase investment.

Table 5 presents the distribution of countries by geographic group, in 2022, with a total of 31.565,62 ounce.

On the one hand, the region of Europe with 20 countries of the European Union and Norway, Iceland and United Kingdom characterizes the biggest representation group with 11,776.47 ounce, for example, Germany with 3335.14 ounce, Italy with 2451.84 ounce, France with 2451.84 and Portugal with 382.57 ounce. On the other hand, North American (the US and Canada) represents the biggest country representation group with 8133.48 ounce, because there are less countries with highest values of gold reserves.

Table 5 Distribution of countries by geographic group, 2022

Group	Number of countries	Gold Reserves (Ounce)	Gold Reserves (%)
1. Australia-Fiji	2	79,88	0,25%
2. Eastern Europe	18	3.491,71	11,06%
3. Central Asia	6	785,38	2,49%
4. East Asia	6	3.394,56	10,75%
5. Latin America	21	614,67	1,95%
6. Arab States	17	1.507,64	4,78%
7. North America	2	8.133,48	25,77%
8. South Asia	5	874,54	2,77%
9. Southeast Asia	9	734,96	2,33%
10. Africa	14	172,33	0,55%
11. Europe	23	11.776,47	37,31%
Total	123	31.565,62	100,00%

Source: Euromonitor International (2023)

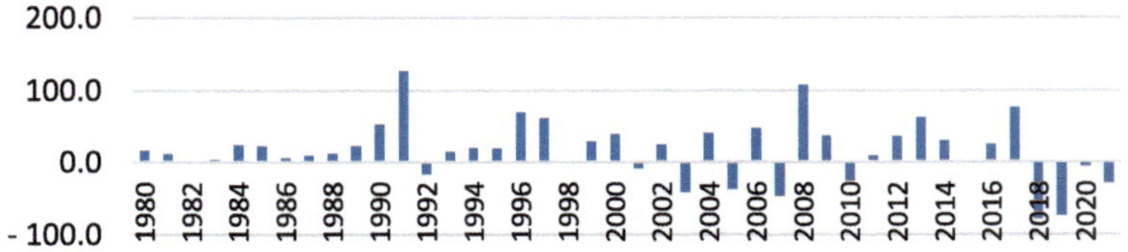

Fig. 1 Distribution of difference between production and selling reserves of gold by total countries, from 1980 to 2022 (in tonnes). *Source*: Euromonitor International (2023)

5 Discussion

Indeed, for the economic system, where producers as economic agents influence markets due to the production and selling process that allows gold to be available at markets with best price. Figure 2 presents the gold price, in gram, in USD, between June 2013 and 2023 and the strong tendency of growth only stopped by small decrease.

For the economic system, citizens live in the environment facing social and economic rules of gold circulation. Fig. 3 presents the Geopolitical Accountability of the Gold Reserve and extends to previous studies by using the IMF (2023).

Figure 3 confirms the tendency of the research which is the importance of the United States on the geopolitical accountability of the gold reserve showing its relevance all over the world. The relative absence of information on gold reserves of several countries does not reduce the uncertainty of the gold price or level of gold reserves, but the knowledge of the major and minor distributions explicated demand more disclosure on the annual report of central banks which may predict good or bad news to the monetary and financial system.

6 Conclusions

The results of this research show the history, the theory, and the practice related with gold reserves. Retracing the demand of gold reserves from central banks is difficult because the practice is linked with the institutional arrangements between several countries which misrepresenting the financial system all over the world. Over the time, gold is always an asset with complex markets involved, but has sufficient robustness in terms of value (Hillier et al. 2006; Jaffe 1989). So, investing in gold reserves by central banks could be in the framework of several regulations, but it will diminish the precision to mitigate precisions and robustness of the monetary system.

The sample of central banks researched shows:

Implications of the economic system, due to the efficiency and the effectiveness of gold on the central bank strategy.

Inequalities in the distribution level of quantities of gold between countries.

Collective obligation of preserving a sustainable gold system for the present and future generations.

From the investors' perspective, the authors defend that gold must be in one's investment portfolio so that it helps investors in reducing losses arising from inflation (Fama & Schwert 1977). Part of this understanding is based on the value that the private and public investors with knowledge get to deal with crises, shocks, and expansion times and allow constant monitoring of the financial and monetary system which reduces the compelling reasons to fail.

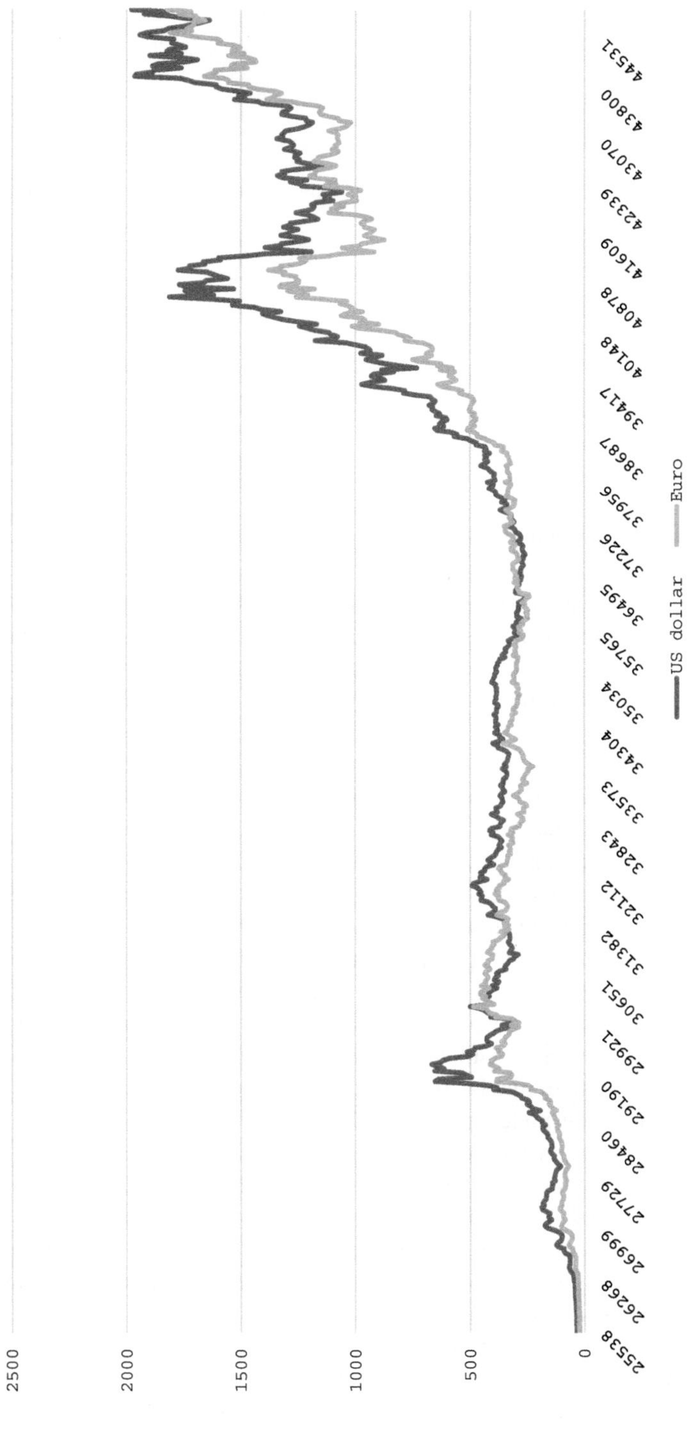

Fig. 2 Distribution of the gold price, in gram, in USD, June of 2013 and 2023. *Source*: World Gold Council (2023)

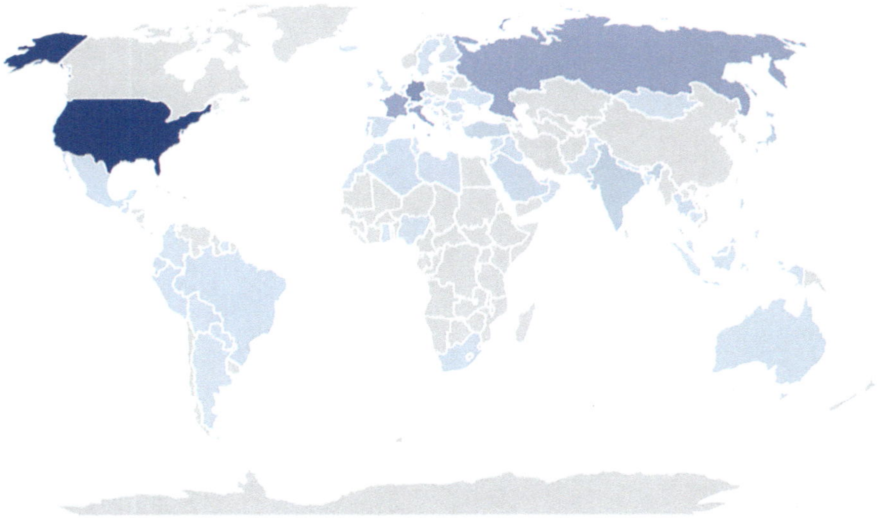

Fig. 3 Geopolitical accountability of the gold reserve. *Source*: IMF (2023)

For the monetary system, the authors consider that central banks need to disclosure in their financial report all the information about gold reserves to allow the society to identify their own investments and that this should be driven mainly by social responsibility from the other stakeholders that operate as a public service (Bordo & Eichengreen 1998).

For the education system, curriculum must include financial stability that protects threats against the global financial system using surveillance and information, communication, and technology functions. Certainly, the financial and monetary systems promote the stable prices and confidence on the currency to improve the economic stability. Students and researchers must research about the evolution of commodities markets and the accounting systems to achieve a more sustainable evolution.

Despite these contributions, this chapter presents two limitations. First limitation is related to role played by several stakeholders, such as the European Central Bank, the Central Bank of Portugal, Commercial, Investment and Saving banks, regulators, legislators, politicians, society, and each citizen in the gold market. Indeed, it is widely perceived as important, that is, to promote the financial literacy. This limitation deals with the financial understanding and the role of basic skills to fight against illiteracy and innumeracy has become ubiquitous knowledge.

Second limitation is the existence of an enormous body of laws, regulations and codes that have emerged and been enforced to reform central banks all over the world, which represents the monetary and financial systems. The challenge is to provide an understanding of gold reserve to devise a true regulatory framework that enables the gold market to be a more resilient absorber of shocks and to become a truly safe investment despite the gap between the private and public investors.

Future research may explore another approach of this research that is fundamental to deal with the volatility of the demand and the supply of the gold market with competitive objectives. Also, to reduce uncertainty of monetary and financial system because central banks must promote the safeguarding of stability of these systems. Even more hard to diminish is the complexity associated with the production of gold because of the powerful mine sector that all over the world must promote social responsibility rules as primary reasons to work in such destructive environment. And the last, but not the least is the ambiguity associated with the geopolitical accountability of the gold reserve that demand more accurate control of the production and selling of gold and the ability for the central banks to invest in gold as an asset with strategic value for the future. So, this chapter opens the door to analysis.

Acknowledgments The authors aim to thank Professor José Ángel Pérez-López of Seville University (Spain) and Professor David Crowther for the Social Responsibility Research Network (UK) for their comments and improvements and the valuable comments of two anonymous reviewers. Also, the first author thanks the Accounting and Taxation Research Center of IPCA for having financed the registration and the trip to participate in the Annual Conference of the Global Corporate Governance Institute with national funds through FCT—Foundation for Science and Technology, I.P., under the multi-year funding UIDB/04043/2020.DFBR.

References

Adrangi, B., Chatrath, A., & Raffiee, K. (2003). Economic activity, inflation, and hedging: the case of gold and silver investments. *Journal Wealth Management, 6*(2), 60–77.

Aggarwal, R., & Lucey, B. M. (2007). Psychological barriers in gold prices? *Review of Financial Economics, 16*(2), 217–230.

Aggarwal, R. (1992). Gold markets. In P. Newman, M. Milgate, & J. Eatwell (Eds.), *The new Palgrave dictionary of money and finance* (pp. 257–258). Macmillan.

Aizenman, J., & Inoue, K. (2012). *Central banks and gold puzzles*. National Bureau of Economic Research, Working Paper no. 17894.

Ariovich, G. (1983). The impact of political tension on the price of gold. *Journal for Studies in Economics and Econometrics, 16*(1), 17–37.

Ashton, R. H., Graul, P. R., & Newton, J. D. (1989). Audit delay and the timeliness of corporate reporting. *Contemporary Accounting Research, 5*(2), 657–673.

Bampinas, G., & Panagiotidis, T. (2016). Are gold and silver a hedge against inflation? A two-century perspective. *International Review of Financial Analysis, 41*, 267–276.

Banco de Portugal (BP). (2023). *Annual report 2022*. BP.

Batchelor, R., & Gulley, D. (1995). Jewellery demand and the price of gold. *Resources Policy, 21*(1), 37–42.

Baur, D. G., & Lucey, B. M. (2010). Is gold a hedge or a safe haven? An analysis of stocks, bonds, and gold. *The Financial Review, 45*(2), 217–229.

Baur, D. G., & McDermott, T. K. (2010). Is gold a safe haven? International evidence. *Journal of Banking & Finance, 34*(8), 1886–1898.

Baur, D. G. (2013). *Gold—Fundamental drivers and asset allocation*. Working Paper. University of Technology Sydney.

Bazot, G., Bordo, M. D., & Monnet, E. (2016). International shocks and the balance sheet of the Bank of France under the classical gold standard. *Explorations in Economic History, 62*, 87–107.

Beckmann, J., & Czudaj, R. (2013). Gold as an inflation hedge in a time-varying coefficient framework. *The North American Journal of Economics and Finance, 24*, 208–222.

Bindseil, U. (2004). *Monetary policy implementation: Theory, past, and present*. Oxford University Press on Demand.
Blose, L. E. (2010). Gold prices, cost of carry, and expected inflation. *Journal of Economics and Business, 62*(1), 35–47.
Bordo, M. D., & Eichengreen, B. (1998). *The rise and fall of a barbarous relic: The role of gold in the international monetary system. (no. w6436)*. National Bureau of Economic Research.
Bordo, M. D. (1981). *The classical gold standard: Some lessons for today* (pp. 2–17). Federal Reserve Bank of St Louis.
Borio, C., & Lowe, P. (2002). Assessing the risk of banking crises. *Bank of International Settlements (BIS) Quarterly Review*, 43–54.
Borio, C. & Disyatat, P. (2015). Capital flows and the current account: Taking financing (more) seriously. Bank of International Settlements (BIS) Working Paper n° 525.
Borio, C. (2014). *Monetary policy and financial stability: what role in prevention and recovery?* Bank of International Settlements (BIS) Working Paper, n° 440.
Carduff, K. C. (2022). Traditional content analysis. In G. J. Previts (Ed.), *Corporate Reporting: From Stewardship to Contract, the Annual Reports of the United States Steel Corporation 1902–2006 (Studies in the Development of Accounting Thought)* (Vol. 26, pp. 33–59). Emerald Publishing Limited.
Cassis, Y. (2011). *Crises and opportunities: The shaping of modern finance*. Oxford University Press.
Chalu, H. (2021). Board characteristics, auditing characteristics and audit report lag in African Central Banks. *Journal of Accounting in Emerging Economies, 11*(4), 578–609.
De Grauwe, P. (2009). *Economics of Monetary Union*. Oxford University Press.
Euromonitor International. (2023). *Gold Statistics. São Paulo Database System*. Euromonitor International.
Fama, E. F., & Schwert, G. W. (1977). Asset returns and inflation. *Journal of Financial Economics, 5*(2), 115–146.
Fantacci, L., & Gobbi, L. (2023). The future of the international monetary system: Geopolitics and technology. In N. Bilotta & F. Botti (Eds.), *Digitalisation and Geopolitics: Catalytic Forces in the (Future) International Monetary System* (Istituto Alfari Internazionali (IAI) Research Studies) (Vol. 10). Edizioni Nuova Cultura.
Ghosh, D., Levin, E. J., Macmillan, P., & Wright, R. E. (2004). Gold as an inflation hedge? *Studies in Economics and Finance, 22*, 1–25.
Gliner, J., Morgan, G. A., & Leech, N. L. (2009). *Research methods in applied settings: An integrated approach to design and analysis*. Routledge.
Gorry, G. A., & Morton, M. S. S. (1971). A framework for Management Information Systems. In *Working Paper Alfred P. Sloan School of Management*. Institute of Technology.
Gray, S. J. (1988). Towards a theory of cultural influence on the development of accounting systems inter-nationally. *Abacus, 24*(1), 1–15.
Harmston, S. (1998). *Gold as a store of value*. World Gold Council, Research Study, No. 22.
Heywood, I., & Sandywell, B. (2012). *Handbook of visual culture*. Berg.
Hillier, D., Draper, P., & Faff, R. (2006). Do precious metals shine? An investment perspective. *Financial Analysts Journal, 62*(2), 98–106.
Hofstede, G. (1980). *Culture's consequences*. Sage.
Hoffmann, A. (2013). *The euro as a proxy for the classical gold standard? Government debt financing and political commitment in historical perspective, Working Paper, No. 119, Universität Leipzig, Wirtschaftswissenschaftliche Fakultät. Leipzig*. Available at: https://www.econstor.eu/bitstream/10419/74607/1/747342059.pdf.
International Monetary Fund (IMF). (2023). *Gold and the IMF*. IMF.
Jackson, M. (1993). *Literacy*. David Fulton Publishers.
Jaffè, J. (1989). Gold and gold stocks as investments for institutional portfolios. *Financial Analysts Journal, 45*(2), 53–59.
Kirshner, J. (1995). *Currency and coercion. The Political Economy of International Monetary Power*. Princeton University Press.
Kolluri, B. R. (1981). Gold as a hedge against inflation: An empirical investigation. *The Quarterly Review of Economics and Business, 21*(4), 13–24.
Krippendorff, K. (2019). *Content analysis: An introduction to its methodology*. Sage Publications.

Lawrence, C. (2003). *Why is gold different from other assets? An empirical investigation*. World Gold Council.
Levin, E. R., & Wright, R. E. (2006). *Short-run and long-run determinants of the price of gold*. World Gold Council, Research Study, No. 32.
Michaud, R., Michaud, R., & Pulvermacher, K. (2006). *Gold as strategic asset*. World Gold Council.
Morris, S., & Shin, H. (1999). Risk management with interdependent choice. *Bank of England Financial Stability Review, 7*(November), 141–150.
Obstfeld, M., & Taylor, A. M. (2017). International monetary relations: Taking finance seriously. *Journal of Economic Perspectives, 31*(3), 3–28.
Oxford Analytica. (2020). Rising geopolitical concerns will help gold gain more. *Expert Briefings*. https://doi.org/10.1108/OXAN-DB249852
Parker, L. (2005). Social and environmental accountability research: A view from the commentary box. *Accounting, Auditing & Accountability Journal, 18*(6), 842–846.
Posen, A., & Juluis, D. (2012). *What the return of 19th century economics means for 21st century geopolitics*. Chatham House.
Reynard, S. (2023). Central bank balance sheet, money and inflation. *Economic Letters, 224*, 111028.
Rose, G. (2013). Visual methodologies: An introduction to the interpretation of visual materials. In G. Griffin (Ed.), *Research methods for English studies*. University Press.
Samano, A. (2022). International reserves and central bank independence. *Journal of International Economics, 139*, 103674.
Shafiee, S., & Topal, E. (2010). An overview of global gold market and gold price forecasting. *Resources Policy, 35*, 178–189.
Sherman, E. (1986). *Gold investment: Theory and application*. Prentice Hall.
Sinclair, P. J. N. (2005). Central banks and financial stability. *Bank of England Quarterly Bulletin*, (November 2000).
Tower, G. (1993). A public accountability model of accounting regulation. *British Accounting Review, 25*(1), 61–85.
Tracy, S. J. (2020). *Qualitative research methods*. John Wiley & Sons.
Tukey, J. W. (1977). *Exploratory data analysis*. Addison-Wesley Publishing Company.
von Landesberger, T., Kuijper, A., Schreck, T., Kohlhammer, J., van Wijk, J. J., Fekete, J.-D., & Fellner, D. W. (2011). Visual analysis of large graphs: State-of-the-art and future research challenges. *Computer Graphics Forum, 30*(6), 1719–1749.
White, M. D., & Marsh, E. E. (2006). *Content Analysis: A Flexible Methodology. Library Trends, Baltimore 55 (1, Summer)*, 27–34. https://doi.org/10.1353/lib.2006.0053.
Widdowson, D., & Hailwood, K. (2007). Financial literacy and its role in promoting a sound financial system. *Reserve of Bank of New Zealand Bulletin, 70*(2), 37–47.
World Gold Council. (2023). World gold council publications archive. Available at https://www.gold.org/goldhub/data/gold-prices
Worthington, A. C., & Pahlavani, M. (2007). Gold investment as an inflationary hedge: Cointegration evidence with allowance for endogenous structural breaks. *Applied Financial Economics Letters, 3*(4), 259–262.

Rute Abreu is Coordinator Professor, with tenure, of Accounting and Finance at the *Instituto Politécnico da Guarda (*Portugal), Department of Management and Economy. Rute teaches financial analysis, corporate finance, schedule and appraisal investment, auditing, financial accounting, taxation, firm valuation, quality, and social responsibility management. Actually, Rute is the Accounting Degree Director and the Integrated Management System master's degree Director. Rute holds a master's degree in industrial engineering at the *Universidade Nova de Lisboa (*Portugal) and PhD in Accounting and Finance at the Universidad de Salamanca (Spain). Their scientific research is based as an integrated researcher at the Center for Research in Accounting and Taxation of the Cávado and Ave Polytechnic Institute, Portugal and as collaborate researcher at the Center for Research in Digital Services and CiTUR. Rute, also, collaborates with MackPesquisa of Universidade Presbiteriana Mackenzie, Brasil. Rute develops scientific activities with Social Responsibility Research Network and Global Corporate Governance Institute and her research focuses on CSR, corporate governance, accounting and firm valuation and it has been published in several journals and participates in the organization, all over the world, of conferences, seminars, and meetings. Also, Rute participates in the blind review process for several journals and helps as Associate Editor on The Social Responsibility Journal and Accounting and Management Review of Ordem dos Contabilistas Certificados (Portugal). Particularly, Rute is involved in projects with higher impact on social reintegration on Higher Education on Accounting. Very relevant as public servant always promotes the transfer of knowledge to the society related to Agriculture Sustainability (Olive oil in Portugal and autochthonous race (Burro-de-Miranda-AEPGA)), Accounting Education (Accountant 5.0), Tax and Auditing Citizenship, Management Quality Systems in Social Economy and Accounting Firms, and Performance Analysis at Beauty Firms.

Carlos Pinho has a PhD in Applied Economics from the University of Santiago de Compostela, an MSc in Finance, and a degree in Management from the Portucalense University. He is an Associate Professor in the University of Aveiro, at the Department of Economics, Management, Industrial Engineering and Tourism. He lectures under-graduated and graduated courses of Finance and Economics. Presently, he is coordinator of the research group on Decision Support Systems integrated in the research unit on Competitiveness, Governance and Public Policy (GOVCOPP). He was member of research teams of the University of Aveiro participating in several national sponsored projects in the fields of Economics and Finance, Regional Development, Decision Support Tools development. He is author and co-author of more than 100 papers presented in national and international conferences or published in scientific journals and books.

Value Challenge: The Role of Sustainability as an Open Innovation Approach

Francesco Martielli, Antonio Salvi, and Emanuele Doronzo

1 Introduction

Today, companies are increasingly focused on implementing responsible behaviors to achieve their business goals and improve performance. Sustainability has become a corporate responsibility, offering different ways of thinking and behaving. This approach to sustainable business brings significant benefits to businesses, society, and the environment (Camilleri, 2019). In this evolving landscape, open innovation is gaining traction as a valid approach to address sustainability challenges (Troise et al., 2021). Previous research suggests that sustainability can provide a competitive advantage when companies establish proper relationships with various stakeholders (Camilleri, 2017). These stakeholder relationships are valuable for accessing external sources of knowledge, which can enhance the organization's competencies and performance. However, the acquisition of new knowledge must be accompanied by dissemination mechanisms, even involving competitors (Markovic et al., 2021).

The growing interest of stakeholders in a company's performance and non-financial activities, driven by community sentiment and new categories of stakeholders expressing implicit claims through specific political maneuvers (Cornell & Shapiro, 1987, 2021; Schaltegger & Burritt, 2018), highlights the need for additional non-quantitative information to identify the drivers and proxies of company value. As a result, corporate strategies and intellectual debates have increasingly

F. Martielli (✉) · A. Salvi
University of Turin, Turin, Italy
e-mail: francesco.martielli@unito.it; antonio.salvi@unito.it

E. Doronzo
University of Molise, Campobasso, Italy
e-mail: emanuele.doronzo@unimol.it

B. Díaz Díaz et al. (eds.), *Building Global Societies Towards an ESG World*, CSR, Sustainability, Ethics & Governance,
https://doi.org/10.1007/978-3-031-56619-6_7

focused on the triple dimension of sustainability: environment, social, and governance (ESG) (Fatemi et al., 2015).

Existing literature argues that if sustainability, represented by non-financial performance, is achieved and evaluated precisely as an open innovation approach, it can have an impact on financial performance and ultimately on corporate value and its estimation. This consideration introduces new variables that need to be taken into account in the economic evaluation of the organization and its business (Chaurasia et al., 2020; Dalal & Thaker, 2019; Eccles et al., 2014). Pursuing goals and activities related to social responsibility and environmental sustainability can generate value and be beneficial for long-term business management (Cornell & Damodaran, 2020).

Therefore, there is no universally accepted measure of sustainability. In this study, we utilize the ESG disclosure score from Bloomberg and the ESG performance score from Refinitiv. Our first research question is:

RQ1: Which score, between the ESG performance score and the ESG disclosure score, is the most suitable for measuring sustainability as an open innovation approach?

Furthermore, our understanding of the potential impact of ESG performance and ESG disclosure on firm value, as well as the proxies and drivers of value, is still limited. Thus, our second research question is:

RQ2: Does sustainability as an open innovation approach have a significant impact on firm value?

To test our hypotheses, we collected data from 572 listed European companies operating in various utility, manufacturing, and service sectors over a period of 10 financial years (2011–2020). We employed Akaike's information criterion (AIC) to identify the best estimator of sustainability as an open innovation approach. Once the best score was determined, we conducted a two-stage least squares regression analysis with instrumental variables (IV-2SLS) to examine how sustainability affects value. Additionally, we validated the results obtained from the AIC and the econometric model (IV-2SLS) through robustness tests.

In conclusion, this study contributes to addressing gaps in the literature. First, it enhances the understanding of sustainability as an open innovation approach in conjunction with ESG factors, identifying the most effective score for capturing the sustainable strategies implemented by companies. Second, through empirical evidence, it demonstrates the positive relationship between sustainability as an open innovation approach and firm value.

2 Literature Review and Hypotheses

2.1 Open Innovation

The research and development (R&D) function has traditionally served as a barrier to entry for potential competitors, providing companies with a competitive advantage. However, changes in the competitive landscape, driven by technological progress, globalization, and shorter product lifecycles, have necessitated new approaches to innovation. Lean, flexible, and dynamic models that can quickly adapt to market needs, such as the open innovation approach, have become crucial (Cheng & Chen, 2013).

Open innovation has gained significant attention in academia, as companies increasingly rely on external information and research collaborations to enhance their competitive advantage by improving processes, products, and services (Popa et al., 2017. The open innovation paradigm emphasizes the utilization of both external and internal sources of technologies, ideas, and knowledge to drive innovation and create value. It involves the flow of knowledge, both inward and outward, to accelerate internal innovation and expand external markets (Chesbrough, 2003). By embracing external and internal ideas and pathways to market, companies can advance their technology and enhance value creation (Chatain & Mindruta, 2017). Additionally, open innovation, coupled with a focus on core competencies, leads to lower innovation costs and improved development of innovations (Chesbrough & Appleyard, 2007).

Furthermore, governments can play a vital role in accelerating innovation processes by providing various forms of support such as tax deductions, financing, soft loans, and training (Mason & Brown, 2013). Despite potential challenges associated with cooperation and competition (coopetition), rivals are recognized as valuable innovation partners, as they can offer complementary resources necessary for innovation (Markovic et al., 2021).

2.2 *Sustainability as an Open Innovation Approach*

Sustainability has emerged as a prominent perspective for understanding the role of businesses in society (Barkemeyer & Figge, 2014). Achieving sustainable development requires innovative approaches, and sustainable innovation provides insights into how technologies and social practices enable sustainability (Hahn et al., 2007). Sustainable innovation encompasses the ideal balance condition that aligns with sustainable development goals and involves re-proposing, improving, or renovating existing ideas or practices in a sustainable manner (Demirel & Kesidou, 2019; Sarkis et al., 2010). It entails the implementation of ideas, methods, or practices that have a significant impact on sustainable development (Cillo et al., 2019).

While the literature on open innovation has primarily focused on economic benefits, innovativeness, and financial performance (Troise et al., 2021), recent research has highlighted the potential of using open innovation to drive sustainable practices within companies (Bogers et al., 2020). Open innovation for sustainability involves merging open innovation practices with the concept of sustainability, recognizing their complementary nature within the contemporary environmental and economic framework (Arcese et al., 2015; Bogers et al., 2020). This convergence is particularly relevant in the face of complex and uncertain challenges like climate change, which demand coordinated and collaborative efforts among multiple organizations sharing expertise to effectively address the issues at hand (George et al., 2016). Moreover, the systemic and complex nature of environmental innovations necessitates substantial external interdependencies, emphasizing the importance of inbound open innovation (Adams et al., 2016).

Sustainability, defined as meeting the needs of the present without compromising future generations' ability to meet their own needs (Brundtland, 1987), and open innovation, characterized as a distributed innovation process utilizing managed knowledge flows across organizational boundaries (Chesbrough & Bogers, 2014), can be viewed as interconnected concepts. The literature suggests that sustainability challenges often converge with open innovation activities to reduce costs and time, highlighting the notion that sustainability can be considered an open innovation approach (Troise et al., 2021).

2.3 ESG Practices

The traditional focus of businesses on shareholder satisfaction, as advocated by the Shareholder Theory (Frideman, 1970), has been challenged by corporate scandals and the financial crisis, leading to a decline in its relevance (Bottenberg et al., 2017). In response, the Stakeholder Theory emerged, emphasizing the identification and satisfaction of the interests of various stakeholders and recognizing their influence on a company's success (Freeman, 1984). The Stakeholder Theory suggests that considering the interests of all stakeholders, rather than solely focusing on shareholders, can lead to superior company performance (Matuleviciene & Stravinskiene, 2015).

ESG practices in companies represent the culmination of this evolutionary process, stemming from various theories. It begins with the Shareholder Theory, which prioritizes maximizing profits for shareholders, and transitions to the Stakeholder Theory, incorporating the satisfaction of other stakeholder interests (Renouard & Ezvan, 2018). The Legitimacy theory, which asserts that corporations must align their actions with societal values and norms to maintain their existence, also influences the Stakeholder Theory (Dowling & Pfeffer, 1975; Suchman, 1995). The evolution toward sustainable practices is further guided by the triple bottom-line approach, which emphasizes the economic, social, and environmental dimensions of a company's activities (Elkington & Rowlands, 1999).

This approach paves the way for the concept of corporate social responsibility (CSR), which recognizes that companies are complex entities embedded in their environments (Boulding, 1956). CSR encompasses environmental, social, and governance criteria, capturing the essence of sustainability and promoting a virtuous entrepreneurial system where profit aligns with ethical principles such as environmental protection and social inclusion (Tonello & Singer, 2015). By integrating ESG considerations into their operations, companies can foster a holistic approach to sustainability and contribute to a more sustainable future.

2.4 ESG and Firm Value

The evaluation of a company's performance cannot be reduced to a pure consideration of the economic and financial results but must include the impacts on the environment and the community. In this regard, it is necessary to integrate economic and financial performance with socio-environmental performance, to reach a framework as complete as possible and consistent with the company's operations. In the literature, the debate on environmental, social, and governance criteria and corporate social responsibility is based on the idea that it is possible to identify socially and environmentally good and bad companies, but in actuality, this is not true. That is because, in contrast to profitability, where there are long-accepted measures, social responsibility is often linked to subjective considerations of the analyst (Dortfleitner et al., 2015). There are multiple problems in interpreting the results of assessing non-financial performance through ESG rating schemes. One among many relates to the assessment of ESG information on sustainability investment performance, as there are numerous organizations involved in assessing non-financial performance through ESG criteria (Li & Polychronopoulos, 2020): at the end of 2019, around 70 companies were providing an ESG rating. The fact that so many organizations are involved in providing ESG ratings would not be a problem if all ratings were similar or comparable, but this is often not the case. Some of the literature on environmental, social, and governance criteria documents the divergence of ESG ratings for the same companies (Berg et al., 2019). Ensuring that a focus on ESG factors lead to a positive payoff in terms of value is difficult because there is no consistency as to what characterizes a good company since there are different scores for the same company resulting from different metrics and measures. The ESG performance score reflects an assessment of what companies do in terms of environmental, social, and governance issues and not just what they disclose (Gutsche et al., 2017). The literature often refers to the Refinitiv database to find measures of non-financial performance (Nirino et al., 2019). The ESG disclosure score reflects an assessment of what companies disclose about environmental, social, and governance issues. The literature often reports a higher value than the performance score (Gutsche et al., 2017). The database often referred to for sustainability disclosure values is Bloomberg's (Fatemi et al., 2018). Therefore, the analysis of the literature leaves room for different unresolved issues to be explored both theoretically and empirically: Do companies that pay attention to environmental, social, and governance issues create more value than companies that do not contemplate these issues? Do markets price sustainable companies better? Does investing in sustainable companies lead to higher returns? (Cornell & Damodaran, 2020). According to the existing literature, the value of a company can be estimated using different methodologies, each characterized by different drivers and proxies (Capelle-Blancard & Petit, 2019). Several empirical studies show that the impact of environmental, social, and governance factors on companies' prospects can be detected at the level of cash flows and/or discount rates to make company valuations as real as possible (Zerbib, 2020).

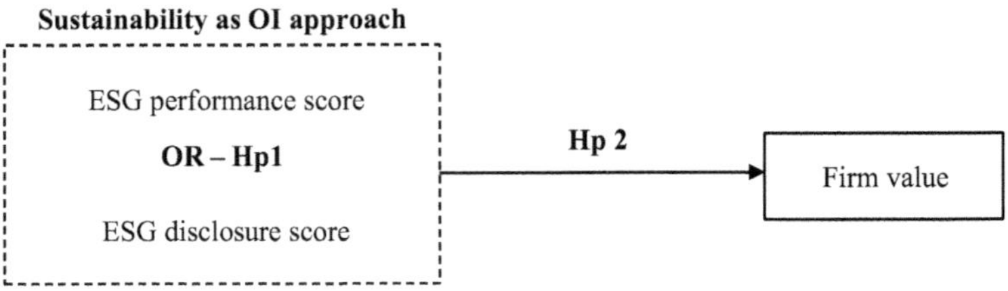

Fig. 1 Conceptual model and hypotheses

2.5 *Greenwashing: ESG Disclosure Score and ESG Performance Score Magnitude*

Sustainability activities implemented by companies should be disclosed externally with intensity to have a positive effect. Therefore, sustainability performance and disclosure are closely related and interdependent (Crespi & Migliavacca, 2020). The intensity of corporate social performance reporting differs greatly between organizations: companies with positive sustainability performance choose to report often and in detail on their ESG activities, while those with negative ESG performance often choose to report less (Zhang, 2022).

In this regard, companies report their ESG performance to distinguish themselves from those with less relevance in terms of ESG criteria, to avoid the consequences of adverse selection (Akerlof, 1978). Finally, a company might choose to report information on sustainable performance because of, for instance, serious environmental damages that negatively affect the company's reputation (greenwashing).

Based on these considerations, we lead the following hypothesis and the conceptual model (Fig. 1):

Hp1: ESG performance score is the best way to measure sustainability as an open innovation approach, rather than ESG disclosure score.
Hp2: Sustainability as an open innovation approach creates firm value.

Specification model

$$\begin{cases} \text{FirmValue}_{i,t} = \alpha + \beta \text{SustainabilityProxy}_{i,t} + \gamma_1 \text{Lev}_{i,t} + \\ \quad \gamma_2 \text{MktCap} / \text{TA}_{i,t} + \gamma_3 \text{Size}_{i,t} + \varepsilon_{i,t} \\ \text{SustainabilityProxy}_{i,t} = \delta_0 + \delta_1 \text{SustainabilityProxy}_{i,t-1} + \\ \quad \delta_1 \text{SustainabilityProxySector}_{j-i,t} + \eta_{i,t} \end{cases}$$

3 Methodology

3.1 *Research Design and Sample*

The objective of the research is to identify the most suitable proxy for measuring sustainability as an open innovation practice and its impact on firm value. To achieve this, the empirical analysis begins by determining the optimal model specification that links corporate value and sustainability as an open innovation practice.

While previous literature emphasizes the positive relationship between sustainability and corporate value creation, the process of selecting the appropriate model is not always clear. Therefore, the empirical analysis employs the Akaike Information Criteria (AIC) in the first step to identify the best model specification (Burnham and Anderson, 2002; Andrew and Currim, 2003; Wahba, 2008.

The goal of the empirical analysis, as stated by Burnham and Anderson (2002), is to establish a "parsimonious model" that includes only the variables that effectively explain the relationship. The AIC, a multimodal inference method, serves as a comprehensive tool to achieve this goal (Burnham and Anderson, 2002; Andrew and Currim, 2003; Wahba, 2008).

The study places particular emphasis on selecting and analyzing two main proxies provided by leading data providers, Thomson Reuters and Bloomberg. These proxies are known as ESG performance and ESG disclosure scores, respectively. They are constructed using different types of data, as explained in the "Variables" section of the chapter.

After determining the best model specification, the next step involves testing the relationship between firm value and sustainability. It is important to consider endogeneity, as highlighted by El Ghoul et al. (2011). To ensure the reliability of the estimates, the empirical analysis employs a 2SLS panel regression fixed effect approach, where the independent variable is instrumented using its own lagged values and the sector average, excluding the i-th firm (El Ghoul et al., 2011; Kelejian, 1971).

The sample analyzed in the study consists of the STOXX Europe 600 index, comprising the 600 largest European public companies. The financial performance data used is sourced from Bloomberg, which aligns with the data from both databases.

3.2 *Variables*

To measure firm value, the research incorporates various drivers and proxies that are considered representative of firm fundamentals (Bardos et al., 2020; Buchanan et al., 2018; Wong et al., 2021). As drivers of firm value, the study includes the cost of equity, cost of debt, and free cash flow (Cornell & Damodaran, 2020). The proxy for firm value used in the analysis is the EBITDA multiple. The ESG scores are

Table 1 Variables description

Independent variables			
ESG_P	ESG Performance score	Refinitiv	Velte (2017)
Env_P	Environmental performance score	Refinitiv	Gutsche et al. (2017)
Soc_P	Social performance score	Refinitiv	Lahouel et al. (2019)
Gov_P	Governance performance score	Refinitiv	Nirino et al. (2019)
ESG_D	ESG disclosure score	Bloomberg	Fatemi et al. (2018)
Env_D	Environmental disclosure score	Bloomberg	Hussain et al. (2018)
Soc_D	Social disclosure score	Bloomberg	Atan et al. (2018)
Gov_D	Governance disclosure score	Bloomberg	Ould Daoud Ellili (2020)
l.ESG_P	InstrumentalVariabletemporal lag	Authors	El Ghoul et al. (2011)
l.ESG_P	InstrumentalVariabletemporal lag	Authors	El Ghoul et al. (2011)
ESG_Psecj-i	IV-sector mean excluded i-esim	Authors	El Ghoul et al. (2011)
ESG_Dsecj-i	IV-sector mean excluded i-esim	Authors	El Ghoul et al. (2011)
Dependent variables			
EVEBITDA	Enterprise value/EBITDA	Bloomberg	Majer (2019)
Re	Cost of equity	Bloomberg	Gregory et al. (2021)
Rd	Cost of debt	Bloomberg	La Rosa et al. (2018)
FCF/SALES	Free cash flow	Bloomberg	Giese et al. (2019)
Control variables			
LnTA	Total asset	Bloomberg	Zhang et al. (2020)
MktCap/TA	Market capitalization	Bloomberg	Dang et al. (2018)
LEV	Financial leverage	Bloomberg	Zhao et al. (2018)
SIC_N	Industry number	Bloomberg	

regarded as the most appropriate parameters for measuring sustainability practices within firms (Nollet et al., 2016). The research considers two types of ESG scores: the ESG performance score from Refinitiv and the ESG disclosure score from Bloomberg. To ensure sample homogeneity, the study incorporates several control variables (Dang et al., 2018; Nirino et al., 2019; Zhang et al., 2020). A description of the variables can be found in Table 1.

4 Empirical Results

The main objective of this research is to determine the most suitable proxy for measuring sustainability as an open innovation approach. To address this research question, a two-phase empirical model is employed: (1) the identification of the best model specification based on the AIC criterion and (2) the implementation of a 2SLS model that examines the relationship between the proxy and the drivers of firm value, using instrumented ESG scores.

The literature on the relationship between sustainability as an open innovation approach and firm value is limited, and this study aims to contribute to filling this gap. The empirical analysis is carried out by conducting univariate tests in Sect. 4.1, comparing the cost of equity of firms with below-median CSR scores to those with above-median CSR scores. Subsequently, in Sect. 4.2, a multivariate regression analysis is performed, regressing firms' cost of equity on various CSR proxy and control variables. Sensitivity tests are presented in Sect. 4.3.

4.1 Step 1: Model Specification

To determine the best model specification, three different fixed effect panel models are implemented, following the verification of multicollinearity using the VIF test and Hausman test (Bell et al., 2019). The model specifications are as follows:

M1: This model includes only the control variables as explanatory variables.
M2: This model incorporates ESG performance as an explanatory variable for each driver and proxy of the firm value.
M3: This model includes ESG disclosure as an explanatory variable for each driver and proxy of the firm value.

Model selection in fixed effect panel data can be challenging due to incidental parameters that can impact the performance of information criteria such as Akaike's Information Criterion (AIC) and the corrected Akaike's Information Criterion (AICc) (Yum, 2022). To address this issue, Yum (2022) conducted a Monte Carlo simulation to assess the reliability of these information criteria.

Based on the simulation results, Yum (2022) concluded that AIC and AICc are suitable for selecting the most parsimonious specification. Therefore, in this study, AICc is used to identify the best model specification. Multiple models are estimated and their respective AICc scores are calculated (Table 2).

The AICc is a useful tool for identifying the most appropriate model given the available data. While the true relationship cannot be known, the model that best represents the true relationship with the given data is indicated by the lowest AICc score (Burnham and Anderson, 2002; Andrew and Currim, 2003; Wahba, 2008). The results presented in Table 2 indicate that model M2 is the best specification based on the AICc scores.

Consequently, according to AICc test, the best proxy of sustainability as open innovation is ESG performance.

Table 2 Model selection with AICc

	EVEBITDA	Re	Rd	FCFTA
M1	1165.664	1200.634	1197.032	1198.229
M2	1137.688	1149.065	1145.618	1146.763
M3	1126.032	1137.292	1133.880	1135.014

The table reports the AICc scores of the models specification

4.2 *Step 2: Multivariate Regression Analysis*

The two-stage least squares with instrumental variables (IV-2SLS) panel model is utilized in this study to examine the research hypothesis. This methodology is appropriate for evaluating the relationships between variables due to the presence of endogeneity issues that can arise between dependent and independent variables (El Ghoul et al., 2011; Kelejian, 1971). In the context of the analyzed relationship, various sources of endogeneity can emerge simultaneously, such as the omitted variables problem (Suriyapongprapai et al., 2022) and reverse causality (Bruna & Lahouel, 2022; El Ghoul et al., 2011; Esposito et al., 2022; Waddock & Graves, 1997).

The concept of reverse causality between ESG performance and financial performance is proposed by Waddock and Graves (1997). According to the good management hypothesis, enhancing CSR performance improves a firm's relationships with key stakeholders, leading to higher firm value. Conversely, the slack resource hypothesis suggests that better financial performance provides firms with the resources to enhance their CSR performance.

While examining the drivers and proxy that influence firm value, it is important to acknowledge that the evidence of the significance of ESG scores for firm value may be influenced by omitted variables that are associated with both ESG scores and firm value drivers and proxy. Therefore, omitting certain variables from the regressions could introduce an unknown bias in the ESG scores. Additionally, the decision of a firm to engage in activities supporting ESG issues may not be independent of its firm value, which introduces the possibility of reverse causality issues in the analysis.

4.2.1 Instrumental Variables

The instrumental variables used in this study are twofold: (1) the temporal lag of the sustainability scores and (2) the sector average of sustainability scores excluding the i-1 firms (El Ghoul et al., 2011). These instrumental variables are employed to address endogeneity concerns and ensure the reliability of the estimates.

Before conducting the linear regression analysis, the relevance of the instruments is tested to ensure their appropriateness for the IV-2SLS panel model. The relevance of instruments is evaluated to determine whether they are statistically significant in explaining the variation in the endogenous variable (Wooldridge, 2002). The results indicating the relevance of the instruments are presented in Table 3, providing support for the implementation of the IV-2SLS panel model in testing the research hypotheses.

4.2.2 2SLS-IV Regressions

To examine the influence of the ESG performance score on the drivers and proxy of firm value, we constructed the following models. The estimated results using 2SLS-IV panel data regressions with fixed effects are presented in Table 4. Each

Table 3 Test of relevance of instrumental variables

	ESG_P	ESG_D
l.ESG_P	0,909*** (0,000)	
l.ESG_D		0,918*** (0,000)
ESG_Psecj-i	0,579*** (0,000)	
ESG_Dsecj-i		0,603*** (0,000)
R2	0,894	0,917

The table reports the result of the test of reliability and relevance of Instrumental Variables
*Statistical significance 10% level
**Statistical significance 5% level
***Statistical significance 1% level

Table 4 ESG performance score (Refinitiv) Regression panel with instrumental variables

	EVEBITDA	Re	Rd	FCF/Sales
	(1)	(2)	(3)	(4)
$\hat{ESG}$_P	0,0161** (0,0081)	−0,0794*** (0,0079)	−0,0142*** (0,0033)	0,0080*** (0,0022)
lnTA	0,9761*** (0,1785)	−15344*** (0,1725)	0,3848*** (0,0717)	−0,4365*** (0,0491)
LEV	0,0164*** (0,0043)	0,0162*** (0,0042)	0,0059*** (0,0017)	−0,0012 (0,0012)
Marketcap/TA	−0,0206*** (0,0065)	0,0047 (0,0063)	0,0027 (0,0026)	0,0044** (0,0018)
Const.	10,082 (14267)	27,580*** (13792)	−15508** (0,5735)	77779*** (0,3923)
R2_within	0,2202	0,20,765	0,25,435	0,2133
R2_between	0,3169	0,337	0,3245	0,3616
R2_overall	0,25,888	0,25,939	0,28,241	0,27,262
F test (prob > F)	0,000	0,000	0,000	0,000
H test (prob > χ2)	0,000	0,000	0,000	0,000
N	4404	4404	4404	4404
N_groups	578	578	578	578

This table reports the 2SLS-IV regressions between proxy and drivers of firm value and ESG performance score instrumented by l.ESG_P and ESG_Psecj-i. In particular, the dependent variable is: in column (1) EVEBITDA; column (2) Re; column (3) Rd.; column (4) FCF/Sales; and the independent variable is ESG performance score
*Statistical significance 10% level
**Statistical significance 5% level
***Statistical significance 1% level

column in models 1–4 represents the association between the ESG performance score and specific variables, namely, EV/EBITDA, cost of equity, cost of debt, and free cash flow/total assets.

The findings reveal that there is a significant positive relationship between ESG performance and both EV/EBITDA and FCF/TA at a 1% level of significance. On the other hand, there is a significant negative relationship between ESG performance and both the cost of equity and the cost of debt. These results indicate that the research hypothesis, which proposes a positive association between sustainability implemented as an open innovation approach and firm value creation, is supported.

The overall goodness-of-fit of the models can be considered acceptable, as indicated by the R-squared within values of approximately 30%.

4.3 *Robustness*

4.3.1 Robustness Step 1

To assess the robustness of our model specification selection, we compared the "R-squared between" values of the M2 and M3 specifications. The "R-squared between" is a measure that indicates the proportion of variability in the dependent variables explained by the independent variables, considering the differences between entities (Portet, 2020; Vuong, 1989; Wooldridge, 2002).

The results clearly demonstrate that the ESG performance score is more appropriate for explaining the variation in the dependent variables used as drivers of firm value. The "R-squared between" values of M2 are consistently higher than those of M3, suggesting that the inclusion of ESG performance as an explanatory variable leads to a better fit of the model and a stronger relationship with the drivers of firm value, as stated in Table 5.

4.3.2 Robustness Step 2

To further validate the significant relationships between ESG performance and firm value, a robustness test was conducted using Pooled Ordinary Least Squares (POLS). This test aims to address any concerns related to instrumental variable selection, particularly regarding the satisfaction of relevance and exogeneity conditions (Larcker & Rusticus, 2010). As a result, the analyses were replicated using the POLS model, and the findings are presented in Table 6.

Table 5 Model selection with "R squared between different models"

	EVEBITDA	Re	Rd	FCFTA
M1	0.168	0.166	0.175	0.176
M2	0.317	0.337	0.325	0.362
M3	0.173	0.171	0.180	0.181

The table reports the R squared between different models selection

Table 6 ESG performance score (Refinitiv) regression robustness check

	EVEBITDA	Re	Rd	FCF/Sales
	(1)	(2)	(3)	(4)
ESG_P	0,0140*** (0,0047)	−0,0544*** (0,0046)	−0,0116*** (0,0018)	0,0051*** (0,0013)
lnTA	0,9369*** (0,1462)	−18948*** (0,1442)	0,2555*** (0,0576)	−0,3939*** (0,0410)
LEV	0,0151** (0,0069)	0,0164** (0,0068)	−0,0016 (0,0027)	−0,0050** (0,0019)
Marketcap/TA	0,0199*** (0,0064)	0,0033 (0,0063)	−0,0010 (0,0025)	0,0045** (0,0018)
Const.	21396* (12816)	29,887*** (12640)	−0,2890 (0,5049)	7546*** (0,3594)
R2_	0,3254	0,3224	0,3104	0,3270
R2_Adj	0,2175	0,2762	0,2903	0,2641
F test (prob > F)	0,000	0,000	0,000	0,000
N	4736	4736	4736	4736
N_groups	587	587	587	587

This table reports the PooledOLS regressions between proxy and drivers of firm value and ESG performance score instrumented by l.ESG_P and ESG_Psecj-i. In particular, the dependent variable is: in column (1) EVEBITDA; column (2) Re; column (3) Rd.; column (4) FCF/Sales; and the independent variable is ESG performance score
*Statistical significance 10% level
**Statistical significance 5% level
***Statistical significance 1% level

The robustness check conducted using the POLS model supports and confirms the empirical findings obtained from the 2SLS-IV panel data regression. The relationships between ESG performance and firm value remain significant and consistent across both models. Additionally, the R-square and adjusted R-square values obtained from the POLS model are also deemed acceptable, at approximately 30% (Wooldridge, 2002).

5 Discussion, Contribution, and Conclusions

The COVID-19 pandemic has highlighted the importance of collective efforts and open innovation to address global challenges (Bertello et al., 2022). In response to the pandemic, initiatives leveraging distributed knowledge sources have emerged to accelerate scientific and technological advancements in areas such as healthcare instrumentation and online meeting platforms. These initiatives embody the principles of open innovation by tapping into diverse sources of knowledge beyond individual organizations.

Sustainable and responsible solutions are increasingly crucial as societies face major challenges (Bogers et al., 2020). Companies play a pivotal role in sustainable development by utilizing economic, environmental, and social resources to meet society's needs (Hahn et al., 2007). To enhance their role as drivers of sustainable development, organizations are exploring ways to align their economic operations with resource preservation and the well-being of the planet and its inhabitants (Cagliano et al., 2016).

This chapter aims to determine the most suitable ESG score for measuring sustainability as an open innovation approach and to examine its impact on firm value. Analyzing firms within the Euro STOXX 600, the study demonstrates that the Refinitiv ESG performance score outperforms the Bloomberg ESG disclosure score as a proxy for sustainability, based on the corrected Akaike's information criterion (AICc). Furthermore, the research reveals a significant positive relationship between sustainability as an open innovation approach and firm value, utilizing the 2SLS-IV estimation method.

The findings have implications for the calculation of sustainability scores. ESG performance scores reflect the strategies implemented by companies, while ESG disclosure scores pertaining to how companies communicate their sustainability policies. The study contributes to the literature by enhancing understanding of sustainability as an open innovation approach and its impact on enterprise value. Additionally, it sheds light on issues such as greenwashing and stakeholder theory, offering empirical evidence on the potential opportunistic use of sustainability disclosure (Kim & Lyon, 2015).

5.1 Managerial Implications

From a practical standpoint, both sustainability scores have their uses, albeit for different purposes. The ESG performance score is more suitable for long-term investment strategies as it is less susceptible to greenwashing, making it a reliable proxy. On the other hand, the ESG disclosure score is more relevant for investors with a short-term perspective, as it captures market dynamics and stock market trends more effectively. ESG disclosure scores are commonly employed by practitioners for investment evaluations, while ESG performance scores are predominantly utilized by researchers for academic studies. Thus, from an open innovation perspective, the Refinitiv ESG performance score is deemed to be the superior representation of managerial sustainability strategies implemented by companies. Ultimately, engaging in sustainability initiatives can generate long-term value and prove to be profitable for businesses' management activities.

5.2 Limitations and Future Research

This study provides valuable insights for future research, but it is important to acknowledge its limitations. There are several interesting avenues for further investigation. First, testing the research hypothesis on a global sample would enhance the generalizability of the findings. Second, analyzing ESG scores from other data providers would provide a broader perspective on sustainability measurement. Lastly, incorporating additional explanatory variables, such as Hofstede's cultural variables, could deepen our understanding of the relationship between sustainability and firm value. Additionally, the issue of information asymmetry, reflected in the coefficients of sustainability measures, ESG disclosure scores, and ESG performance, and their impact on firm value, particularly in relation to greenwashing, remains an open question.

References

Adams, R., Jeanrenaud, S., Bessant, J., Denyer, D., & Overy, P. (2016). Sustainability-oriented innovation: A systematic review. *International Journal of Management Reviews, 18*(2), 180–205.

Akerlof, G. A. (1978). The market for "lemons": Quality uncertainty and the market mechanism. In *Uncertainty in economics* (pp. 235–251). Academic Press.

Anderson, D. R., & Burnham, K. P. (2002). Avoiding pitfalls when using information-theoretic methods. *The Journal of wildlife management*, 912–918.

Andrews, R. L., & Currim, I. S. (2003). Retention of latent segments in regression-based marketing models. *International Journal of Research in Marketing*, 20(4), 315–321.

Arcese, G., Flammini, S., Luccetti, M. C., & Martucci, O. (2015). Open sustainability innovation in the food sector. *Sustainability, 7*(7), 8067.

Atan, R., Alam, M. M., Said, J., & Zamri, M. (2018). The impacts of environmental, social, and governance factors on firm performance: Panel study of Malaysian companies. *Management of Environmental Quality: An International Journal, 29*(2), 182–194.

Bardos, K. S., Ertugrul, M., & Gao, L. S. (2020). Corporate social responsibility, product market perception, and firm value. *Journal of Corporate Finance, 62*, 101588.

Barkemeyer, R., & Figge, F. (2014). CSR in multiple environments: The impact of headquartering. *Critical Perspectives on International Business, 10*(3), 124–151.

Bell, A., Fairbrother, M., & Jones, K. (2019). Fixed and random effects models: Making an informed choice. *Quality and Quantity, 53*(2), 1051–1074.

Berg, F., Koelbel, J. F., & Rigobon, R. (2019). Aggregate confusion: The divergence of ESG ratings. Forthcoming. *Review of Finance, 26*(6), 1315–1344.

Bertello, A., Bogers, M. L., & De Bernardi, P. (2022). Open innovation in the face of the COVID-19 grand challenge: Insights from the Pan-European hackathon 'EUvsVirus'. *RandD Management, 52*(2), 178–192.

Bogers, M., Chesbrough, H., & Strand, R. (2020). Sustainable open innovation to address a grand challenge: Lessons from Carlsberg and the green Fiber bottle. *British Food Journal, 122*(5), 1505–1517.

Bottenberg, K., Tuschke, A., & Flickinger, M. (2017). Corporate governance between shareholder and stakeholder orientation: Lessons from Germany. *Journal of Management Inquiry, 26*(2), 165–180.

Boulding, K. E. (1956). General systems theory—The skeleton of science. *Management Science, 2*(3), 197–208.

Bruna, M. G., & Lahouel, B. B. (2022). CSR and financial performance: Facing methodological and modeling issues commentary paper to the eponymous FRL article collection. *Finance Research Letters, 44*, 102036.

Brundtland, G. (1987). *Report of the world commission on environment and development: Our common future*. United Nations.

Buchanan, B., Cao, C. X., & Chen, C. (2018). Corporate social responsibility, firm value, and influential institutional ownership. *Journal of Corporate Finance, 52*, 73–95.

Cagliano, R., Worley, C. G., & Caniato, F. F. (2016). The challenge of sustainable innovation in agri-food supply chains. In *Organizing supply chain processes for sustainable innovation in the agri-food industry*. Emerald Group Publishing Limited.

Camilleri, M. A. (2017). Corporate sustainability and responsibility: Creating value for business, society and the environment. *Asian Journal of Sustainability and Social Responsibility, 2*(1), 59–74.

Camilleri, M. A. (2019). Measuring the corporate managers' attitudes towards ISO's social responsibility standard. *Total Quality Management and Business Excellence, 30*(13–14), 1549–1561.

Capelle-Blancard, G., & Petit, A. (2019). Every little helps? ESG news and stock market reaction. *Journal of Business Ethics, 157*(2), 543–565.

Chatain, O., & Mindruta, D. (2017). Estimating value creation from revealed preferences: Application to value-based strategies. *Strategic Management Journal, 38*(10), 1964–1985.

Chaurasia, S. S., Kaul, N., Yadav, B., & Shukla, D. (2020). Open innovation for sustainability through creating shared value-role of knowledge management system, openness and organizational structure. *Journal of Knowledge Management, 24*(10), 2491–2511.

Cheng, C. C., & Chen, J. S. (2013). Breakthrough innovation: The roles of dynamic innovation capabilities and open innovation activities. *Journal of Business and Industrial Marketing, 28*(5), 444–454.

Chesbrough, H. W. (2003). *Open innovation: The new imperative for creating and profiting from technology*. Harvard Business Press.

Chesbrough, H. W., & Appleyard, M. M. (2007). Open innovation and strategy. *California Management Review, 50*(1), 57–76.

Chesbrough, H., & Bogers, H. (2014). Explicating open innovation: Clarifying an emerging paradigm for understanding innovation. In *New frontiers in open innovation* (pp. 3–28). Oxford University Press.

Cillo, V., Petruzzelli, A. M., Ardito, L., & Del Giudice, M. (2019). Understanding sustainable innovation: A systematic literature review. *Corporate Social Responsibility and Environmental Management, 26*(5), 1012.

Cornell, B., & Damodaran, A. (2020). *Valuing ESG: Doing good or sounding good?* NYU Stern School of Business.

Cornell, B., & Shapiro, A. C. (1987). Corporate stakeholders and corporate finance. *Financial Management*, 5–14.

Cornell, B., & Shapiro, A. C. (2021). Corporate stakeholders, corporate valuation and ESG. *European Financial Management, 27*(2), 196–207.

Crespi, F., & Migliavacca, M. (2020). The determinants of ESG rating in the financial industry: The same old story or a different tale? *Sustainability, 12*(16), 6398.

Dalal, K. K., & Thaker, N. (2019). ESG and corporate financial performance: A panel study of Indian companies. *IUP Journal of Corporate Governance, 18*(1), 44–59.

Dang, C., Li, Z. F., & Yang, C. (2018). Measuring firm size in empirical corporate finance. *Journal of Banking and Finance, 86*, 159–176.

Demirel, P., & Kesidou, E. (2019). Sustainability-oriented capabilities for eco-innovation: Meeting the regulatory, technology, and market demands. *Business Strategy and the Environment, 28*(5), 847–857.

Dortfleitner, G., Halbritter, G., & Nguyen, M. (2015). Measuring the level and risk of corporate responsibility–An empirical comparison of different ESG ratings approaches. *Journal of Asset Management*, 17(7), 450–466.

Dowling, J., & Pfeffer, J. (1975). Organizational legitimacy: Social values and organizational behavior. *Pacific Sociological Review, 18*(1), 122–136.

Eccles, R. G., Ioannou, I., & Serafeim, G. (2014). The impact of corporate sustainability on organizational processes and performance. *Management Science, 60*(11), 2835–2857.

El Ghoul, S., Guedhami, O., Kwok, C. C., & Mishra, D. R. (2011). Does corporate social responsibility affect the cost of capital? *Journal of Banking and Finance, 35*(9), 2388–2406.

Elkington, J., & Rowlands, I. H. (1999). Cannibals with forks: The triple bottom line of 21st century business. *Alternatives Journal, 25*(4), 42.

Ould Daoud Ellili, N. (2020). Environmental, social, and governance disclosure, ownership structure and cost of capital: Evidence from the UAE. Sustainability, 12(18), 7706.

Esposito, P., Doronzo, E., & Dicorato, S. L. (2022). The financial and green effects of cultural values on mission drifts in European social enterprises. *Business Strategy and the Environment, 32*(1), 1–29.

Fatemi, A., Fooladi, I., & Tehranian, H. (2015). Valuation effects of corporate social responsibility. *Journal of Banking and Finance, 59*, 182–192.

Fatemi, A., Glaum, M., & Kaiser, S. (2018). ESG performance and firm value: The moderating role of disclosure. *Global Finance Journal, 38*, 45–64.

Freeman, E. R. (1984). Stakeholder theory. *California Management Review*.

Frideman, M. (1970). *The social responsibility of business is to increase its profits*. The New York Times.

George, G., Howard-Grenville, J., Joshi, A., & Tihanyi, L. (2016). Understanding and tackling societal grand challenges through management research. *Academy of Management Journal, 59*(6), 1880–1895.

Giese, G., Lee, L. E., Melas, D., Nagy, Z., & Nishikawa, L. (2019). Foundations of ESG investing: How ESG affects equity valuation, risk, and performance. *The Journal of Portfolio Management, 45*(5), 69–83.

Gregory, R. P., Stead, J. G., & Stead, E. (2021). The global pricing of environmental, social, and governance (ESG) criteria. *Journal of Sustainable Finance and Investment, 11*(4), 310–329.

Gutsche, R., Schulz, J. F., & Gratwohl, M. (2017). Firm-value effects of CSR disclosure and CSR performance. In *EFMA-conference proceedings, June* (pp. 1–31). EFMA.

Hahn, T., Figge, F., & Barkemeyer, R. (2007). Sustainable value creation among companies in the manufacturing sector. *International Journal of Environmental Technology and Management, 7*(5–6), 496–512.

Hussain, N., Rigoni, U., & Cavezzali, E. (2018). Does it pay to be sustainable? Looking inside the black box of the relationship between sustainability performance and financial performance. *Corporate Social Responsibility and Environmental Management, 25*(6), 1198–1211.

Kelejian, H. H. (1971). Two-stage least squares and econometric systems linear in parameters but nonlinear in the endogenous variables. *Journal of the American Statistical Association, 66*(334), 373–374.

Kim, E. H., & Lyon, T. P. (2015). Greenwash vs. brownwash: Exaggeration and undue modesty in corporate sustainability disclosure. *Organization Science, 26*(3), 705–723.

La Rosa, F., Liberatore, G., Mazzi, F., & Terzani, S. (2018). The impact of corporate social performance on the cost of debt and access to debt financing for listed European non-financial firms. *European Management Journal, 36*(4), 519–529.

Lahouel, B. B., Gaies, B., Zaied, Y. B., & andJahmane, A. (2019). Accounting for endogeneity and the dynamics of corporate social–corporate financial performance relationship. *Journal of Cleaner Production, 230*, 352–364.

Larcker, D. F., & Rusticus, T. O. (2010). On the use of instrumental variables in accounting research. *Journal of Accounting and Economics, 49*(3), 186–205.

Li, F., & Polychronopoulos, A. (2020). What a difference an ESG ratings provider makes. Research Affiliates. https://www.researchaffiliates.com/documents/770-what-a-difference-an-esg-ratings-provider-makes.pdf.

Majer, A. L. (2019). The effect of corporate social responsibility on the profitability of publicly traded firms within the United States.

Markovic, S., Koporcic, N., Arslanagic-Kalajdzic, M., Kadic-Maglajlic, S., Bagherzadeh, M., & Islam, N. (2021). Business-to-business open innovation: COVID-19 lessons for small and medium-sized enterprises from emerging markets. *Technological Forecasting and Social Change, 170*, 120883.

Mason, C., & Brown, R. (2013). Creating good public policy to support high-growth firms. *Small Business Economics, 40*(2), 211–225.

Matuleviciene, M., & Stravinskiene, J. (2015). Identifying the factors of stakeholder trust: A theoretical study. *Procedia-Social and Behavioral Sciences, 213*, 599–604.

Nirino, N., Miglietta, N., & Salvi, A. (2019). The impact of corporate social responsibility on firms' financial performance, evidence from the food and beverage industry. *British Food Journal, 122*(1), 1–13.

Nollet, J., Filis, G., & Mitrokostas, E. (2016). Corporate social responsibility and financial performance: A non-linear and disaggregated approach. *Economic Modelling, 52*, 400–407.

Popa, S., Soto-Acosta, P., & Martinez-Conesa, I. (2017). Antecedents, moderators, and outcomes of innovation climate and open innovation: An empirical study in SMEs. *Technological Forecasting and Social Change, 118*, 134–142.

Portet, S. (2020). A primer on model selection using the Akaike information criterion. *Infectious Disease Modelling, 5*, 111–128.

Renouard, C., & Ezvan, C. (2018). Corporate social responsibility towards human development: A capabilities framework. *Business Ethics: A European Review, 27*(2), 144–155.

Sarkis, J., Brust, D. V., & Cordeiro, J. J. (2010). *Facilitating sustainable innovation through collaboration: A multi-stakeholder perspective*. Springer.

Schaltegger, S., & Burritt, R. (2018). Business cases and corporate engagement with sustainability: Differentiating ethical motivations. *Journal of Business Ethics, 147*(2), 241–259.

Suchman, M. C. (1995). Managing legitimacy: Strategic and institutional approaches. *Academy of Management Review, 20*(3), 571–610.

Suriyapongprapai, T., Chatjuthamard, P., Leemakdej, A., & Treepongkaruna, S. (2022). Stakeholder engagement, military ties, and firm performance. *Corporate Social Responsibility and Environmental Management, 29*(2), 469–479.

Tonello, M., & Singer, T. (2015). The business case for corporate investment in ESG practices. In *The conference board, July*.

Troise, C., Tani, M., Dinsmore, J., Jr., & Schiuma, G. (2021). Understanding the implications of equity crowdfunding on sustainability-oriented innovation and changes in agri-food systems: Insights into an open innovation approach. *Technological Forecasting and Social Change, 171*, 120959.

Velte, P. (2017). Does ESG performance have an impact on financial performance? Evidence from Germany. *Journal of Global Responsibility, 8*(2), 169–178.

Vuong, Q. H. (1989). Likelihood ratio tests for model selection and non-nested hypotheses. *Econometrica: Journal of the Econometric Society*, 307–333.

Waddock, S. A., & Graves, S. B. (1997). The corporate social performance–financial performance link. *Strategic Management Journal, 18*(4), 303–319.

Wahba, H. (2008). Does the market value corporate environmental responsibility? An empirical examination. *Corporate Social Responsibility and Environmental Management*, 15(2), 89–99.

Wong, W. C., Batten, J. A., Mohamed-Arshad, S. B., Nordin, S., & Adzis, A. A. (2021). Does ESG certification add firm value? *Finance Research Letters, 39*, 101593.

Wooldridge, J. M. (2002). *Econometric analysis of cross section and panel data* (Vol. 108(2), pp. 245–254). MIT Press.

Yum, M. (2022). Model selection for panel data models with fixed effects: A simulation study. *Applied Economics Letters, 29*(19), 1776–1783.

Zerbib, O. D. (2020, October). A sustainable capital asset pricing model (S-CAPM): Evidence from green investing and sin stock exclusion. In: Proceedings of Paris December 2020 finance meeting EUROFIDAI-ESSEC.

Zhang, D. (2022). Are firms motivated to greenwash by financial constraints? Evidence from global firms' data. *Journal of International Financial Management and Accounting, 33*(3), 459–479.

Zhang, F., Qin, X., & Liu, L. (2020). The interaction effect between ESG and green innovation and its impact on firm value from the perspective of information disclosure. *Sustainability, 12*(5), 1866.

Zhao, C., Guo, Y., Yuan, J., Wu, M., Li, D., Zhou, Y., & Kang, J. (2018). ESG and corporate financial performance: Empirical evidence from China's listed power generation companies. *Sustainability, 10*(8), 2607.

Francesco Martielli is PhD candidate in Business and Management at the Department of Management, University of Turin (Italy). His studies focus on the concepts of sustainability, digitalization, and ethics within corporate finance decisions. His research efforts have allowed him to publish in important international journals. He also acted as a reviewer for several academic journals, and he participated as a presenter at different international conferences.

Antonio Salvi is Full Professor in Corporate Finance at the Department of Management, University of Turin (Italy) and Senior Professor at SDA Bocconi (Milan, Italy). His research focuses on corporate finance, Mergers & Acquisitions, corporate social performance, corporate valuation, risk management, financial markets, and corporate disclosure. He is author of books and several articles for refereed academic journals (e.g., Journal of Business Research, Technological Forecasting and Social Change, Global Finance Journal, Finance Research Letters). He is member of the editorial boards for relevant international academic journals.

Emanuele Doronzo is Research Fellow in Accounting at the Department of Management, University of Molise (Italy). His studies focus on the concepts of sustainability, ethics, social enterprises, impact investing, and the role of cultural value. His research efforts have allowed him to publish in important international journals such as Business Strategy and Environmental Journal and International Journal of Business and Management. He also acted as a reviewer for several academic journals and he participated as a presenter at different international conferences.

Analysis of the Emerging Contribution of the Spanish Insurance Sector to the Development of Sustainable Finance

Elena Sevilla Sanromán and Manuel Fernández López

1 Introduction

The notion of sustainable finance refers to the incorporation of environmental, social, and good governance principles into financial businesses' strategy, operations and decision-making processes, particularly those connected to investments. If linked to the Bruntland Commission's traditional definition of sustainability, its goal would be to mobilise financing for the global economy while "meeting the needs of the current generations without jeopardising future generations' ability to meet their own needs," favouring the transition to a low-carbon and more sustainable economy.

As suggested by the Spanish Network of the Global Compact, the financial sector, which insurance companies are a part of, is called upon to be a channel of economic resources to "invest in the transformation of the world," and thus be a part of and act as an accelerator to this vital solution. According to the World Bank, an estimated 3% of global GDP is required to fund sustainability, and states are unable to achieve this task without the assistance of the private sector. At this stage, insurance companies must make a significant contribution from their triple role as risk managers, providers of insurance products and services, and investors.

Due to the nature of its operations, insurance does not directly harm the environment or society. However, according to the World Economic Forum's report *The Global Risk Report 2023*, five of the ten most prominent risks in the next decade are

E. Sevilla Sanromán (✉) · M. Fernández López
Universitat Oberta de Catalunya (UOC), Barcelona, Catalunya, Spain
e-mail: esevillasanroman@uoc.edu; mfernandezlopez14@uoc.edu

B. Díaz Díaz et al. (eds.), *Building Global Societies Towards an ESG World*, CSR, Sustainability, Ethics & Governance,
https://doi.org/10.1007/978-3-031-56619-6_8

environmental, including natural disasters and external climate events, failure to mitigate climate change, large-scale environmental damage, failure to adapt to climate change, and natural resource crises. Two of these risks are associated with the social dimension: the cost-of-living crisis and erosion of social cohesion.

These risks would have an impact on economic sectors such as industry, agriculture, energy, transportation, construction, pharmaceuticals, and others that are insurance company clients, either as legal entities or as natural individuals. Investors, on the other hand, require sustainability information in order to make judgements and analyse companies' exposure to ESG or sustainability risks in addition to financial risks. These elements are also connected to the existence of a palpable shift in the preferences of more conscious and well-informed consumers who take action by incorporating social and environmental values into their purchasing decisions, which were previously defined rather by variables such as quality or price.

Aside from these facts, sustainability is entering the heart of financial institutions, in general, and insurers, in particular, are offering up new business opportunities. It is no longer a question of choosing between ethics and profitability and solvency, but rather of finding a way to include ESG features into products and investments that provide value to shareholders and to society.

Sustainable finance is already a material issue for insurance companies' strategy and business. The international framework, as well as European and Spanish regulations, are pushing to take a step forward in considering and taking action on the environmental, social, and economic ramifications. As a result, the impacts are no longer simply about how companies are managed internally but also about how to actively contribute to minimising the effects of economic activity in general in order to benefit society and the planet. The position that entities take in this regard may have an influence on their value as a company.

According to the notion of double materiality, sustainable finance may thus be viewed in terms of impact and also financial consequences. This also entails taking into account financial and non-financial challenges and opportunities, with increasingly ambiguous limits, for example, proper integration of ESG risks and generation of sustainable products can increase insurer profitability or reduce their competitiveness.

2 International and Normative Framework

The UN Summit on Sustainable Development in 2015 established the so-called 2030 Agenda and the SDGs, which serve as the foundation for humanity's efforts to create a more sustainable world. Almost simultaneously, the Conference of the Parties, COP 21, held in Paris, concretised the global goal of limiting global temperature to 1.5 °C above pre-industrial levels, calling for increased "financial flows" towards sustainable development with lower emissions.

These two milestones positioned humanity in the face of its greatest challenge of its conscious history, highlighting the necessity for private funding to supplement state funding. However, it was the European Commission which included, amongst other measures, a description of the concept of sustainable finance in its Action Plan and began to establish a classification system of sustainable actions and products, known as Taxonomy. Further legal developments include the Sustainable Finance Disclosure Regulation (SFDR), and the recently enacted Corporate Sustainability Reporting Directive (CSRD). Almost simultaneously, the European Financial Reporting Advisory Group (EFRAG) approved the first set of Sustainability Reporting Standards (ESRS) covering environment, social issues, and governance in November 2022.

As a result, we are confronted with a unique challenge that appears to have an unprecedented national and international consensus, but not without obstacles. The financial sector's contribution to the 2030 Agenda includes banks, insurance companies, and investment firms.

The United Nations Finance Programme's most recent initiative is Net-Zero, a coalition that strives to decrease and eliminate greenhouse gas (GHG) emissions from economic activity. The Net-Zero Insurance Alliance and *Net-Zero Insurance Alliance* and *Net-Zero Asset Owner Alliance programmes* are applicable to the insurance industry.

Most large insurers adhere to the Principles of Sustainability in Insurance (PSI) that comprise the concept of sustainable insurance, which include managing ESG risks and opportunities in a "responsible and forward-looking manner" throughout the business value chain and in relationships with stakeholders.

The UN-PRI (Principles of Responsible Investment) serves as a guide for sustainable investments. Its goal is to encourage the integration of ESG criteria into investment decision-making and asset management for a more sustainable global financial system, as a result of the collaboration between the United Nations Programme Finance Initiative and the Global Compact (UN Global Compact).

In Spain, the Law on Climate Change and Energy Transition, as well as the Sustainable Development Strategy form the framework for a path that will continue to move forward and has no way back. In this context, sustainable finance attempts to shift financing and investments towards more sustainable projects and enterprises, thus contributing to the decarbonisation of a more social economy and assuring long-term equitable growth through the incorporation of ESG standards.

3 Results

The investigation was conducted utilising a mixed research strategy that combined collection of quantitative and qualitative data. In addition to consulting nonempirical secondary sources and bibliography, the qualitative section includes a series of interviews with institutional and corporate executives as a primary empirical source. The main conclusions are summarised below.

3.1 The Sight of the Experts

In her public speeches, UNESPA President Mirenchu del Valle asserts that the insurance industry is well-established in society, with a strong and profound capillarity. It also emphasises the sector's key role in sustainable finance as a risk expert, focusing on the prevention and mitigation of ESG risk events. She highlights the commitment of a sector that, while emitting minimal pollution, is currently contributing and has the potential to contribute significantly more to the goal of decarbonisation of the economy, both by itself and by assisting others in their transition process.

According to Alfredo Yagüe, consultant and sustainability manager at Analistas Financieros Internacionales (AFI), specialised in insurance, sustainability, in general, and sustainable finance, in particular, are the sector's most transversal challenges, the only ones that apply to the entire value chain until the end customer is reached.

Del Valle provides the fact that, in its role as an investor, the industry has invested 22 million euros per day for the past 25 years, so it can become a natural ally of Social Responsible Investments (SRI) if the required legal clarity is supplied. Currently, this is not happening more decisively because the regulatory framework is incomplete, and there are contradictions such as the obligation to report indicators on ESG issues that are still in development, according to schedules that put a lot of pressure on private operators, who need time to adapt their own internal structures.

This is stated by Raúl del Pozo, UNESPA's head of economy and finance department. In his opinion, regulatory certainty is one of the main outstanding issues, as is the homogenisation of criteria across analysts and ESG rating agencies in order to produce a similar shared framework and non-financial accounting using the same rigour as financial accounting.

Much related to this topic, the need for reliable and traceable data based on realities is also identified. Currently, according to Ricardo Pedraz, technical secretary of FinResp, investments in ESG assets can be made based on estimates, which create concern amongst insurers due to their nature and the application of the sector's prudence principle. As a result, the industry invests below its real potential.

Transparency obtained from compliance with European taxonomy, according to Mariluz Catilla, strategic business advisor and benchmark for ESG and sustainability, is one of the primary levers to push the industry in its active contribution to sustainable finance. In accordance with the CSRD Directive, this standard demands the publishing of the percentage of income, Opex (operation or operating expenses), and Capex (capital expenditure) of eligible and aligned activities, and therefore considered sustainable.

Patricia Reverter, partner of ESG and sustainability at KPMG, believes that the industry has significant potential as a manager of investment and insurance products, a point which is shared by the rest of the interviewees. In her opinion, sustainable finance has an influence on business because it completely integrates risk analysis and may be an attractive argument from a commercial point of view in the face of new social.

According to del Pozo, insurance has great potential to influence companies through their role as service providers or customers. Indeed, they are included in scope 3 of the carbon footprint measurement as part of the value chain of insurance products, thus they must provide data that insurers require for reporting. They can demand said information in accordance with their internal policies. In this way, they assist them in their shift to a decarbonised activity.

On the other hand, the experts emphasise the critical social dimension that must be monitored in these providers companies, which is manifested in respect to labor rights and the adoption of equality and diversity measures. This is in response to the demands that will arise as a result of the future social Taxonomy and the newly adopted Directive on the submission of sustainability information, both of which will be applied proportionality to them. According to Silvia Agulló, responsible business manager and reputation at DKV, part of the Munich Re group, insurance will be in social matters where insurance can demonstrate its real potential because it is an aspect inherent to the origin and nature of its activity.

According to Yagüe, the sector is called to take the lead by raising awareness of its consumers and suppliers. In addition, its shareholders already demand a clear positioning and strategic plans outline everything that is to be done, including risk management, subscription policy, product governance and investment strategy. In the same vein, Ignacio Lerga, sustainability director of Axa in Spain, highlights the commitment of the insurance European leading corporations, with ambitious objectives in this regard that are concretised in internal policies, programmes, and projects, to the point of including them in the variable remuneration of management.

In summary, Del Pozo believes that we are still in a development phase, not even transitional, of the integration of sustainability in the insurers' strategies for activating their full potential within sustainable finance. For Pedraz, the most pressing priority at the moment, in addition to awaiting greater regulatory certainty from the European and Spanish authorities, is to review the public partnership between the Insurance Compensation Consortium and insurance companies in order to include new events caused by climate change.

Reverter emphasises insurers' huge potential to bring new well-built products to the market, as well as the need to have well-trained experts. Reinforcing this argument, Castilla highlights the need for companies to invest in innovation in order to provide solutions that help prevent and cover ESG risks that benefit their customers, since their own solvency depends on it.

Agulló points out the challenge posed by the new European requirements for all entities, even for those whose positioning has long been constructed, by his own conviction, around the Corporate Social Responsibility (CSR). Lerga emphasises the requirement of uniting all areas of the company behind a shared vision, led by senior management and which must be communicated effectively.

Finally, Yagüe insists on the sector's leadership capability and the significance of establishing good governance because sustainability is not a passing issue, but will have long-term consequences.

3.2 Quantitative Results Are Still Limited

Because the existence of data on sustainable finance in the Spanish insurance sector is recent, there is no way to conduct a historical comparison. The main study available was carried out in 2022 with data from 2021 by the insurance sector statistics and studies service in Spain, ICEA, at the request of UNESPA, within the framework of their collaboration agreements.

Under the heading "*Sustainability Statistics in the Insurance Sector,*" 300 indicators from 126 entities belonging to 69 insurance business groups were presented. Representativeness reached 92% of the total volume of premiums in Spain, a high figure that legitimises its results.

Specifically, the "Survey on Sustainable Investments and Products, Emissions from Entity Activity" was carried out for the first time, *and the "Sector's Contribution to Sustainable Development Goals and the Vision by Goals*" was carried out for the second time. As a result, we are facing the most relevant study at sectoral level to date, to which new indicators will be added in the coming years (2023–2024) relating to sustainable investments, the financial impact of climate change on insurance activity and, in the opposite direction, from the climate and society insurance business. The main key results are given in Figs. 1, 2, and 3.

The results are self-explicit. The insurance sector has embarked on a path of no return in integrating ESG factors into its business and decision-making, which is formalised through Sustainability Policies and whose progress is accounted for through ad hoc reports that respond to a commitment of transparency in relation to their stakeholders. On the other hand, the precise indicators assessing their active contribution to sustainable finance through products and investments do not provide such a clear reading. Although three-quarters of the entities declare that sustainability criteria are incorporated in the relevant policy, the number of those who claim to have at least one product that promotes environmental or social characteristics is less than 25%, and we do not currently have investment data.

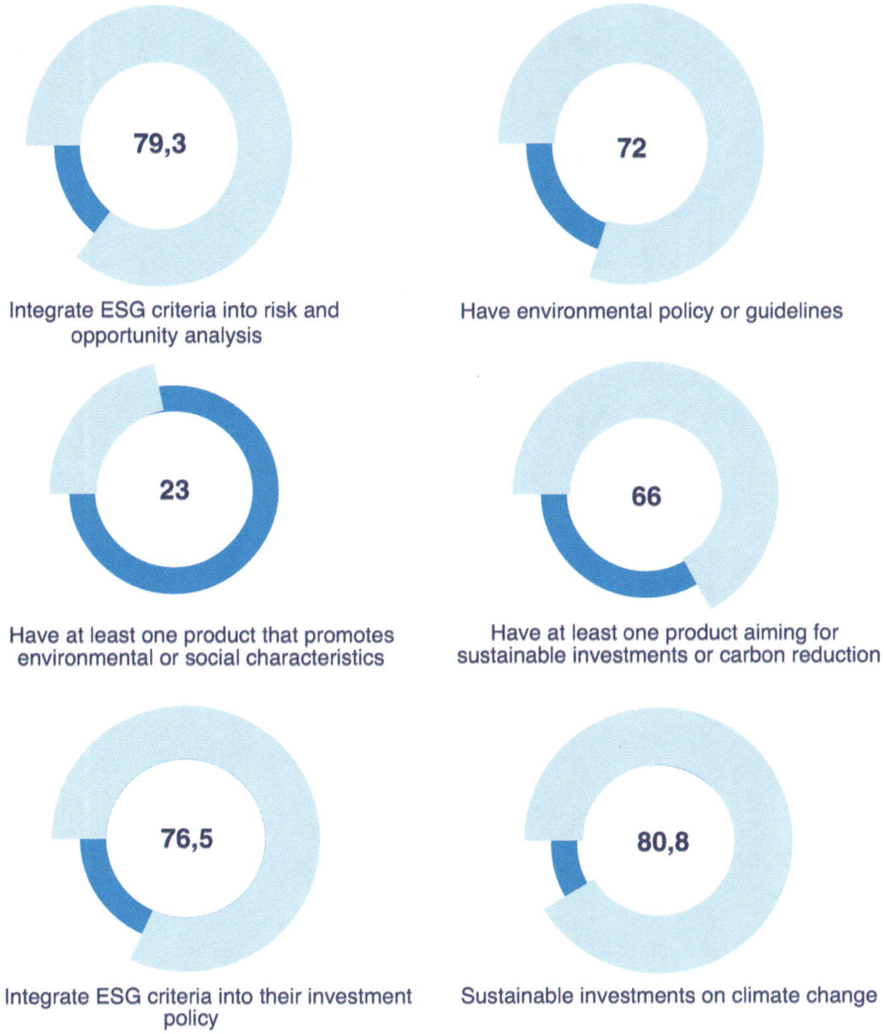

Fig. 1 Management of environmental factors

3.3 *Sustainable Finance Challenges and Opportunities in the Insurance Sector*

The transition to sustainability and sustainable finance presents challenges and opportunities arising from the perspective of double materiality, which refers to the impacts of business on the environment and society, as well as the same external conditions that can influence the financial results.

Fig. 2 Social factors GSA government and transparency

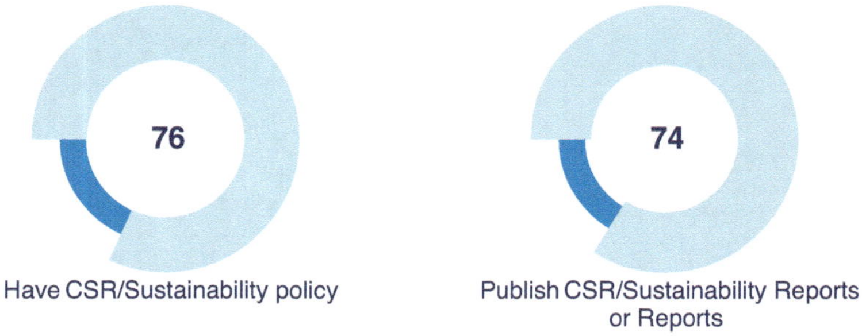

Fig. 3 Management of corporate government and transparency

Opportunities	*Challenges*
– The opportunity to make a committed contribution to the financing of the United Nations 2030 Agenda, demonstrating an active commitment to society and the environment, and boosting the sector's reputation. – The opportunity for leadership if suitable adaptation measures are taken, including the development of a decision-making governance system that incorporates ESG issues. Those that understand how to make sound judgements will be at the forefront of the industry. – The opportunity for profitability, because investments with integrated ESG considerations have proved to be more resilient to risk, particularly in times of crisis. – The opportunity to reduce costs by predicting and properly managing the effects of ESG risks. – The opportunity to reach new consumer groups through the development of products with environmental and/or social aspects. It reaches an audience more aware about sustainability who take into account the balance of profitability/risk/ESG.	– The challenge to transparency stems from one's personal conviction as well as the desire of interest groups. It manifests itself via reporting obligations that must be met in a timely manner and, in many circumstances, validated. – The challenge of trusting stakeholders, particularly regulators, supervisors, shareholders, investors, analysts, ESG rating agencies and clients. In terms of suppliers, the challenge is to provide support for them to make their own ESG transition, in addition to the trust factor. – The challenge of business model change, traditionally oriented towards economic benefits, toward a new model that also includes ESG factors in its management. – The challenge of connecting digitisation and sustainability, with the goal of producing marketable, comparable, and rigorous management and control models of sustainability data. – The challenge of protecting reputation and reducing the possible impact of systemic risks—with external causes, operations connected to stems in processes and/or entity personnel due to external causes, as well as those derived from their commercial ties.

Insurers may contribute to the transition to a decarbonised and fairer economy while also taking advantage of market opportunities and boosting their business figures.

3.4 The Triple Role of the Sector in Relation to Sustainable Finance

At this point, we can already assess the insurance sector's emergency contribution to sustainable finance based on three core business functions: risk management, insurance activity, and asset investment, all of which have a high capacity to mobilise financial resources.

3.4.1 Insurance as an ESG Risk Manager

Sustainable finance impacts insurance companies that act as risk managers and must now include ESG risks into their system, in particular those associated with climate change, as well as the analysis of adverse sustainability implications. Insurance companies contribute to economic and social stability, as well as to environmental protection by absorbing the probability and the hypothetical consequences of the materialisation of such risks.

EU Regulation 2019/2088 on the disclosure of sustainability information in the European Union's financial services sector establishes a definition for the concept of sustainability risk, which is understood as "an environmental, social or governance fact or condition that, if produced, could cause a negative material impact on the value of the investment"as defined in the current regulations."

This standard, in particular, requires insurers to incorporate ESG risks into their risk management, including their identification and evaluation. This has an influence on the actuarial function when it comes to measuring the "uncertainty associated with estimates made when calculating technical provisions." Consideration is also required in the remuneration policy and in the application of the principle of prudence.

ESG risks are incorporated into the conventional risk map, at the same level and importance as underwriting, market, operational, counterparty, financial and credit risks, as well as risks arising from the political and economic environment.

Furthermore, insurers can develop their own models that incorporate actuarial assessments, taking into consideration not only ESG criteria but also market factors, social trends, and stakeholder's expectations.

ESG Risk Classifications

Environmental risks fall into three categories: physical risks, transition risks, and liability risks.

Physical risks are caused by weather events due to climate change that can damage company assets and even the value chain. They are further categorised as follows:

- acute risks, such as hurricanes or floods;
- chronic risks resulting from the medium- and long-term increase in global temperature, such as the increasing heat waves or sea level rise.

The transition risks stem from the necessary adjustment to a low GHG or "net-zero"economic model.

Finally, liability risks are associated with claims, as well as potential penalties, related to weather events, particularly under liability insurance.

Social and governance risks lack this level of specificity. Depending on the model, they can be considered to be covered by traditional risks, such as compliance and reputational risks, which are managed through compliance policies, internal control, good corporate governance, ethical codes, and human resources.

- Social risks: they are those resulting from the observation and respect of human rights, labour rights, human resources, social factors, such as the demographic composition of the population or health hazards such as pandemics.
- Governance risks: these are resulting from compliance with regulations, including reporting obligations; of reputation towards stakeholders as shareholders, rating agencies and public opinion; innovation and digital transformation, cyber risks, etc.

In a similar way, insurers create their risk strategy based on the level of risk that the Board of Directors agrees to accept (risk appetite) and integrate into the business according to the objectives that each of them has set. The highest governing bodies receive regular information on exposure to risk and observation of limits defined by the entity. An SFCR (*Solvency and Financial Condition Report)* and an ORSA (*Own Risk and Solvency Assessment)* report are also generated.

Risk management also entails developing, revising and, if necessary, modifying the underwriting policy, as well as the policy on provisions and reserves to account for the potential negative consequences of ESG risks.

3.4.2 Insurance as a Supplier of ESG Products and Services

The contribution of insurance activity to sustainable finance extends, both in a real and potential way, along with the most important phases of its value chain as a generator of products and services that are critical for society.

Underwriting

The harmful effects of climate change on the planet are evident through the rising frequency of extreme natural events that cause damage, which, of course, have an impact on insurance activity. These climatological events cause more accidents and, as a result, a greater need for financial and non-financial resources for their management. On the other hand, environmental risks linked to climate change lead to a reconsideration, adaptation, or modification of underwriting policies where, as a rule, the criterion of technical rigour is applied to ensure solvency.

In the social realm, factors such as population ageing in Spain, the potential emergence of pandemics defined geographically or globally and the economic crisis also have an impact on the likelihood of insurance-covered cases occurring.

Underwriting in insurance is the process of carefully assessing the risk of any product, taking into consideration market conditions, claims, the possibility of occurrence, losses, etc. Underwriting professionals facilitate, through their work, the decision of the risk limit that a company can accept. Although much of the work is now automated, expert human control is still essential to determine if something is outside the normal parameters. The process is completed by designing the included guarantees and premium pricing.

Climate change risks underwriting is based on detailed reports that include loss estimates if these potentially catastrophic events occur, as well as on risk limit control systems, which can be stress tested.

It is common for insurers to outsource the excess risk they are willing to manage to reinsurance if they believe that they will exceed the limits defined by management, thereby safeguarding their level of solvency and liquidity.

Insurers may contribute to the goal of sustainable finance by including commitments associated with the Paris Agreement, the EU Plan and, in coherence, facilitate the transition to a low-carbon economy through underwriting policies.

Underwriting Exclusion Criteria

Leading companies in the sector in Spain and Europe have established general exclusion criteria affecting polluting industries such as fossil fuels (coal and oil). In particular, they refer to activities such as those listed below, which is not an exhaustive list:

- Construction of new coal-based power plants
- Operation of new coal mines
- Service infrastructure for coal mines or coal-fired power stations
- Enterprises with revenues from coal-fired energy
- Undertakings or entities with plans to increase coal-based energy consumption
- New mining companies
- New projects for extracting or transporting tar sands
- Gas and/or oil extraction and transport projects in the Arctic Ocean

In relation to the existing portfolio, the most common trend is to conduct a reassessment aimed at assisting the transition of the above-mentioned industries, including, for example, the requirement to address energy-efficiency measures, reduction of greenhouse gas emissions, alignment with the objectives of the Paris Agreement, etc.

The ethical conflict that arises in these cases is the risk of insurers failing to meet their civil liability obligations if they refuse to contract with particular sectors. It is one thing to assist them in their transition to decarbonise their activity and another to refuse to provide products and services that can prevent and, in the event of a disaster, rectify a mishap that would otherwise have far worse implications.

Sustainable Insurance Products and Services

Sustainable insurance products are defined in existing European legislation. In general, the European Taxonomy establishes the criteria for an economic activity to be considered environmentally sustainable.

(a) It must contribute to one or more of the defined objectives of mitigation, adaptation to climate change, water and marine resources conservation, transition to a circular economy, pollution prevention, and biodiversity and ecosystem protection.
(b) It must not cause any material damage to the aforementioned objectives.
(c) It is carried out in compliance with the Regulation's minimum guarantees.
(d) It adheres to the technical selection criteria defined by the European Commission.

If a product meets these four criteria, it could be eligible as sustainable and would be aligned according to the Taxonomy.

Given this legal framework, we could refer to environmental insurance products and services such as those whose objective is adaptation to risks and opportunities related to climate change. This typology would be incorporated into the concept of sustainable finance.

In parallel, and pending a forthcoming regulation through the development of the Social Taxonomy regulation, social insurance products and services would be aimed at responding to the people's needs through life and health protection or to vulnerable groups such as individuals with disabilities or low income, etc. In the absence of knowledge about the objectives to be included in the standard, consistent with the SDGs, it is apparent that criteria of diversity, non-discrimination, respect for human rights and labour rights will be included.

Third, good governance insurance products and services are those that provide coverage to companies, such as through cyber-attack protection.

Following the terminology used in the insurance sector, examples of sustainable non-life products that promote sustainable mobility, renewable energy, energy efficiency, reducing emissions in agriculture or the circular economy.

The European Insurance Taxonomy

The European Commission Delegated Act 2021/2139 refers specifically in paragraph 10 to such insurance covering climate-related risks and to those using the substantial contribution criteria to climate change adaptation, health insurance, income protection, workplace accidents, civil liability, motor vehicle liability, maritime, aviation and transport, fire and other damage to property and assistance are specifically addressed.

Relevant leadership inputs in climate risk measurement models, product design, innovative coverage solutions, data sharing, and quality of service following disasters are amongst the technical selection criteria.

Supplier Management within the Value Chain

The insurance sector's role in prescribing and supporting the transformation of the economy has great potential in the management of its network of collaborators and suppliers within its value chain.

Specialised collaborators are those suppliers that provide services required for insurance activity performance, such as mediators and brokers, experts, lawyers, doctors, workshops, and repairers. There are other general providers who supply products and/or services outside the insurance process. Maintenance, cleaning, hardware and computer support, stationery, food, etc. could all fall into this category.

Suppliers' policies often contain selection and relationship criteria with this relevant stakeholder, as well as the commitments of objectivity, equal treatment, quality, and transparency.

The traditional management model has incorporated ESG aspects to accompany and even demand changes with the aim of aligning the actions of suppliers with the insurance company's sustainability positioning. Measures such as the engagement to compliance with the code of ethics and sustainability policies, accountability for internal and external audits and the implementation of continuous improvement systems are examples of these improvements.

3.4.3 Insurance as a Responsible Investor

Insurance plays a dual role in long-term investments. On the one hand, it is a sector that demands this type of investment and, on the other hand, acts as a manager of sustainable investment assets through the marketing of its own products. This role is mostly fulfilled through PIBS, insurance-based investment products, which are incorporated with life products.

A sustainable investment is, according to the European Taxonomy, "an investment that finances one or more economic activities that can be considered sustainable". The criteria and objectives defined by the commission for what is considered sustainable have been outlined above.

In addition, the SFDR classifies financial products into three categories based on their degree of sustainability:

- Article 6 products, which incorporate sustainability risks.
- Those referred to in Article 8, which promote environmental characteristics.
- Those aimed at sustainable investments, as outlined in Article 9, to which we shall refer below.

PBSs are the primary financial products through which the insurance sector contributes to the objective of sustainable finance. They are defined as products that offer "a maturity or redemption value that is exposed in whole or in part, directly or indirectly, to market fluctuations" according to EU Regulation 1286/2014.

Investment funds, pension plans and funds, and green, social, and sustainable bonds are examples of sustainable savings and living products included in the offer of insurers and their asset managers.

Social Responsible Investment (SRIs) include the purely economic criteria of risk, profitability, and liquidity, other non-financial factors, in particular environmental, social, and good corporate governance.

The ESG Investment Strategies

According to Spainsif, the following strategies are used in the investment policy of insurers committed to sustainability:

- Exclusion excludes certain activities, sectors, or geographical areas because they do not meet ESG criteria, such as the arms industry, anti-personnel mines, cluster bombs, pornography, tobacco, animal abuse and most recently, the extraction of fossil fuels, coal and oil.
- *Policy Screening* entails adhering to the international framework on sustainability, selecting assets that adhere to OECD standards, the United Nations and its organisations such as the International Labour Organization (ILO) and the Global Compact.
- *Best in class* invests in companies or assets with better performance and greater ESG commitment within a sector or category. The analysis carried out by sustainability indices such as the Dow Jones Sustainability Index, MSCI, Morningstar, or S&P serves as a reference to facilitate the indexed management of the portfolio.
- Thematic investment selects companies or assets that help to improve climate or social objectives. The former may include topics such as the fight against climate change, renewable energies, or sustainable mobility. The latter may cover human rights, diversity, and corporate accountability.
- Impact investment refers to positive investments aimed at actively contributing to generating a social or environmental benefit. They are implemented through investment instruments, such as green bonds, social bonds, and others that are linked to the SDGs.
- ESG integration complements traditional return/risk analysis when selecting and managing investment portfolios. The *non-financial analysis is based on ratings* and external and/or internal assessments of environmental, social, and governance criteria.
- *Engagement and voting* involves dialogue and influence in those participating companies through the right to vote to support their transition to decarbonisation of activity and the improvement of other ESG practices.

These strategies can be used independently or in combination. According to the aforementioned study by Spainsif, 77% of the entities claim to incorporate five or more criteria into their investment policy compared to the 64% they said they did last year, a figure that reflects the progressive maturity of the Spanish economy, and can be extrapolatable to the insurance sector.

3.5 Impact of Sustainable Finance and the Insurance Sector on the SDGs

Another factor to consider is the role of sustainable finance development to the achievement of the SDGs. In fact, one of the challenges for the financial sector in this area, aside from incorporating ESG factors into its decision-making, is to act as a funding vehicle for the United Nations 2030 Agenda and the European Community's own Sustainable Finance Action Plan, which proposes an emissions-neutral economy in the old continent by 2050.

It is projected that the contribution to the SDGs would amount to between 5 and 7 million euros, with just 3 being allocated in 2019. The insurance's ability to act as an engine of capital flows within the financial services sector is supported by its great penetration, capillarity, and economic muscle.

The primary objectives in this case that we can see in Fig. 4 would be:

- SDG8 Decent Work and Economic Growth refers to access to financial services including insurance, as well as *compliance*, due diligence and ESG aspects as requirements within the value chain.
- The SDG10 Reducing inequalities call for the inclusion of ESG aspects in decision-making to invest in developing countries, as well as in projects that seek equality and improvement of the living conditions of the most vulnerable groups.
- The ODS12 Responsible production and consumption is linked to the objective of prescription and active influence in the value chain and in the choice of investment assets based on companies or ESG projects to contribute to the transformation of the economy.
- SDG13 Climate Action is directly linked to the international framework and European climate change regulation, as well as to the role of the financial sector as a channel of funds to achieve the goal of a carbon-neutral economy.
- Finally, SDG17 relates to the mobilisation of resources for development in the most challenging countries and the institutional framework that integrates the development of sustainable finance, primarily the United Nations and the European Union.

The European Union Action Plan supports this alignment. In line with this, it has devised instruments to facilitate this, such as the Taxonomy Regulation, with the goal of mobilising €1 trillion of capital through SRI. According to the Spanish

Fig. 4 SDGs impacted by sustainable finance

Fig. 5 Linking the SDGs to EU taxonomy

Global Compact Network, the current Environmental and Social Taxonomy, currently under development, are linked to the SDGs as follows in Fig. 5:

The link between sustainable finance and the SDGs may be extended to the insurance sector, specifically through the incorporation of ESG criteria into risk management, underwriting policies, the development of new products, and of course sustainable investments. These activities are geared towards contributing to the goals when they are included in the business strategy and endorsed by senior management.

4 Conclusions

This chapter has demonstrated the high exposure of insurance companies to environmental, social, and governance factors, as well as their emerging contribution to sustainable finance from their triple role as risk managers, insurers themselves and investors in ESG assets, who are also held accountable under current regulations.

Sustainable finance is, as proved, a significant issue for insurance companies. This means that they have a significant weight that influences the situation and the development of the business, as well as its results. This is acknowledged by the international reference bodies, the legislators, the market, and the insurance entities themselves, which are adapting their business and investment models to align with the Paris Agreement, the SDGs, and the European Union Action Plan. In particular, the sector has potential to make a substantial contribution to climate change adaptation.

The call to align the ESG criteria applied to investments and the underwriting policy presents an ethical dilemma with regard to economic reality. On the one hand, industry actors generally believe that there are not enough issuers of sustainable assets that are accredited and operating in a secure legal framework, as this is still incomplete. On the other hand, reviewing the portfolio by introducing sustainability strategies may limit some industries considered brown, causing a liability and ethical problem. It is part of the insurance DNA to provide coverage for its activities, whose risks of damaging the environment and society would be even greater if they were not insured. Another issue is that the insurance sector encourages and accompanies its clients in their own process of decarbonisation, including specific conditions to achieve it.

The sector's potential role is more than evident in all aspects of its operation. However, the implementation of the criteria derived from the European legal framework is still recent and its development is incomplete. Therefore, while there has been progress in disclosure according to recognised standards, we still lack global and reliable data on sustainable products that are eligible and aligned with the Taxonomy or ESG investments.

Similarly, it is still difficult to find information on sustainability risk management and its integration into companies' traditional risk models. The analyses are still at an early stage and lack historical, reliable, and comparable data.

In terms of the market, there are almost unlimited opportunities in the design of new products, adaptation of existing ones with bonuses or price benefits, development of data management models, and response to the demands of greater responsibility for current and future customers.

Overall, the Spanish insurance sector is eager to contribute to the United Nations SDGs. These are easily linked to ESG criteria and aligned with sustainable finance objectives through contribution to SDG8 Decent Work and Economic Growth, SDG10 Reducing Inequalities, SDG12 Responsible Production and Consumption, ODS13 Climate action, and ODS17 Partnerships to achieve the goals.

In conclusion, insurers must position themselves, or have already done so, on environmental issues by realistically reviewing their portfolios, but also including risks arising from climate change and enhancing the transition to an emissions neutral commitment. In terms of social aspects, establishing the target audience, supporting insurance that promotes equality, and integrating stakeholders through relationships of transparency and trust. Finally, in terms of governance through the adoption of policies at the highest level, with the active involvement of the Board of Directors, and accountability that incorporates compliance while ideally demonstrating greater commitment.

Going forward, we may see how the consolidation of sustainability models in insurance companies evolves in the future. That is, what projects and initiatives they are implementing, how much funding they are contributing to the achievement of the SDGs and, by extension, to the 2030 agenda and the European Union Action Plan. Beyond declarations and adhesions to reference organisations, which define the formal commitment, this would be the way to measure the real contribution of the sector to the challenges of society and the planet. Finally, it would also be interesting to see how interest groups assess the effort to adapt and transform the sector.

The insurance sector has an excellent opportunity to demonstrate with facts and data that its activity can promote climate adaptation, articulating solutions to the consequences of global warming and benefiting the transition to a more respectful and fairer decarbonised economy.

Interviews with Experts

- Silvia Agulló, responsible business manager and reputation. DKV Insurance Group, ERGO, Munich Re
- Mariluz Castilla, strategic business advisor and expert in ESG and sustainability
- Pedro del Pozo, head of the Economy and Finance Department. UNESPA
- Ignacio Lerga, Sustainability manager. AXA Spain
- Ricardo Pedraz, Public Finance. AFI. General Secretariat. FinResp
- Patricia Reverter, ESG Partner and Sustainability. KPMG
- Alfredo Yagüe, consultant and manager of the insurance sector. AFI International Financial Analysts

Bibliography

Afi. (2022). Sustainability in insurance companies. https://www.afi-research.es/InfoR/descargas/2208838/1612403/Jornada-Impactos-de-sostenibilidad-en-el-sector-seguros-Alfredo-Yague.pdf

Afi, finReg360, & Allianz Global Investors. (2020). Sustainability and asset management. Practical guide II. https://media.afi.es/afi/libre/PDFS/Grupo/Documentos/2020/1111_2031242.pdf

Allianz. (2022). Sustainability report 2021. https://www.allianz.com/content/dam/onemarketing/azcom/Allianz_com/sustainability/documents/Allianz_Group_Sustainability_Report_2021-web.pdf

AXA. (2022). Sostenibilidad. https://www.axa.es/corporativo#
AXA Investment Managers. (2022). *Sustainable finance*. SFDR. https://www.axa-im.com/important-information/sfdr
Blasco, J. L., & Delrieu, J. C. (2021). *The role of finance in a sustainable economy*. Foundation of Financial Studies, Spanish Institute of Financial Analysts. https://dokumen.tips/documents/el-rol-de-las-finanzas-en-una-economa-sostenible.html?page=1
CNMV. (2022). Sustainable finance. https://www.cnmv.es/
DKV. (2022). Integrated corporate report 2021. https://dkv.es/corporativo/informe-anual
European Commision. Platform on Sustainable Finance. (2021). Transition finance report. https://finance.ec.europa.eu/sustainable-finance/overview-sustainable-finance/platform-sustainable-finance_en
European Commission. (2018, March 8). *Action plan: Financing sustainable development*. Commission communication to the European Parliament, the Council, the European Economic and Social Committee and the Committee of the Regions. https://eur-lex.europa.eu/legal-content/ES/TXT/PDF/?uri=CELEX:52018DC0097
European Commission. (2021). *Strategy for financing the transition to a sustainable economy*. Commission communication to the European Parliament, the Council, the European Economic and Social Committee and the Committee of the Regions. https://eur-lex.europa.eu/resource.html?uri=cellar:9f5e7e95-df06-11eb-895a-01aa75ed71a1.0012.02/DOC_1&format=PDF
European Commission. Commission Delegated Regulation (EU) 2021/1253 of 21 April 2021 amending Delegated Regulation (EU) 2017/565 as regards the integration of factors, sustainability risks and preferences in certain organisational requirements and operating conditions of investment firms. *Official Journal of the European Union, OJ L 277* (2021). https://www.boe.es/doue/2021/277/L00001-00005.pdf
European Commission. Commission Delegated Regulation (EU) 2021/1256 of 21 April 2021 amending Delegated Regulation (EU) 2017/35 as regards the integration of sustainability risks into the governance of insurance and reinsurance undertakings. *Official Journal of the European Union, OJ L 81065* (2021). https://www.boe.es/doue/2021/277/L00014-00017.pdf
European Commission. Delegated Regulation (EU) 2021/2139 supplementing Regulation (EU) 2020/852 of the European Parliament and of the Council establishing technical selection criteria for determining the conditions under which an economic activity is considered to contribute substantially to climate change mitigation or adaptation, and to determine whether that economic activity does not cause significant harm to any of the other environmental objectives. *Official Journal of the European Union, OJ L 81725* (2021). https://www.boe.es/doue/2021/442/L00001-00349.pdf
European Commission. Platform on Sustainable Finance. (2021). Platform on Sustainable Finance's draft report on a social taxonomy. https://finance.ec.europa.eu/system/files/2021-07/sf-draft-report-social-taxonomy-july2021_en.pdf
European Parliament and Council. Regulation (EU) 2020/852 on the establishment of sustainable investments and amending Regulation (EU) 2019/2088. *Official Journal of the European Union*, DOUE-L-2020-80947. https://www.boe.es/doue/2020/198/L00013-00043.pdf
European Parliament and Council. Directive (EU) 2022/2464 of 14 December 2022 amending Regulation (EU) No 537/2014, Directive 2004/109/EC, Directive 2006/43/EC and Directive 2013/34/EU as regards the submission of sustainability information by undertakings. *Official Journal of the European Union, OJ L 322* (2022). https://www.boe.es/doue/2022/322/L00015-00080.pdf
European Parliament. Regulation (EU) 2019/2088 on the disclosure of sustainability information in the financial services sector. *Official Journal of the European Union, OJ* 2019-*81907*. https://www.boe.es/doue/2019/317/L00001-00016.pdf
Fajans-Turner, V. (2018). *Filling the finance gap. SDG's transforming our world*. UNA UK. https://www.sustainablegoals.org.uk/filling-the-finance-gap/
FC4S. (2021). Sustainable finance in insurers. https://www.fc4s.org/viewpdf.php?f_file=wp-content/uploads/2021/08/Deck_05_01_LQ-Spa.pdf

Ferrarini, G., Grünewald, S., & Busch, D. (Eds.). (2021). *Sustainable finance in Europe* (Corporate governance, financial stability and financial markets. EBI studies in banking and capital markets law). Palgrave Macmillan. https://link.springer.com/book/10.1007/978-3-030-71834-3

Global Compact, & Red España. (2022). *Sustainable finance and the 2030 agenda. White Paper n° 1. Update 2022.* https://www.pactomundial.org/biblioteca/white-paper-no-1-finanzas-sostenibles-y-agenda-2030-invertir-en-la-transformacion-del-mundo/#descargar_frm

Gómez-Jover, M. F. (2022). *Sustainability impacts in the insurance sector*. Afi. https://www.afi-research.es/InfoR/downloaded/2208836/1612403/Jornada-Impacts-sustainability-in-the-safe-sector-Francisca-Gomez-Jover.pdf

Head of State. (2018). *Law 11/2018, of 28 December, amending the Commercial Code, the consolidated text of the Capital Companies Law approved by Royal Legislative Decree 1/2010, of 2 July, and Law 22/2015, 20 July, Audit of Accounts on non-financial reporting and diversity*. Official State Gazette. https://www.boe.es/boe/dias/2018/12/29/pdfs/BOE-A-2018-17989.pdf

ICEA. (2022). *Estadística sobre Sostenibilidad en el Sector Asegurador*. ICEA.

Insurance Europe. (2022). Annual report 2021–2022. https://reports.insuranceeurope.eu/annual-report-2020-2021/contents/

Mapfre. (2022a). Integrated report 2021. https://www.mapfre.com/media/shareholder/2021/informe-mapfre-2021.pdf

Mapfre. (2022b). TCFD report. https://www.mapfre.com/media/sostenibilidad/informe-TCFD-mayo-2022.pdf

MM Mutual Group. (2022). Responsible and sustainable management. https://www.grupomutua.es/sostenibilidad/

Munich Re. (2022). Sustainability report 2021. https://www.munichre.com/en/company/sustainability/news/2022/2022-04-22.html

Pacto Mundial, & Red España. (2021). Banking and insurance financial services: contributing to the 2030 agenda. https://www.pactomundial.org/biblioteca/servicios-financieros-de-banca-y-seguros-contribuyendo-a-la-agenda-2030-digitalizacion-y-finanzas-sostenibles/

Scholer, M., & Cuesta, L. (2020). *The sustainable finance taxonomy from the perspective of the insurance and reinsurance sector*. EIOPA, European Insurance and Occupational Pensions Authority. https://www.eiopa.europa.eu/document-library/thematic-article/eu-sustainable-finance-taxonomy-perspective-of-insurance-and_en

Spainsif. (2022). Sustainable and responsible investment in Spain 2022. https://www.spainsif.es/wp-content/uploads/2022/1javascript:void(0);0/Market-Research-Spainsif-2022.pdf

Spanish Agency for International Cooperation for Development. (2017). Study on the contribution of business to the Sustainable Development Goals (SDGs) Agenda. https://www.aecid.es/Centro-Documentation/Documentos/Publications%20AECID/Abstract%20executive%20study%20contributory%C3%B3n%20de%20la%20enterprise%20a%20los%20ODS.pdf

Swiss Re. (2022). Partnership for progress. https://reports.swissre.com/2021/assets/pdf/AR21_SURE_Sustainability_Report_2021.pdf

Tejero, E. (2021). *Sustainable finance in the insurance sector*. Directorate-General for Insurance and Pension Funds.

UNEP; PSI Principles for Sustainable Insurance. (2015). *Insurance 2030 enhance insurance for sustainable development*. Fasecolda. https://fasecolda.com/cms/wp-content/uploads/2019/10/insurance-2030.pdf

UNEP-FI. (2021). Leadership Council. Annual meeting summary. https://www.unepfi.org/about/structure/leadership-council/

UNEP-FI. (2022a). Net-zero insurance alliance. https://www.unepfi.org/net-zero-insurance/

UNEP-FI. (2022b). Principles for sustainable insurance. https://www.unepfi.org/insurance/insurance/

UNEP-FI. (2022c). UN convened net-zero asset owner alliance. https://www.unepfi.org/net-zero-alliance/

UNESPA. (2020). *Insurance and the sustainable development goals*. Verbal analysis and working document of the Sustainability Commission. UNESPA.

UNESPA. (2023). *Memoria Social del Seguro 2022*. UNESPA. https://www.unespa.es/que-hacemos/publicaciones/informes-2023/
UN-PRI. (2022). Principles for responsible investment. https://www.unpri.org/
Wbcsd. (2018). Sectoral roadmaps to achieve the SDGs. https://www.wbcsd.org/contentwbc/download/5735/76504/1
World Bank. (2022). Finance for equitable recovery. https://www.bancomundial.org/es/publication/wdr2022
World Economic Forum. (2023). The global risks report *2032* (18th edn). https://www3.weforum.org/docs/WEF_Global_Risks_Report_2023.pdf
Zurich. (2022). Sustainability report 202. https://www.zurich.com/de-de/reports/2021/sustainability-report

Elena Sevilla Sanromán, Strategy Manager at Anthesis Lavola, professor of and freelance. Master Degree in Corporate Social Responsibility by Universitat Oberta de Catalunya (UOC), her final work on Sustainable Finance of the insurance sector received an Honour Mention and was awarded as the best of the course 2022/23. Graduate in Law in Universidad de Barcelona, she got a Master's Degree in Advertising and Corporate Communication by ESIC Business and Marketing School and a Master's Degree in International Relations by Ortega y Gasset University Institute, recognized by Universidad Complutense de Madrid, where Elena also studied a post grade on Socioeconomic Journalism. She has developed her professional career as CSR/Sustainability and Communication Manager in companies of the Spanish insurance sectors such as the Groupama, Allianz Global Assistance, and Grupo Catalana Occidente. Within her functions on sustainability, she has carried out materiality analysis, strategic plans, reporting, external assurement, relationship with investors and ESG rating agencies, Sustainable Development Goals (SDG) integration, and communication on sustainability. Currently, Elena works as Strategy Manager at Anthesis Lavola.

Manuel Fernández López, Assistant Professor, Dublin City University at the Institute of Education. Contributor to the Master in Sustainability and Social Responsibility at the Open University of Barcelona. Master Degree in Sustainable Development (Dublin Institute of Technology), postgraduate diploma in Environmental Impact Assessment (University College Dublin, UCD), and international doctorate (University of Barcelona, UB—Social Psychology). In the context of sustainable development, Manuel has been lecturing in the Master degree program in Ecological Economics and Environmental Management in Norway (Nord University) and in Educational Innovation (Polytechnic University of Catalonia, UPC) and Responsible Communication (Open University of Catalonia, UOC) in Spain. He has worked in international environmental consulting and foresight and has spent over 11 years as a resident in various European countries. He collaborates with the United Nations in the context of climate change resilience. The countries where Manuel have developed or participated in projects include Ireland, the United Kingdom, Spain, Norway, Mexico, Cuba, and the Seychelles. Currently, he is assistant professor at the Dublin City University (DCU), where he is researching on future studies and sustainable development in education.

Sustainability in the Main Spanish Banking Entities: A Comparative Analysis

Antonio Baraybar Fernández, Sandro Arrufat Martín, and Cristina Gonzáliez Oñate

1 Introduction

Both academia and the business world have shown a clear interest in issues relating to corporate social responsibility (CSR). This interest has been promoted by governmental entities incentivizing it in policy and through society also demanding responsible behaviour from organizations. Sustainable growth is a central issue in today's society and the financial system must play a leading role in achieving the ambitious objectives set.

As a point of interest, it is worth noting that the term CSR first appeared at the Stockholm Conference of 1972, promoted by the UN under the title Environment and Development (Janicka & Sajnóg, 2022). At around the same time, the first academic research into CSR was taking place, although it was not widely broadcast due to its not being central to the lines of investigation at the time. Latterly, the concept of sustainable development was defined more concretely in 1987 in the report titled 'Our Common Future' by the World commission on environment as "a development that enables the current needs of societies to be met without limiting this possibility for future generations" (Report by the World Commission, 1987). As such, it is evident that from the outset this term has related to concerns about environmental degradation and its impact on the development of future generations. Over recent years however, the scope of the term has been broadened to include social aspects and corporate governance as well.

A. Baraybar Fernández · S. Arrufat Martín (✉)
Universidad Rey Juan Carlos, Madrid, Spain
e-mail: antonio.baraybar@urjc.es; sandro.arrufat@urjc.es

C. Gonzáliez Oñate
Universitat Jaume I, Castellon, Spain
e-mail: onate@uji.es

B. Díaz Díaz et al. (eds.), *Building Global Societies Towards an ESG World*, CSR, Sustainability, Ethics & Governance,
https://doi.org/10.1007/978-3-031-56619-6_9

Political concerns about these issues have been growing over the last decade and have been mirrored in legislation. In 2014, the European Union adopted a directive on non-financial reports which obliged large corporations to publish information on those aspects of their business related to sustainability and their environmental impact. One of its main objectives was to facilitate the incorporation of those matters into the investor decision making processes beyond just the financial metrics of business.

In September 2015, the United Nations presented the document 'Transforming our world: the 2030 Agenda for Sustainable Development'. In it, the 17 sustainable development goals (SDGs) were clearly defined. In December of that year during the Paris climate conference, the first binding global climate change agreement was approved by the signatory countries and came into force in November 2016. It was principally concerned with the adoption of urgent measures to raise public consciousness of and to also slow down the effects of global warming. However, due to the relevance of the financial system as a key factor in global economic development, sustainability was relegated to a secondary position. That could well be considered erroneous given the need to channel significant resources. Such resources allow for the provision of long term funds for sustainable investment and to fulfil the objectives set out in the 2019 Europe Green Deal; a deal that seeks to make Europe a carbon net-zero continent by 2050.

The proposals in Agenda 2030 can be grouped into three columns that implicate both the internal and external stakeholders of any given organization. They are identified by the acronym ESG: Environmental (E), Social (S), and Governance (G). From the adaptation of the concept of sustainable development into the ambit of finance comes the concept of sustainable finance. Generally this term goes beyond considerations of financial flows or risk management and includes aspects related to the stability of the system in contributing to sustainable social development (Migliorelli, 2021). Currently, sustainable development is an essential element in corporate strategy. At least this is so in the European space and it has become a starting point for decision making and in action taken by directors. It is accepted that good ESG management leads to better market capitalization with investor decisions considering those ESG related indicators as relevant (Migliorelli, 2021). As a consequence of this, businesses complying with these demands and certifying their adherence to them, enjoy a better financial valuation. ESG reports are carried out for the most part by large entities (Janicka & Sajnóg, 2022) and the number of companies publicly reporting their ESG information is rising continuously.

Within the financial world, ESG criteria has been growing in importance since the 2008 financial crisis and the subsequent loss of trust in both brokers and financial markets. The recognition and dissemination of good practice is used as a narrative in recovering from the damage done to credibility and transparency and in giving value to efficiency and social commitment (Baraybar-Fernández & Arrufat-Martín, 2022).

However, the mere fact that companies are ever more linked with concepts of responsibility for social reasons is not enough for real development to actually happen. Although the social component is relevant, the company is also interested in the economic dimension which should not be jeopardized by the adoption of good practices.

There is no unified academic opinion on the relationship between business profitability and CSR compliance. From the start of this century, various studies have established a positive relationship that justifies the profitability of solid and efficient CSR management. Among other criteria, the improvement in both social and financial perceptions has allowed for gains in competitivity, the potential increase in the economic value of the company, a reduction in possible risk derived from irresponsible social behaviour and by association, a commitment to quality management. Other authors however have not identified any specific relationship either favourable or negative from commitments in this field, financial results, and SRI. Furthermore, SRI has drawn criticism attributing it to lower profits and higher costs and as even being a product of conjunctural marketing (Charlo Molina & Moya Clemente, 2010: 16–17).

2 Dow Jones Sustainability World Index (DJSI)

Actors making up any competitive market economy need references that allow for the evaluating of the management of organizations. To live up to the commercial maxim that only what is measured can be managed, the increase in activity in investments that proactively integrate ESG has led to the emergence of metrics to measure and validate those efforts. ESG ratings and indices have multiplied in number, improving in both quality and complexity. An example of this is that of the 21 ESG rating systems registered in 2000, 108 were subsequently registered in 2010 (Pagano et al., 2018: 341). The development of the rating systems was something that began with little sophistication but which today has been incorporated into the strategic business consulting industry.

There is an obvious problem in establishing diachronic comparisons of the indices over the medium and long term due to significant changes produced in their development over time. What is more, there is no agreement between academia and real world application on the precise definitions of ESG and the correct ways to measure it.

The Dow Jones Sustainability World Index (DJSI) has been selected as the source for the sample choice included in this study. Among other reasons, the said index is regarded as one of the main sustainability related indices globally. This index is calculated by Standard & Poor's and RobecoSam. It was first published in 1999, and since 2017 it has assessed the sustainability actions of the 2500 largest corporations on the Dow Jones Global Total Stock with the inclusion of all industries. The methodology behind the evaluation of corporate sustainability (Corporate Sustainability Assessment methodology) (CSA) is designed to capture the general and specific criteria of any industry fitting within the parameters of ESG. The information compiled provides a hybrid approach combining the specific information requested and provided by the company along with publicly available information, followed by a third party audit of the process.

In the DJSI list published in December 2022, there were 332 organisations of which 15 were based in Spain:

Amadeus, Acciona, BBVA, Bankinter, CaixaBank, Enagás, Endesa, Ferrovial, Grifols, Iberdrola, Inditex, Indra, Red Eléctrica, Santander, and Siemens Gamesa Renewable Energy.

It was significant that Acciona was included though left the European DJSI list following its publication.

The inclusion of an organization in these lists allows for, among other things, three benefits. Firstly there is an increase in their appeal to and the confidence they impart to investors. Secondly it internally generates continuous improvement processes which apply constant assessment of the economic, social, and environmental behaviour. Lastly, it allows for an enhanced perception and social acceptance by the stakeholders.

3 Results

As previously mentioned, the S&P Global Sustainability 2023 establishes a ranking sorted by industry. One of them is the banking sector with 506 financial entities evaluated. Spain, as a country shows good results with four financial entities in the top 5% and top 10% of the S&P Global ESG score. BBVA came out as best positioned followed by Santander, Bankinter, and CaixaBank. With the aim of establishing the comparative approach with other European financial entities, it is worth mentioning that BBVA is positioned ahead of such prestigious entities as BNP Paribas (France) or indeed that Santander outperformed the results of Intesa Sanpaolo (Italy). It is also important to highlight the case of Banco Sabadell which from among a total of 75 financial entities in the ranking, entered the Sustainability Yearbook Members with a score of 74/100 points, though without the formal recognition received by the four other Spanish entities. Following here below is an assessment of the four entities according to the three columns making up the ESG.

3.1 BBVA

BBVA ranks as the highest positioned Spanish bank in the S&P Global Sustainability Yearbook 2023 with a result of 86 points from a possible 100. It is placed ahead of Santander, Bankinter, and CaixaBank. It stands out in the areas of Social and in Governance and Economic. Its score has remained stable over the last 5 years although it has dropped slightly in the last two: 88 points (2020) and 89 points (2021). Currently BBVA is the highest placed Spanish and European bank in the financial entity rankings occupying fifth place in the general ranking and second in the category of Top 5% S&P Global ESG score. BBVA Peru has also managed to be included in the ranking with 67 points.

BBVA's commitment to sustainability has a long history, beginning with its adhesion to the United Nations Global Pact in 2002, and it is reflected in the Bank's various corporate policies and regulations. This is especially so in the Corporate Social Responsibility Policy updated in 2020 and in the General Sustainability Policy approved by the Board of Directors the same year.

3.1.1 Criteria E: Environmental

This is the area in which the financial entity has room to improve and currently sits an appreciable distance behind the financial institution with the best score, E.SUN Financial Holding Company, Ltd. However, BBVA is nonetheless committed to responsible and sustainable growth. As such, one line of action is the 2025 Commitment to which BBVA has mobilized 100,000 million euros between 2018 and 2025 to green financing and sustainable infrastructure. Furthermore, it was the first financial institution in the world to issue contingently convertible, perpetual, bonds—the so-called 'CoCos'—with green bonds of 1000 million euros destined for the finance of eligible green assets in BBVA's portfolio. They were diversified into assets from various green sectors related to energy efficiency, renewable energies, sustainable transport, waste management, and water management. In relation to their indirect environmental footprint, the Group announced in 2021 that it would reduce its exposure to coal-related activities to zero. It said it would cease to finance the companies involved and do so before 2030 in developed countries and 2040 in the rest of the world.

3.1.2 Criteria S: Social

This is a fundamental pillar in the politics of the financial entity and as such BBVA has a strong commitment to all forms of diversity and inclusion. In this context, it is worth highlighting that BBVA received a "2021 Gallup Exceptional Workplace Award" as one of the 30 most exceptional businesses worldwide. This award distinguishes organizations committed to developing the human potential of their workforce. The social programs of BBVA act as an opportunity driver for people and are a key pillar of its responsible banking policy. In 2022, BBVA benefited over 12 million people with the allocation of 142.2 million euros to community investment through the promotion of financial education, social entrepreneurship and knowledge, education, and culture.

3.1.3 Criteria G: Governance

BBVA's Corporate Governance System is designed to guarantee the solidity and effectiveness of the Group's management and supervision. It is one of the most highly valued parameters, ahead even of the Social area and just two points below the best score in the sector. In terms of diversity and inclusion, it has clearly defined initiatives to promote a diverse and inclusive work environment and works actively to incorporate more women into processes of recruitment and the promotion of talent (Rooney rule). In the company there is pay parity for men and women which guarantees internal equity. Additionally there is full integration of indicators linked to sustainability in the remuneration scheme of all employees and is oriented towards climate action for 2021. Furthermore, the Board has approved a governance model for sustainability in full alignment with the Group's global strategy, a new Global Standard for Responsible Procurement, and a Code of Ethics for suppliers.

3.2 *Santander*

Santander is the second placed Spanish bank in the S&P Global Sustainability Yearbook 2023 rankings with a result of 83 points out of 100. This entity stands out in the areas of Social and Governance and Economic and even surpasses its direct competitor BBVA in the Environmental area. Over the past 5 years, its score has remained stable, down just three points with respect to its highest score achieved in 2021 (86 points). Furthermore, Santander Chile (78 points) and Santander Mexico (66 points) have also managed to be included in the ranking. Santander was one of the founding financial institutions of the United Nations Principles for Responsible Banking and based its Sustainability and Responsible Banking policies on the acronym ESG. It was able to reinforce its public commitments during 2022 thanks to the results obtained prior to that year.

3.2.1 Criteria E: Environmental

Santander has made a clear commitment to the transition to a low-carbon economy. To this end, from among the most noteworthy actions carried out, we highlight the financing of more than 150,000 electric vehicles with a volume of 4800 million euros and the setting of three new objectives for the decarbonization of portfolios by 2030. These include a 29% reduction in absolute emissions financed in the energy sector, a 33% reduction in emission intensity in the aviation sector, and a 32% reduction in emission intensity in the steel sector. This comes together with the launch through Santander Universities of the Santander X Global Challenge/Countdown to zero, to aid society in finding innovative and sustainable solutions in the fight against climate change. They represent just three items from a list of other environmental initiatives the financial institution is engaged in.

3.2.2 Criteria S: Social

The entity stands out for the social impact of its activities and initiatives that have the purpose of promoting inclusive growth. This is one of the key areas in its sustainability strategy and is reflected in the breakdown of its score in the S&P Global Sustainability 2023 ranking. Santander took on the commitment to financially empower 10 million people between 2019 and 2025 through its financial education initiatives, developing accessibility programs for vulnerable groups and in particular the elderly. This objective was achieved 3 years ahead of schedule. The bank is also recognized as Best Bank in Financial Inclusion by Euromoney and The Banker. Another noteworthy aspect that demonstrates its dynamism and ability to adapt to unforeseen events, is in its support for the humanitarian crisis generated by the war in Ukraine. This is especially so in Poland, where it has collaborated with the UN refugee agency (UNHCR) and the Red Cross. It has a network of Santander volunteers to carry out social action and financial inclusion work.

3.2.3 Criteria G: Governance

Undoubtedly, this is the most outstanding and recognized aspect for Santander. The entity has carried out various actions in the field of internal governance from among which the following are most noteworthy:

- An update of the General Code of Conduct.
- The inclusion of ESG criteria in long-term incentives and short-term remuneration systems.
- Improved due diligence with revised socio-environmental surveys for customer operations and supplier certification.
- The implementation of a data ethics guide and employee training courses on how to use data and advanced analytics ethically and responsibly.
- The development of internal regulations to define roles and responsibilities in the development of the responsible banking strategy.

3.3 Bankinter

Bankinter occupies third place among Spanish banks in the S&P Global Sustainability Yearbook 2023 ranking with 80 out of 100 points and it is tied in fourth place with another Spanish entity, CaixaBank. The bank stands out in the Social area, though it is weaker with respect to its direct competitors in the areas of Governance and Economic and Environmental. Over the last 5 years its score has remained stable, although it has decreased slightly compared with 2023 (−3 points). It is recognized in the Top 10% S&P Global ESG Score category and first entered this index in 2017.

3.3.1 Criteria E: Environmental

It is in this area that Bankinter is weakest with lower results compared to its Spanish competitors. The transition towards a more sustainable and inclusive economy in line with the Sustainable Development Goals (SDGs) provides new windows of opportunity to offer innovative products and services which, in addition to being profitable, generate positive social and environmental impacts. Bankinter Group's strategy is based on this aspect, as evidenced by the increase in sustainable business volume with different products alongside sustainable investment funds. In addition, the entity works in line with alternative investment vehicles, green financing for housing, and financing for the improvement of energy efficiency. Bankinter has also continued to roll out its Sustainability Training Plan, which is developed through various programmes aimed at different sectors of the bank. In regard to this last point, Bankinter promoted a training course on sustainability management for its entire workforce which counted on the participation of the president and other members of the Management and Sustainability Committee.

3.3.2 Criteria S: Social

Social is the area of greatest strength for Bankinter, even outperforming Santander in its score. The management of social criteria is divided into the external and internal sphere. The bank has a strong commitment to maintaining employment and between 2012 and 2022 it organically increased its workforce in Spain by 1000. This commitment is also amplified when going beyond quantitative data and it has seen the promotion of quality employment. To this end, it has developed advanced people management programs such as those related to talent attraction and retention, family conciliation, human capital development, and health and safety.

In external social management, it is worth noting the relationship established with stakeholders such as customers to whom Bankinter seeks to provide a quality and accessible service in the physical, digital, and cognitive fields. Also noteworthy is the applying of ESG criteria to suppliers in the contracting process and the collaborating with NGOs and foundations to develop their social action strategy. Within this strategy, it is worth highlighting the management lines related to financial inclusion programs, the updating of the procedures of the Human Rights Map in its Social Action strategy and in the development of advanced people management programs that promote corporate volunteering.

3.3.3 Criteria G: Governance

Governance is the second highest rated factor for Bankinter. The sustainability policy was approved by the Board of Directors and it aims to contribute, together with the rest of the bank's internal policies, to sustainable, inclusive, and healthy development based on Bankinter's three strategic pillars: quality, innovation, and technology. Bankinter adheres to the principal international alliances on sustainability, such as the United Nations Environment Programme Finance Initiative (UNEP FI). It has also subscribed to the Principles of Responsible Banking, accepting among other things, the commitment to align its business strategy with the Sustainable Development Goals (SDGs) and the Paris Agreement. In 2021, the bank joined the Net Zero Banking Alliance sponsored by UNEPFI, with the aim of reaching net zero emissions by 2050 through the direct impact of its activities and the aligning of loan and investment portfolios to this end. The bank also established new environmental policies and regulations regarding climate change and accessibility for its stakeholders.

3.4 *CaixaBank*

CaixaBank is fourth placed among Spanish banks in the S&P Global Sustainability Yearbook 2023. It scored 80 out of 100 points which puts it level with third-placed Spanish bank Bankinter. The entity stands out in the areas of Social and Governance and Economic. Over the past 5 years, its score has varied considerably. In 2018, it achieved 79 points before going on to score higher points in 3 subsequent years: 81 points (2019), 85 points (2020), and 86 points (2021). However, in 2022, it slid six points compared to the previous year. It is recognized in the top 10% of the S&P Global ESG Score category.

3.4.1 Criteria E: Environmental

The environmental criteria is one of the lowest parameters for CaixaBank scoring just 68 points. The entity's objective is to advance in the decarbonization of its portfolio and reach net-zero emissions by 2050. It also aims to reduce the average intensity of its electricity sector loan portfolio by 30% and absolute emissions financed for the oil and gas sector by 23% by 2030. The bank has mobilized 64,000 million euros in sustainable finance and one of its main objectives is to maintain category 'A' in the synthetic sustainability indicator. One of the milestones reached in 2022 was the certification through guarantees of renewable origin of all the energy consumed by the group. CaixaBank has five buildings certified with ISO 14001, one certified with ISO 50001, and another certified under the EMAS Regulation. It also has the Environmental Quality Label across the entire Catalonian branch network. Its objective is to continue strengthening this factor and adopting a socially responsible banking model based on the sustainable and efficient management of natural resources.

3.4.2 Criteria S: Social

This is one of the two strongest areas for CaixaBank and it reaffirms its commitment to people and the senior community through the implementing of initiatives that meet customer needs. As such, it is the first entity certified by AENOR as an organization committed to the elderly. Some of its figures are: 1016 million euros in microcredits and other finance with a social impact, 1000 million euros issued in its own social bonds, and 25,000 million euros of the La Caixa Foundation aimed at social entities and channelled through its network of offices. Its main objective is to contribute to the progress and well-being of the most vulnerable groups through access to financial services, social action, and an active housing policy. This is also together with the boosting of economic activity through the promotion of investment in innovation, entrepreneurship, and the growth of microenterprises and SMEs. The social actions of the entity make up one of the central pillars of its corporate communication.

3.4.3 Criteria G: Governance

Governance is the area in which CaixaBank scored highest and it is evidenced by a corporate sustainability/ESG risk management policy. The Board of Directors is the most senior body responsible for approving the sustainability strategy and principles of action and then to oversee their implementation. CaixaBank is a voluntary member of Autocontrol, the Association for Commercial Self-Regulation, in favour of good advertising practices. Currently, 42% of female employees hold managerial positions. The entity has developed an ethical and transparent culture among its professionals through a code of ethics and integrity. In addition, based on the principles and values of this code, CaixaBank has developed a series of rules of conduct that apply to all companies in the CaixaBank Group. In line with this, they work hand in hand with suppliers who are asked to share the same ethical, social, and environmental commitment principles held by the entity.

4 Conclusions

In recent years, the relevance of sustainability has increased significantly, making the term a widely used symbol of reflection on the current socio-economic model. The pandemic crisis, the manifestation of environmental phenomena related to climate change and geopolitical conflicts, together with their impact on a globalized environment, have accelerated a process that questions the system of production in the quest for sustainable economic development.

According to the Bank of Spain in its report titled Financial Innovation for a sustainable economy, we are witnessing a "broad current dispersion of the available environmental and social ratings" (Alonso & Marqués Sevillano, 2019: 11). This is reflected in the dispersion and inequality in the results each rating offers to those brands presented for evaluation in terms of ESG.

We can identify six megatrends related to sustainability which set the criteria for estimating the principal and most recognized sustainability indices:

- Climate change.
- Pressure on limited natural resources.
- Maintenance of the planet's biodiversity and its different ecosystems.
- Inequality and human rights.
- Demography, health.
- Decision-making nuclei and governance.

The signing in 2015 of the Paris Agreement and the 2030 United Nations Agenda for Sustainable Development was the definitive impulse for public and institutional commitment by financial institutions in their respective business commitments to sustainability and ESG criteria. Socially responsible performance has a positive impact on societal perception of the organization (Stanaland et al., 2011). However, beyond these possible benefits, an effort is required on the part of the organization to align its strategies with its environment.

Currently Spain is one of the best represented countries in terms of financial entities on the S&P Global Sustainability 2023. Together with Brazil and the Republic of Korea, it is represented by four banks while Taiwan leads the ranking with seven entities. Spanish financial institutions still have some way to go to achieve the highest positions of a Top 1% S&P Global ESG Score, which is currently led by E.SUN Financial Holding Company and Ltd. and First Financial Holding Company Ltd—both Taiwanese. Hana Financial Group Inc. (Republic of Korea) occupies third place with BBVA as the highest ranked Spanish bank in fifth place.

The results analysed demonstrate the commitment and effort made by the four banking institutions and is reflected in their scores. Competitors also follow the same management policies, which is reflected in the decrease in levels of recognition in some of the parameters of the S&P Global Sustainability ranking.

The five financial institutions analysed still have considerable room for improvement in the Environmental criteria, with CaixaBank the most penalized here in its score. The Spanish regulator itself, in the Alonso and Marqués (2019: 8) report, establishes that "climate change risk management is one of the elements to which increasing attention is being paid by the authorities, economic agents and the academic world". In the environmental criterion, Spanish banks remain well outside the highest positions and until they make progress in this field, they will not overtake their main competitors in the S&P Global Sustainability.

The Governance and Economics practices of the five Spanish financial institutions highlighted in the ranking are of the highest levels and compare favourably with other large and reputable international financial institutions. Spanish banks also stand out well in the Social criteria in which they invest economic, human, and material resources to develop concrete actions. These are linked to financial inclusion, support for non-profit organizations, and contributing to the progress and well-being of groups and people. However, despite the dedication and investment, they have still proven unable to reach the maximum score in the sector nor those of their international competitors. The case of CaixaBank is even more surprising with results showing it has been unable to capitalize on the Social factor when up against its direct competitors despite significant investment having been made and the transcendence of actions carried out by La Caixa Foundation.

The work carried out by the Spanish brands BBVA and Santander in positioning their subsidiaries in this type of international indicator is significant. Currently, BBVA Peru and Santander Mexico and Chile are recognized in the Sustainability Yearbook Members section in the Banking category of the S&P Global Sustainability 2023.

ESG has become a vital aspect of the core business of any organization that wants to operate in the EU; it is no longer an option, it is an obligation. The EU has been particularly active in developing regulations and policies to facilitate the achievement of sustainability goals.

In terms of the contribution of compliance with ESG criteria to brand value, its relevance differs according to the audience involved. For both investors and shareholders it has become key to decision-making. In the management of product or service communications focused on the potential customer, it still however remains of secondary importance. They are considered pillars of communication or advertising campaigns in those markets in which the brand has an auctoritas (Baraybar-Fernández, 2022: 82), while also having a secondary, preventive, or reactive condition when facing vulnerability or any crisis scenarios that might arise. In general, they believe the consumer does not consider this information a priority when informing themselves about the product or service. Consequently, it will not significantly affect a purchase decision unless there is a scandal related to ESG that causes them to reflect on and reject the commercial proposal. This would explain why brands such as McDonald's, Nike, or Amazon are loved and desired despite having a somewhat moderate reputation in terms of sustainability and values (Brand Finance Spain, 2022: 45).

From a media and reputational point of view, banks have tried to change the way the public perceive them. They have tried to alter the view that they are strongly oriented to economic benefit and the belief that it is the way they must continue (Ruiz & del Bosque, 2012: 27). The Spanish banking sector needs to build a greater emotional bond with society and generate admiration and trust. In striving for this, one opportunity is through working and valuing their commitment and progress to ESG. As such, Spanish banking can become a reference and aspirational example for all those companies and sectors that wish to boost the reputation of the Spanish business tapestry and, consequently the Spain brand as well.

References

Alonso, A., & Marqués Sevillano, J. M. (2019). Innovación financiera para una economía sostenible. *Documentos ocasionales/Banco de España, 1916.*

Baraybar-Fernández, A. (2022). The evolution of the influence business. In J. M. Álvarez Monzoncillo (Ed.), *The dynamics of influencer marketing* (pp. 80–98). Routledge. https://doi.org/10.4324/9781003134176-6

Baraybar-Fernández, A., & Arrufat-Martín, S. (2022). Narrativas económicas. In A. Baraybar & S. Arrufat (Eds.), *Comunicación, economía y finanzas* (pp. 9–23). Fragua.

Brand Finance. (2022). *España 100 2022. Informe anual de las marcas valiosas y fuertes de España (marzo).* Accessed January 12, 2023, from https://static.brandirectory.com/reports/brand-finance-spain-100-2022-preview.pdf

Charlo Molina, M. J., & Moya Clemente, I. (2010). El comportamiento financiero de las empresas socialmente responsables. *Investigaciones Europeas de Dirección y Economía de la Empresa., 16*(2), 15–25.

Janicka, M., & Sajnóg, A. (2022). The ESG reporting of EU public companies—Does the company's capitalization matter? Sustainability, 14, 4279. https://doi.org/10.3390/su14074279

Migliorelli, M. (2021). What do we mean by sustainable finance? Assessing existing frameworks and policy risks. *Sustainability, 13*, 975. https://doi.org/10.3390/su13020975

Pagano, M. S., Sinclair, G., & Yang, T. (2018). Understanding ESG ratings and ESG indexes. In *Research handbook of finance and sustainability* (pp. 339–371). Edward Elgar Publishing.

Report of the World Commission. (1987). Accessed January 21, 2022, from https://sustainabledevelopment.un.org/content/documents/5987ourcommon-future.pdf

Ruiz, A. P., & del Bosque, I. A. R. (2012). La imagen de Responsabilidad Social Corporativa en un contexto de crisis económica: El caso del sector financiero en España. *Universia Business Review, 33*, 14–29.

Stanaland, A. J. S., Lwin, M. O., & Murphy, P. E. (2011). Consumer perceptions of the antecedents and consequences of corporate social responsibility. *Journal of Business Ethics, 102*, 47–55.

Antonio Baraybar Fernández, Full Professor of Audiovisual Communication and Advertising at the Rey Juan Carlos University. Ph.D. in Information Sciences from the Complutense University of Madrid. Member of the high-performance research group at URJC: INFOCENT. His research interests are related to Communication Economics, Communication Management in Organizations, and Neuroscience applied to Communication. He has published his studies and research in prestigious international and Spanish publishing houses, as well as in academic journals indexed in the world's leading databases. He has served as the Vice-Dean of Technology and Resources for the Faculty of Communication Sciences and as the head of the Department of Communication and Sociology Sciences at URJC. He has also been the director of the Francisco Villamartín chair (CESEDEN-URJC).

Sandro Arrufat Martín, Doctor Cum Laude in Communication Sciences from Rey Juan Carlos University (2021). Master's in Protocol, Communication, and Comprehensive Event Organization from URJC (2018) and Master's in Corporate Communication Management from EAE Business School (2017). Bachelor's in Journalism from UDIMA (2016). Currently, an associate professor at Rey Juan Carlos University, having won a competitive selection in the Department of Audiovisual Communication and Advertising. He teaches at both undergraduate and master's levels at EAE Business School, UNIR, and the Madrid Chamber of Commerce. Moreover, he is an author in journals indexed in the Arts and Humanities Citation Index (A&HCI) of Web of Science, Scopus, Emerging Sources Citation Index (ESCI), Latindex, among others. He has also published book chapters listed in the Scholarly Publishers Indicators (SPI). In addition, he has been involved in various research projects related to digital communication management and strategies, social networks, and corporate reputation. Similarly, his research areas include public relations, branding, and corporate communication.

Cristina Gonzáliez Oñate, Associate Professor in the Department of Communication Sciences at the Universitat Jaume I in Castellón. Doctorate in Business and Institutional Communication

(February 2007); Bachelor's degree in Advertising and Public Relations (June 2003); Bachelor's degree in Audiovisual Communication (June 2007); and Master's in Strategic Communication Management (June 2005) from Jaume I University. Currently, she has two six-year research periods recognized by CNEAI (2007–2012, 2013–2018), teaching both core and mandatory courses at both undergraduate and official postgraduate levels. In 2016, she received the Young Researchers Award given by Banco Santander for her research trajectory, and she also received the Teaching Excellence Award from Jaume I University. She has supervised several doctoral theses and numerous Master's and Bachelor's final projects. Her research focuses on the management of audiovisual brands from the perspective of advertising across different mediums and platforms. She also dedicates her research to digital advertising, specifically on the social influence of advertising messages across different consumer profiles as well as on the management of intangible assets of territorial brands.

Part III
Corporate Governance

Self-Regulation and Code of Conduct in the Community: Four Pilots on Utilising Decentralisation Technologies for Improving Sustainability and Collective Governance

Esko Hakanen, Joel Wolff, Ville Eloranta, and Claire Shaw

1 Introduction

Technology development has provided exciting possibilities for improving the sustainability of actions and decisions in our everyday lives. One example of such prospects is the opportunity to coordinate cooperative actions and contributions among independent actors through decentralisation technologies, such as blockchains (Lovett & Thomas, 2021; Swan, 2015). These technologies provide means to operationalise and concretise rules that define the code of conduct for community members and create incentive mechanisms to motivate self-regulation among individuals. These rules are specified in the formal protocols that lay the technological foundation of the blockchain (Berg et al., 2020; De Filippi et al., 2020). The protocol and its rules are accessible and open to anyone willing to review the smart contract or the white paper of the project.

However, while such technologies provide means to increase alignment and guide members to more collaborative actions, they are often perceived as technologically complex and challenging to comprehend (Hakanen et al., 2022; Lovett & Thomas, 2021). Instead of attracting new participants to join communities, thanks to more egalitarian and fair governance structures enabled by the decentralisation protocol (De Filippi et al., 2020; Dierksmeier & Seele, 2018), these solutions may have

E. Hakanen (✉)
Aalto University, Espoo, Finland

University of Vaasa, School of Management, Vaasa, Finland
e-mail: esko.hakanen@aalto.fi

J. Wolff · V. Eloranta · C. Shaw
Aalto University, Espoo, Finland
e-mail: joel.wolff@aalto.fi; ville.eloranta@aalto.fi; claire.shaw@aalto.fi

B. Díaz Díaz et al. (eds.), *Building Global Societies Towards an ESG World*, CSR, Sustainability, Ethics & Governance,
https://doi.org/10.1007/978-3-031-56619-6_10

the opposite effect of alienating people who are not familiar with the technology or do not feel confident exploring it (Atzori, 2015). This digital divide (Greco & Floridi, 2004) separates participants and non-participants based on their technological savviness. Consequentially, despite having the potential for empowering social movements on a global scale, decentralisation technologies and blockchains are rarely used when solving collective, practical, or social problems. This chapter addresses that deficiency and shows how novel decentralisation technology can engage community members to achieve more sustainable operations and collective benefits.

In this work, we demonstrate how decentralisation technologies can prove valuable in coordinating cooperative actions and contributions of independent actors in different contexts. We provide evidence from four practical pilot experiments that demonstrate how blockchains support highly different communities to attain social goals. First, the "Tracey" pilot illustrates how blockchains can be used for reliable catch and trade data on tuna fishing, combining data provenance and user incentivisation. Second, the pilot on "Barcelona Green Shops" uses a similar technology to encourage more sustainable shopping behaviour with the support of a similar technology. Third, "Food Futures" uses blockchains to accurately measure the environmental sustainability of our collective meal choices and enable more informed choices. Last, the "Streamr Community" pilot utilises decentralisation technology to align and motivate collective efforts toward open-source software development. A distinctive characteristic in all the pilots is the ensured approachability of the solution for the intended audience. Simplifying the technological complexity related to the underlying technological protocols requires a careful translation between the leading team and the community members they represent (Callon, 1984; Hakanen et al., 2022). However, the successes of these experiments illustrate how, when successful, the translation practices can facilitate self-regulation and a shared code of conduct for a diverse community with local and global impact.

This paper is organised as follows. Next, we shortly explicate the conceptual background of our study: digital commons and decentralisation technology, their relevance for community regulation and governance, and the translation processes behind them. The methodology section describes the ethnographical approach that provides the data for our insights. The results and discussion section presents the four pilots and their main implications in relation to past research. We conclude by highlighting the promise of decentralisation technology for a more equal, sustainable, and better-functioning society for all individuals.

2 Background

2.1 Developing and Maintaining Digital Resources Within a Community

This study focuses on a specific type of organising that relies on emerging decentralisation technologies: digital commons. It is "*a subset of the commons, where the resources are data, information, culture and knowledge which are created and/or maintained online*" (de Rosnay & Stalder, 2020, p. 2). In turn, "commons" refer to common-pool resources that are accessible to society's members, with typical examples ranging from clean air and fresh water to natural resources or stocks of ocean fish (Ostrom, 1990). Accordingly, digital commons can support more sustainable societies (Ascui et al., 2018; Lovett & Thomas, 2021) that increase the societal value created while decreasing the environmental impact. Like their physical counterparts, digital commons are affected by social connections and trust among members, who benefit from an aligned community which allows them to pursue collective goals. A "community" is a collection of people, who—in this context—rely on digital structures to provide coordinated actions among its members for collective benefits (de Rosnay & Stalder, 2020; Ostrom, 1990).

The digital commons often utilise decentralisation technology or distributed ledger technologies (DLTs), for example blockchains, to create digital tokens that account for the value created in the community and facilitate the governance of the commons through a process of tokenisation (Dal Mas et al., 2020; Hakanen et al., 2022). In its most simple form, a "digital token" refers to a concrete representation of a member's share, contribution, or achievement for a specific community that is recorded and maintained via a digital protocol. As such, digital commons build on the characteristics of digital technologies and goods, as they rely on resources that are easy and cheap to copy, distribute and combine across various instances (Birkinbine, 2018; de Rosnay & Stalder, 2020). These possibilities easily lead to benefits that grow and accrue in practically an exponential manner (Olleros, 2018).

Many communities behind the digital commons have proclaimed to be on a mission for the common good and to pursue various social values (Dierksmeier & Seele, 2018; Kleineberg & Helbing, 2016). Such an approach can attract hobbyists and open-source activists (de Rosnay & Stalder, 2020; Stalder, 2010) and investors intrigued by the ideological or social objectives (Fisch et al., 2021). To give an example of a DLT protocol-enforced digital commons, consider SolarCoin. It is a project that aims to facilitate a solar-powered planet with its cryptographic token of value for incentivising solar panel installations. The goal is to drive action to enable free, abundant solar energy to humanity (Solarcoin, 2021). Similarly, projects such as Single. Earth or Efforce look to tokenise the value created in natural carbon capture processes or when improving companies' energy efficiency, respectively. The Single. Earth project looks to bridge nature and finance and help to protect climate and biodiversity by valuing and monetising the intrinsic value of nature. They incentivise action by minting "MERIT" tokens for landowners who commit to conserving their lands, maintaining biodiversity and driving carbon sequestration. The project encourages us to consider the forests, nature, and Earth as more than just raw materials to be exploited at will. In turn, Efforce tries to shape a sustainable future for mankind by providing a possibility to fund and commit to projects that improve energy efficiency. Their protocols tokenise saved energy measured in kilowatt-hours (kWh). Efforce has introduced a decentralised platform that allows anyone to invest in energy efficiency projects worldwide, attaining profits based on realised energy savings. With the help of DLT protocols, such digital commons initiatives try to establish socio-digital capital around collective goals, promote diversity in the system to maximise innovation, and, at the same time, mitigate the risk of monopolistic control (Kleineberg & Helbing, 2016; Stalder, 2010).

Nevertheless, similar to the commons in the physical realm, digital commons exhibit social struggles over access to and command of space, territory, place, region, and resources. The members of the community face uncertainty regarding the behaviour and motives of their fellow participants in their environment (Hardin, 1968), exaggerated the anonymous or pseudonymous settings of the online environment (Fisch et al., 2021; Skågeby, 2010). Such challenges shape collective action since it may be difficult to identify actors who silently deviate from the collective frontier. This is at the heart of the tragedy of the commons, where "*the greediest herdsmen would gain–for a while*" (Hardin, 1998, p. 682) before all would be ruined. However, the reality is that it is impossible to surely know the total cost or even the direction of impact of specific actions on all the other members before the consequences have been realised. Instead of the true impact of individual actions, the members of the community require a more functional proxy for evaluating the morality and motives of the behaviour of other members. Therefore, transparent and easily understood norms and rules in the community are vital for the sustainability of the commons, in addition to setting transparent policies on how the rules are set or can be changed (Aligica & Tarko, 2012). An essential feature of any (decentralised) community, such as for digital commons, is the ability to form a collective consensus within the group. Coincidentally, the decentralisation technology also provides a means for attaining self-regulation and setting the desired code of conduct for the community.

2.2 Self-Regulation and Code of Conduct Using Decentralisation Technology

We have now suggested that modern accounting technologies can address the issues of governing the commons or forming a consensus. However, while the protocol-enforced tokenised value creation and sharing, in principle, offer means to organise around collective aims in the digital commons, the practice is often far less egalitarian (Dierksmeier & Seele, 2018). Paradoxically, the DLT protocols that were initially used to avoid monopolistic power centres and capitalistic enclosure often result in systems with high economic centralisation, to the extent of being plutocratic (De Filippi et al., 2020). Moreover, although decentralised protocols and accounting systems offer a solution to prevent freeriding and vandalism, such technologies increase institutional and technological complexity, resulting in an increased digital divide (Greco & Floridi, 2004). Not surprisingly, then, the state-of-the-art critique against protocol-enforced value tokenisation in the digital commons context is that such technologies not only replicate the problems of financial enclosure and centralisation but boost such issues by rendering the institutional structures too challenging to comprehend and regulate (e.g. Dierksmeier & Seele, 2018; Hakanen et al., 2022; Zavolokina et al., 2020).

Put differently, the decentralisation protocols rely on a sense of togetherness, social relationships, and mutual understanding that are considered difficult, even impossible, to obtain without face-to-face interaction (Aligica & Tarko, 2012; Berlant, 2016; Marshall et al., 2020; Ostrom, 2009; Skågeby, 2010). Yet, the examples such as SolarCoin, Single.Earth, and Efforce illustrate that digital commons enabled by decentralisation protocols can emerge and evolve in a setting without traditional social relationships. The traditional means of creating togetherness and trust with social interactions, communication, and personal encounters (Ostrom, 2000) are unattainable in the contexts of these projects. Digital commons can even be anonymous if made-up nicknames or randomly generated strings of letters and numbers (e.g. specifying wallet addresses in a blockchain transaction) protect the user identities. If so, the digital commons may lack personal, bonding relationships.

Instead of personal touch and relationships, decentralisation technology can provide digital commons with tailor-made accounting systems that establish governance systems, rewarding mechanisms, policy management processes, and dispute resolution systems without a centralised authority. Additionally, DLT protocols can be enforced at the community level to avoid excessive centralisation (Birkinbine, 2018; Stalder, 2010) or to prevent the risk of freeriding and vandalism (Greco & Floridi, 2004). In detail, the technological protocols define member-to-member relationships, automatically reward contributions to commons, and deterministically punish malicious actions—thereby aligning collective actions toward a joint goal (Swan, 2015). However, the resulting system must have clear structures to evade the tragedy of the commons that guide the self-regulation and code of conduct within the community (Aligica & Tarko, 2012; Ostrom, 1990). While setting these structures in the form of coded DLT protocols, one must carefully balance the diverse voices of the community members.

2.3 *Representing the Diverse Voices of a Community*

While decentralisation protocols provide the basis for digital institutions and more collective governance mechanisms, their development is highly centralised. Especially in the first stages of growing the community for digital commons, the formulation, facilitation, and interpretation of signals rely on the decisions of a small group of entities, affecting everyone in the community. Interestingly, such challenges resonate with Callon's (1984) work on the "sociology of translation". In the following, we explain the connection between these discourses.

Callon's sociology of translation focuses on the mechanisms of power and the resulting controversies over social explanations. In more practical terms, the sociology of translation explores the full range of consensual and coercive mechanisms of enrolment and disenrolment (Best & Walters, 2013). Such actions bring notable challenges to the translation process when single individuals act as the representatives of a much larger community (Callon, 1984). Paradoxically, to "*speak for others is to first silence those in whose name we speak*" (Callon, 1984, p. 216), as the aspiring leaders present the whole community's views with one voice. Moreover, a single community may have multiple overlapping, even contesting, identities (Ingram Bogusz & Morisse, 2018). Thus, an unsuccessful translation process can cause the community members to feel alienated from the group's social identity and endanger the sense of togetherness vital for the community. The sociology of translation is a process—not an outcome to be accomplished (Callon, 1984)—that can be aided by compelling narratives and other processes that reduce complexity and make the systems more approachable and understandable.

Digital commons are initially based on the vision of the leading consortium, materialised in the project's white paper and other documentation. However, while the public documentation is the primary source of information behind the supporter's participation decisions, not all the participants read and understand the documents in full detail (Fisch et al., 2021). Additionally, the actual implementation of the digital commons project may change considerably from what is described in the documentation (May, 2017), and the participants generally lack control over their resource investments and the implementation of the project (Zook & Grote, 2020). Therefore, it is conceivable that the participation decisions in this setting are considered more from an emotional point of view than the more traditional investment instruments, increasing the role of ideological motives, new financial logic, and compelling narratives behind the participation decisions (Fisch et al., 2021; Gasparro & Monk, 2020; Zook & Grote, 2020). From this perspective, the view of the leading consortium significantly shapes the digital commons.

Yet, when successful, decentralisation technology and digital commons can prove highly effective as tools for empowering a community to generate global impact. It has been suggested that the DLT protocols can "*create new foundations for our economic and social systems*" (Iansiti & Lakhani, 2017, p. 121). Accordingly, past research has noted that decentralisation technology and blockchains can lead to more sustainable and socially inclusive business models (Dal Mas et al., 2020), for instance, by helping to close material loops and increase resource efficiency throughout value chains (Rajala et al., 2018). In general, sustainable business models focus on capturing economic, social, and environmental value across various stakeholders (Bocken et al., 2014; Boons & Lüdeke-Freund, 2013). Examples involving decentralisation technology feature blockchain-based solutions increasing stakeholder involvement and transparency, eliminating middlemen, and democratising entrepreneurial investments (Dal Mas et al., 2020). More generally, decentralisation technologies can help create "ecosystem-level" business models (Eloranta et al., 2019; Hakanen, 2021) that create and align complex incentive structures by motivating collaboration among multiple parties. The most audacious initiatives present solutions that challenge our fundamental economic structures; for instance, by defining constitutional rules for the decentralised community (Berg et al., 2020) or suggesting an alternative means of accounting better suited for digital goods (Elo et al., 2023; Hakanen et al., 2023).

While connecting to the discussions above, this paper explores the potential of decentralisation technologies and the DLT-enabled decentralised protocols in aligning diverse groups of people and their collective efforts in digital commons. In addition, we address the potential of such an approach in providing a novel organisational form (Morrison et al., 2020), increasing sustainability (Lovett & Thomas, 2021), establishing a group identity (Ingram Bogusz & Morisse, 2018), and developing governance models (Zavolokina et al., 2020). The processes for establishing alignment among the members in digital commons differ significantly from conventional social mechanisms (Etzioni, 2019; Lovett & Thomas, 2021). Our insights are based on qualitative evidence from four pilot experiments using DLT protocols for collective action.

3 Methodology

3.1 Research Design

Our insights are based on the ground-breaking ATARCA project (Accounting Technologies for Anti-Rival Coordination and Allocation, https://atarca.eu), which explored decentralisation technologies to facilitate collective action. This project was funded through the European Commission's instrument on Future Emerging Technologies, which funds "*early-stage science and technology research exploring new foundations for radically new future technologies by challenging current paradigms and venturing into unknown areas*". The project challenged many of the foundational structures and institutions of our economic systems, such as the focus on the appropriability of scarce rival goods (e.g. money or natural resources). Instead, ATARCA focused on resources like knowledge, reputation, and practically any digital good. These "anti-rival" goods increase in value with use, challenging the scarcity logic of our current global economy (Elo et al., 2023; Hakanen et al., 2022; Olleros, 2018). Hence, the project signals a transformative shift in our global economy towards sustainability and collaboration. The project was considered successful, as demonstrated by multiple "Innovation Radar Prices" by the European Commission.[1] Accordingly, the pilot experiments conducted in this project were likely to provide novel insights about the implications of emerging decentralisation technologies.

The results of this study are based on four pilot pilots that exhibit the potential impact of decentralisation technologies for attaining collective goals. The pilots are

[1] Find out more at the European Commission's page for Innovation Radar Prizes: https://innovation-radar.ec.europa.eu/resultbykeyword?keyword=atarca

considered preliminary feasibility studies or pilots documenting the potential for subsequent, more extensive studies. All authors have worked on the project and have first-hand knowledge about the design, implementation, and results of the experiments. We worked closely with members from Streamr and TX, who implemented and led the Tracey pilot that preceded the ATARCA project. Before that, we have collected public material on the Streamr project and analysed its progress based on this material, starting from this effort in 2018. During the ATARCA project, we have explored the potential of decentralisation technologies in various contexts but have continuously reflected on the work conducted for the Tracey project.

3.2 Data Collection and Analysis

Our research data collection and analysis build on ethnographic observations in various forms that differed slightly between the four pilots. Since one of the pilots, Tracey (on collecting reliable fishing catch and trade data), took place prior to the primary data collection period for this research, this experiment provided us with a contrasting perspective to the three other pilots (Barcelona Green Shops, Food Futures, and Streamr Community) for which we have followed the whole process across designing, executing, and evaluating the results of the obtained experiments. Moreover, since the people leading the Tracey pilot planning have also been involved in the ATARCA project, we have been able to obtain ethnographic observations on how they have retrospectively evaluated the pilot, its results, and, in hindsight, what could or should have been done differently. The obtained data contain project meeting minutes, project-wide instant messaging (Slack business account), recorded online workshops and meetings (Zoom), and outputs created with collaborative online tools (e.g. Miro boards mapping the process on ecosystem design).

In line with the principles of ethnographic research, the authors have been personally involved with the social context being studied (Gioia & Chittipeddi, 1991). However, since the studied social fabric is largely guided by digital resources and online (or non-personal) communication, the conventional approaches to ethnographic research have required some adaptations to be fitted to such contexts (for an extended discussion, see e.g. Kozinets, 2022). Our purpose is not theory generation, per se, but rather theory elaboration (Ketokivi & Choi, 2014) with the support of the abductive analysis process (Dubois & Gadde, 2002, 2014).

While the ethnographic investigation provides an opportunity to become deeply involved in the study context and collect rich data through interviews, participant observations, and field notes, it is also adamant that the researcher(s) are able to distance themselves from the immersion to their context (Gioia & Chittipeddi, 1991). Adequate distance allows for a more objective and generalisable account of their findings and conclusions by extending from the intricacies of the study in hand (Dubois & Gadde, 2014; Ketokivi & Choi, 2014). In our work, we did not involve external researchers (as suggested by e.g. Gioia & Chittipeddi, 1991) but instead extended our ethnographic analysis with cross-case comparison and analysis, a style more commonly utilised in qualitative case research (Eisenhardt & Graebner, 2007). We found such an approach helpful in demonstrating how the observed practices deviate from the past, more predictable trajectories. The result can be a "*weak theory*" that "*observes, interprets, and yields to emerging knowledge*" with the prospect of having "*small facts speak to large concerns*" (Gibson-Graham, 2014), such as when challenging and rethinking the very foundation of our economic structures. Next, we will present the key findings of the four pilot experiments and discuss their implications in coordinating cooperative actions and contributions of independent actors in favour of more sustainable operations.

4 Results and Discussion

The four pilot cases showed promising results on the effectiveness of decentralisation technologies for improving sustainability and collective governance. All cases rely on decentralisation technology and DLT-protocols as the core foundation providing collective governance mechanisms. However, it should be noted that all cases exemplify effective translation processes in which a small group of people have taken a leading role in specifying the key issues of the represented community and shaping a decentralisation protocol (a DLT) that operationalises collective means to address those issues.

DLTs are crucial to facilitate sustainability and collective governance in all cases. They are used to set and formalise incentives for member self-regulation. In practice, the respective DLT specifies incentives for actions that are considered valuable for the community (while disincentivising actions that likely increase the identified issues of the represented community). This DLT also formalises the rules and code of conduct for all participating members. Thanks to the technological reliability of its implementation, it is practically impossible to forge records or otherwise cheat when using these DLT systems. This enables the members to reliably observe the impact on collective action that the documented actions produce for the community. The key results and insights indicate that the decentralisation protocol has a slightly different impact across cases.

The main results are summarised in Table 1. Overall, the results from the pilot case are promising and indicate that, in fact, DLTs can be effective for facilitating collective action in various use cases. Based on our findings, we argue that decentralisation technologies can foster sustainable, collective governance for a more prosperous future of partnerships, people, and the planet. In the following section, we briefly explain each pilot and discuss the obtained results and key implications.

Table 1 Summary of the cases

Pilot Case	Tracey	Barcelona Green Shops	Food Futures	Streamr Community
Purpose/aim	Provide reliable catch and trade data on tuna fishing to support wildlife conservation	Encourage more sustainable shopping and local production	Measure the environmental sustainability of individuals' meal choices	Incentivise open-source software development through non-monetary rewards
Data collection period	2018–2021 (secondary data) 10/2021–06/2022 (primary data, retrospective reflection)	10/2021–03/2023 (primary data, observations from planning to obtained results)	03/2022–03/2023 (primary data, observations from planning to obtained results)	10/2022–05/2023 (primary data, observations from planning to obtained results)
Leaders and their role	TX & Streamr employees (program lead developer), WWF (sponsor & client)	Novact (program lead), Qbit (developer), REC (promote)	Aalto/UoH (program lead and education), Unicafe (vendor), Flowa (developer)	Streamr team (program lead), Ethereum network (evaluate and facilitate)
Sociology of translation	What are the main issues of fisherfolk in rural areas and developing countries	Challenges of small business owners Unmet customer demand and shopping preferences	Climate impact of specific meal choices Interpreting the observed consumption habits and preferences of consumers	Defining the community vision Shaping the community future by choosing the contributions to endorse
Use of DLT protocol	Document catch and trade data Accumulate reliable data to monitor fish stock levels Ensure audit trail and provenance of data	Document customer choices in participating shops Facilitate knowledge sharing among shop owners	Document individual meal choices Accumulate collective consumption data Increase transparency and enable more conscious choices	Recognise and acknowledge member contributions Share merit on collective work
Set incentives for self-regulation	Rewards (micro-payment subsidies) for data inputs Create and maintain a working history record Participate in data union by pooling created data	Reward customers for making sustainable choices in shops Reward shop owners for sharing best practices (e.g. on reducing packaging waste)	Customers get to know the true impact of their daily consumption Vendors get feedback on rationale behind meal choices Gamified rewards for making better choices	Contributing members gain higher visibility for their valuable efforts Easier to align collective work Contribute to the sense of unity and togetherness among members

Table 1 (continued)

Pilot Case	Tracey	Barcelona Green Shops	Food Futures	Streamr Community
Defined rules and code of conduct	Catch and trade data must be documented with the Tracey app	Customers got rewards for participating (cf. gamification) Shop owners gain visibility and stature in their network for shared insights	Buy your lunch using the app (instead of over the counter) Sustainability data provided for each lunch option Possibility to self-report other meals consumed at remote locations	Leading team members credit contributions they see worthy Receivers can share merit with contributing members Any member can upvote contributions they see as valuable
Observed impact on collective action	Participants (fishers, traders, other stakeholders) valued the system's potential Subsidies were effective in engaging fishers	Customer participation and engagement increased over time Shop owners liked and used the system, despite not receiving subsidies or other direct rewards	App users made more sustainable meal choices than non-users People reacted positively to non-monetary incentives Vendors found the solution promising	Community members appreciated the system Members felt more motivated to contribute DLT system can increase alignment on contributions
Key results and insights	User participation relied largely on subsidies → System design could be improved	Increasing transparency on user actions motivated participation to the community	DLT systems can guide consumer behaviour with non-monetary incentives	The non-monetary incentives can be effective in guiding and attracting member contributions

4.1 Tracey: Collecting Reliable Fishing Catch and Trade Data

Tracey is a grassroots-level application that explores the use of blockchains for organising artisanal tuna fishing and trading (Marttila et al., 2019). It is a collective effort among WWF Philippines (a local branch of the World Wildlife Foundation), Union Bank (universal bank in the Philippines looking for technological innovations), and TX (a consultancy partner of Streamr, which, in turn, is a distributed open-source software project). In addition, the project engages existing fishing communities in the Lagonoy Gulf and Mindoro Strait area in the Philippines and joins them in the prospect of a blockchain-based solution for documenting and verifying the catch and trade data of tuna fishing.

Tuna fishing provides the main economic income to thousands of small-scale fishers, who often use artisanal, handline techniques for their catch. While the area provides an ideal environment for many valuable tuna species, many of the area's tuna fisheries are severely overfished (WWF Philippines, 2017). Therefore, the future of the fishers' lifestyle and livelihood has become threatened, because of disconcerting depletion rates in tuna stocks since 2000 (Llanto et al., 2018). Tracey is connected to the work conducted by the WWF-Philippines' labelled as the Fishery Improvement Project (FIP) (WWF Philippines, 2017) and provides an example of *problematisation*, in which the leading consortium characterises the represented actors and their problems (Callon, 1984).

The Tracey project gave highly promising initial results, while also some challenges. The fishers felt motivated to participate in the system, indicating that the leading team had succeeded in designing a system that addresses problems relevant for the represented community. The DLT system had implemented effective incentives for self-regulation and code of conduct rules. The fishers used the created mobile phone app to log their catch and trade data and were subsidised for data creation with micro payments. The system was found promising in enticing actions that were aligned with the project's purpose and aim. However, further examination also showed challenges that could mean the system might not be completely self-sustaining in the long run.

While the system benefitted from interlinked activities that were complementary to one another, it relied on a considerable part on subsidising the fishers for their data inputs. The original plan involved an idea of pooling data among the fishers into comprehensive data products that could be sold to subsequent users (e.g. environmental research agencies or regulation monitors) but that aspect did not proliferate as planned. Hence, the system became a reflection of a sponsor-based platform with a strong reliance on its leaders (Boumgarden et al., 2012) rather than a vibrant community among ecosystem members (Hakanen, 2021). While the system had a strong emphasis on digital commons (i.e. catch and trade data), its implementation still largely relied on monetary rewards for the participating members. Additionally, not all members were found equally motivated in changing the status quo (e.g. the "Casa", vendors buying the fish). In result, the pilot results suggest that system design could be improved to motivate and facilitate more collective governance structures that better account for the non-monetary incentives for participation (Elo et al., 2023; Hakanen, 2021).

4.2 Barcelona Green Shops: Facilitating Sustainable Shopping

The Barcelona Green Shops case focused on encouraging consumers to shop more sustainable and local products in their neighbourhood shops. Led by ATARCA project partners Novact and Qbit, the experiment focused on the identified challenges of small business owners and combined those with the unmet customer demands among residents. It connected to the REC platform (Real Economic Currency, Barcelona's social currency that complements the euro, see https://rec.barcelona). Concrete goals were set for improving sustainable and responsible conduct among shop owners, for example, by reducing plastic packaging waste with the products sold and to help consumers choose products that are better for them and the environment.

The DLT system was designed to document consumer choices in participating shops and to facilitate the sharing of best practices among shop owners. It rewarded customers for making "better" consumer choices and shop owners for sharing their knowledge with their peers. The system provided visibility and stature benefits to more active shop owners or other members who gave valuable community contributions.

The initial results of the experiment were encouraging. The quantitative evidence showed that the use of DLTs had a positive effect on customer engagement. In addition, the shop owners considered the system valuable, despite its inability to provide them with direct monetary benefits. Hence, the system showed the effectiveness of non-monetary rewards as motivating factors for guiding user behaviour (cf. gamification, see Deterding, 2012). Based on our findings, we argue that the increased transparency of actions conducted by the community members helped to increase motivation for value-creating activities. These results suggest that, indeed, digital commons can greatly benefit from accounting solutions that widely acknowledge non-monetary transactions and interactions (cf. Elo et al., 2023; Hakanen et al., 2023).

4.3 Food Futures: Measuring the Impact of Our Meal Choices

Food Futures was a pilot designed as a feasibility study to see if individuals' diets can be affected by providing them with more transparent and accurate data on the sustainability impact of their meal choices. The pilot was led and designed by researchers from Aalto University and the University of Helsinki, and conducted in collaboration with a Finnish vendor focused on university student lunches, Unicafe, and an external software developer (Flowa). To address the overall aim, the project spent considerable effort establishing reliable criteria for evaluating the overall impact of each meal option on various criteria, including water usage, CO_2 emissions, animal welfare, etc. This stage involved translating the problems to address and resulted in an *interessement* and *enrolment* device (the DLT system) that stabilised and consolidated the relationship and identity of stakeholders and actors through a shared intermediary platform while defining roles and coordinating actions among them (Callon, 1984).

The Food Futures DLT system was utilised to document individual meal choices, accumulate collective consumption data, and increase the transparency behind different options. With these factors, the system generated clear incentives for user self-regulation toward common goals. In essence, the system generated gamified rewards for making better choices that facilitated subsequent benefits: The consumers got to know the true impact of their daily consumption habits while the vendors got detailed feedback on the rationale behind individuals' meal choices. These benefits were enabled by the DLT system rules, which encouraged consumers to use the app to buy their meals by having the additional benefit of accruing historical data on past choices. The system-generated lunch meal data collection was complemented with the option to add user-generated data on other meals consumed throughout the day by a self-reporting function. This combination of data sources provided a more comprehensive account from which to infer the participants' habits and preferences.

Overall, we found that the app users made more sustainable meal choices than the non-users in the same lunch venue. This indicates that the DLT system and the non-monetary rewards in place can, in fact, incentivise members of the digital commons to favour more ethical options (Etzioni, 2018) or engage in collective action for the betterment of the environment (Ostrom, 2000). Following the pilot, other vendors have found the system promising for supporting causes not motivated strictly by economic rationale. For instance, it has been suggested that such systems could help fast-food restaurants entice consumers to choose more plant-based options. Thus, the DLT systems offer non-monetary incentives which can effectively guide consumer behaviour.

4.4 Streamr Community: Aligning Digital Commons for Open-Source Software

Last, the Streamr Community case was focused on creating non-monetary incentive structures to encourage open-source software development. Like any leading team shaping responsible open-source development and the growth of digital commons, the key problem for Streamr is to concretely and accurately define a vision for the future that attracts a wide group of followers that feel united by a joint goal and a shared identity (Ingram Bogusz & Morisse, 2018), defined by problematisation and interessement (Callon, 1984). For this purpose, Streamr developed a DLT system that complements the existing Ethereum network (Hakanen et al., 2023). The goal is to help Streamr define and test their vision for the community's future.

The DLT system enables recognising and acknowledging member contributions (through tokens awarded by Streamr) and allows the token recipients to share the merit of their contributions with other participating members. In addition, other community members can shape the community's future by endorsing contributions. This system has clear incentives for self-regulation: Contributing members get visibility on their valuable efforts, Streamr gets wide support for aligning future work, while all members giving endorsements of other inputs benefit from the sense of unity and togetherness of such a collective governance system. The code of conduct and rules of enrolment (Callon, 1984) follow a similar logic as Streamr credits contributions that they see worthy but with a transparent system that enables sharing the merit collectively with other contributors, who might not have been otherwise recognised by the leading team. Moreover, since any member can upvote practically any contribution, the system is well-suited for mapping the community's collective vision with a decentralisation technology.

The results of this experiment were highly encouraging. The community members appreciated the system as it increased their motivation to participate. In addition, by increasing transparency between collaborators on past work and future demands, the DLT system can greatly improve the alignment of member contributions for the digital commons. The non-monetary incentives and the attribution of tokens were found to be effective in guiding and attracting member contributions by creating signals about an individual's skills, knowledge, and efforts in service to the community (Ingram Bogusz & Morisse, 2018).

5 Implications for Theory and Practice

From a theoretical point of view, the ATARCA pilot experiments demonstrated the effectiveness of the DLT protocols for supporting different causes. However, the translation process must accurately define the problems addressed with the solution and how the DLT protocol can help in resolving them (Callon, 1984). All pilots demonstrated such designs by supporting self-regulation and a code of conduct guided by non-monetary incentives. Our findings corroborated the arguments that blockchains can facilitate more sustainable economic foundations for future businesses (Iansiti & Lakhani, 2017). In addition, the experiments demonstrated that increasing transparency can be essential in attracting community members for collective action. Our findings indicated that DLT protocols add tools for gamification and for creating more engaging, supportive, and satisfying systems (Deterding, 2012).

Our results connect to multiple discussions. First, our findings elaborate the discourse on the digital commons (de Rosnay & Stalder, 2020; Stalder, 2010) and illustrate how they can facilitate more sustainable behaviour within a community and its members (Dal Mas et al., 2020; Lovett & Thomas, 2021; Mindel et al., 2018). Second, despite the lack of traditional, social relationships in developing a consensus and social norms (Ostrom, 2000), our results demonstrated that the decentralisation technology can, indeed, prevent the tragedy of commons through structures that guide the self-regulation and code of conduct among the community members (Aligica & Tarko, 2012; Ostrom, 1990). Third, while the decentralisation technologies for solving a community's collective action problem are often formalised via complicated technical solutions, coded by actors external to the community being helped (Callon, 1984), we found that a careful translation of the implemented technology and its problem-solving potential can lead to more sustainable and socially inclusive behaviour (Dal Mas et al., 2020; Iansiti & Lakhani, 2017).

In particular, our findings elaborate theory on Callon's work on sociology of translation (1984). All cases utilised an intricate DLT protocol to coordinate collective action for digital commons but were able to provide a simple and intuitive solution for the members. Thus, these simplified user interfaces provided devices of *interessement* and *enrolment* between the members of the community and the digital commons (Callon, 1984). For interessement, they defined and stabilised clear roles and identities for the members, whether they relate to catching or trading fish, enabling a more sustainable shopping experience, monitoring individual meal choices and their collective impact, recognising and rewarding member contributions, or practically any activity that support the digital commons. Simultaneously, the DLT protocols established the role of the leading team as an invaluable member of the whole network (Ascui et al., 2018; Callon, 1984). The mechanisms for self-regulation and code of conduct set in the DLT had an important role in enrolment by coordinating the members' actions. They enabled the enforcement of rules, persuaded members with concrete incentives, handled transactions securely, and ensured that participation was always consensual (Ostrom, 2000). In addition, all cases utilised narratives and digital storytelling to support the *mobilisation* phase of the translation (Callon, 1984). The narratives helped to build a positive reputation for the project, growing the legitimacy of the solution and forming a group identity within the community (Ingram Bogusz & Morisse, 2018; Marshall et al., 2020) and, subsequently, establishing a sustainable decentralised collective (Mindel et al., 2018).

From a practical point of view, our insights highlighted the potential of decentralisation technology in fostering a more sustainable community guided by more collective governance. As our findings and the considerations above illustrate, the DLT can engage community members more actively toward joint targets. Our suggestions to anyone considering their application are as follows:

1. *Invest in stakeholder analysis*. Understanding the problem at hand requires considerable effort to hear and learn from the voices of the represented community members. Clearly define the *mission to be solved*.
2. *Analyse the interactions and incentives*. Consider how the community's mission could be translated into concrete actions, interactions, and even strategic interactions among the members. The more detailed the better.
3. *Attract and engage stakeholders*. As "decentralised" implies, such a structure is not a centralised structure with a focal orchestrator. The designed system should represent and work for the community, not its original creator.

6 Conclusion

> The moral values of a society are not self-enforcing. They rely on two very different modes of engendering compliance. One is informal social controls, which draw on people's quest for approval and acceptance by others, on peer pressure, and voices of clergy and secular moral leaders. The other draws on the state's means of coercion (Etzioni, 2018, p. 4).

As the quote above from Amitai Etzioni succinctly illustrates, the moral values of a society (or a community) cannot be taken for granted, but require constant efforts to maintain. Decentralisation technology, such as blockchains, provide interesting possibilities to support self-regulation and codes of conduct for various collectives through formal DLT protocols (Berg et al., 2020; De Filippi et al., 2020). Hence, DLT protocols can provide new mechanisms for safeguarding the society's moral values. They can foster sustainable, collective governance to facilitate more prosperous collaboration for the good of the society, the environment, and the planet.

Hence, the set incentives for self-regulation and code of conduct in the studied cases were considerably more guided to support the psychological processes of self-efficacy, group identity, and social approval (Hakanen et al., 2022; Ingram Bogusz & Morisse, 2018). We found the evidence particularly promising for suggesting how the developed DLT protocols enabled complex incentive structures that motivated collaboration among multiple parties. All cases provided evidence for the notion that decentralisation technology can support more equal and sustainable digital institutions to solve complex practical problems (de Rosnay & Stalder, 2020; Lovett & Thomas, 2021; Mindel et al., 2018). Hence, we argue that the decentralisation technology, such as alternative accounting mechanisms aimed for facilitating the creation and sharing of digital goods (Elo et al., 2023; Hakanen et al., 2023), provide the basis for developing more equal, inclusive, and sustainable business models (Eloranta et al., 2019; Hakanen, 2021) with global impact.

References

Aligica, P. D., & Tarko, V. (2012). Polycentricity: From Polanyi to Ostrom, and beyond. *Governance, 25*(2), 237–262. https://doi.org/10.1111/j.1468-0491.2011.01550.x

Ascui, F., Haward, M., & Lovell, H. (2018). Salmon, sensors, and translation: The agency of big data in environmental governance. *Environment and Planning D: Society and Space, 36*(5), 905–925. https://doi.org/10.1177/0263775818766892

Atzori, M. (2015). Blockchain technology and decentralized governance: Is the state still necessary? Available at SSRN 2709713, 1–37.

Berg, A., Berg, C., & Novak, M. (2020). Blockchains and constitutional catallaxy. *Constitutional Political Economy, 31*(2), 188–204. https://doi.org/10.1007/s10602-020-09303-9

Berlant, L. (2016). The commons: Infrastructures for troubling times*. *Environment and Planning D: Society and Space, 34*(3), 393–419. https://doi.org/10.1177/0263775816645989

Best, J., & Walters, W. (2013). Translating the sociology of translation. *International Political Sociology, 7*(3), 345–349. https://doi.org/10.1111/ips.12026_5

Birkinbine, B. J. (2018). Commons praxis: Towards a critical political economy of the digital commons. *TripleC, 16*(1), 290–305. https://doi.org/10.31269/triplec.v16i1.929

Bocken, N. M. P., Short, S. W., Rana, P., & Evans, S. (2014). A literature and practice review to develop sustainable business model archetypes. *Journal of Cleaner Production, 65*, 42–56. https://doi.org/10.1016/j.jclepro.2013.11.039

Boons, F., & Lüdeke-Freund, F. (2013). Business models for sustainable innovation: State-of-the-art and steps towards a research agenda. *Journal of Cleaner Production, 45*, 9–19. https://doi.org/10.1016/j.jclepro.2012.07.007

Boumgarden, P., Nickerson, J., & Zenger, T. R. (2012). Sailing into the wind: Exploring the relationships among ambidexterity, vacillation, and organizational performance. *Academy of Management Journal, 33*, 587–610. https://doi.org/10.1002/smj

Callon, M. (1984). Some elements of a sociology of translation: Domestication of the scallops and the fishermen of Saint-Brieuc Bay. *The Sociological Review, 32*(S1), 196–233. https://doi.org/10.22394/0869-5377-2017-2-49-90

Dal Mas, F., Massaro, M., Verde, J. M., & Cobianchi, L. (2020). Can the blockchain lead to new sustainable business models? *Journal of Business Models, 8*(2), 31–38. https://doi.org/10.5278/ojs.jbm.v8i2.3825
De Filippi, P., Mannan, M., & Reijers, W. (2020). Blockchain as a confidence machine: The problem of trust & challenges of governance. *Technology in Society, 62*, 101284. https://doi.org/10.1016/j.techsoc.2020.101284
de Rosnay, M. D., & Stalder, F. (2020). Digital commons. *Internet Policy Review, 9*(4), 1–22. https://doi.org/10.14763/2020.4.1530
Deterding, S. (2012). Gamification: Designing for motivation. *Interactions, 19*(4), 14–17. https://doi.org/10.1145/2212877.2212883
Dierksmeier, C., & Seele, P. (2018). Cryptocurrencies and business ethics. *Journal of Business Ethics, 152*(1), 1–14. https://doi.org/10.1007/s10551-016-3298-0
Dubois, A., & Gadde, L. (2002). Systematic combining: An abductive approach to case research. *Journal of Business Research, 55*, 553–560. https://doi.org/10.1016/S0148-2963(00)00195-8
Dubois, A., & Gadde, L.-E. (2014). 'Systematic combining'–A decade later. *Journal of Business Research, 67*(6), 1277–1284. https://doi.org/10.1016/j.jbusres.2013.03.036
Eisenhardt, K. M., & Graebner, M. E. (2007). Theory building from cases: Opportunities and challenges. *Academy of Management Journal, 50*(1), 25–32.
Elo, T. M., Marttila, J., Cutillas, S., & Hakanen, E. (2023, July). Elements of antirival accounting with sNFT. *International Conference on Computational Science*.
Eloranta, V., Hakanen, E., Töytäri, P., & Turunen, T. (2019). Aligning multilateral value creation and value capture in ecosystem-level business models. *Academy of Management Proceedings., 2019*, 18966.
Etzioni, A. (2018). Apple: Good business, poor citizen? *Journal of Business Ethics, 151*, 1–11. https://doi.org/10.1007/s10551-016-3233-4
Etzioni, A. (2019). Cyber trust. *Journal of Business Ethics, 156*, 1–13. https://doi.org/10.1007/s10551-017-3627-y
Fisch, C., Masiak, C., Vismara, S., & Block, J. (2021). Motives and profiles of ICO investors. *Journal of Business Research, 125*, 564–576. https://doi.org/10.1016/j.jbusres.2019.07.036
Gasparro, K., & Monk, A. (2020). Demystifying "localness" of infrastructure assets: Crowdfunders as local intermediaries for global investors. *Environment and Planning A: Economy and Space, 52*(5), 878–897. https://doi.org/10.1177/0308518X19887181
Gibson-Graham, J. K. (2014). Rethinking the economy with thick description and weak theory. *Current Anthropology, 55*(S9), S147–S153. https://doi.org/10.1086/676646
Gioia, D. A., & Chittipeddi, K. (1991). Sensemaking and sensegiving in strategic change initiation. *Strategic Management Journal, 12*(6), 433–448.
Greco, G. M., & Floridi, L. (2004). The tragedy of the digital commons. *Ethics and Information Technology, 6*(2), 73–81. https://doi.org/10.1007/s10676-004-2895-2
Hakanen, E. (2021). What is a business model—For products, platforms, or ecosystems? *Journal of Business Models, 9*(4), 1–12.
Hakanen, E., Eloranta, V., & Shaw, C. (2022). Forming digital commons: The role of signaling and sociology of translation in decentralized systems. *Academy of Management Proceedings, 2022*, 11067.
Hakanen, E., Eloranta, V., Marttila, J., & Amadae, S. M. (2023). Digital protocols as accounting and incentivization mechanisms in anti-rival systems—Developing a shareable non-fungible token (sNFT). In T. Seppälä, T. Mucha, & J. Marttila (Eds.), *The fifth wave*. BRIE-ETLA Collection of Articles.
Hardin, G. (1968). The tragedy of the commons. *Science, 162*, 1243–1248.
Hardin, G. (1998). Extensions of the tragedy of the commons. *Science, 280*(5364), 682–683.
Iansiti, M., & Lakhani, K. R. (2017). The truth about blockchain. *Harvard Business Review, 95*(1), 119–127. https://doi.org/10.1016/j.annals.2005.11.001

Ingram Bogusz, C., & Morisse, M. (2018). How infrastructures anchor open entrepreneurship: The case of bitcoin and stigma. *Information Systems Journal, 28*(6), 1176–1212. https://doi.org/10.1111/isj.12204
Ketokivi, M., & Choi, T. (2014). Renaissance of case research as a scientific method. *Journal of Operations Management, 32*(5), 232–240. https://doi.org/10.1016/j.jom.2014.03.004
Kleineberg, K.-K., & Helbing, D. (2016). A 'social bitcoin' could sustain a democratic digital world. *SSRN Electronic Journal, 1–7*. https://doi.org/10.2139/ssrn.2771326
Kozinets, R. V. (2022). Immersive netnography: A novel method for service experience research in virtual reality, augmented reality and metaverse contexts. *Journal of Service Management, 34*, 100. https://doi.org/10.1108/JOSM-12-2021-0481
Llanto, G. M., Ortiz, M. K. P., & Madriaga, C. A. D. (2018). The Philippines' tuna industry. In J. Gross & P. Intal Jr. (Eds.), *Reducing unnecessary regulatory burdens in ASEAN: Country studies* (pp. 210–238). ERIA.
Lovett, M., & Thomas, L. (2021). A fork in the road: Perspectives on sustainability and decentralised governance in digital institutions. *First Monday, 26*(11).
Marshall, D. J., Staeheli, L. A., & Čelebičić, V. (2020). Why are "we" called "them"?: Storytelling and the contested terrain of post-conflict public formation. *Environment and Planning D: Society and Space, 38*(2), 306–324. https://doi.org/10.1177/0263775819852124
Marttila, J., Nousiainen, M., Sheppard, B., Malka, M., & Karjalainen, R. (2019). *Tracey—Your traceability and trade data companion* (pp. 1–52). TX.
May, R. (2017). *Scrap the white paper: How to evaluate tokens and blockchains*. CoinDesk. https://www.coindesk.com/scrap-white-paper-evaluate-tokens-blockchains
Mindel, V., Mathiassen, L., & Rai, A. (2018). The sustainability of polycentric information commons. *MIS Quarterly, 42*(2), 607–631. https://doi.org/10.25300/MISQ/2018/14015
Morrison, R., Mazey, N. C. H. L., & Wingreen, S. C. (2020). The DAO controversy: The case for a new species of corporate governance? *Frontiers in Blockchain, 3*(25). https://doi.org/10.3389/fbloc.2020.00025
Olleros, F. X. (2018). Antirival goods, network effects and the sharing economy. *First Monday, 23*(2).
Ostrom, E. (1990). Governing the commons. In J. E. Alt & D. C. North (Eds.). Cambridge University Press.
Ostrom, E. (2000). Collective action and the evolution of social norms. *Journal of Economic Perspectives, 14*(3), 137–158. https://doi.org/10.1080/19390459.2014.935173
Ostrom, E. (2009). Beyond markets and states: Polycentric governance of complex economic systems, Prize lecture, December 8, 2009. *The Nobel Prizes*, 408–444.
Rajala, R., Hakanen, E., Seppälä, T., Mattila, J., & Westerlund, M. (2018). How do intelligent goods shape closed-loop systems? *California Management Review, 60*(3), 20–44. https://doi.org/10.1177/0008125618759685
Skågeby, J. (2010). Gift-giving as a conceptual framework: Framing social behavior in online networks. *Journal of Information Technology, 25*(2), 170–177. https://doi.org/10.1057/jit.2010.5
Solarcoin. (2021). *SolarCoin is a cryptocurrency that incentivizes a solar-powered planet*.
Stalder, F. (2010). Digital commons. In K. Hart, J.-L. Laville, & A. D. Cattani (Eds.), *The human economy* (pp. 313–324). Polity Press. https://doi.org/10.1017/cbo9780511707964.019
Swan, M. (2015). *Blockchain–Blueprint for a New Economy*. O'Reilly Media.
WWF Philippines. (2017). *Partnership program towards sustainable tuna*. https://wwf.org.ph/what-we-do/food/pptst/
Zavolokina, L., Ziolkowski, R., Bauer, I., & Schwabe, G. (2020). Management, governance, and value creation in a blockchain consortium. *MIS Quarterly Executive, 19*(1), 1–17. https://doi.org/10.17705/2msqe.00022
Zook, M., & Grote, M. H. (2020). Initial coin offerings: Linking technology and financialization. *Environment and Planning A, 52*(8), 1560–1582. https://doi.org/10.1177/0308518X20954440

Esko Hakanen is a postdoctoral researcher in the areas of digitalization, platforms, and ecosystems. He is employed by two Finnish institutions: Aalto University and University of Vaasa. His work builds on an interdisciplinary background that combines operations management with contextual knowledge of the manufacturing industry and is particularly interested in elaborating how emerging technological practices map against the theoretical models in the academic literature. In addition to his research activities, he has had various organizational responsibilities. He served as the Project Manager of the H2020-funded ATARCA project, which explored the means for a more efficient digital economy by leveraging the prospect of anti-rivalry (i.e., replicability and value amplifying properties) of digital goods. He is the Research Manager for his research group on Service Engineering and Management. He has also acted as the Academic Coordinator for the Department of Industrial Engineering and Management at Aalto University.

Joel Wolff, MA in Arts and Design, is a doctoral candidate at Aalto University School of Science's Department of Industrial Engineering and Management. His research focuses on business ecosystems, particularly their potential to foster sustainable innovation, with a special emphasis on stakeholder dynamics. His broader research interests encompass sustainability transformation, socio-technical systems, and transdisciplinary innovation, with a particular emphasis on mobility services and cross-sectoral collaboration. Wolff is a representative member of the MaaS Alliance, reflecting his research involvement in Mobility as a Service. His background in strategic service design and sustainability studies equips him with co-creative design skills to facilitate sense-making and strategic development in complex environments. Wolff applied these skills as a Coordinator for the recent EU-funded interdisciplinary innovation project, ATARCA.

Ville Eloranta is a Senior University Lecturer who possesses a broad academic and industry background. In education, he leads Aalto's interdisciplinary IDBM flagship master's program, focusing on leadership for creativity. In research, he investigates business ecosystems, digital commons, and platform business models. Dr. Eloranta has led several big EU projects as Principal Investigator.

Claire Shaw is a doctoral student in organization and management at Aalto University, Finland. Her research focuses on the relationship between decentralized technologies and values. She has a background in education and education research, specifically focused on developing contexts.

Empowering Change: Female External Directors and the Evolution of Corporate Governance in Japan

Naoe Imura

1 Introduction

This research aims to explore the integration of diversity within corporate governance in Japan, contextualized by international practices and norms of corporate governance. The spotlight is on female external directors. Whitley (1999) and Guillen (2000) have established that corporate governance systems are institutionalized nationally. Countries such as the United States and the United Kingdom are characterized by shareholder-oriented systems, in contrast to the stakeholder-oriented approaches of Japan and Germany (Fiss & Zajac, 2004; Ahmadjian & Robbins, 2005; Imura, 2017; Hirano, 2020). The discourse on national trends in corporate governance systems pivots around two dimensions: the robustness of market-oriented factors in capital markets and the solidity of employee relations within the labor market (Akaoka, 2013; Hirano, 2020). Up until the 1980s, Japanese corporations were lauded for their stakeholder orientation and strong employee relations, juxtaposed with weaker market-oriented facets. Nevertheless, the late 1990s saw a pivot towards the Anglo-American management model, characterized by a shareholder orientation and diminished employee relations—a shift that also influenced the restructuring of intermediary relationships within Japanese corporations. Yet, the adaptability of Japanese labor practices to swift transitions was limited, necessitating a reinvigoration of employee relations post-2010 (Akaoka, 2013). Parallel shifts were observed in German management systems. In both scenarios, the impetus to align with global shifts, inclusive of corporate governance alterations in capital markets, was palpable. Nonetheless, domestic labor markets were challenged by rapid transitions, culminating in a renewed emphasis on fortifying worker

N. Imura (✉)
Nagoya Institute of Technology, Nagoya, Japan
e-mail: imura.naoe@nitech.ac.jp

B. Díaz Díaz et al. (eds.), *Building Global Societies Towards an ESG World*, CSR, Sustainability, Ethics & Governance,
https://doi.org/10.1007/978-3-031-56619-6_11

relations. The focus on worker relations bears significant pertinence to the dynamics of female labor in Japan. While a direct causative link between the acceptance of diversity as a heterogeneous entity and corporate performance is not explicitly established, numerous studies have identified associative correlations.

Globally, the structural frameworks and norms of corporate governance are increasingly acknowledging the pivotal role of boards of directors—not solely on the principles of equity but also on their critical influence in decision-making and the enhancement of corporate performance. This global inclination, however, reveals a disparity in the proportion of women serving as independent directors, a variance that is pronounced across nations. Since the inception of the Corporate Governance Code in 2015, corporate governance within Japanese enterprises, particularly large corporations, has undergone considerable transformations. Nonetheless, the proportion of female external directors continues to trail behind that of Western corporations. Thus, an in-depth examination of the Japanese context is imperative to discern the prospective opportunities and impediments for amplifying gender diversity on the boards of Japanese firms.

The architecture of national-level management systems is sculpted by both formal and informal institutions (North, 1990; Aguilera & Jackson, 2003). Institutions are malleable, subject to the introduction of novel practices by predominant actors or through exerted pressures. In recent times, investors with a predilection for environmental, social, and governance (ESG) criteria have assumed a salient role, underscoring corporate accountability on societal matters such as gender inequality. Various countries have adopted non-mandatory guidelines on board diversity or instituted gender quota systems with a degree of enforceability. Predominant Western institutional investors wield considerable sway over the corporate governance practices and institutions of numerous countries. These investors are proponents of the Anglo-American paradigm, which accentuates agency relations (Geng et al., 2016) and are propelling Japanese firms to refurbish their corporate governance practices in alignment with the fluid 'global' standards. The amalgamation of external pressure and intrinsic organizational traits unveils the diversity in corporate responses to institutional transformations. In response to such external impetus, Japanese and German corporations have been and continue to be prompted to transition towards a market-oriented management framework.

This investigation delves into the evolving challenges and transformations of corporate governance among Japanese corporations, framed by the backdrop of international corporate governance practices and diversity norms. By probing the relatively uncharted territory of female external directors in Japan, this study aspires to incite policy and pragmatic reforms, fostering further research and the amelioration of gender representation, thereby augmenting the echelons of corporate governance within Japan.

2 Theoretical Background

2.1 Agency Theory and Stakeholder Theory in Corporate Governance

The agency theory has been a cornerstone in corporate governance scholarship, illuminating the contractual dynamics within firms. Jensen and Meckling's (1976) foundational work defines the agency relationship as a contract where principals employ agents to perform services on their behalf, acknowledging the potential for agents to act against the principals' interests if it benefits them (p. 308). This framework resonates within corporate structures where directors (principals) rely on managers (agents) to execute company strategies.

Conversely, Japan exemplifies a stakeholder-oriented governance model, markedly distinct from the shareholder-focused models of the United States and the United Kingdom. (Aoki et al., 2007; Jacoby, 2018). This model integrates a spectrum of stakeholder interests into corporate decision-making, diverging from the shareholder primacy observed in US governance (Jacoby, 2018).

Freeman (2010) describes stakeholder theory as a web of complex relationships between groups vested in a firm's operations. It posits that a business' core lies in the value generated by interactions among customers, suppliers, employees, financiers, communities, and managers (p. 7). Fernández-Gago et al. (2016) extend this to include a multilateral relation among all stakeholders, broadening the purview beyond the dyadic agency relationship.

The dichotomy between the Anglo-American and Japanese systems manifests in both market orientation and corporate relationships with employees and directors. The former is characterized by short-term stock financing, dispersed ownership, robust shareholder rights, active markets for capital control, and flexible labor markets, emphasizing shareholders, stock prices, stock repurchases, and mergers (Aguilera & Jackson, 2010). In contrast, Japan's system features corporate ownership by banks, cross-shareholdings, lifetime employment, and internal director promotions (Jackson & Miyajima, 2007). However, this system has faced criticism for impeding corporate performance, prompting a reevaluation of employment and labor relations (Akaoka, 2013).

Historically, Japan's employment structure has revolved around lifelong employment and seniority-based promotions. Companies valuing collective ethos and employee loyalty function akin to community firms, with senior management prioritizing the company's long-term health and employee welfare (Inagaki & Whittaker, 2005; Dore, 2004). Yet, this framework has perpetuated gender disparities, with women often relegated to supportive roles, exacerbating workplace inequality (Inagaki & Whittaker, 2005; Nemoto, 2016). Nemoto (2022) further examines gender bias in Japanese corporate culture. The Japanese stakeholder model's treatment of employees includes comprehensive training, economic downturn protection, and a focus on human capital equivalent to financial equity. An internal promotional structure is central, with seniority-based compensation and hierarchical promotions leading to lengthy average job tenures and making mid-career recruitment rare (Jacoby, 2018; Sarra & Nakaghigashi, 2002; Gilson & Milhaupt, 2005; Shishido, 2000; Aoki et al., 2007). The board of directors often emerges as the pinnacle of this internal progression ethos.

2.2 Female (Outside) Directors and Firm Performance

A critical aspect of the discourse on female directors is the influence they wield on corporate governance performance. Adams and Ferreira (2009) examined the role of women in boardrooms and identified that boards with female representation tend to have better attendance records and are more vigilant in CEO monitoring. Additionally, they found a positive correlation between the number of female directors and firm value, particularly in firms with less stringent governance.

Campbell and Mínguez-Vera (2008) also explored the link between gender diversity on the board and firm financial performance, establishing a positive association between the two. Terjesen et al. (2016) supported these findings in a multi-country study, which provided evidence that gender-diverse boards contribute positively to firm performance.

The topic of gender diversity in the boardroom and its impact on firm performance is a central focus in corporate governance studies. Researchers exploring the effectiveness of diversity in different countries have generally found a positive effect of female directors on firm performance. Lückerath-Rovers (2013) conducted studies in the Netherlands, Reguera-Alvarado et al. (2017) in Spain, Salloum et al. (2017) in France, Torchia et al. (2011) in Italy, and Elstad and Ladegard (2012) in Norway. Positive effects were also observed in India by Das (2019) and in Turkey by Kılıç and Kuzey (2016).

Further, female directors influence corporate decision-making and innovation. Terjesen et al. (2009) posited that women directors could enhance market understanding, noting the significant proportion of women in the consumer base. In China, board gender diversity positively affected corporate innovation, as measured by various patent applications (Ain et al., 2022).

However, this relationship can be influenced by national business cultures and practices. Studies in Asia by Chua et al. (2018) found a negative association between board gender diversity and firm performance in Malaysia. Ren and Zeng (2022) suggested that gender diversity could decelerate internationalization speed, varying with the characteristics of female directors. In Italy, female CEOs had a negative association with the number of female directors, which may reflect cultural impediments to female inclusiveness in corporate governance (Galavotti & D'Este, 2023).

The influence of female directors varies under different conditions. Mogbogu (2016) found a negative impact of female directors in US technology firms. Conversely, during the Great Recession in the United States, female directors had a positive impact (Papangkorn et al., 2019). Radulovic et al. (2019) reported positive effects on market performance but negative impacts on micro-enterprises in India.

Conyon and Lerong (2017) observed that female presence on boards positively affected firm performance, with a more substantial effect in high-performing firms. Ciavarella (2017) found no overall impact of board diversity on firm performance in EU (European Union) countries; however, more female and foreign executive directors correlated with positive outcomes. Nur and Darvin (2023) highlighted that female directors significantly mitigated negative impacts on firm profitability during the pandemic in Indonesia.

In summary, literature generally supports the positive role of female directors in corporate governance, correlating with better governance, performance, financial results, and enhanced decision-making. As the conversation on gender equality advances globally, the role of female directors becomes increasingly relevant in developing effective corporate governance practices.

Nonetheless, the impact of government-mandated gender diversity on boards has also been scrutinized. Ahern and Dittmar (2012) found that such mandates caused a significant short-term drop in firm value, indicating that abrupt changes in board composition might disrupt existing corporate governance dynamics.

3 Changes in Japanese Corporate Governance and Diversity of Boards of Directors

3.1 Changes of the Independent Director Issues in the Japanese Corporate Governance Code

The Japanese Corporate Governance Code, introduced as a corrective measure against corporate misconduct and to fill the transparency void in Japan, was aimed at aligning the nation's corporate governance with international standards, thereby improving transparency, accountability, and performance.

Pre-2015, Japan's corporate governance faced criticism for favoring insiders over shareholders, marked by inadequate oversight and weak boards. The administration under Prime Minister Shinzo Abe recognized these issues, initiating reforms as part of the economic strategy known as "Abenomics," with corporate governance reform being a pivotal element.

The 2015 Code advocates for the appointment of at least two independent directors and adopts a "comply or explain" approach, mandating companies to adhere to the code or disclose reasons for non-compliance (Council of Experts Concerning the Follow-up of Japan's Stewardship Code and Japan's Corporate Governance Code, 2015). The 2018 revision accentuated the enhancement of corporate governance for long-term corporate value and stakeholder engagement (Council of Experts Concerning the Follow-up of Japan's Stewardship Code and Japan's Corporate Governance Code, 2018).

Subsequent amendments in 2018 built upon these principles, introducing significant changes aimed at reinforcing governance (Council of Experts Concerning the

Follow-up of Japan's Stewardship Code and Japan's Corporate Governance Code, 2018). While 'outside director' and 'independent director' are terms commonly interchanged in the United States, the 2015 Code delineated a clear distinction. An outside director, as per the definition, does not hold specific roles such as executive director within the company or its subsidiaries (Tokyo Stock Exchange, 2018, p. 11). An independent director, however, is an outside director who meets additional criteria ensuring no conflict of interest with shareholders (Tokyo Stock Exchange, 2018, p. 21). Hence, the number of external directors in Japanese corporate governance is, by definition, equal to or greater than that of independent directors.

The revisions in June 2021 further underscored the effective use of independent external directors and set forth prerequisites for the efficacy of both the Board of Directors and the Board of Corporate Auditors (Council of Experts Concerning the Follow-up of Japan's Stewardship Code and Japan's Corporate Governance Code, 2021). With the Tokyo Stock Exchange's reorganization in April 2022 into three market segments, the Prime Market now requires advanced governance, specifically targeting large corporations.

The oversight responsibilities of the board have expanded beyond enhancing the board's supervisory function to also include the qualitative and quantitative augmentation of external directors. These directors play a critical role in oversight, addressing societal shifts such as sustainability. However, simply increasing the number of external directors does not suffice. There is an exigent need for corporations to promote diversity among these directors and to seek candidates capable of addressing supervisory issues, posing an urgent challenge for corporate management.

3.2 Comparison with United States and United Kingdom

Understanding the nuances of corporate governance on a global scale, this research delves into the board composition of American corporations (S&P100), British corporations (FTSE100), and Japanese corporations (TOPIX100). The analysis by Yamada (Yamada, 2022a, 2022b) utilizes the agency theory to explain the practices in the United States and United Kingdom, whereas the stakeholder theory elucidates the Japanese approach.

In American and British corporations, the board structure excludes the appointment of statutory auditors, a practice seen in Japanese companies with nominations committees. Instead, these Western companies opt for a unitary system with established committees, such as audit committees (see Table 1). Typically, boards comprise approximately 11–12 directors, with only 1–2 being executive directors and the remainder serving as non-executive external directors, thus endorsing a monitoring model that concentrates on executive oversight. Operational execution is delegated to a management team led by the CEO and inclusive of various CxOs. In the United States, it is common for the CEO to double as the Chairman, with a Lead Independent Director appointed to synchronize the activities of external directors.

Table 1 Board of Directors in United States, United Kingdom, and Japan

	United States (S&P 100)	United Kingdom (FTSE 100)	Japan (TOPIX 100)
Companies	100	100	100
Board of directors	11.8	10.3	11
External directors	10.2	8.1	5.3
Board of directors + auditors	n.a.	n.a.	13.7
Total external directors	n.a.	n.a.	6.9
Female directors ratio	32.5%	38.5%	16.1%
(Female external directors ratio)	36.1%	45.1%	29.5%
Ave. age (external)	62.5 (62.9)	59.8 (60.9)	63.8 (65.9)
Ave. length of tenure (external)	7.7 (7.3)	4.4 (3.9)	5.0 (3.3)
Concurrent positions other than in-h	1.2	1.1	1.1

Source: Yamada (2022a, 2022b)

British companies appoint an external director as Chair, ensuring neutrality in execution and oversight, and similarly to the United States, a Senior Director is elected to organize the external directors.

The contrast in corporate governance structures between Japanese companies and those in the United States and United Kingdom is most apparent in the appointment of external directors. US and UK firms tend to appoint a greater number of external directors, aiming for a diverse and comprehensive oversight of intricate operational landscapes. These companies also feature a higher count of advisory committees within their boards.

Both the United States and United Kingdom are actively pursuing board diversity, considering various attributes such as race, nationality, gender, age, tenure, and skills. It is particularly noted that the ratio of female directors is significantly higher in these countries compared to Japan, where women occupy 16.1% of director roles.

Regarding the directors' age, Japanese board members tend to be older than their US and UK counterparts, with a notably higher average age among Japanese external directors as compared to those in the United Kingdom. Japan also holds the highest proportion of directors aged 61 and above.

Tenure among directors also varies by country. UK firms show the shortest average director tenure, whereas US companies exhibit longer tenures, which may be attributed to their board structure and the operation of multiple committees. In Japan, directors have an average tenure of 5 years, but for external directors, the tenure is only 3.3 years, reflecting the impact of recent governance reforms.

4 Challenges in Japanese Corporate Governance and Responses to Change

4.1 The Current State of Japanese Companies

Post-implementation of the Corporate Governance Code in 2015 and its revisions, the Financial Services Agency, alongside the stock exchanges, has been instrumental in enhancing the diversity and transparency among Japanese corporations. This endeavor is aimed at bolstering the global competitiveness of Japanese firms. This chapter scrutinizes the status of female (external) directors in Japanese companies, confronts the challenges, and debates the responses of Japanese stakeholders to these challenges, thereby assessing the effectiveness of the Corporate Governance Code and contemplating prospective challenges.

The non-coercive establishment of the Corporate Governance Code, which embraces the "comply or explain" principle, has significantly influenced Japanese corporations. The changes post the 2015 introduction of the Code are examined here, drawing on information from the Financial Services Agency, corporate securities reports, quarterly board member reports, and a survey of TOPIX 100 companies by Yamada (2022a, 2022b).

There has been a noticeable uptick in the number of female directors since the Code's introduction, with the 2018 revision—which underscored the necessity of diversity—acting as a catalyst. Disclosure of policies and objectives concerning the elevation of women to managerial roles has contributed to this progression. The rise

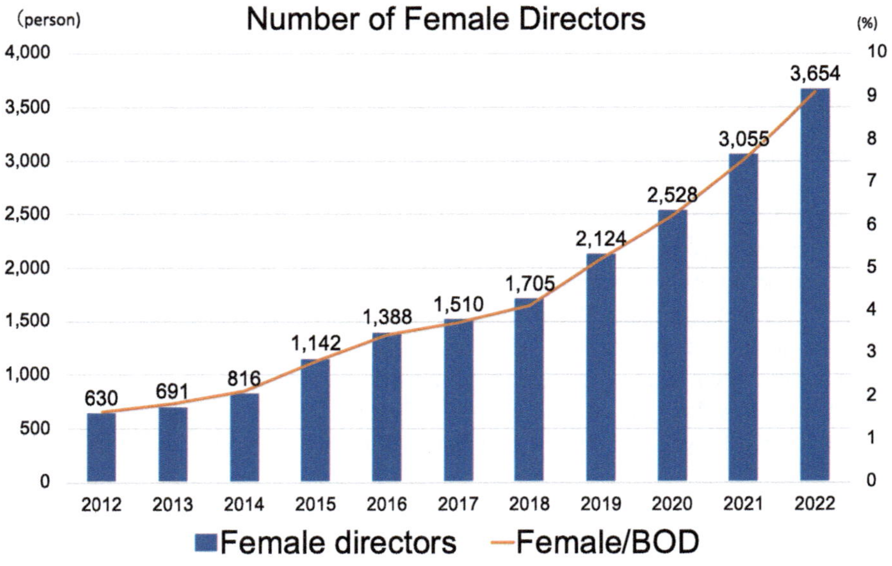

Fig. 1 Female directors in listed companies. Source: Quarterly Report of the Board of Directors, 2023

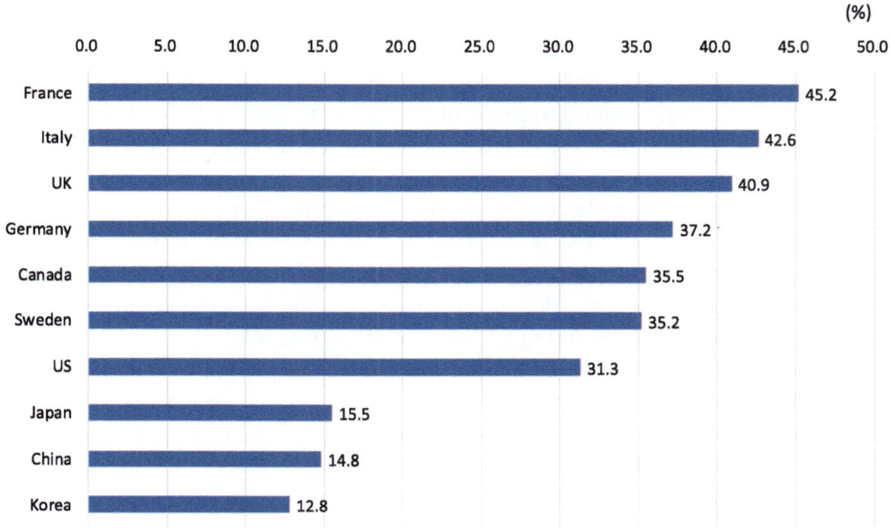

Fig. 2 Female directors in major countries. Source: OECD Social and Welfare Statistics, 2022

in female director numbers, as well as their proportion, affirms the Code's success in one of its aims: increasing female directorship (see Fig. 1). Nevertheless, when compared to Western nations like France, Italy, and the United Kingdom, where female external directorship exceeds 30%, Japan lags with a mere 15.5% in 2022 (see Fig. 2). Moreover, the efficacy of the board's monitoring function is contingent upon a majority of external directors. The 2021 revision mandates that prime-listed companies appoint external directors to make up at least one-third of the board. The proportion of external directors in TOPIX 100 companies has since surpassed this threshold, reaching 36.7% in the 2019 survey and escalating to 48.2% in 2022, nearing a majority (Yamada, 2022a, 2022b). Over 87% of companies listed in the JPX Nikkei 400 now meet this requirement, indicating that the reinforcement of the Corporate Governance Code has fostered an increase in external directors among leading corporations. However, the trend is predominant among companies adopting the Anglo-American board structure, such as those with committees. In contrast, firms with statutory auditors—a hallmark of the traditional Japanese governance system—remain behind in both the proportion of external directors and the number of companies with a majority of external directors. The primary difference lies in the orientation; the former is monitoring-focused, while the latter is management-focused (Yamada, 2022a, 2022b). More than half of the companies still opt for the statutory auditor system, suggesting that a transition to a monitoring-focused board will take time.

The board composition is evolving, with an emphasis on the appointment of women and international directors. Yet, the ratio of female directors stands at 16.1% and that of foreign directors at 7.6%, which, despite showing an increase from the 2021 survey, still indicates a predominance of female and foreign appointments in external director roles (Yamada, 2022a, 2022b). Since the enactment of the Equal Employment Opportunity Law for Men and Women in 1986, there has been ample time to cultivate internal female director candidates. The dearth of such candidates might stem from inadequate development aligned with the requisite skills matrix, suggesting that internal promotion and nurturing of female officers within Japanese companies are wanting.

For Japanese firms, traditionally uniform in composition, acclimating to the inclusion of heterogeneous female external directors is essential for harnessing the benefits of diversity. Incorporating diversity-conscious external directors is in line with the Corporate Governance Code's recommended skills matrix and bolsters the quality of directorship, reinforcing corporate market principles.

The prevalence of women holding multiple directorships signifies a high demand for female external directors and a limited pool of qualified candidates, with some occupying positions in more than four companies. Although the percentage of female external directors is on the rise, it remains at a meager 10%. Despite the steady increase since the Code's inception, Japan still trails other nations in female director representation.

For a long-term enhancement of women in directorial roles, companies must embrace strategic initiatives spanning immediate actions and sustained efforts. Short-term solutions include appointing female external directors to rectify gender imbalances. However, establishing a continuous flow of qualified female leaders necessitates a long-term commitment to developing and promoting internal talent, ensuring a gradual ascension of women to roles of internal directorship and statutory auditors. Such comprehensive strategies address not only the immediate diversity needs but also lay a sustainable foundation for gender parity in corporate leadership.

In the broader scheme, incremental diversification from external to internal directors reflects a strategic adaptation to Japan's corporate realities, fostering a diverse governance framework. This progression mirrors the changing ethos in Japanese business, where inclusive governance is increasingly valued. By systematically integrating these principles, Japanese corporations can methodically redress gender disparities, setting the stage for a governance model that not only meets modern standards of corporate responsibility but is also primed for the global market's evolving demands for diversity and inclusion.

4.2 Business Environmental Changes in Japan

As mentioned, the increase in the introduction of female external directors in Japan is a result of the functioning Corporate Governance Code. However, the shortage of female external director candidates is a serious issue due to the lack of cultivation of skilled and experienced female executive candidates by Japanese corporate practices and culture. In response, the Cabinet Office has implemented a female executive candidate training program annually in 2–3 locations nationwide since 2017 and created a database of candidates who completed the program. Higher education institutions such as Kyoto University, Waseda University, Kwansei Gakuin University, Kyoto Women's University, Showa Women's University, and Fukuoka Women's University, as well as corporations like Nikkei BP, have launched numerous female executive candidate training programs. The development of female executive candidates and the completion of databases reflect a rising awareness and eagerness for reskilling in society, with many companies and organizations engaging in the training of executive candidates. However, many training programs for executive candidates remain limited to individual applications. Considering the need for Japanese companies to undergo a change in mindset and the importance of corporate cultures that foster internal development, it becomes essential to promote training either through corporate sponsorship or internally within the companies.

If this awareness has emerged following the introduction of the Corporate Governance Code, it is speculated that it may take about 10 years to cultivate executive candidates from the internal labor market. As such, while the shareholder market principle aspect tolerates Anglo-Saxon corporate governance, on the personnel and labor market aspect, strengthening the relationship with workers represents one of the future management systems toward which Japanese companies are heading. Akaoka (2013) has pointed this out as the "Omega" management system concept.

Embracing the shareholder market principle, the Code has set a trajectory towards an "Omega" management system, as delineated by Akaoka (2013), which underscores the importance of reinforcing worker relations in future Japanese management structures. While the integration of Anglo-Saxon governance principles is acknowledged, it does not diminish the significance of cultivating a robust worker relationship.

The discourse on diversity in Japanese corporations is longstanding, extending back to the enactment of the Equal Employment Opportunity Law for Men and Women in 1986. Scholars such as Taniguchi (2011), Sato and Takeishi (2017), and Sato et al. (2022) have consistently explored this theme. Historically, research predominantly focused on enhancing the work environment, framed within the labor logic context. The recent pivot towards diversifying corporate governance reflects a shift to capital logic discussions. However, these facets are interconnected; the amplification of labor logic invariably fosters a more diverse and sustainable capital logic framework, underscoring the multifaceted nature of corporate governance evolution in Japan.

Acknowledgement This research is funded by the JSPS Scientific Research Grants 17H02571.

References

Adams, R. B., & Ferreira, D. (2009). Women in the boardroom and their impact on governance and performance. *Journal of Financial Economics, 94*(2), 291–309.

Aguilera, R. V., & Jackson, G. (2003). The cross-national diversity of corporate governance: Dimensions and determinants. *Academy of Management Review, 28*, 447–465.

Aguilera, R. V., & Jackson, G. (2010). Comparative and international corporate governance. *The Academy of Management Annals, 4*(1), 485–556.

Ahern, K. R., & Dittmar, A. K. (2012). The changing of the boards: The impact on firm valuation of mandated female board representation. *The Quarterly Journal of Economics, 127*(1), 137–197.

Ahmadjian, C. L., & Robbins, G. E. (2005). A clash of capitalisms: Foreign shareholders and corporate restructuring in 1990s, Japan. *American Sociological Review, 70*, 451–471.

Ain, Q. U., Yuan, X., & Javaid, H. M. (2022). The impact of board gender diversity and foreign institutional investors on firm innovation: Evidence from China. *European Journal of Innovation Management, 25*(3), 813–837.

Akaoka, I. (2013). Strategies and organizational relationships of Japanese companies—organizational set strategy. In N. Kanbayashi (Ed.), *The transformation of Japanese-style management: The advancement of global market principles (6th chapter, pp. 125–141)*. Chuo Keizai Sha.

Aoki, M., Jackson, G., & Miyajima, H. (Eds.). (2007). *Corporate governance in Japan: Institutional change and organizational diversity*. Oxford University Press on Demand.

Campbell, K., & Mínguez-Vera, A. (2008). Gender diversity in the boardroom and firm financial performance. *Journal of Business Ethics, 83*(3), 435–451.

Chua, M. S., Razak, A., Hisyam, N., Ali, S., & Bin, A.. (2018). The Impact of Board of Directors' Characteristics and Remuneration on Companies' Performance in Malaysia (December 9, 2018). *Indian Journal of Public Health Research and Development*, Available at SSRN: https://ssrn.com/abstract=3317189

Ciavarella, A., Board Diversity and Firm Performance Across Europe (December 7, 2017). *CONSOB Working Papers* No. 85, Available at SSRN: https://ssrn.com/abstract=3084114 or https://doi.org/10.2139/ssrn.3084114.

Conyon, M., & Lerong, H. (2017). Firm performance and boardroom gender diversity: A quantile regression approach. *Journal of Business Research, 79*, 198–211. https://doi.org/10.1016/j.jbusres.2017.02.006

Council of Experts Concerning the Follow-up of Japan's Stewardship Code and Japan's Corporate Governance Code. (2015). Japan's Corporate Governance Code [Original edition]. Financial Services Agency.

Council of Experts Concerning the Follow-up of Japan's Stewardship Code and Japan's Corporate Governance Code. (2018). Japan's Corporate Governance Code [Revised edition]. Financial Services Agency.

Council of Experts Concerning the Follow-up of Japan's Stewardship Code and Japan's Corporate Governance Code. (2021). Japan's Corporate Governance Code [Revised edition]. Financial Services Agency.

Das, P. K. (2019). Impact of women directors on corporate financial performance–Indian context. *American Journal of Humanities and Social Sciences Research, 3*(2), 29–36.

Dore, R. (2004), "Innovation for whom? Institute for technology, enterprise and competitiveness", Research Paper 04-01, Doshisha University.

Elstad, B., & Ladegard, G. (2012). Women on corporate boards: Key influencers or tokens? *Journal of Management & Governance, 16*(4), 595–615.

Fernández-Gago, R., Cabeza-García, L., & Nieto, M. (2016). Corporate social responsibility, board of directors, and firm performance: An analysis of their relationships. *Review of Managerial Science, 10*(1), 85–104.

Fiss, P. C., & Zajac, E. J. (2004). The diffusion of ideas over contested terrain: The (non) adoption of a shareholder value orientation among German firms. *Administrative Science Quarterly, 49*, 501–534.

Freeman, R. E. (2010). Managing for stakeholders: Trade-offs or value creation. *Journal of Business Ethics, 96*(1), 7–9.

Galavotti, I., & D'Este, C. (2023). Female CEO and board composition: A gender rivalry approach to family firms. *Corporate Board Role Duties and Composition, 19*(1), 8–19.
Geng, X., Yoshikawa, T., & Colpan, A. M. (2016). Leveraging foreign institutional logic in the adoption of stock option pay among Japanese firms. *Strategic Management Journal, 37*, 1472–1492.
Gilson, R. J., & Milhaupt, C. J. (2005). Choice as regulatory reform: The case of Japanese corporate governance. *The American Journal of Comparative Law, 53*(2), 343–377.
Guillen, M. (2000). Corporate governance and globalization: Is there convergence across countries? *Advances in International Comparative Management, 13*, 175–204.
Hirano, T. (2020). Transition of the German management system and Omega management. *Hiroshima Prefectural University Faculty of Business and Information System, 13*, 65–75.
Imura, N. (2017). Changes in the Japanese management system in core industries and the relationship with strategy and business performance: An analysis from the omega management model. *Information Management*, 133–136.
Inagaki, T., & Whittaker, D. H. (2005). *The new community firm: Employment, governance and management reform in Japan*. Cambridge University Press.
Jackson, G., & Miyajima, H. (2007). Introduction: The diversity and change of corporate governance in Japan. Corporate governance in Japan: Institutional change and organizational diversity, (pp. 1–47).
Jacoby, S. M. (2018). *The embedded corporation: Corporate governance and employment relations in Japan and the United States*. Princeton University Press.
Jensen, M. C., & Meckling, W. H. (1976). Theory of the firm: Managerial behavior, agency costs and ownership structure. *Journal of Financial Economics, 3*(4), 305–360.
Kılıç, M., & Kuzey, C. (2016). The effect of board gender diversity on firm performance: Evidence from Turkey. *Gender in Management: An International Journal, 31*(7), 434–455.
Lückerath-Rovers, M. (2013). Women on boards and firm performance. *Journal of Management & Governance, 17*(2), 491–509.
Mogbogu, O. (2016). *Women on the Board of Directors and their impact on the financial performance of a firm: An empirical investigation of female directors in the United States Technology Sector* [Illinois State University].
Nemoto, K. (2016). *Too few women at the top: The persistence of inequality in Japan*. IRL Press Book/Cornell University Press.
Nemoto, K. (2022). Revisiting Japan's stakeholder-based system and foreign ownership: IR managers' view of foreign shareholders in corporate governance reform in Japanese companies. *Corporate Governance: The International Journal of Business in Society, 23*(3), 534–562.
North, D. (1990). *Institutions, institutional change and economic performance*. Cambridge University Press.
Nur, T., & Darvin, Q. (2023). Gender diversity and firm profitability, before and during the Covid-19 pandemic. 2023 international conference on cyber management and engineering (CyMaEn), (pp. 408–412).
Papangkorn, S., Chatjuthamard, P., Jiraporn, P., & Chueykamhang, S. (2019). The effect of female directors on firm performance: Evidence from the great recession. *SSRN Electronic Journal*.
Radulovic, B., Bhaskarabhatla, A. S., & Wang, Z. (2019). Women on board and the impact on financial firm performance-A case study in India. MSc. Economics and Business-Industry, Dynamics and Strategy Master Thesis.
Reguera-Alvarado, N., de Fuentes, P., & Laffarga, J. (2017). Does board gender diversity influence financial performance? Evidence from Spain. *Journal of Business Ethics, 141*(2), 337–350.
Ren, G., & Zeng, P. (2022). Board gender diversity and firms' internationalization speed: The role of female directors' characteristics. *Baltic Journal of Management, 17*(1), 72–88.
Salloum, C., Azoury, N., El Khoury, R., & Sleiaty, F. (2017). Female representation on boards of directors: A study of financial performance and risk in the French market. *European Management Journal, 35*(3), 367–376.

Sarra, J., & Nakaghigashi, M. (2002). Balancing social and corporate culture in the global economy: The evolution of Japanese corporate structure and norms. *Law & Policy, 24*(4), 299–354.
Sato, H., & Takeishi, E. (2017). *Diversity management and talent utilization: Corporate efforts to support diverse work styles*. University of Tokyo Press.
Sato, H., Takeishi, E., & Sakazume, Y. (2022). *Management of diverse talents*. Chuo Keizai Sha.
Shishido, Z. (2000). Japanese corporate governance: The hidden problems of corporate law and their solution. *Delaware Journal of Corporate Law, 25*, 189.
Taniguchi, M. (2011). *Diversity management: Organizations that leverage diversity*. Hakuto-Shobo Publishing.
Terjesen, S., Couto, E. B., & Francisco, P. M. (2016). Does the presence of independent and female directors impact firm performance? A multi-country study of board diversity. *Journal of Corporate Finance, 41*, 183–204.
Terjesen, S., Sealy, R., & Singh, V. (2009). Women directors on corporate boards: A review and research agenda. *Corporate Governance: An International Review, 17*(3), 320–337.
Tokyo Stock Exchange. (2018). *Japan's corporate governance code* [revised edition]. Japan Exchange Group. https://www.jpx.co.jp/english/news/1020/20210611-01.html.
Torchia, M., Calabrò, A., & Huse, M. (2011). Women directors on corporate boards: From tokenism to critical mass. *Journal of Business Ethics, 102*(2), 299–317.
Whitley, R. D. (1999). *Divergent capitalisms: The social structuring and change of business systems*. Oxford University Press.
Yamada, E. (2022a). Reading trends in corporate governance reform (part 1) impact of TSE reorganization and revision of corporate governance code, Japan Research Institute https://www.jri.co.jp/column/opinion/detail/13871/.
Yamada, E. (2022b). Reading trends in corporate governance reform (part 2): Analysis of board structure and director skills in three countries: Japan, the U.S., and the U.K., Japan Research Institute https://www.jri.co.jp/page.jsp?id=104157.

Naoe Imura is a Professor at the Graduate School of Engineering, Nagoya Institute of Technology. She completed her doctoral program in economics at the Graduate School of Economics, Kyoto University, and holds a Ph.D. in Economics. Since 2023, she has been teaching Management of Technology (MOT) at the Graduate School of Engineering, Nagoya Institute of Technology. Her research interests include strategies in the design industry, corporate innovation, and management systems.

Part IV
Global Perspectives and Cases

Third Sector's Corporate Social Responsibility: In Portuguese Law

João de Sousa Assis

1 Introduction to CSR

Not-for-profit organisations (furthermore referred as "NFPs") are often regarded as organisations whose main purpose is to pursue relevant interests which must not be connected with the pursue of profit for their members and stakeholders. On the contrary, NFPs are perceived as organisations pursuing the public interest, or the interest of the community at large.[1]

In other words, NFPs are perceived, in opposition to for-profit organisations, as players in the pursue of the general interest, either directly, or through the pursuit of the interest of its members, users, and/or its beneficiaries. For-profit organisations, such as companies, are often connected to the concept of 'firm' or 'enterprise' (which signifies any economic activity developed by the entrepreneur in a professional and organised fashion towards the distribution of what was produced or the exchange of goods or services[2]), while NFPs are associated with charity and pursue of the public good.[3]

[1] As stated under article 2 of the Portuguese Basic Law on Social Economy, enacted by Law n. 30/2013, of 8 May.

[2] Following the definition of business organisation as an "activity" by Pupo Correia, M., 'Direito Comercial', Ediforum and Almedina Editora (14 ed. 2018), 43.

[3] For more see Assis, J., 'Responsabilidade Social e organizações sem fins lucrativos—uma reflexão legal', *in* Estudos em Homenagem ao Professor Doutor Manuel Pita, Almedina (2022), 287.

J. de Sousa Assis (✉)
Lisbon Accounting and Business School, Polytechnic University of Lisbon, Lisbon, Portugal
e-mail: jpassis@iscal.ipl.pt

B. Díaz Díaz et al. (eds.), *Building Global Societies Towards an ESG World*, CSR, Sustainability, Ethics & Governance,
https://doi.org/10.1007/978-3-031-56619-6_12

Different ways to perceive the action of these organisations also lead to different legal approaches to the rules guiding their action, and the duties imposed to those who decide how NFPs use their resources or even interact with the communities that surround them. A perceived difference in regulation exists, where the law imposes (sometimes) heavy duties on directors of companies and other for-profit organisations but abstains itself from regulating NFP's decision makers.

Rules and regulations exist, in order to regulate how directors of for-profit organisations use the company's assets, or are meant to impose duties of conduct, guiding directors of for-profit organisations on their decision making process, in order to protect company itself, its shareholders, and other stakeholders such as employees or creditors, by imposing duties of care and loyalty to those who decide.[4] This does not happen with NFP's decision makers in Portugal—organisations where these internal proceedings are often often not regulated, by the law.

1.1 CSR Evolution

Corporate Social Responsibility (furthermore referred to as "CSR") is often regarded as a frame of ethical/moral practices guiding the way how for-profit organisations conduct their business,[5] while in the pursuit of profit.[6] However, there are opposing views in the literature as to whether CSR comprises an actual set of moral rules, which should or must be followed.[7]

For example, Idowu states that CSR "overlaps with other concepts such as corporate citizenship, sustainable business, environmental responsibility, the triple bottom line, social and environmental accountability, business ethics, and corporate accountability",[8] while other authors disagree with this approach, by disassociating CSR with a 'moral' or 'ethical' approach, and by connecting CSR with the way

[4] As an example, under the UK Companies Act 2006, directors hold the duty to act within powers; the duty to promote the success of the company; the duty to exercise independent judgment; the duty to exercise reasonable care, skill and diligence; the duty to avoid conflicts of interest; the duty not to accept benefits from third parties; the duty to declare interest in proposed transaction or arrangement; among others. Similar provisions may be found, for example, under article 64.° of the Portuguese Companies Code, where directors (or other managers) must observe duties of care and loyalty towards the company and other stakeholders such as its workers, customers, and creditors.

[5] Argandoña & Hoivik (2009), Bainbridge (2008), Banerjee (2014), Berle & Means (1991), Blair (1995), Clark (2007).

[6] Assis (2022).

[7] González (2017), Idowu (2009), Kroszner & Putterman (2009), Littler (2008), McWilliams & Siegel (2001), Meira (2013), Orlitzky (2015), Rahim (2013), Silberhorn & Warren (2007), Thorne et al. (2014), Tricker (2009), Van Marrewijk (2003).

[8] Idowu, S., 'The United Kingdom of Great Britain and Northern Ireland', *in:* Idowu, S., Filho, W. (Eds.), Global Practices of Corporate Social Responsibility. Springer Berlin Heidelberg (2009), 14.

companies organise themselves in the long-run, establishing practices that enable them to actively pursuit their mission in their community.[9]

One thing is sure, CSR and how it is perceived has evolved over time, allowing for it to encompass multiple definitions.[10] Several CSR models have been developed, following different objectives, such as pursuing primarily the interest of those who own the capital, pursuing the interest of the community at large, or a combination of both. But one thing is clear, CSR is intertwined with corporate governance—the mechanism designed to control the means of production of an organisation.[11]

But this control over an organisation which dwells in the market is complex, and it may pursuit different interests.[12] In a simplified fashion, it is possible to identify two relevant corporate governance models: the (1) the principal–agent model, and (2) stakeholder theory; but others exist as well.

Under the principal-agent model, the interests of the shareholders (as owners of the capital) are to be protected because a "shareholder is the only corporate participant with the residual, unfixed, ex post claim on corporate investment and future return, and therefore plays an important role in corporate governance".[13] It is perceived that this model may lead to a practice where the interests of stakeholders who are not the shareolders are disregarded.[14]

Under the stakeholder theory, not only the interests of those who own the capital are taken into consideration, on the contrary, the interests of employees, creditors, or suppliers are deemed relevant. Under this model, directors should actively work on the reputation of the organisation, protecting other stakeholder's interests such as the employees' right to a work-life balance, fair salaries, as well as reducing as

---

[9] See authors such as Silberhorn, D., Warren, R.,'Defining Corporate Social Responsibility: a view from big companies in Germany and the UK', Eur. Bus. Rev. 19 (2007), 352–372; or Van Marrewijk, M., 'Concepts and Definitions of CSR and Corporate Sustainability: Between Agency and Communion', J. Bus. Ethics 44 (2003), 95–105, who connect CSR with corporate social performance, encompassing voluntary for-profit organisations' activities which are guided by social and environmental concerns when interacting with their stakeholders.

[10] As examples see Wood, D. J., 'Corporate Social Performance Revisited', *in* Academy of Management Review (1991), Vol16, 4, 691–718; Visser, W., 'Corporate Social Responsibility in Developing Countries', *in* The Oxford Handbook of Corporate Social Responsibility, Oxford University Press (2008), 473–502; Villers, C., 'Corporate Reporting and Company Law', *in* Cambridge Studies in Corporate Law, Vol 5, Cambridge University Press (2006); Tricker, B., 'Corporate Governance-Principles, Policies and Practices', Oxford University Press (2009); McWilliams, A., Siegel, D., 'Corporate Social Responsibility: A Theory of the Firm Perspective', Academy of Management Review (2001), Vol 26, 1, 117–127; among others.

[11] Kroszner, R. S. and Putterman, L., 'The Economic Nature of the Firm: A Reader', 3rd Edition, (ed.), originally published 1986, Cambridge University Press (2009), 7–9.

[12] Clark, T., 'Cycles of Governance', *in* International Corporate Governance: A Comparative Approach, Routledge (2007), 1–3.

[13] Bainbridge, S. M., The New Corporate Governance in Theory and Practice, Oxford University Press (2008), 49–51.

[14] Berle, A. A. and Means, C. G., 'The Legal Position of "Control"', The Modern Corporation and Private Property, originally published in 1932, Transaction Publishers (1991), Book II, Chapter VI, 235–239.

much as possible the negative footprint of the organisation in the environment. Under Tricker's words, under this model "the success of a corporation is judged on the motivation of employees, the close relationship with customers, maintaining good relations with suppliers and even the positive reputation of the corporation in the community".[15]

It should be noted that some authors believe that CSR should be a tool used by organisations to address social problems, in other words, a tool that should be used by the organisations to achieve 'social good'.[16] This idea is often pursued by authors who connect CSR with the idea of philanthropic action, where the organisation is expected to conduct activities outside of the organisation's core social objective[17] in the pursuit of moral (or ethic) responsibilities. For this reason, it is therefore possible to find, in the relevant literature, CSR defined as a "set of moral duties towards other social actors and towards society that the firm assumes".[18]

1.2 CSR in a For-Profit Context

A vast portion of literature on CSR focuses on the eventual contributions of companies and other for-profit/business organisations to improve the lives of its stakeholders or even the community they are based, by contributing to the 'common good'.[19] But this perspective is starting to shift, through the writings of new thinkers, who criticise this approach, by regarding the current relation between CSR and the law as unsuitable "to address complex social and environmental issues" and the "limited business accountability; and business rhetoric on giving back" that may be found in legal provisions regulating the action of decision makers.[20]

This connection between CSR and for-profit organisations may even be further criticised considering the reason why for-profit organisations exist in the first place. In fact, their core objective holds values that are objectively different from values pursued by not-for-profit organisations, or even the idea of 'common good'.[21] For

[15] Tricker, B., Corporate Governance: Principles, Policies and Practices, Oxford University Press (2009), 230.

[16] Orlitzky, M., 'The Politics of Corporate Social Responsibility or: Why Milton Friedman Has Been Right All Along', Ann. Soc. Responsibility, 1 (2015), 5–29.

[17] Halme, M., Laurila, J., 'Philanthropy, Integration or Innovation? Exploring the Financial and Societal Outcomes of Different Types of Corporate Responsibility', J. Bus. Ethics 84 (2009), 325–339.

[18] Argandoña, A., Hoivik, H., 'Corporate Social Responsibility: One Size Does Not Fit All. Collecting Evidence from Europe', J. Bus. Ethics 89 (2009), 221–234.

[19] Van Marrewijk (2003), Visser (2008), Wood (1991).

[20] González, R. (2017), 'Corporate social responsibility and brand value in luxury. Not published. Available at http://theses.gla.ac.uk/8159/, assessed 31/05/2023, 65.

[21] Thorne, L., Mahoney, L.S., Manetti, G., 'Motivations for Issuing Standalone CSR Reports: A Survey of Canadian Firms', Audit. Account. J. 27 (2014), 686–714.

example, a company that produces apples may wish to wash and polish the apples before selling them, in order to make them more appealing, and by doing so, increase the price (and profit margin); on the contrary, some communities based in dry countries consider water a valuable and scarce asset, which must be used with restraint.

It should be noted that some authors also refer that business organisations 'should or need to give back' to the communities which support them a portion of the profits they generate. As an example, Litter refers that these statements on how business organisations should give back to their communities are based in the assumption that they are taking something away, and consequently should return the favour, almost as if consideration is required or expected[22] from them. But this is only one of the justifications to why the decision-making process should follow a certain direction or path in for-profit organisations.

In order to better understand what is expected from those who decide how to use the resources commanded by these organisations, it is necessary to understand if coercive measures are in place to conform and even direct the decision-making process towards one specific goal. To shed light on these rules and regulations, when applicable to NFPs, Portuguese Law will be used as a case study to better understand how CSR is regulated under the law, in what NFP organisations are or should be concerned about.

2 CSR and Not-For-Profit Organisations

2.1 Compatibility of CSR and Not-For-Profit Organisations

CRS is not the same as charity. Charity (or even philanthropy) is often associated with free will and casual benevolence, while CSR is typically regarded as connected with the pursuit of a business organisation's long-term goals.[23] In this sense, while charity involves casual and benevolent impoverishment of the business organisation (by freely sharing its profits with the community), therefore disconnected with the organisation's business, CSR remains connected with the organisation's corporate goals/objectives, allowing it to continue its operations in the future. CSR is, therefore, perceived as a tool used by business organisations to increase their profits.[24]

As mentioned before, it is commonplace to state that business organisations 'should or need to give back' to their communities,[25] as they drain resources from

[22] Littler, J., 'Radical Consumption. Shopping For Change In Contemporary Culture', McGraw-Hill Education (2008).

[23] Rahim, M., M., 'Corporate Social Responsibility, Corporate Governance and Corporate Regulation', Mia Mahmudur Rahim (ed), Legal Regulation of Corporate Social Responsibility, Springer (2013).

[24] European Commission, 'European Competitiveness Report: 2008′ (OOPEC 2009) 107.

[25] Littler, J., 'Radical Consumption. Shopping For Change In Contemporary Culture', McGraw-Hill Education (2008).

their stakeholders (employees, or the community at large). It was also suggested before that "a quid pro quo is therefore (morally and/or legally) perceived as required. Contrary to business organisations, not-for-profit organisations are thought to possess greater social responsibility and 'gratuitously' aid their communities".[26]

But just like for-profit organisations, NFPs also pursue an economic activity, which is used to fund and develop their social objectives. However, portuguese law, in general, does not impose the same duties for decision makers of NFPs and for-profit organisations. On the contrary, it may be argued that for-profit managers, in their pursue of profit, may hurt the interests of all those who are not shareholders, while it is assumed that NFPs decision-makers will not do so. This perspective was dismissed before, as it was argued before that NFPs also drain resources from the communities where they are based and "where they fund their activities (through, as example, voluntary labour, monetary donations or donations of goods, or even by taking advantage of underprivileged populations by paying low wages to their employees)".[27]

2.2 *Decision-Making Accountability*

A common critique found in CSR literature is that for-profit decision-makers lack accountability for their actions, in particular when their decisions hurt values that are considered to be socially relevant (and which are not directly related to the business organisation or its capital holders' interests). As an example, Banerjee argues that public pressure on the establishment of CSR rules was not yet fully converted into coercive regulations under the law,[28] allowing organisations, in this author's opinion, to arbitrarily select what objectives to pursue and report, therefore selecting areas of social life which mostly generate positive feedback for the organisation.[29]

This critique is associated with the voluntarist nature of CSR, where the law does not define or impose social obligations to an organisation, especially if these social endeavours are outside of its scope.[30] If this was the case, then any private

[26] This point was made before in Assis, j., 'Responsabilidade Social e organizações sem fins lucrativos—uma reflexão legal', *in* Estudos em Homenagem ao Professor Doutor Manuel Pita, Almedina (2022), p. 287.

[27] See Assis, J., 'Responsabilidade Social e organizações sem fins lucrativos—uma reflexão legal', *in* Estudos em Homenagem ao Professor Doutor Manuel Pita, Almedina (2022), p. 287.

[28] Banerjee, S., 'A Critical Perspective on Corporate Social Responsibility: Towards a Global Governance Framework', Crit. Perspect. Int. Bus. 10 (2014), 84–95.

[29] Banerjee, S., 'A Critical Perspective on Corporate Social Responsibility: Towards a Global Governance Framework', Crit. Perspect. Int. Bus. 10 (2014), 84–95.

[30] See European Commission (2001) 'Promoting a European Framework for Corporate Social Responsibility', https://ec.europa.eu/commission/presscorner/api/files/document/print/en/doc_01_9/DOC_01_9_EN.pdf, accessed 31st May 2023.

endeavours—such as companies, associations, trusts, charities, and others—would be forced to devote a portion of their resources to the 'common good', therefore depriving these entities of part of their property for the benefit of what the state considered to be the 'common good'. Something which may be regarded as contrary to the rule of law, essential rights, and freedoms, in multiple jurisdictions across the globe and certainly in the EU.[31]

This dichotomy of how private endeavours should participate in social life has found some answers over time, but has gained traction recently in the EU through action of the European Commission, which has set in place multiple frameworks and codes of conduct dealing with the issue,[32] and of the European Parliament and the Council, which together have enacted the Directive (EU) 2022/2464 of the European Parliament and of the Council of 14 December 2022, as regards corporate sustainability reporting, and where it was defined that "sustainability reporting standards should also take account of internationally recognised principles and frameworks on responsible business conduct, corporate social responsibility, and sustainable development, including the SDGs, the UN Guiding Principles on Business and Human Rights, the OECD Guidelines for Multinational Enterprises (…), the UN Principles for Responsible Investment", among others.[33]

But it should be noted that several EU Member States have also decided to adopt laws on social economy, CSR and the third sector, which may impact on the way CSR is perceived in those counties, by mapping which objectives could or should be pursued by private organisations as 'common good'. As examples, Spain and Portugal have enacted framework laws on social economy.[34]

In what concerns to Portugal, it should be mentioned that Law n. 30/2013 (the Portuguese Basic Law for Social Economy) was approved in 2013, setting up a legal framework for the third sector in Portugal, which is to be complemented by further rules and regulations enacted by the Portuguese Government.[35] This law has defined social economy as "the set of economic and social activities, freely carried out by"[36]

[31] See the European Commission's action on 'Corporate sustainability reporting rules', https://finance.ec.europa.eu/capital-markets-union-and-financial-markets/company-reporting-and-auditing/company-reporting/corporate-sustainability-reporting_en, accessed 31st May 2023.

[32] See European Commission (2001) 'Promoting a European Framework for Corporate Social Responsibility', https://ec.europa.eu/commission/presscorner/api/files/document/print/en/doc_01_9/DOC_01_9_EN.pdf, accessed 31 May 2023.

[33] See the Directive (EU) 2022/2464 of the European Parliament and of the Council of 14 December 2022 amending Regulation (EU) No 537/2014, Directive 2004/109/EC, Directive 2006/43/EC and Directive 2013/34/EU, as regards corporate sustainability reporting (Text with EEA relevance) *in* https://eur-lex.europa.eu/legal-content/EN/TXT/?uri=CELEX:32022L2464, assessed 31 May 2023.

[34] As stated by Meira, D, 'A Lei de Bases da Economia Social Portuguesa: do Projeto ao Texto Final', *in* Revista Jurídica n. 24/2013, available at www.ciriec-revistajuridica.es, accessed 31/05/2023, 7, when referring to *Ley n.° 5/2011, de Economía Social.*

[35] Under article 6 of the Portuguese Basic Law for Social Economy.

[36] Free translation of article 2/1 of the Portuguese Basic Law for Social Economy ("*Entende -se por economia social o conjunto das atividades económico-sociais, livremente levadas a cabo pelas entidades referidas no artigo 4.° da presente lei*").

the following organisations: (i) Cooperatives; (ii) Associations; (iii) Mercies; (iv) Foundations; (v) Other private social solidarity institutions under future rules and regulations; or (vi) Other entities with legal personality, registered in the social economy database.[37]

It is also clear that under the Portuguese Basic Law for Social Economy, it is assumed that NFPs undertake and participate in the market economy. However, the decision-making process of NFP managers isn't regulated following the same principles, rules, and regulations, as other (for-profit) organisations in the market, as we will see bellow.[38]

3 The Case of Portugal

Portuguese Law regulates decision-making in what for-profit organisations are concerned under article 64 of the Commercial Companies Code[39] and under the Portuguese corporate governance framework, in line with CMVM Regulation n. 4/2013 (Corporate Governance), applicable to issuers of shares admitted to trading on a regulated market situated, or operating in Portugal, and subject to Portuguese Law.

Article 64 of the Portuguese Commercial Companies Code imposes duties of care and loyalty to managers with executive power, i.e., those who are able to take part in the decision-making process, and who hold the power of attorney to bind the company. Under their duty of care, directors must be available to devote their time to the company, must possess technical competence and knowledge of the company's activities—a level of knowledge which is appropriate to the execution of their job—and finally, they must act with diligence and in the best interest of the company.[40]

---

[37] As defined under Article 4 of the Portuguese Basic Law for Social Economy ("*Integram a economia social as seguintes entidades, desde que abrangidas pelo ordenamento jurídico português: a) As cooperativas; b) As associações mutualistas; c) As misericórdias; d) As fundações; e) As instituições particulares de solidariedade social não abrangidas pelas alíneas anteriores; f) As associações com fins altruísticos que atuem no âmbito cultural, recreativo, do desporto e do desenvolvimento local; g) As entidades abrangidas pelos subsectores comunitário e autogestionário, integrados nos termos da Constituição no sector cooperativo e social; h) Outras entidades dotadas de personalidade jurídica, que respeitem os princípios orientadores da economia social previstos no artigo 5.° da presente lei e constem da base de dados da economia social.*").

[38] For more on this see Assis, J., 'Responsabilidade Social e organizações sem fins lucrativos—uma reflexão legal', Estudos em Homenagem ao Professor Doutor Manuel Pita, Almedina (2022), 287.

[39] The Portuguese Companies Code was enacted under Decree-law n. 262/86 of 2 September.

[40] Article 64 of the Portuguese Commercial Companies Code states that "*os gerentes ou administradores da sociedade devem observar: (...) b) Deveres de lealdade, no interesse da sociedade, atendendo aos interesses de longo prazo dos sócios e ponderando os interesses dos outros sujeitos relevantes para a sustentabilidade da sociedade, tais como os seus trabalhadores, clientes e credores*".

Decision-makers of NFPs are not bound by these provisions and their managers, or those who have the power to bind the NFPs, are not bound by any such duties. On the contrary, looking at associations[41] and foundations,[42] as examples,[43] the decision-making process is freely regulated under their articles of association. If no provisions are established there, then the rules of agency shall apply.[44,45]

Associations may be defined as juridical persons whose social object is not the pursuit of profit,[46] while foundations may be defined "a legal person, who acts not-for-profit, and is endowed with sufficient assets, irrevocably allocated to the pursuit of an aim of social interest".[47] Both of them may be defined as NFP organisations, operating under the Portuguese Law, and defined as part of the Social Economy sector by the Portuguese Basic Law for Social Economy.[48] Both are created by a private juridical act, and in both cases those who create them are free to establish their own rules regarding the decision-making process of the NFPs' managers.

Considering that the decision-making process is freely regulated under the freedom of contract, only if no rules are privately defined in the relevant articles of association, will the rules on the law of agency apply— a set of suppletive rules found in the Portuguese Civil Code.

Civil agency is defined under article 1157 of the Portuguese Civil Code as "the contract by which one of the parties undertakes the obligation to perform one or more legal acts on behalf of the other[49]", and certain generic obligations are imposed upon the agent, such as the obligation to provide information and to be diligent. But no specific duties are imposed on NFP managers and decision makers to act on the best interest of the NFPs' stakeholders. Article 1161 of the Portuguese Civil Code reads as follows:

"Article 1161.° - (Obligations of the agent)

The agent is obliged:

(a) To perform the acts included in the mandate, according to the instructions of the principal;

---

[41] Associations are regulated under articles 167 and 184 of the Portuguese Civil Code.

[42] Foundations are regulated under articles 185 and 194 of the Portuguese Civil Code, and under Law 24/2012 of 25 August, which sets the Legal Framework for Foundations in Portugal.

[43] Associations and foundations are two of the most common types of NFOs in Portugal.

[44] Article 164/1 of the Portuguese Civil Code states that "*as obrigações e a responsabilidade dos titulares dos órgãos das pessoas colectivas para com estas são definidas nos respectivos estatutos, aplicando-se, na falta de disposições estatutárias, as regras do mandato, com as necessárias adaptações*".

[45] Article 29/1 of Law n. 24/2012.

[46] Mota Pinto, C.A., 'Teoria Geral do Direito Civil', Coimbra Editora (4th ed. 2005), 292.

[47] Free translation of article 3/1 of Law n. 24/2021 ("*A fundação é uma pessoa coletiva, sem fim lucrativo, dotada de um património suficiente e irrevogavelmente afetado à prossecução de um fim de interesse social*").

[48] Article 2/1 of the Portuguese Basic Law for Social Economy.

[49] Free translation of article 1157 of the Portuguese Civil Code "*Mandate is the contract by which one of the parties undertakes to perform one or more legal acts on behalf of the other.*"

(b) To provide the information requested by the latter regarding the state of management;
(c) To promptly inform the principal of the execution of the mandate or, if it has not been executed, the reason for doing so;
(d) To render accounts, at the end of the term of office or when required by the principal;
(e) To deliver to the principal what he received in execution of the mandate or in the exercise of it, if he did not normally spend it in the performance of the contract[50]".

The core obligation of the agent, under Portuguese Law, is to follow the principal's orders.[51] However, complementary duties must be observed, such as the duties of diligence (by always providing the relevant information) and the duty of fidelity (by acting in the presumed interest of the principal). The duty of acting with diligence is of prime relevance here, considering that whenever the agent acts in his professional capacity, they should not just act as a bonus pater famîlias.[52]

Carlos Ferreira de Almeida argues that if an agent acts under his professional capacity, the agent simply cannot act under the diligence of an average person, of average intelligence, positioned in that situation. On the contrary, he deems this unsatisfactory. In this case, standard diligence isn't enough. In this case, the agent must bear applicable statutory duties which exist for every professional category, combined with the level of duties expected from him by the principal. This means that the behaviour of the agent must be in line with the legitimate expectations of the principal, in what regards to the level of efficiency, fidelity, and loyalty expected in those specific circumstances.[53]

Considering the above, it is possible to argue that even though the actions of NFPs, managers are potentially regulated under the law, in practice, there is no actual regulation of the NFP decision-making process, considering that:

(i) The obligations of managers and/or those who are able to bind the NFPs are loosely conceptualised, allowing for a wide interpretation of the agent's duties, and therefore, they are not practical to use or enforce as every interpreter may find a different meaning in these concepts.

[50] Free translation of Article 1161 of the Portuguese Civil Code: "*Artigo 1161.° (Obrigações do mandatário)—O mandatário é obrigado: a) A praticar os actos compreendidos no mandato, segundo as instruções do mandante; b) A prestar as informações que este lhe peça, relativas ao estado da gestão; c) A comunicar ao mandante, com prontidão, a execução do mandato ou, se o não tiver executado, a razão por que assim procedeu; d) A prestar contas, findo o mandato ou quando o mandante as exigir; e) A entregar ao mandante o que recebeu em execução do mandato ou no exercício deste, se o não despendeu normalmente no cumprimento do contrato*".

[51] Article 1161 of the Portuguese Civil Code.

[52] Following Almeida, C. F., Contratos III—Conteúdo—Contratos de Troca, Almedina (2007), 193.

[53] Following Almeida, C. F., Contratos III—Conteúdo—Contratos de Troca, Almedina (2007), 194.

(ii) Using the legitimate expectation of the principal (in this case the NFP) as criteria for the accountability of NFP managers does not provide a stable criterion, making it hard to use and easily disputed in court.
(iii) If the duties and obligations of NFP's managers are regulated under the principle of freedom of contract, then the relevant articles of association may simply state that NFP's managers are not liable for their actions.
(iv) Even if NFP's managers are liable towards the relevant NFP under the articles of association, or under the law of agency, they are never liable for their actions towards the NFP's stakeholders under Portuguese law.

4 Concluding Remarks

Given the size and scope of this article, it is not possible to review all statutory rules and regulations, as well as jurisprudence, applicable to the government of NFP organisations under Portuguese Law.

Therefore, the present article focused on how the decision-making process is conducted in associations and foundations under Portuguese Law, looking at these two NFP organisations as case studies, and therefore allowing us to shed light on which duties are imposed by Portuguese Law to NFP's managers and other NFP's decision-makers.

After the review of how Portuguese Law regulates the duties (and liability) of NFP managers (in particular, those who manage associations and foundations), it became clear that Portuguese Law disregards the impact of NFP's managers decision-making in the NFP's stakeholders (those who are not the NFP organisation itself, such as employees, creditors, or even the community at large). As an example, if a relevant association mistreats an employee by decision of a manager, the employee cannot act directly against the manager, being forced to react against the association alone.

But what seems mostly out of balance is the fact that an association/foundation manager may be completely exempt from liability for their actions, if such is inscribed in the NFP's articles of association. And even if nothing is mentioned in the articles of association, the subsidiary law applicable remains based in undetermined concepts such as 'good faith' or 'diligence', which do not allow for a uniform application of the law to all managers of associations and/or foundations in Portugal. This uncertainty may lead to the complete unaccountability of the NFP's manager.

References

Almeida, C. F. (2007). Contratos III—Conteúdo—Contratos de Troca. *Almedina, 194*.
Argandoña, A., & Hoivik, H. (2009). Corporate social responsibility: One size does not fit all. Collecting evidence from Europe. *Journal of Business Ethics, 89*, 221–234.

Assis, J. (2022). 'Responsabilidade Social e organizações sem fins lucrativos—uma reflexão legal'. In Estudos em Homenagem ao Professor Doutor Manuel Pita, Almedina.

Bainbridge, S. M. (2008). *The new corporate governance in theory and practice* (pp. 49–51). Oxford University Press.

Banerjee, S. (2014). A critical perspective on corporate social responsibility: Towards a global governance framework. *Critical Perspectives on International Business, 10*, 84–95.

Berle, A. A., & Means, C. G. (1991). The Legal Position of "Control"', The Modern Corporation and Private Property, originally published in 1932, Transaction Publishers, Book II, Chapter VI, (pp. 235–239).

Blair, M. M. (1995). 'Ownership and control: Rethinking corporate governance for the twenty-first century', Theories of Corporate Governance, the Philosophical Foundations of Corporate Governance, Routledge, (pp. 176–179).

Clark, T. (2007). Cycles of Governance. In *International corporate governance: A comparative approach* (pp. 1–3). Routledge.

González, R. (2017). Corporate social responsibility and brand value in luxury. Not published. Available at http://theses.gla.ac.uk/8159/, Assessed May 31, 2023, 65.

Halme, M., & Laurila, J. (2009). Philanthropy, integration or innovation? Exploring the financial and societal outcomes of different types of corporate responsibility. *Journal of Business Ethics, 84*, 325–339.

Idowu, S. (2009). The United Kingdom of Great Britain and Northern Ireland. In S. Idowu & W. Filho (Eds.), *Global practices of corporate social responsibility*. Springer.

Kroszner, R. S., & Putterman, L. (2009). *The economic nature of the firm: A reader* (3rd ed., originally published 1986, pp. 7–9). Cambridge University Press.

Littler, J. (2008). *Radical consumption. Shopping for change in contemporary culture*. McGraw-Hill Education.

McWilliams, A., & Siegel, D. (2001). Corporate social responsibility: A theory of the firm perspective. *Academy of Management Review, 26*(1), 117–127.

Meira, D. (2013). A Lei de Bases da Economia Social Portuguesa: do Projeto ao Texto Final. In Revista Jurídica n. 24/2013, available at www.ciriec-revistajuridica.es, Accessed May 31, 2023.

Mota Pinto, C. A. (2005). Teoria Geral do Direito Civil, Coimbra Editora (4th ed., p. 292).

Orlitzky, M. (2015). The politics of corporate social responsibility or: Why Milton Friedman has been right all along. *Annual Social Responsibility, 1*, 5–29.

Pupo Correia, M. (2018) 'Direito Comercial', Ediforum and Almedina Editora (14th ed.).

Rahim, M. M. (2013). Corporate social responsibility, corporate governance and corporate regulation. In M. M. Rahim (Ed.), *Legal regulation of corporate social responsibility*. Springer.

Silberhorn, D., & Warren, R. (2007). Defining corporate social responsibility: A view from big companies in Germany and the UK. *European Business Review, 19*.

Thorne, L., Mahoney, L. S., & Manetti, G. (2014). Motivations for issuing standalone CSR reports: A survey of Canadian firms. *Audit Accounts Journal, 27*, 686–714.

Tricker, B. (2009). *Corporate governance-principles, policies and practices*. Oxford University Press.

Van Marrewijk, M. (2003). Concepts and definitions of CSR and corporate sustainability: Between agency and communion. *Journal of Business Ethics, 44*, 95–105.

Villers, C. (2006). Corporate reporting and company law. In *Cambridge studies in corporate law* (Vol. 5). Cambridge University Press.

Visser, W. (2008). Corporate social responsibility in developing countries. In *The Oxford handbook of corporate social responsibility* (pp. 473–502). Oxford University Press.

Wood, D. J. (1991). Corporate social performance revisited. *Academy of Management Review, 16*(4), 691–718.

João de Sousa Assis holds a PhD in Law from the University of Glasgow (Scotland), with the thesis "The Law of Donation and the Market: Scottish,

Portuguese and French Perspectives". During his PhD, he was responsible for teaching Business Organisations at the Faculty of Law of the University of Glasgow (Scotland), while providing regular assistance in the Competition Law classes, taught in Portugal and Brazil by Professor Rosa Greaves. He currently works as Assistant Professor in Law at ISCAL, Polytechnic University of Lisbon (Portugal), where he serves Vice-Dean for International Affairs and as Course Convenor for Commercial Law, Commercial Contracts, and Company Law. Additionally, he regularly collaborates with Thammasat University (Thailand) and Symbiosis Law School Pune (India), where he teaches Comparative Private Law and European Private Law. Furthermore, he is an Integrated Researcher at IJP—Instituto Jurídico Portucalense (Portugal), researching on topics spanning the areas of Private Law and Commercial Law, while devoting his attention to transnational-related topics as Research Fellow at the Center for ASEAN Transnational Studies (CATS) of the Faculty of Law at Chiang Mai University (Thailand).

An Analysis of the Effects of an Absence of Governance & Community Solutions in Combating Environmental Degradation

Olusegun Ehinfun and Paul R. Sachs

1 Introduction

According to Professor Kate Raworth of Oxford University (founder of Doughnut Economics Action Labs—DEAL), humanity is in the era of the anthropocene. We have "become the greatest drivers of change at the scale of the earth system post World War II" (Al- Jazeera English Documentaries, January 2023). Such scholars are of the view that the era of the anthropocene, which we are currently experiencing, became turbocharged when economies began to grow fueled by the availability of cheap fossil fuels coupled with attendant growth in accompanying consumption patterns globally. Ultimately, this process has led to climate and ecological breakdowns with potential catastrophic consequences, with excessive consumption and consumerism patterns impacting the environment adversely. Raworth believes that either by commission or omission, policies geared toward achieving broad-based economic development lacked the forethought of envisaging the underlying environmental externalities that result from such production and expansionist policies (ibid). The question now is how policymakers can avoid further problems and reduce the negative impact of existing climate change and environmental problems (Okunola & Simatale, 2023). It is proposed that implementation of effective environmental resource governance (ERG), management best practices, and joined-up thinking among developing countries is a potential solution. This paper contends that coherent policies can be designed for such implementation. These

O. Ehinfun (✉)
University of York, York, UK

P. R. Sachs
ReidSachs LLC, Montgomery, PA, USA
e-mail: paul@reidsachs.com

B. Díaz Díaz et al. (eds.), *Building Global Societies Towards an ESG World*, CSR, Sustainability, Ethics & Governance,
https://doi.org/10.1007/978-3-031-56619-6_13

policies require and ensure, as a sine qua non, coordinated efforts between cross-regional governments with legal institutional frameworks and backing across Africa.

1.1 Why a Twin-Regional Focus?

This paper illustrates the problem and potential solutions by examining the Lake Chad and Niger Delta regions of West Africa largely because they have similar development challenges and accompanying environmental realities. They are situated geographically within some of Africa's largest River Basin(s) Authorities (RBA) and represent two out of the eight River basins—Benue, Niger, Delta, and Cross River, Osun, Imo-Anambra, Hadejia-Chad, Sokoto-Rima, Owena, and Ogun basins Ita, E.O. (1994)—in a country with Africa's largest population and economy. Both regions are facing erosion of their land and water resources, destruction of local fauna and flora, and either presently or historically suffer from the menace of non-state armed groups. In the Lake Chad Basin (LCB), security and environmental issues were partly aggravated and precipitated by the shrinking of Lake Chad (Serdeczny et al., 2017) within the border areas of the Lake Chad Basin Area (LCBA) countries, with attendant soil erosions and drought extending from the outer edges of the Sahel/Sahara Desert. This area spans the length and breadth of the old Kanem–Bornu old empire. It is described as an oasis within the Sahel region, nestled on the southern edge of the Sahara Desert. It sat at the crossroads of commercial activities from the period of the rule of various El-Kanemi(s)—traditional imperial rulers of their age (Martin, 1969). The Niger River Delta Basin (NRDB) is a vital, at-one-time pristine biodiversity & environmental resource including sources of water, fauna & flora, forests, lakes, rivers, creeks, and coastal areas. The Nigerian state's (mis)management of its extractive land resources (oil, gas, minerals) has had serious security, socio-economic, and constitutional implications for this region and for Nigeria's estimated 213 million people (World Bank IBRD-IDA Data: Nigeria, 2023). There has been alleged illegal oil bunkering by corrupt government officials in the national oil company, perhaps in concert with some parts of its security establishment. This is coupled with indiscriminate oil drilling, refining, and the illegal activities of unemployed youths pilfering crude oil pipelines, which run through host communities (Igwe, 2022). Ultimately selling illegal crude on the black markets, but also leading to extensive environmental and social destruction. This is a consequence of having had their main sources of livelihood (artisanal fishing)—via rivers, creeks, coastal waters—damaged and despoiled by crude oil spillages from pipelines of oil majors/multinational oil corporations (MNOCs), local communities have been devastated.

1.2 Geo-Strategic Implications

These regions are located between the Sahel in the North and the Gulf of Guinea countries in the South geographically, which includes also the tiny country of Sao-Tome and Principe, which has a joint economic and development zone between Nigeria and São Tomé called the Joint Development Zone (JDZ); according to the Wood-Mckenzie Upstream Summary Report (2023). On a geo-strategic level, the country-focus in this paper is on Nigeria, Africa's largest economy and country by population size. The case study regions are vital development basins. The Lake Chad Basin Area (LCBA) is a regional development framework which consists of 4 neighboring countries working together via the Lake Chad Basin Commission (LCBC) in providing solutions to development challenges around transboundary water management and food security. The Niger River Delta Basin (NRDB) spans 6 states within Nigeria with massive oil and gas reserves, but also rich fauna and flora, biodiversity, and natural habitat. The Niger Delta Development Commission (NDDC) administers development programs and solutions for the peoples of the South—Southern region of Nigeria—where most of the oil and gas resources that funds the Nigerian state is derived from. The importance and implications of the LCBA and NRDB are particularly strong due to their socio-economic development potential. The regions highlight governance challenges in terms of balancing environmental and security challenges in West Africa, the Sahel, and Equatorial/Central Africa. Furthermore, the regions illustrate how transboundary issues and environmental issues interplay in their impact on economic and political development.

2 Environmental Impact

2.1 Background & Context

There exists a political impasse akin to a frozen conflict in both the Lake Chad Basin Development Area (LCBA) and Niger River Delta Basin (NRDB) regions. This paper argues that coordinated efforts between government, corporations, local communities, and other stakeholders are key to ameliorating socio-economic challenges, poverty and privations within the transboundary communities embodied by these regions. The Lake Chad region and Niger Delta oil and gas-endowed settlements have had their fauna and flora despoiled by natural and man-made environmental degradation. Ultimately, these are the visible consequences of the dearth of effective environmental management practices by the authorities within both regions. The sources of livelihood in both regions, in the forms of artisanal fishing and farming, have been largely destroyed by a mixture of water erosion and land degradation around the Lake Chad Basin Areas (LCBA), (Bdliya & Bloxom, 2013).

According to Yusuf (2022), there exist long-lasting impacts in terms of curtailed oil production due to a combination of activities of some community members—mainly unemployed youths—who turn into crude oil profiteers damaging oil pipelines to extract oil for sale on the "black market." The realities of patchy economic development in some areas coupled with ongoing environmental deterioration have compounded the well-being of the local communities in both regions with the resultant reality being incessant instability in the regions.

2.2 *Lake Chad Basin Area (LCBA)*

The Lake Chad Basin Area is a geographically low point in the Sahel region. The lake is fed by various rivers and a critical water source amid the dry Sahel region. It is strategically located at a crossroads of the borders of Nigeria, Cameroon, Chad, and Niger Republic. According to some early scholars who tracked the evolution of non-state actors and terrorist groups, one of whom is Dr. Ona Ekhomu in his book "Boko Haram: Security Considerations and the Rise of an Insurgency," Ekhomu (2019), he details the mishandling of security events and the Nigerian authorities' approach in the year 2009 which may have been the critical juncture at which the insurgency in Northeastern Nigeria escalated, as the Boko Haram phenomenon, snowballing into neighboring Lake Chad Basin and Sahelian border nations of Chad, Cameroon, and Nigerian Republic (Channels TV Book Club Review, 2023). Other scholars are of the view that this resulting expansion in influence and notoriety by Boko Haram (The Jama'atu Ahlis Sunna Lidda'awati wal-Jihad-JAS) terrorism resulted in severe community displacements, ultimately disrupting the social, economic, and geo-political balance of the region (Hoinathy & Tayo, 2022), with the entity later splintering and subsequently metamorphosing into the Islamic State in West Africa Province—ISWAP (Wilāyat Garb Ifrīqīyā). This development has been the bane of existence, in terms of sociology-economic instability for agrarian and fishing communities in the 4 countries around the LCBA (ibid.)

2.3 *Niger River Delta Basin (NRDB)*

The Niger River Delta Basin comprises several regions in southern Nigeria. It has historically been an area of varied economic activity and, as a result, is a densely populated area. Petroleum processing began in the region in the 1950s and the area has since developed extensively with the industry making Nigeria a chief oil producer for the world. Catastrophic crude oil spillages in and around the 9 states of the oil polluted riverine areas of the Niger River Delta Basin (NRDB) have occurred. Compounding these problems is the absence of effective participatory governance and an implementation of oil and gas resource devolution (sharing) arguments with the community. Militant restiveness that has developed can be seen as a by-product of this mismanagement within the NRDB. Knowing that they produce most of the foreign exchange income for the Federal Government of Nigeria (FGN), communities in the NRDB understandably dissatisfied with the operations of the oil majors/ MNCs, who are in Joint-Venture (JV) partnerships on oil and gas exploration that has impacted negatively on their environment via oil spillages and gas flaring, without attendant sustainable job opportunities with deep connections to their communities.

Since the discovery of oil in 1956, with production in commercial quantities commencing via Shell in 1958 at Oloibiri (Oshwofasa et al., 2012), within present-day Rivers State, oil despoliation has been the bane of existence of the peoples of the NRDB. Instances of oil spillage have occurred at Oloibiri, Ogoni, Bonga, and most recently in 2022 within Nembe areas of South-Southern Nigeria (Nwafor, 2022). Access to freshwater for communities has been restricted or cut off entirely. Arable farmland for artisanal farmers and fishing waters for fishermen have been destroyed. Consequently, this has negatively impacted the communities in terms of political, socio-economic, and cultural dynamics that underpins these challenges, most notably around resource ownership/control (including water rights and oil/ land derivation policies) and how community solutions could be engendered.

3 Effective Environmental Management

The communities that suffer disproportionately from development challenges, including pressing ones like those brought on by climate change, need the state, responsive governments, and institutions to take proactive actions in their domains to help the communities manage these challenges. Long-standing political duties such as the capacity to deliver for constituents and proper allocation of resources, along with contemporary burgeoning ones like environmental governance (Environmental Resource Governance or ERG) are critical to arresting environmental externalities associated with climate change. Effective, systematic, and concerted implementation of development pathways and solutions toward addressing these challenges will serve the state and its citizens well in ameliorating the extant challenges of environmental degradation. The authors suggest that a confluence of factors within the political economy ultimately threw up the effete and ineffective governance system. According to Towwalola Kasali, "factors such as poor socio-economic performance, human rights abuses, widespread poverty, insecurity, corruption, and lack of trust in the political system have led to disenchantment amongst the electorate, especially the youth" (Kasali, 2020). There is a burgeoning youth profile with the potential to power up the economy as they constitute about 51% of the population and with over 60% of the vast population of an estimated 213 million (World Bank IBRD-IDA Data: Nigeria, 2023). This reality coupled with attendant environmental degradation probably led to the rise of terrorism and insurgency in these regions (Omeje, 2004). The effect has been that pre-existing sources of livelihood in both regions, artisanal fishing and farming, have been largely destroyed by a mixture of terrorism, lake erosion, drought, water despoliation, and land degradation around the LCBA and NRDB. Journalist Kabir Yusuf's analysis in a Premium Times publication showed how and why a combination of the production activities of multinational oil corporations (MNOCs), the Federal (central) and State governments' neglect all ultimately led to displaced fishermen, farmers, and unemployed youth turning to crude oil profiteering by damaging oil pipelines to extract oil for sale on the black market—commonly referred to as "oil bunkering"—which affected the host communities' environments (Yusuf, 2022). This is arguably one of the main contributors to the catastrophic despoliation of fauna and flora, including biodiversity loss.

One of the reservations regarding the Nigerian state's management of its resources is the local institutional context (state's legislation and policies) from which resources are derived. That is, the lifecycle from prospecting of mineral resources to processing and export (Omeje, 2004). Communities from where these resources are extracted believe a sizeable share of revenues accruable from such activities within their communities must be ploughed back into their communities via instruments and structures provided for by the constitution, for example the Nigerian Consolidated Revenue Fund (CRF) Exclusive, Legislative and Concurrent lists, largely based on a Federation sharing formula for derivable revenues. This is because Nigeria relies so heavily on oil-related revenues. However, some scholars underscore that it only allocates a paltry 13% of the derivation fund to the nine local states (state governments) in the Niger Delta/oil-producing areas (Adebowale, 2021). This disparity has been a major issue since 1958 when oil, gas, and bitumen were first discovered in commercial quantities by Shell and continued through the upheavals of the 1990s and the noughties when the renowned poet and environmentalist, Ken Saro-Wiwa and other Ogoni environmental activists were summarily tried for high treason and executed by the military dictatorship of General Sanni Abacha (Earthrights, 2018). Local governance and institutional context are key for any successful and effective management of resources. Supporting and fortifying local governance will aid the federal government in managing the community fallout from the oil spillages and crude oil pipeline damages. Trust and community buy-in are key elements of participatory governance. Governments engaging in effective environmental cleaning operations must consider these elements. Without them, it is arguable and likely that both the state/Federal government and the oil majors/multinational oil companies (MNOCs) will fail.

4 Governance and How It Has Led to Problems

Upon gaining its independence in 1960 during the First Republic, Nigeria's first and only Federal Parliamentary government (governance system) consisted of the "Central" government and other semi-autonomous regional governments and vestiges of the colonial native authority system. They somehow held on to convenient levers and "artifices" of governance which supposedly worked well for the previous colonial administrations in some regions. The few local participatory powers of governance were devolved to regional governments and municipal authorities, which were themselves further absorbed and consolidated into a unitary style of governance by the military. Two successive military coups and administrations took place in 1966 which truncated the short era of parliamentary and democratic rule post-independence. An interplay of the politics of military coups and suboptimal governance took hold in the Nigerian body-polity over several decades. Persistent maladministration by successive governments ensued: From the short-lived civilian second Republic (1979–1983) to the ill-fated but truncated military controlled third Republic (1989–1993). These iterations of governance (colonial, military, and civilian) both had long-lasting deleterious effects on socio-economic well-being and environmental governance, severely impacting the nascent politics of the Nigerian state (Nyangoro, 1994).

Arguably, therefore, weak governance and a poorly managed development regime affected both the development pathways of both the Niger River Delta Basin (NRDB) and the Lake Chad Basin Area (LCBA). This impact occurs in the context of pressures from oil and gas extraction/exploration and black-market profiteering activities, population growth, environmental degradation and climate change, including the ever-expanding Sahara Desert on the edges of the Sahel region within LCBA countries (Bonzanigo et al., 2022). In evaluating the current situation, one must acknowledge the impact of colonialism. Colonial rule by European powers in West Africa brought two chief (and alien) cultural legacies in that area: Christianity and Capitalism. Doing so implanted the values inherent in these legacies: the sovereignty of man over the earth and its other creatures, and the commoditization of human and natural resources to make a profit. The legacy of centralized control regardless of local issues was essentially maintained through native authority "indirect rule" by the British Colonial government. This had the deleterious effect of keeping public and lower rungs of government disempowered and disenfranchised. Participatory governance that would have empowered local communities and given them a sense of place and ownership was disabled by this power structure, ultimately leaving the lower rungs of governance closest to the people disempowered (Egbe, 2014).

5 Community Solutions and the Limitation of that Approach

Positive community action in creating environmental sustainability and strengthening the will of politicians to do so begins from the grassroots. However, such grassroots support for participatory governance must come from a public that has confidence in existing structures and systems. Hence, community interventions, in of themselves, cannot substitute for a proactive and responsive governance regime. An exclusive focus on such community programs risks letting various governmental authorities shirk their own responsibilities. An agile political system should put in place environmental communication structures. Doing so engages the community and curtails and redirects community restiveness. Doing so lets the community know that the government is attuned to community concerns, empathetic and willing to act. These interventions should be thoughtfully planned, designed, and implemented by a cross-section of local/municipal, state, and Federal strata of government. Such robust environmental education and engagement could be driven through community elders, imams, priests, chiefs, and civic leaders. Their messages could be delivered via the various existing Rural Education Authority (REA) and Community Outreach Programs. According to some scholars, this communication system could be administered by the Ministries of Education and Environment of governments. An example of this model focused on teaching and imparting cognitive and empathic critical thinking skills, effectively demonstrated in Chile: "The findings reveal a significant benefit in using empathy strategies to engage students regarding the thinking processes involved with solving environmental problems. Using these elements as teaching techniques for environmental education courses can be very helpful in reaching the aims of creating a sustainable citizenry." (Ampuero et al., 2013). Other examples of community-based sustainable programs include the Casa Pueblo positive intervention during Hurricane Maria in Puerto Rico. The power of community was clearly displayed when, according to Artur Massol-Deya, Executive Director of the community-based organization, Casa Pueblo, it helped communities across Puerto Rico (to) install solar panels for a more sustainable and independent futures (Aljazeera English Magazine Programme, 2022). According to other scholars of community interventions like Torres et al. (2022) empathy, civic commitments and contributions of young people partly aided a quik recovery of natural disasters that severely impacted the island: "…During the past four years, Puerto Rico has experienced compounding disasters beginning with the landfall of Hurricane Maria in September 2017. While many of the archipelago's residents were still recovering from the hurricane in late 2019 and early 2020, Puerto Rico suffered a series of earthquakes, mainly affecting the southwestern portion of the main island…." (Torres et al., 2022). In sum, the devastating effects of such climate externalities led to Casa Pueblo's positive intervention in 2020. The lesson is that galvanizing community participation (including the young) can aid sustainable impact in the aftermath of such natural disasters, especially by groups of committed community-based organizations. Such efforts are worthy of emulation, perhaps with the possibility of their replication in other parts of the global south and other developing economies.

6 Proposed Public–Private Partnerships and Participatory Governance

In the quest for development many resource-rich countries (like Nigeria) have tended to focus, almost exclusively, on how the end justifies the means. They ignore the socio-economic, political, and environmental displacements associated with prospecting for minerals, rare earth metals, hydrocarbons, and water management, to name a few. Resource politics and environmental resource governance (ERG) have been understood and operationalized in limited ways, particularly among least developed countries. Public–private partnership (PPP) model best exemplifies how participatory governance could be effective. Public sector (local, state, and federal governments) development frameworks and initiatives can be combined with community participation, engagements, and buy-ins, as well as other stakeholders such as: non-governmental organizations (NGOs) and private sector local industry players and multinational corporations (MNCs). Such collaboration might yield the most economically, politically, and environmentally sustainable projects. This kind of development and participatory governance framework requires a level of openness to collaboration among all parties, especially around corporate governance. It is also vital and important to have an educated and engaged public. A veritable governance framework that advocates the participation of third sector/non-governmental organizations (NGOs) in the effective management of natural resources for the benefit of many is the "Institutional Analysis and Development Framework" proposed by Elinor Ostrom. She posits that the "exploration of solving common pool resources problems" is key as neither the state nor the market had been universally successful in the proper administration of the commons. This alternative is opposed to the other scholarly postulations characterized by the "tragedy of the commons narrative." Her considered view, backed up by theoretical and empirical analyses over the years, is that "common pool problems sometimes are solved by voluntary organizations rather than by coercive states" (Ostrom, 1990, 2015).

7 Transboundary/Tansnational Competition and Collaboration

Due to the discovery of oil and natural gas off the coasts of Senegal and Mauritania in 2015, it can be argued that the discovery and exploitation of this resource, far from being a source of cooperation, could potentially be a source of transboundary tensions. However, if both governments choose to continue cooperating in protecting the existential biodiversity and environmental resources, it could engender transnational cooperation between the West African neighbors on the outer Western stretch of the Sahel. In a situation not dissimilar to the Niger Delta River Basin of South-Southern Nigeria, the Saint-Louis region of Senegal has always been a bastion of the fisheries industry in Senegal. However, over the past number of years, the diattara or fertile fishing lands on the ocean bed in local Wolof parlance have become susceptible to sea erosion, washing away settlements and homes, due to the externalities associated with the effects from climate change (Mednick, 2023). Ultimately, a combination of the building of gas exploration rigs and the aftereffects of COVID-19 pandemic pushed the local populace into desperation, poverty, and in some cases, destitution having lost access to some of their most productive fishing waters. Commercial fishing hauls dwindled, and the promised economic recovery and rejuvenation have failed to materialize, as the Gas partnership cooperation between the Multinational Oil Corporations (MNOCs)—Kosmos Energy and BP—and respective governments of Senegal and Mauritania has not yet been realized. For the second largest fishing economy, after Nigeria, in West Africa the Senegalese fisheries industry is being negatively impacted by a confluence of factors including the warming waters off the coast of Senegal leading to the migration of Sardinella species of fish—a mainstay of Senegalese fisheries industry—northwards toward the coasts of Mauritania and Morocco (Moody, 2023). However, the oil and gas exploration almost heralds a death knell for its economy and puts immense pressures on the socio-economic fabric of society in these regions. This case study might have been a classic transboundary cooperation regime prior to the arrival of the oil and gas companies, a cooperative mechanism along the lines of the Lake Chad Basin Commission (LCBC) co-opting Lake and land reclamation policies from Cameroon, Chad, Niger Republic, and Nigeria. Senegal, Mauritania, and Guinea might be able to coalesce around a potential tripartite-type common River basin authority commission/authority toward managing depleting fish stocks, stopping overfishing from transcontinental fishing trawlers allegedly from Europe and China. This form of cooperation model can make such countries attractive to accessing the World Bank's funding facility; The Cooperation in International Waters in Africa (CIWA) program, d esigned as a bespoke multi-donor fund backing sub-Saharan African nations in engendering "sustainable, climate-resilient growth by addressing constraints to cooperative water resources management." (Bonzanigo et al., 2022).

8 Conclusion and Recommendations

Multiple historical and present-day factors have jeopardized economic and political sustainability in two African regions. Modifying some of these factors, such as climate change, requires a global, multi-tiered effort. Other factors, however, such as balancing local, regional, and federal priorities are more amenable to modification. This balance can be addressed by a commitment to participatory governance and greater community-business collaboration. West Africa is the focus of this paper, but the political, economic, and social concerns raised by climate change apply to the entire planet. Some participatory governance interventions may work better in some parts of the world than others. Understanding what works where and the underlying reasons for successful or unsuccessful interventions can guide the design of future interventions. It will also be valuable to identify any industry-specific factors that affect the success of governance interventions. The examples in the present paper focused on water/fishery and oil/gas resources. Different model development and implementation may be needed for other industries, such as mining, manufacturing, and agriculture. Studies comparing and contrasting industry interventions will also be useful. The relative prominence of localism vs. globalism or, in some cases, nationalism vs. regionalism is a dynamic seen in the twenty-first century events. This paper has given examples of this dynamic as it affects resource utilization and allocation. How nation-states and governments balance these sometimes-competing areas of focus in managing climate change and other resources also presents an important area for research. Do the colonial and national histories of African countries and others in the Southern Hemisphere facilitate or detract from transboundary collaboration? According to a collection of forward-thinking climate governance professionals at the Swedish Environment Institute (SEI) and the IDDRI (Institut De Recherche Indépendant, L'Institut Du Développement Durable Des Relations Internationales—Independent Research Institute, The Institute for Sustainable Development and International Relations): there are factors to be explored, studied, and ultimately to be understood now and into the future to facilitate or undermine such collaboration (Adaptation without Borders, 2021).

In the final analysis, the impending task might be making commitments to new ways of managing risks and facilitating collaboration which would require a change in the culture for business stakeholders and political leaders. Nevertheless, to be able to manage growth and sustain the well-being of citizens and the environment simultaneously, it will be easier to make these changes now than wait to make them under the pressure of an environmental or political catastrophe.

References

Al- Jazeera English Documentaries. (January 2023). *Earthrise - business critical: Can companies inspire a sustainable future?* Available at: https://www.aljazeera.com/program/earthrise/2023/1/7/business-critical-can-companies-inspire-a-sustainable-future

Bdliya, H. H. & Bloxom, M. (2013). Transboundary diagnostic analysis of the Lake Chad Basin, Dr. Hassan Harlan Bdliya, Federal Ministry of Environment and Housing (Federal Secretariat, Maitama, Abuja, Nigeria) and Dr. Martin Bloxom. Published on: International Waters Learning Exchange and Resource Network (IW Learn) (pp. 19, 20). [Under the aegis of the Global Environment Facility - GEF International Waters Learning Exchange and Resources Network - IW LEARN]. Available at https://iwlearn.net/resolveuid/9470ff35bbc5e0205dc364a8322a0f36; https://sustainabledevelopment.un.org/partnership/?p=13864; https://sdgs.un.org/partnerships. Additional sources available at https://reliefweb.int/report/world/lake-chad-living-example-devastation-climate-change-wreaking-africa

Channels TV Book Club. (2023). *Book review of: 'Boko haram: Security considerations and the rise of an insurgency* (1st ed.). By Ekhomu, Ona. CRC Press, Taylor Francis Group. ISBN-13: 978-1032084336.

Igwe, U. (2022). Wake-up call: Nigeria must fight the oil thieves that are wrecking its economy, Uche Igwe, PhD., London School of Economics and Political Science (LSE). *African Report Magazine*, September 29, 2022. Available online at https://www.theafricareport.com/245471/nigeria-must-fight-the-oil-thieves-that-are-wrecking-its-economy/?fbclid=IwAR3tEFDIuJKx8u06UM2lJ7R3ijW6SjqHKMNKlgsIhOUxmHySsoW-4AuF4ho

Ita, E. O. (1994). *Aquatic plants and wetland wildlife resources of Nigeria, National Institute for Freshwater Fisheries Research New Bussa, Niger State* (CIFA Occasional Paper. No. 21, pp. 52). FAO. Available at https://www.fao.org/3/t3660e/t3660e01.htm

Martin, B. G. (1969). Kanem, Bornu, and the Fazzān: Notes on the political history of a trade route. Journal of African History, X, I, (1969), Published online by Cambridge University Press, 22nd January 2009. pp. 15–27. (pp. 15–17, 22–23, 26–27). Available at https://www.cambridge.org/core/services/aop-cambridge-core/content/view/2472FC74F3B7C178F5994EDD38AAF92E/S0021853700009257a.pdf/kanem-bornu-and-the-fazzan-notes-on-the-political-history-of-a-trade-route.pdf

Okunola, O. H., & Simatele, M. D. (2023). Climate change in Urban Nigeria - 4 factors that affect how residents adapt. *The Conversation*. Published on: February 26, 2023. Available at https://www.un.org/en/climatechange/what-is-climate-change

Serdeczny, O., et al. (2017). Climate change impacts in sub-Saharan Africa: From physical changes to their social repercussions. *Regional Environmental Change, 17*, 1585–1600. https://doi.org/10.1007/s10113-015-0910-2

The World Bank IBRD-IDA Data, Nigeria. (2023). Available at https://data.worldbank.org/country/nigeria

Wood-Mckenzie Nigeria - São Tomé Joint Development Zone - JDZ- Upstream Summary. (2023). Available at https://www.woodmac.com/reports/upstream-oil-and-gas-nigeria-sao-tome-jdz-upstream-summary-9014452/

Yusuf, K. (2022). *Analysis: How broke Nigeria lost $10 billion to crude oil theft in seven months*. Published by Premium Times (Special Report), September 8th, 2022. Available at https://www.premiumtimesng.com/news/headlines/552781-analysis-how-broke-nigeria-lost-10-billion-to-crude-oil-theft-in-seven-months.html

Detailed in Book Reading & Interview (Video) on

Adebowale, A. (2021). Analysis: How state governments cheat oil-producing communities in use of 13% derivation fund. Adedugbe Adebowale, Premium Times, April 23, 2021.Under Sections: 'Constitutional Provision', 'Poorly Funded Commissions'. https://www.premiumtimesng.com/news/headlines/456847-analysis-how-state-governments-cheat-oil-producing-communities-in-use-of-13-derivation-fund.html?tztc=1

Aljazeera English Magazine Programme. (2022). Can positivity help tackle the global climate emergency. *The Stream, The Power of Community Segment*, October 25, 2022 at 19:30 GMT (Video: via YouTube - Minutes 18:01–25:25). Available online at https://aje.io/3k45kj; https://www.aljazeera.com/amp/program/the-stream/2022/10/25/can-positivity-help-tackle-the-global-climate-emergency

Ampuero, D., Miranda, C. E., Delgado, L. E., Goyen, S., & Weaver, S. (2013). Empathy and critical thinking: Primary students solving local environmental problems through outdoor learning. *Journal of Adventure Education & Outdoor Learning, 15*(1), 64–78. Published online Taylor & Francis Online 12th November 2013, pp. 64, 65. Available online at https://www.tandfonline.com/doi/abs/10.1080/14729679.2013.848817

Bonzanigo, L., Lajaunie, M. L., & Abdulnour R. (2022). Reflecting on 20 years of transboundary water engagement in Western Africa: Impacts and lessons learned, World Bank Blogs, The Water Blog, Worldbank.org, MARCH 03, 2022. Available online at https://blogs.worldbank.org/water/reflecting-20-years-transboundary-water-engagement-western-africa-impacts-and-lessons-learned

Channels TV Book Club. (2019) Author and Security, Late Dr. Ona Ekhomu's Interview on his book: 'Boko Haram: Security Considerations and the Rise of an Insurgency'. March 8th, 2023. Available at https://m.youtube.com/watch?v=cHBxcfSJauk (Video; YouTube).

Earthrights. (2018). WIWA V. ROYAL DUTCH SHELL: 'Getting away with murder: Shell's complicity with crimes against humanity in Nigeria.' Earthrights.org. Available online at: https://earthrights.org/case/wiwa-v-royal-dutch-shell/; https://earthrightsdefenders.org/story/case-wiwa-v-royal-dutch-shell/

Egbe, E. J. (2014). Native authorities and local government reforms in Nigeria since 1914. Enyi John, Egbe; Department of Political Science, Benue state university, Makurdi, Nigeria. *IOSR Journal of Humanities and Social Sciences (IOSR-JHSS), 19*(3), 113–126. pp. 113, 114, (Ver. V (Mar. 2014), e-ISSN:2279-0837, p-ISSN:2279-0845) www.iosrjournal.org. Available online at https://www.iosrjournals.org/iosr-jhss/papers/Vol19-issue3/Version-5/S01935113127.pdf

Hoinathy, R., & Tayo, T (2022). *Lake Chad Basin, Socio-economic resilience in the Shadow of Boko Haram*. Institute for Security Studies (ISS), West Africa Report 38, March 2022. pp. 3 &6 (pp. 1–23). Available at https://issafrica.org/research/west-africa-report/lake-chad-basin-socio-economic-resilience-in-the-shadow-of-boko-haram

Kasali, T. (2020). 'Bad governance and political selection in Nigeria has a human cost', Toluwalola Kasali, London School of Economics and Political Science (LSE) Blogs; African Elections, Politics. December 18th, 2020. Available at https://blogs.lse.ac.uk/africaatlse/2020/12/18/bad-good-governance-political-selection-in-nigeria-elections-human-cost/

Mednick, S. (2023). Communities can fall apart: Senegal gas project drives locals to desperation, Euro News Green. *Climate*. Updated: 14/04/2023. Available online at https://www.euronews.com/green/2023/04/14/communites-can-fall-apart-senegal-gas-project-drives-locals-to-desperation

Moody, J. (2023). An offshore energy Bonanza spells doom for Senegal's Fishermen, Jessica Moody, World Politics Review (WPR), briefing West Africa, Jan 10, 2023. https://www.world-politicsreview.com/senegal-fishing-industry-oil-gas-reserves-economy-politics/

Nwafor, G. (2022). In Niger delta, oil spill is impoverishing residents, devastating environment, dislocating cultures. Published in Earthjournalism.net on 17 August 2022. Produced with support from Internews Earth Journalism Network. It was first published in the Nigerian Tribune on July 26, 2022. Available at https://earthjournalism.net/stories/in-niger-delta-oil-spill-is-impoverishing-residents-devastating-environment-dislocating

Nyangoro, J. E. (1994). Military Coups d'état in Nigeria Revisited: A Political and Economic Analysis. Julius E. Nyangoro, Published in the American Review of Politics (14:129), April 1993. DOI:10.15763/issn.2374-7781.1993.14.0.129-147. License: CC BY-NC-SA 4.0. Available online at https://www.researchgate.net/publication/308384412_Military_Coups_d'etat_in_Nigeria_Revisited_A_Political_and_Economic_Analysis

Omeje, K. (2004). The state, conflict & evolving politics in The Niger Delta, Nigeria. *Review of African Political Economy, 101*, 425–440. ISSN 0305-6244Print/1740-1720 ONLINE/04/0304425-26, ROAPE Publications Ltd., 2004. PP. 425, 435. Online] Available online at http://41.204.183.105/bitstream/handle/11732/801/omeje.pdf?sequence=4isAllowed=y

Oshwofasa, B. O., Anuta, D. E., & Aiyedogbon, J. O. (2012). Environmental degradation and oil industry activities in the Niger-Delta Region. Ohwofasa, Bright O. (Department of Arts and Social Sciences, Delta State Polytechnic, Oghara, Delta State, Nigeria, brightohwofasa@yahoo.com, Anuta, David E. (Department of Banking and Finance, Delta State Polytechnic, Otefe-Oghara, Delta state, Nigeria), Aiyedogbon John O. (Department of Economics, Nigerian Defence Academy, Kaduna, Kaduna State, Nigeria]. Available at: https://citeseerx.ist.psu.edu/document?repid=rep1&type=pdf&doi=8c4e0768fc3c298d8b128aab5a70af8b206908c1

Ostrom, E. (1990, 2015). *Governing the commons, the evolution of institutions for collective action*. Cambridge University Press. Published 1990, and September 2015.

Torres, M., Hayward, R. A., Meltzer, G., Garcia, C., & Bustos, T. E. (2022). Young adults and the impacts of compounding disaster (!Estamos Bien, Puerto Rico!), Natural Hazards Center (hazards.colorado.edu) 2022. Nellie Torres (New York University), R. Anna Hayward (Stony Brook University), Gabriel Meltzer, Catherine Garcia (Syracuse University), Tatiana E. Bustos (Michigan State University), Alejandro Silva Diaz (Mentes Puertorriqueñas en Acción). Available at https://bit.ly/3WML0Ha

Transboundary Climate Risks: An Overview. (2021). Publisher: Adaptation without borders (Responding to a global challenge).4 Pages. April 2023.Research Report Collaboration between the: Stockholm Environment Institute (SEI) and IDDRI (Institut De Recherche Indépendant, L'Institut Du Développement Durable T Des Relations Internationales - Independent Research Institute, The Institute for Sustainable Development and International Relations). [Updated in 2023]. Available online at https://adaptationwithoutborders.org/sites/weadapt.org/files/2017/transboundary_climate_risks_web-2.pdf

Olusegun Ehinfun is a management consultant with experience, expertise, and knowledge working in emerging and frontiers market economies on issues ranging from: business development consulting (BDC) to stakeholder and sustainability management. Also, currently an Environment and Politics PhD. researcher at the University of York, England. Researching the impacts of transboundary effects and water governance on geo-strategic cooperation among nation-states, with a focus on cooperation, environmental and security challenges within the Lake Chad Basin Area (LCBA) and Sahel regions of West and Central Africa, exploring how climate action, biodiversity, and environmental remediation can be integrated with sustainable social and governance strategies.

Paul R. Sachs is a consultant and licensed psychologist based in Philadelphia, PA, USA. For over 20 years, he was a nonprofit executive at organizations helping underserved individuals with mental health and substance use challenges. He is author of professional articles and chapters in the fields of rehabilitation psychology and CSR. He is co-editor with Dr. Shame Mjugova of the volume: Opportunities and Pitfalls of Corporate Social Responsibility: The Marange Diamond Mines Case Study (Springer 2019). Currently, Dr. Sachs works independently providing business consultation, training, and coaching.

ESG 2.0: The New Perspectives for Human Rights Due Diligence

Iury Prado Muci de Lima and Diego Costa Fernandes

1 Introduction

This paper examines the concept of Environmental, Social, and Governance (ESG) and its increasing prominence in contemporary business practices. While companies' voluntary adoption of ESG principles has gained significant traction, this trend has been largely driven by the absence of comprehensive regulations in the field. Consequently, companies often measure ESG impacts solely based on financial risks and the potential benefits to their business, thereby potentially limiting the real-world impact of ESG initiatives. However, the future trajectory of ESG is expected to be influenced by emerging laws and regulations that aim to establish clearer human rights obligations for companies.

Drawing upon academic research and insights from business practices, this paper presents an analysis of two approaches to integrating mandatory human rights into business ESG frameworks: the recent European Commission directive on Corporate Sustainability Due Diligence and the Strategic Climate Change Litigation practices within the realm of international private law.

Moreover, this study delves into the historical context of business and human rights, encompassing discussions surrounding the dichotomy between a legally binding treaty and a voluntary approach. It examines the divergent perspectives among developing and developed countries regarding the necessity of a mandatory approach in addressing human rights concerns. Additionally, the paper highlights

I. Prado Muci de Lima (✉)
Università degli Studi di Torino, Turín, Italy
e-mail: iury.pradomucidelima@unito.it

D. Costa Fernandes
Researcher, Planetary Collaboration, Geneva, Switzerland
e-mail: diegoc@planetarycollaboration.com

B. Díaz Díaz et al. (eds.), *Building Global Societies Towards an ESG World*, CSR, Sustainability, Ethics & Governance,
https://doi.org/10.1007/978-3-031-56619-6_14

the diverse criticisms raised against voluntary and non-binding human rights mechanisms for companies, such as the Global Compact, the UN Guiding Principles, ESG practices, and Corporate Social Responsibility (CSR) initiatives.

Furthermore, this research pays specific attention to recent developments in the field of business and human rights. It investigates two prominent mechanisms that have gained prominence. Firstly, it examines the Directive on Corporate Sustainability Due Diligence, which was endorsed by both the European Parliament in March 2021 and the Council in December 2020, highlighting its potential impact on the business landscape within the European Union. Secondly, the study explores Strategic Climate Change Litigation as an innovative approach to compelling companies to adhere to human rights and environmental standards.

Overall, this paper provides a comprehensive analysis of the evolving landscape of business and human rights, shedding light on the historical context, criticisms of voluntary mechanisms, and emerging mandatory approaches.

2 International Context and Discussions on a Legally Binding Treaty vs. Voluntary Approach

The discussions surrounding business and human rights emerged during the 1970s at the United Nations, evolving through distinct phases. According to S. Deva (2021), the debate initially focused on the balance between rights and responsibilities,[1] with developing countries seeking to impose obligations on corporations and developed countries prioritizing fair treatment for companies in host states. In the 1990s, the discussion centred on the choice between voluntary vs. binding regulations which resulted in another failure to elaborate a norm on the responsibilities of corporations (Draft UN Norms) and the launch of the UN Global Compact in 2000. From 2005 to 2011, the third phase focused on developing the UN Guiding Principles on Business and Human Rights (UNGPs), which were unanimously endorsed by the Human Rights Council in 2011 (Deva, 2021, pg. 145).

The term "Environment, Social, and Governance" (ESG) first emerged in a report titled "Who cares wins: Connecting financial markets to a changing world" (Global Compact, 2017), released by the United Nations Global Compact in a joint initiative with diverse actors of the financial sector in 2004. In the subsequent year, the United Nations Environment Programme (UNEP) Finance Initiative published a report titled "A legal framework for incorporating environmental, social, and governance issues into institutional investment" with the objective of analysing if investment policies could be integrated voluntarily, under legal requirements, or be hindered by laws and regulations (UNEP, 2005). In 2006, the Principles for

[1] The discussion was related to the 'Draft United Nations Code of Conduct on Transnational Corporations' (1984) 23 ILR 626 which was suspended by the UN.

Responsible Investment (PRI) was launched as a voluntary framework by which investors can incorporate ESG issues into their decision-making.

2.1 *Oppositions for a Legally Binding Treaty Between Developing and Developed Countries*

On the one hand, there was a divide between developed countries, backed up by companies, for a voluntary approach and developing countries favouring a legally binding treaty. On the other hand, there is a discussion about the legal basis to make businesses accountable in international Human Rights law.

A recent example was the divide on the Human Rights Council (HRC) to adopt a resolution to establish an intergovernmental working group on transnational corporations and other business enterprises with respect to human rights, led by the UN delegation from Ecuador and supported by a large number of NGOs and states (UN General Assembly, 2014). A division among the 47 members of the HRC, markedly between developing states and the developed ones, "within the 47-members-large Human Rights Council, it was supported by 20 member states[2] and opposed by 14 states (including the United States and the Member States of the European Union),[3] whereas 13 member states of the HRC abstained[4]" (Schutter, 2015). Opposing the Ecuador initiative, there was a draft resolution proposed by Norway supporting the UN Guiding Principles which lacked enough support and was abandoned. Therefore, an intergovernmental working group was established in 2014 "to elaborate an international legally binding instrument to regulate, in international human rights law, the activities of transnational corporations and other business enterprises" (UN Human Rights Council A/HRC/26/9, 2014).

Similarly, there was also a divergence in the Draft United Nations Code of Conduct on Transnational Corporations (1983). While "developing countries stressed the need for a legally binding international instrument, developed countries preferred a voluntary code" (Sauvant, 2015, pg. 46). According to TH Moran, the failure of the UN Code was due to a clash between government-oriented development and the primacy of the market mechanism (Moran, 2009). Also, because developing countries wanted to attract foreign investment and due to a shift from "investor responsibility to investor protection in the early 1990s" (Hamdani & Ruffing, 2021).

---

[2] Algeria, Benin, Burkina Faso, China, Congo, Cote d'Ivoire, Cuba, Ethiopia, India, Indonesia, Kazakhstan, Kenya, Morocco, Namibia, Pakistan, Philippines, Russia, South Africa, Venezuela, and Vietnam voted in favour of the resolution.

[3] The states who voted against the resolution are Austria, Czech Republic, Estonia, France, Germany, Ireland, Italy, Japan, Montenegro, South Korea, Romania, Macedonia, the United Kingdom, and the United States of America.

[4] Argentina, Botswana, Brazil, Chile, Costa Rica, Gabon, Kuwait, Maldives, Mexico, Peru, Saudi Arabia, Sierra Leone, and the United Arab Emirates abstained.

The second prevailing arguments are about the legal basis. Regarding the Draft UN Norms, the Sub-commission approved the text, but as it "has not been requested by the Commission and, as a draft proposal, has no legal standing" (UN Commission on Human Rights, 2004, pg. 15). Also, Krajewski describes the public-private divide in Human Rights Law. According to him

> "A rejection of the notion of 'direct horizontal effect', i.e. an obligation of non-state actors under international law, and the establishment of the state duty to protect are thus the cornerstones of the public–private divide in conventional human rights law doctrine. Yet the state's duty to protect is also the reaction of this doctrine to the problem that rights are often infringed by private actors. The state duty to protect establishes indirect duties for corporations as it relies on states to adopt legislative, administrative, or judicial measures to establish and implement obligations for non-state actors. (...) This question has played a significant role in many domestic debates as proponents of these laws, in particular *civil society organisations, have argued that companies need to be bound to direct human rights obligations, while business associations reject such legislative instruments*." (Krajewski, 2023, pg. 6)

"Ruggie (2015), argues that those obligations derive from societal expectations, not from legal norms. Therefore, possibly their most striking shortcoming is that they recognise that businesses do not have legal obligations to respect, but only 'responsibility to respect', which 'is not an obligation under international human rights law imposed directly upon companies'" (Woods, 2015, pg. 649). Ruggie, former Special Representative of the Secretary-General (SRSG), is known as the biggest defender of a voluntary approach for business and human rights which favoured the private sector. Some scholars place him in an antagonistic position (Deva, 2021) or the most prominent public voice opposing a comprehensive treaty (Bilchitz, 2016).

2.2 Criticism About a Voluntary Approach

Based on this historic overview until 2010, it is clear that voluntary initiatives prevailed over mandatory ones. However, diverse criticism is made about the voluntary and non-binding human rights mechanisms for companies, such as the Global Compact, the UN Guiding Principles, ESG, Corporate Social Responsibility (CSR) and others. Even the European Commission (2022) mentioned that voluntary action does not appear to have resulted in large-scale improvement across sectors which had, as a consequence, negative impacts on EU production inside and outside of the Union.

The UN Global Compact has become the largest corporate sustainability initiative but has had limited success in driving meaningful changes in corporate conduct. Many companies join the Compact for its association with the UN (Deva, 2021). The UN Global Compact Progress Report shows that "only 13 per cent of the surveyed companies have reported requiring their suppliers to commit to the ten principles" (UN Global Compact, 2019). According to the Corporate Human Rights

Benchmark report of 2020, a significant portion of assessed corporations (46.2%) across five sectors failed to obtain any points for their implementation of Human Rights Due Diligence (World Benchmarking Alliance, 2020). This finding indicates a notable gap in these companies' efforts to assess and address potential human rights impacts within their operations.

The UN Guiding Principles do not provide sanctions for corporate human rights abuses, giving corporations a free hand in incorporating human rights into their business activities (Černič, 2018). Additionally, some widely spread concerns are that companies measure ESG impacts based on financial risks vs. the opportunities posed to their business which can lead to greenwashing; the reduction of ESG's positive effect in the real world as companies may prioritize what is easier and what benefits more their brands; and limited transparency as companies do not disclose the more sensitive and controversial issues in their own operations and their value chain. "While businesses are encouraged to consider risks to people, in practice this has led to corporations focusing mostly on risks to themselves, especially if they rely on traditional due diligence tools" (Fasterling, 2017, pg. 233).

On the other side of the spectrum, the defenders of a voluntary approach mention that the UN Guiding Principles were essential to promote a human rights culture in the daily activities of business—it is particularly true in the case of the European Union as described in the next section.

3 New Developments in Business and Human Rights

In addition to the UN Human Rights Council initiative for transnational corporations mentioned before, there are two other initiatives that are still under development with the attempt to create a regulation with Human Rights responsibilities for companies. The first, at the European Union, is the Directive on corporate sustainability due diligence[5] called by both the Parliament in March 2021 and the Council in December 2020. The second prominent mechanism is the Strategic Climate Change Litigation as an attempt to oblige companies to comply with human rights and environmental standards.

[5] European Commission. "Just and sustainable economy: Commission lays down rules for companies to respect human rights and environment in global value chains". *Corporate sustainability due diligence*, 2022, https://ec.europa.eu/commission/presscorner/detail/en/ip_22_1145 (accessed 03 March 2023).

3.1 Corporate Sustainability Due Diligence Directive (CSDDD)

The European Union has a longstanding history of establishing standards for companies, with notable examples dating back to 1999 and 2006. These efforts include compliance with the UN Guiding Principles on Business and Human Rights. The latest addition to this ongoing progress is the introduction of the Corporate Sustainability Due Diligence Directive (2022).

Historically, the European Parliament played a significant role in advancing corporate responsibility. In 1999, it called for the development of a European multilateral framework governing the operations of European enterprises worldwide (European Parliament, Resolution A4-0508/98, 1999). Similarly, in 2006, the European Parliament approved a report emphasizing the need for improved access to justice for victims seeking accountability of European corporations for human rights abuses (Corporate Social Responsibility: A New Partnership, 2006). In 2016, the Parliament adopted a resolution urging member states to take appropriate steps to ensure access to effective remedies for victims of human rights abuses by corporations operating in third countries. The Council of Europe has aligned its approach with the UN Guiding Principles on Business and Human Rights, with European states supporting the work of the UN Working Group on Business and Human Rights. With that, National Action Plans implementing the UN Guiding Principles have been adopted by several European states, although many have lagged behind in developing their plans and strengthening their national systems to ensure greater corporate human rights accountability (Černič, J., 2018).

These examples illustrate the continuous efforts within the European Union to promote responsible business conduct and enhance human rights standards for companies operating both within and beyond its borders. The introduction of the Corporate Sustainability Due Diligence Directive represents a significant step forward in this regard.

However, concerns regarding the existing imbalance in human rights protection between individuals and businesses have also been raised. While companies have the ability to bring cases before the European Court of Human Rights, individuals alleging violations of their rights by private corporations face challenges in effectively pursuing their claims within this jurisdiction (Parliamentary Assembly, 2010).

The demand for the EU economy to address adverse impacts, as expressed by its citizens during the Conference on the Future of Europe, has been a driving force behind existing and upcoming national legislation on human rights and environmental due diligence. Debates at the national level, along with calls for action from the European Parliament and the Council (European Commission directive 2019/1937, 2022), have further reinforced the need for wider rules on corporate due diligence.

At the time of this paper's publication, the Corporate Sustainability Due Diligence Directive (CSDDD) is still being negotiated. Despite ongoing discussions, it is possible to identify four main points of disagreement regarding the proposal (European Parliament—Plenary Session, 2023): the inclusion of financial institutions; directors' responsibility; the burden of proof; and the breadth of coverage across the value chain.

One significant area of contention has been the extent to which financial institutions would fall under the directive's scope. This point aims to prevent large investment funds from evading responsibility and emphasizes the need for these institutions to acknowledge their global impact. During the parliamentary vote, the committee's position was supported, indicating that financial institutions will be included in the directive. However, while the Parliament agreed to mandatory due diligence checks for financial services and institutions, member states would prefer to keep them optional.

Another point of discussion concerns the responsibility of directors. For large companies with over 1000 employees, meeting the targets set by the directive could affect directors' variable remuneration. However, the broader proposed rules that would hold directors legally responsible for implementing and overseeing the due diligence process within their companies did not pass. Although this is a controversial topic, the Dutch Child Labour Due Diligence Law (2019) contemplates criminal liability with the responsible company director liable for up to 2 years of imprisonment under the Dutch Economic Offences Act.

Regarding the burden of proof, EU lawmakers reached an agreement that the claimants, rather than the companies, bear the responsibility of proving the existence of adverse impacts associated with a company's activities. This means that victims will need to demonstrate the link between adverse impacts and a company's actions. Therefore, it is a barrier added to victims of human rights violations.

Furthermore, the directive aims to focus not only on the value chain but also on business processes. Although member states have agreed on a narrow definition of the 'chain of activities', the Parliament has supported the application of due diligence rules not only to the organization and its supply chain but also to the sale, distribution, transport, storage, and waste management of products and services.

The procedure for approving the CSDDD involves a co-decision process, in which the European Commission submits the proposal to both the Council and the European Parliament. The legislative proposal can be adopted at the first, second, or even third reading. If, at the third reading, an agreement is not reached even with the support of a conciliation committee, the proposal is not adopted, and the procedure comes to an end. Even though some points may change in the final text of the CSDDD, it is evident that there is no consensus and that companies have a huge say in the process.

3.2 Strategic Climate Change Litigation Practices in Private International Law

Litigation refers to processes conducted by two competing parties to enforce or defend a legal right. Litigation is 'strategic' in human rights when it is purposefully aimed to promote the clarification, respect, protection, and fulfilment of rights.

The identification and pursuit of legal matters as part of a human rights promotion strategy are known as strategic litigation. It concentrates on a single example to effect greater social change. These instances established significant legal precedents by publicly exposing abuses, increasing awareness, and influencing policy, practice changes, and legislation. Strategic litigation on a national, regional, or worldwide scale can have a long-term impact on a huge number of individuals. In that regard, many strategic climate change litigations or impact litigations are now well-known worldwide. This new term aims to raise awareness of climate change and sustainability issues by adding references to the Corporate Social Responsibility (CSR) and Environmental, Sustainability, and Governance (ESG) framework.

Climate change litigation has escalated considerably since the Paris Agreement was signed in 2015. The Grantham Research Institute on Climate Change and the Environment compiled a 2021/2022 Report that included over 1000 new court cases filed in the previous 6 years.

A narrow definition of climate change litigation can be described as follows:

> *'[A]ny piece of federal, state, tribal, or local administrative or judicial litigation in which the party filings or tribunal decisions directly and expressly raise an issue of fact or law regarding the substance or policy of climate change causes and impacts.' (David Markell and J.B. Ruhl, 'An Empirical Assessment of Climate Change in the Courts: A New Jurisprudence or Business as Usual?' 64 Fla. L. Rev. (2012) 15, 27).*

But a broader definition can also be stated as follows:

> *'there is a need for concepts of climate litigation that are able to capture lower profile cases where climate change is more peripheral to arguments in, or the motivation for, the lawsuit.' (Jacqueline Peel and Jolene Lin 'Transnational Climate Litigation: The Contribution of The Global South' 113 AJIL (2019) 679, 691).*

Explaining the functions of litigation comes as a way to limit GHG (greenhouse gas) emissions, adapting to the impacts of climate change by observing that the government can take into account climate change in its decision-making, ordering the government to take stronger climate action, compensation for the victims of climate change damages, and also to raise public awareness. In addition to that, the sources of law such as the violations of international law, international norms for interpretive purposes (ex: Leghari, Urgenda), and National law (ex: Clean Air Act, Endangered Species Act in the USA; Access to Environmental Information Act in Germany) are useful to understand about climate change litigation.

It is worth noting, from the perspective of private international law, that one complaint of this type speaks the language of conflicts of laws. Milieudefensie et al. v. Royal Dutch Shell plc., resolved by the Hague District Court in May 2021, is a class action initiated by seven non-governmental organizations (NGOs) and 17,379 individuals against a private firm headquartered in the Netherlands.

The lawsuit called into question whether a private firm might breach its duty of care and human rights obligations by failing to make necessary efforts to reduce greenhouse gas emissions. Before proceeding to the merits of a case including multiple cross-border components, The Hague District Court had to determine its own jurisdiction over the defendant and the applicable law. The Brussels I bis Regulation and the Rome II Regulation were deemed applicable in this case.

Strategy is the ambitious pursuit of a plan of action that will create and compound a competitive advantage in order to enable the achievement of the desired objectives. The Grantham Research Institute on Climate Change and the Environment defines "strategic litigation" as lawsuits "where the claimants' motives for bringing the cases go beyond the concerns of the individual litigant and aim to bring about some broader societal shift, such as 'advancing climate policies, creating public awareness, or changing the behaviour of government or industry actors'"(Setzer & Higham, 2021).

Such lawsuits exist at the crossroads of 'shaping' and 'enforcing' domestic laws. This is demonstrated by the lack of global consensus among the applicants on critical aspects of such litigation, such as the criterion for allocating the burden of mitigating measures among states and by the emphasis placed by NGOs on efforts made to adopt, for the purposes of human rights-based litigation, a common scientific standard regarding emission reductions, on the assumption that such standard is not satisfactory.

Following in the footsteps of Milieudefensie et al. v. Royal Dutch Shell plc., some developments in climate change litigation point to the evolution of new court strategies in which climate activists direct their claims towards large transnational corporations.

The Dutch Urgenda case has contributed to the creation of a strong incentive for national climate trials: The Court decided that the Dutch government owed more aggressive mitigation measures under national, European, and international law.

Recent advances in climate change litigation support this approach. The Four Islanders of Pari case in Indonesia utilizes common private law techniques (tortious responsibility) to hold a foreign transnational firm accountable for its overall CO2 emissions creating a very intriguing situation. The factor of the timing and nature of the damage alleged by the applicants make this case fit into a larger context of litigation that involves several international bodies and tribunals, demonstrating a certain complementarity of action, or at least a commonality of end goals, between private and public international law.

The claim is made against Holcim, a company based in Switzerland that specializes in cement production. Specifically, the plaintiffs are attempting to demonstrate a direct link between Holcim's considerable pro-rata contribution to such emissions and the negative effects of the Pari Island ecosystem.

However, there is a significant distinction between the two scenarios. While Lliuya is subject to the Brussels I bis and Rome II Regulations, the Four Islanders of Pari will be controlled by the 1987 Swiss Act on PIL (SwAPIL). Given the Swiss legislator's significantly divergent choice in this regard, the identification of the applicable legislation may perhaps be the key point of argument in the Four Islanders of Pari case from the position of Private International Law. In its second paragraph, Article 133 SwAPIL mentions that the place where the parties to a dispute are not normally resident in the same State, torts are governed by the law of the State where the tort was committed.[6]

A relevant important factor in this matter is jurisdiction, which is, in fact, the most complex and important area of Private International Law as it can adjudicate, prescribe, or enforce, and the first conclusion to be drawn from Lliuya is that establishing jurisdiction in these types of proceedings is relatively simple, considering the well-known principle of actor sequitur forum rei. Suing at the defendant's domicile ensures access to a (European) forum under Article 4 of the Brussels Ibis Regulation.

Pragmatically, the fact that (economically disadvantaged) third-country plaintiffs may be required to pay court fees or warranties to access the local forum should not be particularly problematic in cases where litigation is supported by external funding through NGOs or other means.

A recent example is FossielVrij NL v. KLM, in which a group of environmental organizations is suing (in the Netherlands) the national airline KLM for its 'Fly Responsibly' advertisement campaign (which is based on allegedly false claims of 'climate neutrality' or 'CO2ZERO').

It simply notes that "because both [the applicant] and KLM have registered offices in the Netherlands, the Dutch court has jurisdiction over this dispute. As a result, Dutch law will apply to Fossil Free's claims against the defendant".

It is important to conclude that National climate disputes, on the other hand, benefit from international talks and State promises, as well as new clarifications on the customary 'no harm' criterion. Claimants count on factual data collected in accordance with the Paris Agreement scientific arguments mainly with the reliability of Intergovernmental Panel on Climate Change (IPCC) reports that are widely recognized and legal arguments such as the goals of limiting global warming.

They can also rely on legislation that implements a state's international commitments in a less direct way. In this regard, the Paris Agreement serves as a fertile ground for national lawsuits rather than legal issues in and of themselves.[7] While the

[6] EAPIL, "Private International Law and Climate Change: the "Four Islanders of Pari" Case".2023, https://eapil.org/2023/01/10/private-international-law-and-climate-change-the-four-islanders-of-pari-case/ (accessed 26 October 2023).

[7] Sandrine Maljean-Dubois. Climate litigation: The impact of the Paris Agreement in national courts. The Taiwan law review, 2022, 324, pp. 211–222. ffhalshs-03679086f.

Paris Agreement does not allocate each country a carbon budget, it does provide a framework for calculating one based on national pledges.[8]

4 Conclusion

The discussions surrounding the responsibility of businesses to respect, protect, and fulfil human rights have been ongoing for a considerable period of time. However, a consensus about the obligation of businesses in this regard remains elusive, as it is generally perceived as the duty of states under international law. Nevertheless, progress has been made through voluntary initiatives aimed at promoting human rights in business practices, although attempts to create a legally binding instrument have been unsuccessful until 2010. The current landscape, however, is witnessing notable changes.

The emergence of the UN Human Rights Council initiative for transnational corporations, the Corporate Sustainability Due Diligence Directive (CSDDD), and the increasing prominence of Strategic Climate Change Litigation practices within international law are raising the bar for human rights. These developments suggest a shifting paradigm where business obligations to respect human rights are being re-evaluated and may potentially become more legally enforceable.

There is a clear historical pattern of *progressive realization* of human rights over time. These advancements are now paving the way for a new phase in the integration of environmental, social, and governance (ESG) factors, which are referred to in this paper as ESG 2.0 encompassing a clearer commitment to all human rights due diligence (HRDD). Yet, it is crucial for regulators and policymakers to critically assess the practical limitations of HRDD and move beyond simply mandating its implementation. Merely making HRDD mandatory does not guarantee significant improvements in the situation of rights holders or lead to a fundamental transformation in business operations (Deva, 2023).

Regardless of whether human rights due diligence obligations are perceived as obligations of conduct or of result, it is important to note that they do not establish a direct horizontal effect on human rights. Based on the European Corporate Sustainability Due Diligence Directive, victims of human rights violations may not directly claim a violation of their rights by a company. "Instead, they could claim that the violation of a particular right protected by an applicable domestic law (e.g. right to life, health, freedom, property, etc.) was caused by a violation of a due diligence obligation" (Krajewski, 2023, pg.13). However, based on Strategic Climate Change Litigation practices in international private law, there is the emergence of

[8] Jaise Kuriakose, Chris Jones, Kevin Anderson, Carly McLachlan, John Broderick, What does the Paris climate change agreement mean for local policy? Downscaling the remaining global carbon budget to sub-national areas, Renewable and Sustainable Energy Transition, Volume 2, 2022, 100030, ISSN 2667-095X, https://doi.org/10.1016/j.rset.2022.100030. (https://www.sciencedirect.com/science/article/pii/S2667095X22000149).

new court strategies in which climate activists direct their claims towards large transnational corporations.

Nevertheless, it is imperative to recognize that human rights due diligence laws do not replace the state's responsibility to respect, protect, and fulfil human rights; rather, they complement it.

In light of these considerations, ongoing efforts to promote business accountability for human rights must navigate the complex legal and practical challenges involved. By pursuing a balanced approach that incorporates both voluntary initiatives and regulatory measures, it may be possible to foster a corporate culture that genuinely respects and upholds internationally recognized human rights standards.

References

Bilchitz, D. (2016). The necessity for a business and human rights treaty. *Business and Human Rights Journal, 1*(2), 203–227. https://doi.org/10.1017/bhj.2016.13

Woods, C. (2015). It Isn't a state problem: The Minas conga mine controversy and the need for binding international obligations on corporate actors. *Georgetown Journal of International Law*, 629–683. 649.

Černič, J. (2018). European perspectives on the business and human rights treaty initiative. In J. Letnar Cernic & N. Carrillo-Santarelli (Eds.), *The future of business and human rights: Theoretical and practical considerations for a UN treaty* (pp. 229–250). Intersentia. https://doi.org/10.1017/9781780686455.012

Commission on Human Rights. Report on the 60th session, 15 March-23 April 2004 para. (c). Available at https://digitallibrary.un.org/record/537775, Accessed May 21, 2023.

Deva, S. (2023). Mandatory human rights due diligence laws in Europe: A mirage for rightsholders? *Leiden Journal of International Law, 36*(2), 389–414. https://doi.org/10.1017/S0922156522000802

Deva, S. (2021). The UN guiding principles on business and human rights and its predecessors: Progress at a Snail's pace? In I. Bantekas & M. Stein (Eds.), *The Cambridge companion to business and human rights law (Cambridge companions to law)* (pp. 145–172). Cambridge University Press. https://doi.org/10.1017/9781108907293.008

European Commission. (2022). Just and sustainable economy: Commission lays down rules for companies to respect human rights and environment in global value chains. Corporate sustainability due diligence, Available at https://ec.europa.eu/commission/presscorner/detail/en/ip_22_1145. Accessed March 3, 2023.

European Parliament—Plenary Session. (2023). MEPs push companies to mitigate their negative social and environmental impact. Available at https://www.europarl.europa.eu/news/en/press-room/20230524IPR91907/meps-push-companies-to-mitigate-their-negative-social-and-environmental-impact. Accessed June 2, 2023.

Fasterling, B. (2017). Human rights due diligence as risk management: Social risk versus human rights risk. *Business and Human Rights Journal, 2*(2), 225–247. https://doi.org/10.1017/bhj.2016.26

Ruggie, J. G. (2015). Regulating Multinationals: The UN Guiding Principles, Civil Society, and International Legalization. In *Regulatory policy program working paper RPP-2015-04*. Mossavar-Rahmani Center for Business and Government, Harvard Kennedy School, Harvard University.

K. Hamdani, & L. Ruffing (Eds.) (2021). The United Nations Centre on Transnational Corporations: Corporate Conduct and the Public Interest(Routledge 2015) In Deva, S.

Krajewski, M. (2023). Mandatory human rights due diligence Laws: Blurring the lines between state duty to protect and corporate responsibility to respect? *Nordic Journal of Human Rights*. https://doi.org/10.1080/18918131.2023.2195232

de Schutter, O. (2015). *Towards a new treaty on business and human rights*. Cambridge University Press.

Sauvant, K. P. (2015). The Negotiations of the United Nations Code of Conduct on Transnational Corporations: Experience and Lessons Learned. *The Journal of World Investment & Trade, 16*(1), 11–87. https://doi.org/10.1163/22119000-01601002

Setzer, J., & Higham, C. (2021). *Global trends in climate change litigation: 2021 snapshot*. Grantham Research Institute on Climate Change and the Environment and Centre for Climate Change Economics and Policy, London School of Economics and Political Science.

TH Moran (2009). The United Nations and Transnational Corporations: A Review and a Perspective. Transnational Corporations, (pp. 91–112). https://doi.org/10.18356/8cbf8f8c-en

UN General Assembly. (2014). Elaboration of an international legally binding instrument on transnational corporations and other business enterprises with respect to human rights. A/HRC/RES/26/9. Human Rights Council. Available at https://documents-dds-ny.un.org/doc/UNDOC/GEN/G14/082/52/PDF/G1408252.pdf?OpenElement. Accessed May 28, 2023.

UN Global Compact. Progress Report 2019 (UN Global Compact, 2019) 31. In Deva. S (2021) (pp. 154–155).

United Nations Environment Programme Finance Initiative. (2005). A legal framework for incorporating environmental, social and governance issues into institutional investment. Freshfields Bruckhaus Deringer. Available at https://www.unepfi.org/fileadmin/documents/freshfields_legal_resp_20051123.pdf.

United Nations Global Compact(2019). UN Global Compact Progress Report 2019. Available at https://unglobalcompact.org/library/5716

World Benchmarking Alliance. 'Corporate Human Rights Benchmark: 2020 Key Findings'. (2020) Available at www.worldbenchmarkingalliance.org/research/corporate-human-rights-benchmark-2020-key-findings-report/.

Iury Prado Muci de Lima lived in 8 countries so far accumulating global experience in Law by attending his bachelor's degree in Brazil, a master's degree in International and Comparative Law in the United States, and currently attending his Ph.D. in Private International Law with research on Strategic Climate Change Litigation in Italy. His professional background includes International Human Rights, Public International Law, and Private International Law, ESG and CSR practices. All of these past opportunities were gained in the private and public sectors, including NGOs and the Office of the United Nations High Commissioner for Human Rights in Geneva.

Diego Costa Fernandes Diego Costa's work focuses on the nexus between scientific knowledge, policy formulation and policy implementation. He worked in multiple United Nations organisations (UN OCHA, UN Migration - International Organization for Migration, UNESCO, and UN Environment Programme), NGOs and the private sector in six countries. With a degree in Mass Communication, an MBA in Business Intelligence, and a master's in Human Rights at the University of Vienna, Diego specializes in knowledge management to facilitate collaboration and knowledge sharing among diverse stakeholders. Currently based in Geneva, he serves as an international consultant and Executive Director at Planetary Collaboration.

Collaborating for a Sustainable Future: A Case Study of an Energy Conglomerate's Transformation

Heejung Yim, Tae Su Kim, Hyunmin Kang, and Seoyoung Kim

1 Introduction

Korean conglomerates actively adopt sustainability in their businesses and transform their operations in alignment with Environmental, Social, and Governance (ESG) principles. They are setting up their ESG goals and trying to enhance their overall corporate sustainability. Increasing demand for electric vehicles (EVs) is changing the ecosystem of the energy industry as well as mobility. As EVs bring diverse industries to the electromobility (e-mobility) ecosystem, companies face new opportunities to expand or transform their businesses to meet their carbon reduction goals. In this ecosystem, charging infrastructure has the most important role in expanding EVs on the road, and EV charging is required to be public, fast, and convenient. In line with this trend, oil companies are exploring gas station transformation as part of their carbon neutrality initiatives. In this study, we explore how the petroleum industry is making the transition to EV charging and creating a new ecosystem by collaborating with other industries in their green transformation. To understand this transformation in Korea, we examine how a company initiates and collaborates with the government and local entrepreneurs to transform its business while minimizing the risk of investment, using the case of

H. Yim (✉) · H. Kang
Stanford Center at the Incheon Global Campus (SCIGC), Stanford University, Incheon, Republic of Korea
e-mail: hyim@stanford.edu

T. S. Kim · S. Kim
GS Caltex, Seoul, Republic of Korea
e-mail: jennsy@stanford.edu

B. Díaz Díaz et al. (eds.), *Building Global Societies Towards an ESG World*, CSR, Sustainability, Ethics & Governance,
https://doi.org/10.1007/978-3-031-56619-6_15

GS Caltex,[1] a leading petroleum company in Korea. The major factors that support successful collaboration among corporations, industry stakeholders, governments, and institutions to drive innovation are discussed in this paper. The focus is not solely on the success or failure of new green businesses or evaluating the effectiveness of collaboration, but rather on understanding the forms of collaboration and essential factors being pursued as they transition into the e-mobility ecosystem.

1.1 Methodology

To analyze and understand how the collaboration is structured and effectively working, we conducted a literature review, case studies, and interviews targeting stakeholders of the project. We investigated how government incentives are driving the transformation of energy and mobility industries through the case of Jeju Smart City Challenge Project, which sets a goal of being a Carbon-Free Island (CFI) by 2030 and puts efforts into expanding green energy and mobility environments on the island with the private sector. For creating an e-mobility ecosystem, we studied how GS Caltex initiated the gas station transformation with cross sectoral collaboration. Comparing the Government-led consortium and cross-sectoral collaboration provides us an opportunity to explore the early stage of collaboration in energy transition of the conglomerate in terms of collaboration and networking with diverse types of companies and organizations, which is yet underexplored. We discuss how our findings contribute to organically creating the e-mobility ecosystem and increasing the sustainability of our community. The challenges in transformation towards net-zero provide insights that can guide future tools for designing and building new ecosystems.

1.2 About Jeju Smart City Challenge Project

The study begins by examining the recent endeavors of GS Caltex as part of the Jeju Smart City Challenge Project. This initiative, led by the Jeju Island local government and the Ministry of Land, Infrastructure, and Transportation (MOLIT), aims to design a sustainable and eco-friendly urban environment in the fields of energy,

[1] GS Caltex is a South Korean energy and chemical company co-owned by Chevron and GS Group, which is actively leading a transformative process for sustainable management. The company was established in 1967 as the first private oil refining company in Korea and has significantly contributed to the growth of the Korean economy. It exports petroleum, petrochemical, and lubricant products to 57 countries, and its competitiveness as a world-class oil refining company is attributed to its adoption of cutting-edge technologies (GS Caltex, 2020). Since 2021, GS Caltex has actively invested in sustainability fields and has been making proactive efforts to address climate change through diverse business activities. Through various partnerships and investments, GS Caltex is actively building a new mobility ecosystem that integrates energy services, mobility solutions, and lifestyle services. This integrated approach allows the company to cater to a broader customer base and meet their evolving mobility requirements. This ecosystem requires strong partnerships, investments, and collaborative efforts that drive innovation and value creation for the industry and consumers.

mobility, and transportation. The research investigates GS Caltex's role in constructing electric vehicle (EV) charging stations and networks on Jeju Island in alignment with the project's objectives. The research focuses on understanding the characteristics and dynamics of collaboration facilitated by government initiatives and examines the unique features, challenges, and benefits associated with collaborations established under the guidance of government entities. In parallel, the study also explores GS Caltex's Green Transformation to understand the collaboration model with ecosystem players without government involvement. To gain insights into the collaboration strategies of GS Caltex, a wide analysis of its recent endeavors towards green transformation is conducted. This examines the company's strategic shifts, partnerships, and initiatives aimed at sustainability. By analyzing diverse partnerships forged in this process, the study dissects the complexity of collaborations among various sectors of the energy and transportation industries and an e-mobility ecosystem through the gas station transformation.

For this research, qualitative insights are collected through interviews conducted with the companies actively participating in the Jeju Smart City Challenge Project, including GS Caltex. These interviews provide valuable insights on the motivations, challenges, and outcomes of collaborative efforts within the energy and e-mobility sectors. Also, a literature review is performed to understand collaboration models, government-industry partnerships, and sustainable urban development initiatives. During the 2-year period of the Jeju Smart City Challenge Project, direct observations on collaborative interactions are conducted to collect and provide qualitative data. This contributes to a more comprehensive understanding of collaborative dynamics, ecosystem creation, energy transition, and collaborative governance for green transformation. These approaches, qualitative data from interviews, observations, and literature reviews, provide the basis for an analysis of company's collaborative strategies, effectiveness, and implications for the energy sector's shift towards sustainability. Eighteen employees from thirteen companies and the Jeju government office were interviewed in person, taking an average of 60 to 90 min for each interview.

2 Government-Driven Collaboration: Project for Carbon Free Island

Among the four major oil refining companies in Korea, GS Caltex was the first to enter the electric vehicle charging business, to meet its energy transition goals. The company collaborates with the government and continues to actively construct charging infrastructure and transform gas stations to new sources of energy supply. Islands are important in national strategies to reduce carbon emissions and promote renewable energy. Islands are often used as testbeds for new technologies that can benefit the local economy and environment (Kallis et al., 2021). Due to its geographical nature as an island, Jeju faces higher costs for building an EV charging infrastructure and electrical work on transportation facilities in comparison to mainland areas. These higher costs impede economic feasibility, which is the fundamental nature of the companies to exist. This hinders companies from expanding the business of charging infrastructure. Jeju Island has been leading the EV charging infrastructure through Smart Grid projects for more than 10 years, but some operators have failed to operate and maintain the equipment properly. This experience has had a negative impact on many other related projects and businesses, leading companies to be cautious about entering the charging business.

With the recent surge in electric vehicle demand, Jeju Island has proactively initiated and funded pilot projects for transitioning to smart energy and mobility infrastructure aligned with the Carbon Free Island 2030 agenda. A consortium of 15 companies in Jeju wins government funding for the Smart City Challenge project to address urban issues on Jeju Island (Jeju Special Self-Governing Province, 2021). GS Caltex is part of a consortium that has secured USD 20 million in funding from the Ministry of Land, Infrastructure, and Transport (MOLIT) and the Jeju local government to explore and test new businesses for the green transformation of the island, including the gas station transformation. The project aims to implement a personal mobility platform and a Smart Transit system that connect personal mobility with public transportation and demonstrate a power trade model using Energy Storage Systems (ESS) under a regulatory sandbox. It also plans to build smart hubs, which are charging stations for personal mobility and electric vehicles, throughout Jeju to support these services (e-3DA: Jeju Smart City Challenge Project, 2021). The consortium participating companies were selected competitively by the government, mostly local companies from Jeju Island, and they were able to boldly undertake new business with low investment risks through government funding. Especially, by regulatory sandboxes for pilot projects, they could identify and test new business opportunities.

Overall, we gained insights through group discussions during organizational meetings, interactive workshops with consortium companies, and 2 years of field observations. A government-led consortium is swiftly organized with selected companies aligned with project goals and requirements. It employs a streamlined decision-making process, facilitating rapid work progress to achieve project objectives within the timeline. However, their partnerships and collaborations were limited due to the allocated funding, work scope, and timeframe. The project had to operate within these constraints, and it made collaboration with non-consortium partners difficult. Particularly as the project progressed, differences in the pace and outcomes of the project emerged among the companies in the consortium based on their capabilities and conditions.

2.1 Collaboration Dynamics: Government-Driven Consortium

The Jeju Smart City Challenge Project is conducted by the consortium, which is composed of 15 companies and organizations selected by the Jeju government before the project starts (Fig. 1). The project is characterized by closed-group

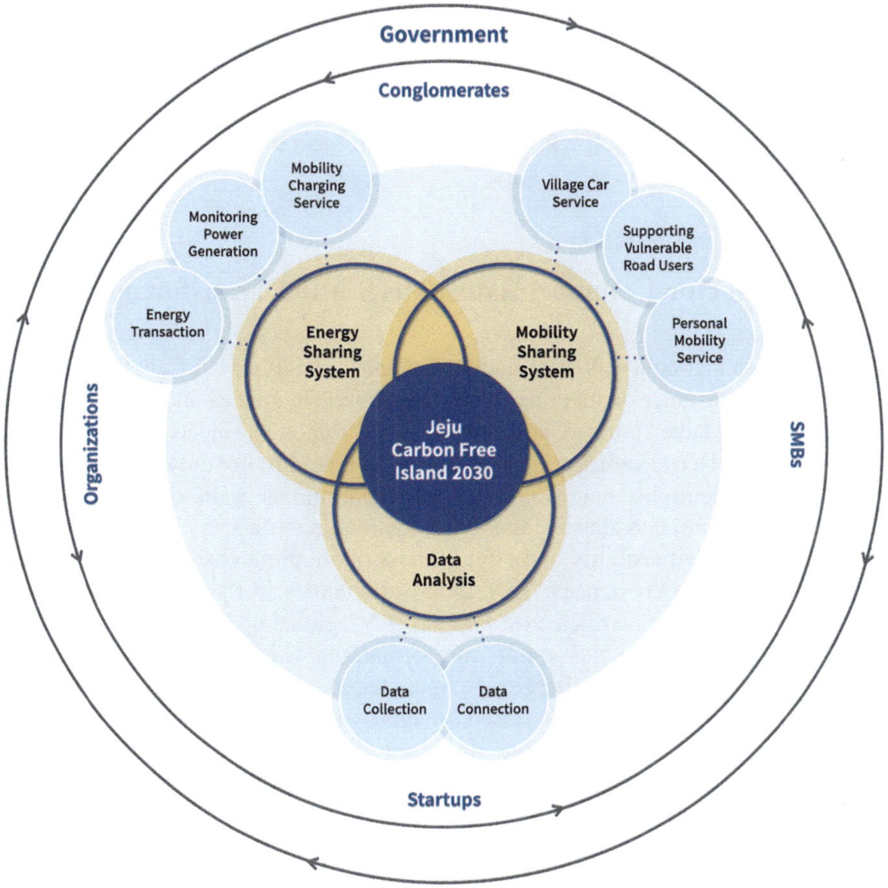

Fig. 1 Dynamics of Jeju Smart Challenge Project Collaboration, government-driven consortium

collaboration, and consortium members are from different sectors and fields and different sizes of businesses, from startups to conglomerates. Jeju local government has authority over decision-making and expenditure approvals for project funding. Mobility and energy sharing system implementation are the main goals of the project to achieve The Jeju Carbon Free Island 2030.

Smart Hub Through the Jeju Smart City Challenge Project, people could access charging and rental services for electric vehicles and personal mobility from gas stations. After 2 years of the project, Smart Hubs have been built in about 50% of existing gas stations, and personal mobility charging equipment is operated as well as fast EV chargers. GS Caltex collaborates with Jeju's local startups in the consortium to offer personal mobility rental services at the Smart Hub. In addition, Jeju Energy Plus Hub, the first multi-complex energy charging station in Korea built by GS Caltex, provides collaborative services with companies from diverse industries.

Energy Storage System with Re-Use EV Batteries Energy Plus Jeju, an e-mobility flagship site of GS Caltex, is currently under construction as an achievement of the Jeju Smart City Challenge. In collaboration with KIA Motors, Energy Storage System (ESS) with re-use EV batteries will be installed in the station and connected to EV chargers. It will be a good pilot project to test future collaboration and investment as well as technology.

3 Cross-Sector Collaborations: Gas Station Transformations

Oil companies that own refineries and gas stations, including GS Caltex, have recognized the importance of adapting to changing energy demands and environmental concerns. They have initiated gas station transformation projects to incorporate renewable and electric vehicle charging facilities. This shift not only aligns with the goal of carbon neutrality but also offers new opportunities in the evolving energy-mobility ecosystem. Gas station transformation requires trials, tests, and pilot projects to evaluate the feasibility and effectiveness of adopting charging technologies and new customer experiences. To respond to changes in the energy sector and contribute to the diffusion of electric vehicles (EV), global oil companies, including GS Caltex, are attempting gas station transformations. GS Caltex has been actively pursuing the electric vehicle charging business based on its existing gas stations for the energy transition since 2019. Based on approximately 2600 gas stations across South Korea, the company is expanding into the network-based mobility business and creating a new space where gas stations are integrated with lifestyle services (GS Caltex CSR Team, 2021).

Escaping from the conventional concept of gas stations, where customers visit to refuel or wash their cars, GS Caltex is redefining the role of gas stations into new platforms that cater daily life related services to customers without cars, provide personal mobility services, and serve as logistics centers for deliveries. The brand "Energy Plus" by GS Caltex was newly created to align with the company's transformation and expansion as an energy company. "Energy Plus Hub," a gas station that integrates various business areas of GS Caltex as well as a fuel service combining mobility infrastructure and lifestyle services such as last-mile delivery services, logistics, and car lifecycle services.

Traditionally, the gas station has been an important customer contact point, and this is still an advantageous factor as it provides and tests new customer experiences and digital technologies that bring new mobility services. With a goal of green transformation, GS Caltex is expanding its presence in the electric vehicle (EV) charging business to various mobility services through collaborations and strengthening strategic partnerships with big tech companies, startups, conglomerates, and public enterprises to develop a comprehensive mobility ecosystem. In this chapter, we examine five cases of GS Caltex collaborations with companies from other sectors to make gas station transformations.

- Charging Station Management Solution Development with LG Electronics
- EV Charging Solution Development with LG Energy Solution
- Mobility Data Sharing System Implementation with Hyundai Motors
- Mobility as a Service (MaaS) Development with Kakao Mobility
- Last-Mile Delivery Efficiency Improvement with IKEA

3.1 *Collaboration Dynamics: Cross-Sector Ecosystem*

To strengthen its position in the evolving mobility landscape, GS Caltex engages in various collaborative models with others in the mobility ecosystem (Fig. 2). Through diverse partnerships and investments, the company is expanding to offer a broad range of energy, mobility, logistics, and lifestyle services while transforming gas stations into digital platforms (GS Caltex, 2020).

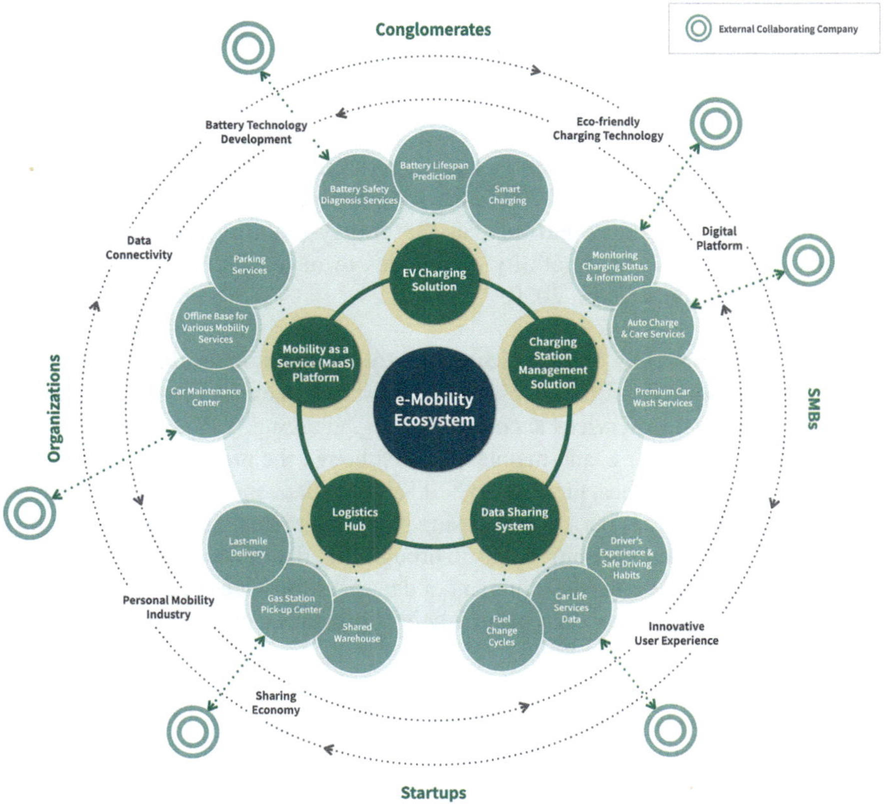

Fig. 2 Dynamics of e-mobility ecosystem collaboration, cross-sector ecosystem

Charging Station Management Solution Development with LG Electronics GS Caltex partnered with LG Electronics in 2020 to develop an integrated charging station management solution. This solution includes monitoring the charging status and real-time charging information, automated charging payments, remote control, and diagnostics for charging stations across the country. By using big data from the solution, GS Caltex can understand charging station usage and customer patterns and provide real-time traffic and lifestyle information to customers. Additionally, once registered, customers' vehicles are automatically recognized, enabling automatic charging and payment processing during future charging sessions (LG Electronics, 2023). LG Electronics, in addition to its energy-related businesses such as Energy Storage Systems (ESS), has been forming networks with global automobile manufacturers. LG Energy Solution, which produces electric vehicle batteries, and LG Innotek, which supplies automotive parts and boards, are among the LG Group affiliates collaborating with GS Caltex to create synergy effects (Jeon, 2022). Recently, GS Energy, the mother company of GS Caltex, has invested in and acquired an EV charging station company with LG Electronics.

EV Charging Solution Development with LG Energy Solution GS Caltex and LG Energy Solution are teaming up to develop charging solutions for the electric vehicle (EV) ecosystem. They use big data generated during the EV charging process to offer battery-related services, develop a battery safety diagnosis service, develop smart charging, and predict battery lifespan to enhance battery longevity (Jung, 2020; Accenture, 2023). To strengthen competitiveness not only in the traditional oil business but also in the energy-mobility sector, GS Caltex expands partnerships with mobility companies to develop innovative customer services based on data (Park, 2020).

Mobility Data Sharing System Implementation with Hyundai Motors GS Caltex and Hyundai Motor Group plan to establish a data exchange system to share data related to car-life services such as refueling, charging (LPG, electric, hydrogen), driving, car washing, and maintenance. Although the project is currently facing data-sharing challenges, they aim to build a stable data-sharing system. The goal is to improve customer experiences by using data on vehicle part replacements, fuel change cycles, and safe driving habits. Through this data cooperation agreement, they expect to accelerate the development of data-based services throughout the car-life domain, creating a new ecosystem where companies can collaborate based on data (GS Caltex Newsroom, 2020).

Mobility as a Service (MaaS) Development with Kakao Mobility GS Caltex and leading domestic mobility platform company, Kakao Mobility, are collaborating to develop Mobility as a Service (MaaS). GS Caltex has invested USD 20 million in Kakao Mobility to leverage its future-oriented technologies and data, such as autonomous driving, to enhance their fuel stations and charging infrastructure (GS Caltex, 2021). Kakao Mobility utilizes GS Caltex's infrastructure as an offline base for various mobility services, including logistics and parking. They will also share data and collaborate on technical development in vehicle maintenance and fuel supply for Kakao Taxi. This strategic partnership drives innovation in the future mobility industry, where diverse technologies like autonomous driving and artificial intelligence (AI) converge through collaborative platforms, making cross-industry cooperation essential for mobility innovation (GS Caltex, 2021).

Last-Mile Delivery Efficiency Improvement with IKEA GS Caltex has begun "Last-Mile Service" through its gas station pickup service with IKEA, the world's largest furniture retailer, since 2021. Last-mile delivery refers to the logistics involved in distributing shipments to customers' homes in urban areas. It begins when the shipment arrives at a starting point in the city and ends when the shipment reaches the customer's desired destination point (Boysen et al., 2021). It is considered the most inefficient operation in the supply chain and comprises up to 28% of total delivery costs (Ranieri et al., 2018). Recently, it has become an important business area for the logistics and distribution industries. GS Caltex offers a pickup service from the Gas Station Pickup Center. IKEA customers can choose a nearby GS Caltex gas station as their delivery point. IKEA delivers the products to the designated gas station, and customers can collect their items there for a 70% lower fee than the standard IKEA delivery cost (Choi, 2021). Gas stations transform into mobility and logistics hubs. Customers can switch to small, shared personal mobility at the gas station to reach their final destination after traveling with other mobility modes, such as public transportation. In logistics as well, gas stations serve as distribution centers or shared warehouses, like in collaboration with IKEA.

To drive gas station transformation in Korea, GS Caltex collaborates on multiple projects with diverse industries, including big tech companies, conglomerates, and startups. The projects described in Table 1 are in different stages of development, and some projects are put on hold for their own business reasons while others are ongoing. In this study, we examine the collaboration partners and their approaches to green transformation, without assessing the success or failure of the project. In this regard, projects that are on hold were not omitted.

Table 1 GS Caltex's cross-sector collaborations for gas station transformation

Industry	Partners	Year of initiation	Collaboration details
Mobility Services	KakaoMobility	2021	Securing fuel supply through the nation's top mobility platform and providing EV charging information
	Lotte Rental	2015	Promotions for long-term rental car customers are in progress
	Green Car	2018	Utilization of gas stations as car-sharing hubs and promotion of EV sharing services
	Cardoc	2016	Utilization of online hubs through a mobile maintenance platform
Electric Vehicle	Kis Motors	2019	Operating Kia Motors-exclusive EV charging stations and used battery energy storage system (ESS)
	LG Electronics	2019	Establishing an EV charging control system and a joint venture with an EV charger manufacturer
	LG Energy Solution	2022	Collaborating on the development of an EV battery management service model
	Softberry	2019	Utilizing the largest domestic EV charging platform (EV infrastructure)
	Hyundai Capital	2023	Collaborating to provide EV charging benefits to EV vehicle purchasers
Logistics	IKEA	2022	IKEA pick-up centers in the current gas stations
	Coupang	2022	Utilizing gas stations as logistics hubs
	Ministry of Land, Infrastructure and Transport	2020	Utilizing gas stations as drone logistics hubs
Digital Transformation (DX)	Naver	2022	Oil refinery, gas station, and EV charging/payment data management using Naver cloud, and enhancing customer service through data integration
	Hyundai Motor Group	2022	Enhancing charging services through the acquisition of connected car data

4 The Factors for Successful Collaboration Toward Green Transformation

One observation from the projects is that collaboration in electromobility (e-mobility) industries is essential to creating new business opportunities, and a single company or sector cannot drive the transformation. It requires a combination of capabilities from different sectors to build an e-mobility ecosystem. To create a new ecosystem, collaboration is not optional but a necessity. This may take the form of mergers, acquisitions, partnerships, or strategic alliances (Simpson et al., 2019).

This chapter presents the authors' findings on the three successful factors of collaboration in a consortium, which are associated with speed of work, government incentives, and open innovation.

- Speed of Implementation
  - Strategic alliances with an appropriate number of partners and flexibility in modifying work scope enhance the speed of progress and minimize project delays.
- Government Incentives
  - Providing a motivation to industries for green transformation reduces the risk of collaborative failure even after the project subsidy period.
- Open Innovation
  - Developing collaborative culture and building agile capability in the organization to implement new ideas into innovation.

4.1 Speed of Implementation

Strategic Alliances Companies traditionally pursued mergers and acquisitions (M&A) to create a new ecosystem or access new capabilities (Rymkovska et al., 2017). However, in the process of acquisition, M&A requires more cautious considerations on diverse aspects, including input of time and resources, control of uncertainty, and transactional cost, and it often hinders prompt decision making and collaborative outcomes (Yin & Shanley, 2008). The transformation in the energy and mobility sectors demands rapid collaboration to respond to the market and drive innovation. Strategic alliances have become an attractive and adaptable option for creating new products and services in this evolving ecosystem, particularly for businesses seeking investment flexibility or unable to commit to large upfront expenditures (Rymkovska et al., 2017).

> *Participating companies in the consortium were selected by the government, so their involvement was determined. As a result, the partnerships and collaborations that companies needed were limited. Due to the allocated funding, the scope of work, and the limited timeframe, it was challenging to collaborate with other entities outside the consortium.*

– Extracted from the interview, Interviewee A

> *It is considered desirable to grant authority and responsibility for consortium participating companies to have additional individual partnerships.*

– Extracted from the interview, Interviewee B

Limited Number of Partners Speed of product development is vital for success in technology-driven industries, and it is influenced by the number of strategic alliances. Not all alliances contribute equally to accelerating product development.

Strategic alliances can boost new product development, but as a company engages in more alliances, some allied firms may have poor capability or a minor impact, leading to diminishing returns (Deeds & Hill, 1996). A government-driven consortium is an appropriate collaboration model to achieve the goals the government is aiming for within a limited time line. Fifteen companies and organizations are involved in the Jeju Smart City Challenge project, and each company has its own scope of work and responsibilities in the project. However, managing 15 companies in the project brought various issues and barriers and ultimately affected the progress of the project and its outcomes. These companies participated in the project consortium under their own business circumstances regarding business capabilities, financial stability, and employee hiring, as well as expectation of the project. With the different interests of the companies and the various roles and capabilities of the participants, project output and schedule management become complicated, which often leads to project delays and eventually affects the speed of innovation. Especially in government projects, due to the strict management of costs, schedules, outputs, and numerous reports resulting from government funding usage, often becomes a burden on companies as they become additional tasks. What we observed from the Jeju Smart City Challenge Project, it is considered that less than 10 companies, about 4 to 6, are appropriate to manage in the consortium. It is desirable to give the consortium participants authority and responsibility to form partnerships with external companies beyond the consortium.

As the project progressed, there were significant differences in the pace and outcomes of projects based on the capabilities and conditions of the companies involved in the consortium. If a company couldn't execute its assigned task within the given timeframe and budget, it had an impact on the overall project.

– Extracted from the interview, Interviewee B

Communication with the consortium's participating companies is difficult. The project concept is complex, involving numerous participating companies, not only from the private sector but also public enterprises, government agencies, and educational institutions. Each sector has different requirements, making it challenging to consolidate these diverse demands into a single framework.

– Extracted from the interview, Interviewee C

Efficient operation and results can be achieved when the consortium consists of 4-5 participating companies with a willingness to collaborate and the competitive capabilities.

– Extracted from the interview, Interviewee D

Flexibility Furthermore, there are procedural issues that require approval from the provincial government and the Ministry of Land, Infrastructure, and Transport (MOLIT) for the project. While the project's goals and direction are driven by the Jeju Provincial Office, the actual authority for permitting the regulations lies with the Jeju City Office. This separation of the project progress supervising authority and the approval authority causes project delays. When the project involves an innovative and disruptive business that contains uncertainties and risks by nature (Banholzer et al., 2023), flexibility is essential to deal with those challenges (Georgsdottir & Getz, 2004), and the ability to find diverse solutions to a problem (Thurston & Runco, 1999). Changing or adjusting the initial plans can often be a better approach than adhering strictly to the original plan, which may lead to new issues and project delays. It is important that the government establishes a structure that allows for more flexible responses to issues such as changes in business plans and budget adjustments that can arise during the actual implementation of the project.

About communication issues, each company has their own business and tasks for the project, and different project schedules and these making it challenging to manage progress collectively. As it is a government-led project, when issues arise in the project, the coordination process for issue resolution often results in delays in specific schedules. This can lead to disruptions in the overall project timeline, causing administrative sanctions and introducing risks, which is inefficient for the project.

– Extracted from the interview, Interviewee A

The Jeju Smart City Challenge was initiated to address urban issues in Jeju Island and to seek new opportunities for businesses. It aimed to promote the use of renewable energy in Jeju, resolve transportation issues through PM(Personal Mobility) and EV(Electric Vehicles), but faced challenges in achieving visible outcomes due to various regulations and procedures.

– Extracted from the interview, Interviewee E

Reduction in Turnover One of the challenges that GS Caltex faces while working on projects with startups and SMBs (Small and medium-sized Businesses) is the frequent turnover of the person in the participating companies who was in charge of the task in the consortium. For example, among the personal mobility companies in the project, there were several changes in a shared e-motorcycle company during the project years. The frequent changes of participating companies caused difficulties in customer acquisition, resulting in a lack of continuity in the business and poor quality of the project. Despite the initial passion and motivation of startups, they often encounter practical challenges related to operational experience and funding. It is critical to align with the company's goals and strategies. Each company has specific roles in the project, and disruptions of work caused by a high turnover rate or poor takeover negatively impact the efficiency and speed of project execution.

Regarding services, since multiple companies are jointly creating a single service, problems can arise if one company decides to withdraw. Coordinating such situations can be challenging.

– Extracted from the interview, Interviewee C

The difficulties encountered when working with startups in a project include the frequent turnover of project personnel, leading to a lack of continuity in the work. Disruptions and less-than-smooth transitions due to departure or job changes of existing personnel can hinder the efficiency of project implementation.

– Extracted from the interview, Interviewee F

4.2 Government Incentives

Reducing the Risk and Motivating the Transformation According to Su et al. (2023), for companies and the private sector, an appropriate institutional environment is a key driver for the adoption of a service-oriented transformation strategy. The government should drive innovation and create an environment that aligns with the transformation that the enterprise tries to make (Su et al., 2023). Interviews conducted with project managers explain that their transformation effort involves significant risks and costs, and local governments have important roles and responsibilities in providing suitable environments for industry's transformation to encourage their active participation. Jeju local government provides supportive measures, government incentives such as financial subsidies and regulatory easing to expedite the Smart City Challenge project and encourage active industry participation. Government incentives can significantly mitigate the risks and costs associated with the transformation of businesses, and these government supports play an important role in motivating industries to invest in creating an environment that drives innovation. By offering timely and well-designed incentives, governments can promote sustainable practices in the energy sector and contribute to a step towards achieving the energy transition.

Participating consortium companies were able to make bold new attempts with reduced investment risks, thanks to government funding. In particular, through various regulatory sandboxes, they could pilot and test new business opportunities.

- Extracted from the interview, Interviewee G

This project can be considered the first case of constructing a Mobility as a Service (MaaS) system in South Korea, particularly the innovative integration with public transportation and Personal Mobility. Projects like this require significant investment and involve substantial risks, making it challenging for companies to initiate with their investments alone. Especially, once a project starts, there are inherent sunk costs, such as infrastructure usage fees, communication expenses, and cloud services, which cannot be reduced, and reducing personnel is not a solution.

- Extracted from the interview, Interviewee H

When implementing new businesses such as the Smart City Challenge, it often becomes challenging to proceed due to violations of existing regulations and procedures or a lack of suitable business grounds, which can result in difficulties in obtaining permits and progressing with the project.

- Extracted from the interview, Interviewee I

Consideration of Operation Capabilities After Subsidy When the project involves public interest, which does not meet economic feasibility, government support is crucial to driving the initiative. In the Jeju Smart City Challenge project, government subsidies were provided with the condition of a 5-year operation of their business after the project. While the government provides support for service design and implementation, there is often a lack of consideration for operational management and maintenance costs after the project, and the burden is shifted to the private sector. Startups and SMBs often encounter situations where they cannot sustain their operations after the subsidy period, and maintaining a consortium can become problematic. In many projects, SMBs struggle as they rely on government grants to sustain their businesses and operations, and there are many cases of business termination when subsidies are cut off. This is one of the inefficiencies of government subsidy projects. On the other hand, conglomerates are able to operate and maintain their new businesses after the government subsidy, which is a trigger for them to make business transformations. When companies with different business purposes and capabilities are involved in a government-led consortium to collaborate on innovative services, creating a new ecosystem becomes challenging. Therefore, to continue the business, consideration of the business plan after the subsidy period is critical in the stage of designing a large and long-term project, including the allocation of subsidies.

> *The obligation for the maintenance of Smart Hub (EV/PM sharing site) over five years is challenging to implement. The government provides support for service design and construction, but the operational management costs after construction are entirely the responsibility of the consortium participants. In this process, if a company cannot sustain the project, it becomes problematic for maintaining the consortium structure.*

– Extracted from the interview, Interviewee J

4.3 *Open Innovation*

Transformation of Organizational Culture GS Caltex is actively exploring the challenges of future mobility and transportation through open innovation. The company recognizes that collaboration with strong and strategic partners is essential to creating an effective ecosystem centered on open innovation. As a conglomerate, the company is in an advantageous position to integrate diverse expertise for producing new forms of knowledge and has applied the design thinking approach to drive transformation. Since 2016, it has been actively incorporating design thinking and open innovation as a creative problem-solving process to achieve sustainable innovation and transform organizational culture in preparation for the changing norms (Won, 2020). Design thinking, a human-centered approach to innovation, has now become a paradigm that involves a set of principles, methods, and tools for creating customer value and market opportunity (Brown, 2008; Verganti et al., 2021; Dorst, 2010). Employees of GS Caltex are encouraged to participate in design thinking workshops or training sessions to change their mindsets when working with people from different departments. This involves reshaping work methods, strengthening shop floor capabilities, and fostering problem-solving skills within the workforce through activities like camps and hackathons. Approximately one-third of the company's workforce has been exposed to open innovation and developed expertise in problem identification and resolution (GS Caltex CSR Team, 2021). Open innovation often faces challenges due to siloed cultures within organizations and issues between internal departments. To address this, various organizational changes are necessary at different stages of business development. In order to effectively engage and collaborate with external parties through open innovation, it is essential to open up internally first (Chesbrough, 2020).

We focused on creating a service flow for the entire process of tourists entering and exiting Jeju Island through the airport. We aimed to establish an ecosystem where transportation, tourism, accommodation, baggage storage, and all available services could be interconnected.

– Extracted from the interview, Interviewee B

Agile Capability Quick response and adaptation of new ideas are especially important for organizations to create value in a rapidly changing environment. For agile transformation to occur within an organization, the members should acquire mindsets to embrace collaboration across different levels and units; moreover, the leadership should share and support a clear vision with practical strategies (Salo, 2017). Through voluntary engagement in design thinking and open innovation programs, employees gain opportunities to raise issues and identify pain points in their work to redefine problems and develop solutions (GS Caltex CSR Team, 2021). Consequently, these kinds of individual efforts to make change not only contribute to bringing innovative outcomes to business but also build an agile capability for conglomerates to promptly implement new ideas.

Various collaborations with different companies are being discussed for the utilization of solar energy, surplus energy utilization, and the reuse of electric vehicle (EV) batteries for applications like energy storage systems (ESS). Quick responses are necessary for these initiatives.

– Extracted from the interview, Interviewee C
– The interview overview is summarized in Table 2.

Table 2 Interview overview

Participating areas of the project	Number of company	Number of interviewee	Interview results: Factors for the successful collaboration
Charging infrastructure construction	1	3	Speed of implementation – Strategic alliances – Limited number of partners – Flexibility – Reduction in turnover Government incentives – Reducing the risk and motivating the transformation Open innovation – Transformation of organizational culture – Agile capability

Table 2 (continued)

Participating areas of the project	Number of company	Number of interviewee	Interview results: Factors for the successful collaboration
Mobile application implementation	1	3	Speed of implementation – Strategic alliances – Limited number of partners – Flexibility Government incentives – Reducing the risk and motivating the transformation – Consideration of operation capabilities after subsidy
Personal mobility services	2	2	Speed of implementation – Flexibility Government incentives – Reducing the risk and motivating the transformation – Consideration of operation capabilities after subsidy
Luggage service	1	0	N/A
UAM (Urban Air Mobility)	1	1	Government incentives – Reducing the risk and motivating the transformation – Consideration of operation capabilities after subsidy
Energy trade system	3	3	Speed of implementation – Flexibility Government incentives – Reducing the risk and motivating the transformation – Consideration of operation capabilities after subsidy
Living lab	1	1	Open innovation – Transformation of organizational culture – Agile capability
Advisory	1	1	Speed of implementation – Strategic alliances – Flexibility Government incentives – Reducing the risk and motivating the transformation – Consideration of operation capabilities after subsidy
Academia	3	2	Speed of implementation – Strategic alliances Government incentives – Reducing the risk and motivating the transformation Open innovation – Transformation of organizational culture

(continued)

Table 2 (continued)

Participating areas of the project	Number of company	Number of interviewee	Interview results: Factors for the successful collaboration
Organization	1	0	N/A
Jeju Government	1	2	Speed of implementation – Flexibility Government incentives – Reducing the risk and motivating the transformation – Consideration of operation capabilities after subsidy

5 Conclusion

Gas station transformations and the expansion of electric vehicle charging infrastructure are challenges that most petroleum companies encounter as the energy landscape changes. These challenges compel them to dedicate themselves to sustainability in their business transformation. Through strategic partnerships and the optimization of their existing infrastructure, petroleum companies are playing a leading role in driving the adoption of electric vehicles and the creation of an e-mobility ecosystem. Customer needs are evolving in new e-mobility environments, prompting corporations and industries to work together to meet these changing demands.

This case study provides experiences and insights on collaboration gained from GS Caltex's green transformation journey. Traditional gas stations were places for mechanical refueling, whereas EV charging stations allow interactions between systems, cars, and chargers. These interactions drive new business collaborations with diverse industries and governments. The transformation of gas stations into charging stations, representing a form of digital transformation, triggers fundamental changes in various aspects of the company, including strategy, organization, processes, business models, culture, communication, and systems. By examining both government-led collaboration as a national project and cross-sector collaboration initiated by the private sector, we can identify key considerations for successful collaboration in the context of green transformation: speed of implementation, government incentives, and open innovation. For disruptive changes in the energy industry, collaboration is not an option but a necessity. Conglomerates need to quickly experiment with new ideas through collaborations with other industries and startups. Simultaneously, they should expedite their transition towards sustainable energy solutions while mitigating business risks through government support mechanisms. Above all, the collaborative culture and capability of organizations are to implement new ideas into innovation. When these three elements are effectively combined, it facilitates an expedited green transformation.

References

Accenture. (March 31, 2023). *Creating value through collaboration.* https://www.accenture.com/us-en/insights/utilities/creating-value-through-collaboration

Banholzer, M., Birshan, M., Doherty, R., & LaBerge, L. (2023, January 10). Innovation: Your solution for weathering uncertainty. McKinsey & Company. Retrieved from https://www.mckinsey.com/capabilities/strategy-and-corporate-finance/our-insights/innovation-your-solution-for-weathering-uncertainty.

Boysen, N., Fedtke, S., & Schwerdfeger, S. (2021). Last-mile delivery concepts: A survey from an operational research perspective. *OR Spectrum, 43*, 1–58. https://doi.org/10.1007/s00291-020-00607-8

Brown, T. (2008). Design thinking. *Harvard Business Review, 86*(6), 84–92.

Chesbrough, H. (2020). *Open innovation results: Going beyond the hype and getting down to business.* Oxford University Press.

Choi, K. (2021, October 5). Why would IKEA's furniture order assistant manager Kim visit GS Caltex gas station on the way home from work? [Newspaper]. Maeil Economy. https://www.mk.co.kr/news/business/10048575

Deeds, D. L., & Hill, C. W. L. (1996). Strategic alliances and the rate of new product development: An empirical study of entrepreneurial biotechnology firms. *Journal of Business Venturing, 11*(1), 41–55. https://doi.org/10.1016/0883-9026(95)00087-9

Dorst, K. (2010). The nature of design thinking. *DTRS8 Interpreting Design Thinking: Design Thinking Research Symposium Proceedings, 1*, 131–139. http://hdl.handle.net/10453/16590

e-3DA: Jeju Smart City Challenge Project. (2021). https://www.e-3da.com/.

Georgsdottir, A. S., & Getz, I. (2004). How flexibility facilitates innovation and ways to manage it in organizations. *Creativity and Innovation Management, 13*, 143–198. https://doi.org/10.1111/j.0963-1690.2004.00306.x

GS Caltex. (2021, July 26). GS Caltex joins with Kakao Mobility to participate in future mobility innovation. [Newspaper]. https://gscaltexmediahub.com/news/kakaomobility-investment/.

GS Caltex. (2020). https://www.gscaltex.com/en.

GS Caltex CSR Team. (2021). GS Caltex sustainability report 2021: Expanding the possibilities of energy. *GS Caltex Corporation.* https://www.gscaltex.com/en/sustainability/sustainabilityreport

GS Caltex Newsroom. (2020, September 24). GS Caltex and Hyundai Motor Group sign a business agreement for data-based service development. [Article]. https://archive.gscaltexmediahub.com/story/mou-hyundai-data-alliance/.

Jeju Special Self-Governing Province. (2021, March 17). Jeju Island's Smart City challenge project. [PowerPoint slides]. Ministry of Land, Infrastructure and Transport. https://smartcity.go.kr/wp-content/uploads/2019/08/제주-스마트시티-챌린지_발표자료.pdf.

Jeon, H. (2022, April 12). LG Electronics, selected electric vehicle charging as a future industry. [Newspaper]. Seoul Economy Daily https://www.sedaily.com/NewsView/264NZQZ1BI.

Jung, H. (2020, July 7). GS Caltex, promote battery-specific service development using big data with LG Chem. [Newspaper]. Industry News. https://www.industrynews.co.kr/news/articleView.html?idxno=38842.

Kallis, G., Stephanides, P., Bailey, E., Devine-Wright, P., Chalvatzis, K., & Bailey, I. (2021). The challenges of engaging Island communities: Lessons on renewable energy from a review of 17 case studies. *Energy Research & Social Science, 81*, 1–11. https://doi.org/10.1016/j.erss.2021.102257. 102257.

LG Electronics. (2023, May 25). LG Electronics, full-fledged EV charging solution business. [Article]. https://live.lge.co.kr/lg-ev-chargingsolution/.

Park, S. (2020, July 7). GS Caltex-LG Chem, development of EV battery specialized service using big data. [Newspaper]. Seoul Finance. https://www.seoulfn.com/news/articleView.html?idxno=388282.

Ranieri, L., Digiesi, S., Silvestri, B., & Roccotelli, M. (2018). A review of last mile logistics innovations in an externalities cost reduction vision. *Sustainability, 10*(3) 782, 1–18. https://doi.org/10.3390/su10030782
Rymkovska, J., Bhaiji, M., Rassloff, J., & Zinke, C. (2017). Strategic alliances: A real alternative to M&A? *KPMG International*. https://assets.kpmg.com/content/dam/kpmg/xx/pdf/2017/11/strategic-alliances-toolkit.pdf
Salo, O. (2017, October 2). How to create an agile organization. McKinsey & Company. Retrieved from https://www.mckinsey.com/capabilities/people-and-organizational-performance/our-insights/how-to-create-an-agile-organization#/.
Simpson, C., Ataii, E., Kemp, E., & Zhang, Y. (2019). Mobility 2030: Transforming the mobility landscape. *KPMG International*. https://assets.kpmg.com/content/dam/kpmg/xx/pdf/2019/02/mobility-2030-transforming-the-mobility-landscape.pdf
Su, X., Mou, C., & Zhou, S. (2023). Institutional environment, technological innovation capability and service-oriented transformation. *PLoS One, 18*(2), e0281403. https://doi.org/10.1371/journal.pone.0281403
Thurston, B. J., & Runco, M. A. (1999). *Encyclopedia of creativity* (Vol. 1). Academic Press.
Verganti, R., Dell'Era, C., & Swan, K. S. (2021). Design thinking: Critical analysis and future evolution. *Journal of Product Innovation Management, 38*(6), 603–622. https://doi.org/10.1111/jpim.12610
Won, H.S. (2020, January 14). Innovate like Silicon-Valley. Maeil Business News Korea. https://www.mk.co.kr/news/business/9163949.
Yin, X., & Shanley, M. (2008). Industry determinants of the "merger versus alliance" decision. *Academy of Management Review, 33*(2), 473–491. http://www.jstor.org/stable/20159408

Heejung Yim is a research director at the Stanford Center at the Incheon Global Campus. She involves in the Jeju Smarty City Challenge Project providing advisory on technology and market dynamics. She is interested in renewable energy market and related technology, and sustainable urban design. She has extensive industry experience and knowledge focusing on the energy sector.

Taesoo Kim is a project leader of Future Strategy Task Force in GS Caltex Corporation. He is leading the Jeju Smarty City Challenge Project as a project director for the past four years. His dedicated efforts have been focused on the expansion of electric vehicle charging infrastructure within the existing network of gas stations across the country. His expertise is focused on development of new network-based services and fostering collaborations with a diverse range of companies and industries.

Hyunmin Kang is a research scientist at the Stanford Center at the Incheon Global Campus. He is interested in the field of AI–human interaction based on human factors and cognitive engineering and has been studying how smart technologies affect human life and society.

Seoyoung Kim is a research scientist of Stanford Center at the Incheon Global Campus. Her research focuses on multidisciplinary design practice and design thinking by collaborating with professionals from diverse fields. Throughout her education and career, she aimed to attain higher level of skills by participating in industry and academia projects with creative approaches and design processes.

Internal Control in Microfinance Institutions in Ecuador

Paola Martina Pucha Medina, Rebeca García-Ramos, and Belén Díaz Díaz

1 Introduction

Over the last decades, the importance of the microfinance sector has boomed (Kendo & Tchakounte, 2022). Despite the difficulties they face, microfinance institutions (MFIs) have increased their presence in the financial sector and have become one of the most useful tools in the fight against poverty in developing countries (Gupta & Sharma, 2023), where they play a crucial role in providing economic support to vulnerable communities.

Internal control is particularly relevant in the context of MFIs, being one of the fundamental pillars to guarantee the stability, transparency, and sustainability of these financial institutions. Considering that public trust is essential for the effective functioning of microfinance, the establishment and maintenance of robust internal control systems becomes imperative to mitigate risks, prevent fraud, and ensure the integrity of financial operations. Proper implementation of internal control not only strengthens the financial position of these institutions, but also enhances the confidence of investors, clients, and other stakeholders. This strengthens the ability of microfinance to fulfil its mission of promoting economic development throughout the world, especially in the most socially and economically vulnerable areas.

This paper addresses the importance of internal control in Ecuador's Popular and Solidarity Sector, which emerges as a fundamental pillar in the country's economic and social structure, playing a crucial role in financial inclusion, community empowerment, and the construction of a more robust social fabric. In the context of Ecuador, the Popular and Solidarity Sector has evolved as an essential

P. M. Pucha Medina · R. García-Ramos · B. Díaz Díaz (✉)
Universidad de Cantabria and SANFI, Santander, Spain
e-mail: paola-martina.pucha@alumnos.unican.es; rebeca.garciaramos@unican.es; diazb@unican.es

B. Díaz Díaz et al. (eds.), *Building Global Societies Towards an ESG World*, CSR, Sustainability, Ethics & Governance,
https://doi.org/10.1007/978-3-031-56619-6_16

counterweight to conventional financial structures, providing accessible and community-oriented financing alternatives. Savings and credit cooperatives, small producers' associations, and other forms of solidarity organisations not only facilitate access to financial services but also promote collaboration and solidarity.

Despite having excellent microfinance models, the traditional mechanisms implemented to boost management are no longer sufficient to solve the growing problems afflicting popular and solidarity sector institutions in Ecuador. These changes are having a serious effect on the management and measurement of the social objectives of microfinance. In this sense, there is controversy about the possible prevalence of commercial objectives over the cooperative mission of the most vulnerable sectors. It is therefore necessary to analyse the internal control of these institutions.

2 Internal Control: Concept and Evolution

Organisations today recognise that adequate internal control is essential to preserve their business, to safeguard their assets, to ensure efficient and effective operations, and to meet the company's objectives, all within the framework of current regulations. Internal control must address what risks the company faces, what risks may lead to the company's objectives not being met, and what internal control activities need to be implemented so that these risks do not occur. Once the risks, whether controllable or uncontrollable, have been identified, control activities are generated, for which an internal control system adapted to the sector where the organisation is located is employed, which will provide reasonable assurance regarding the achievement of business objectives.

The competitive scenario faced by MFIs evidences constant threats in their strategic and operational dimensions, as well as the need to handle highly reliable information and to comply with a series of specific laws and regulations. In this sense, it is urgent for these institutions to optimise risk control and management and to implement an internal control system geared to their reality and needs.

Although internal control has been extensively analysed in some sectors, there are not many studies that address the analysis of internal control within the popular and solidarity-based economic sector in Ecuador. The public economic organisations that make up the Ecuadorian economic system have control tools as a management instrument, established in the Management Audit Manual of the General State Comptroller's Office, which makes it possible to determine the weaknesses and strengths, as well as the risks faced by the institution. The private sector has also relied on this manual in order to manage the development of its organisations through the Committee of Sponsoring Organisations of the Tradeway Commission (COSO).

Internal control arises as a response to the corrupt and fraudulent acts produced in organisations of all kinds from historical times to the present, achieving through this tool to generate reliability in financial information through compliance with applicable laws and regulations and to provide effectiveness and efficiency of operations. The implementation and strengthening of organisations through internal control has had one of its maximum manifestations in the proactive activity to reduce the risks that are generated in the entities, achieving at the same time to comply with the objectives set.

Historically, the concept of "internal control" first appeared in 1929, linked to the area of accounting. The importance of disclosing information on internal controls has been debated since the late 1970s (McMullen et al., 1996), focusing its attention after the accounting scandals of the early twenty-first century, due to public concern about the lack of quality of internal control, giving way to the creation of awareness about the key role of the effectiveness of internal controls in corporate governance (Lin et al., 2014). Taking into consideration the above argument, several definitions and statements are presented that consider internal control as a key element in the decision-making process in organisations (Table 1):

Yu and Neter (1973) review the purpose of internal control systems in organisations and conclude that they focus on preventing, detecting, and eliminating irregularities and fraud in financial reporting, transcending to policies, plans, procedures, processes, systems, activities, functions, projects, initiatives, and undertakings of all kinds at all levels of an organisation, with the active collaboration of the available human talent. According to, the effectiveness of internal control is framed by the ability of companies to ensure compliance objectives—business reporting and strategic goals, while providing tailored and tailored support to the needs of the entity, achieving effective, efficient, and economical controls, being a basic requirement for sustainable operations of companies in complex business environments.

Undoubtedly, the great evolution in internal control thinking has come hand in hand with the growth of economic activity and the emergence of large business organisations, encompassing a wide variety of specialised technical operations. The onslaught of regulatory and competitive forces led to a significant increase in the attention paid to internal controls in organisations in the 1990s, leading to the creation of models and standards with a broad conception of the organisation worldwide, detailed in Table 2.

The COSO report is considered to be a pioneer, reflecting a broad concept of internal control that allows for an effective management assessment of the organisation. It is a document developed by the Committee of Sponsored Organisations of the Treadway,[1] currently available in three versions updated according to the needs of companies over time. The first publication of the Report was in 1992, called Internal Control—Integrated Framework. Subsequently, in 2004, the second version, Enterprise Risk Management—Integrated Framework, was presented, which considers the risks faced by companies. In May 2013, the third version, Internal Control—Integrated Framework, was published, providing a fresh perspective on

[1]American Accounting Association (AAA); American Institute of Certified Public Accountants (AICPA); Institute of Internal Auditors (IIA); Institute of Management Accountants.

Table 1 Chronological definition of internal control

Authors	Year	Definitions
Foreign Corrupt Practices Act (FCPA)	(1977)	Emphasising to companies the importance of developing and maintaining an internal control system for the proper execution and recording of transactions, as well as accountability for the company's assets, is relevant to their long-term survival
Committee of Sponsoring Organisations of the Treadway Commission—COSO	(1992)	The process of control effected by all levels of an entity and designed to provide reasonable assurance regarding the achievement of corporate objectives. Dashtbayaz et al. (2019)
Statement on Auditing Standards—SAS/78	(1995)	Internal control is a process, effected by an entity's board of directors, management, and other personnel, designed to provide reasonable assurance regarding the achievement of objectives in the categories of reliability of financial reporting, effectiveness and efficiency of operations, and compliance with applicable laws and regulations
(Auditing; Accountants; Accountants)	(1991; 1994; 1996)	Internal control is defined as a process designed to provide reasonable assurance regarding the achievement of objectives in the following categories: reliability of financial reporting, effectiveness and efficiency of operations, and compliance with applicable laws and regulations
The Control Objectives for Information Systems and related Technology—CobiT	(1996)	Internal control is the policies, procedures, practices, and organisational structures designed to provide reasonable assurance that business objectives will be achieved and that undesirable events will be prevented or detected and corrected
Millichamp	(2000)	Internal control is a comprehensive system established by the board of directors to conduct the business of an organisation in an orderly manner, ensuring compliance in conjunction with management policies, protection of assets to ensure complete and accurate information, in other words, controlling the entire management system to conduct business operations effectively. Kumuthinidevi (2016)
Control and Audit System—SAC	(2002)	Internal control is the set of processes, functions, activities, sub-systems, and people that are consciously grouped or segregated to ensure the effective achievement of specific objectives that must be translated into measurable targets
Sarbanes-Oxley Act—SOX	(2002)	Internal control is the process of preparing financial statements through the use of information technology, with the objective of ensuring the quality of financial reporting and the definition of a rating agency

internal controls and extending its focus to the role of the board and audit committee. Among the objectives encompassed by COSO III are:

(a) Clarify internal control requirements.
(b) Updating the context of the application of internal control to many changes in business and operating environments.
(c) Broadening its application by expanding operational and reporting objectives.

Table 2 Standards, templates, and reports on internal control

Model	Year	Country	Target group	Internal control system approach	Internal control system principles	Internal control objectives and tasks	Internal control system composition	Evaluation of the effectiveness of the internal control system
AEC (Self-Assessment of Controls Model)	1980	Canada	Administration and staff	Focusing on information security	Methodology for reviewing an organisation's key objectives	Reasonableness in meeting the entity's objectives	1. Definition of improvement actions. 2. Prioritise according to probability of occurrence and impact on objectives. 3. Contribute actions for improvement and consolidate proposals. 4. Dissemination	It provides reasonable assurance of achieving the organisation's objectives
SAS 55, SAS 78	1988	United States	External auditors	Financial report—Financial statements	In general, SAS 55, SAS 78 focus on controls that affect the reliability of an organisation's financial reporting	Reliability of financial reporting. 2. Efficiency and speed of operations. 3. Compliance with applicable laws and regulations	Control of the environment. 2. Risk assessment. 3. Actions to be controlled. 4. Information and communication. 5. Follow-up	1. The internal control system is effective if all five components are functioning in relation to the established requirements. 2. The external auditors report on weaknesses in the internal control system that influence the reports. 3. It is maintained for a certain period of time
Cadbury	1991	United Kingdom	Financial and corporate governance aspects. Broad interpretation of control	Focus on governance policies, analysing the code of ethics on financial aspects of corporate governance	Management tool and its financial package	Effectiveness and efficiency of operations. Reliability of financial information and reporting. Compliance with laws and regulations	1. Surveillance 2. Control environment 3. Control activities 4. Increased risk assessment	To provide reasonable assurance of operations, reliability of financial reporting, compliance with laws and regulations, and safeguarding of assets
COSO (Committee of Sponsoring Organizations of the Treadway Commission)	1992	United States	Administration	The organisation (company) in general	Management tools	The efficiency and effectiveness of operations. Compliance with financial statements. Reliability of financial reporting	1. Control of the environment. 2. Risk assessment. 3. Actions to be controlled. 4. Information and communication. 5. Follow-up	1. Support to management for a better control of the organisation. 2. At a point in time
SAC (Systems Auditability and Control)	1992	United States	Internal auditors	Information system (metadata)	Emphasis on risk assessment, comparison of costs and benefits of control, building control devices into the system, rather than adding them after the introduction of control systems	1. Provide unit of information. 2. Ensure compliance with established requirements. 3. Ensuring reliability measures	1. Control of the environment. 2. Automatic and manual control system. 3. Control procedures. "Content introspection"	Auditor's guide to analysing audit procedures. It is maintained for a certain period of time

(continued)

Table 2 (continued)

Model	Year	Country	Target group	Internal control system approach	Internal control system principles	Internal control objectives and tasks	Internal control system composition	Evaluation of the effectiveness of the internal control system
King	1994	South Africa	Corporate Governance	With a focus on Corporate Governance	Administrative efficiency	Establish principles of good practice for organisations to meet the requirements of company law and changes in international corporate governance trends	1. Ethical leadership and corporate citizenship. 2. Roles and responsibilities of the Board of Directors. 3. Roles and responsibilities of the Audit Committee. 4. Risk governance. 5. Governance of information technologies. 6. Compliance with laws, regulations, codes, and standards. 7. Roles and responsibilities of the internal audit function. 8. Governance of shareholder relations. 9. Integrated reporting and disclosures	Philosophy of leadership, sustainability, and corporate citizenship, including a risk-based approach to internal audit
COCO (Criteria of Control Committee)	1995	Canada	Administration	The organisation in general	Management tools	Development of general guidelines for the design, implementation, evaluation, and reporting on control structures. Encompasses the public and private sector	Four categories (20 criteria) Purpose 2. Commitment 3. Aptitude 4. Evaluation and learning	Simpler and more concise report compared to COSO
Vienot	1995	France	Board of Directors and management	Sociable interest of the company	Management tool	Establish recommendations on rights, obligations, and responsibilities for supervision and control, based on the reflections of the Treadway Commission	Component of the COSO Model adapted to the particular requirements and needs of public entities in France	Emphasises the rights, obligations, and supervisory and control responsibilities, based on the reflections of the Treadway Commission
CobiT (Control Objectives for Information and related Technology)	1996	Europe, USA, and Australia	Management, auditors (information system), users	Information system—Technological tools. System life cycle	It emphasises the role and impact of IT control as it relates to business processes. It represents the control structure for the business process owner	1. The effectiveness of information. 2. The adequacy, completeness, and availability of information. 3. The reliability and validity of the information. 4. Confidentiality of information	Planning and organisation. 2. Procurement and implementation. 3. Delivery and support. 4. Follow-up	1. The grouping of processes into components, which are the areas of responsibility. 2. It is maintained for a certain period of time
Peters	1997	Netherlands	Administration	The organisation in general	It is based on the principles of the COSO model	Establish maturity levels for each control element	Component of the COSO Model adapted to the particular requirements and needs of Dutch public entities	Management through leadership. Continuous innovation, focusing on the present of the negotiation, in order to provide comfort to the client

KONTRAG	1998	Germany	Administration	Board of Directors Management Internal auditors Staff	Management tools	Improving the organisation in order to avoid corporate crises	1.Responsibility for setting up an organisational risk structure based on control and management. 2. Systematic risk analysis and assessment. 3. Information relevant to risk observation	Safeguarding invested resources
TURNBULL	1999	United Kingdom	Administration	Risk-based approach	Management tool (guidelines in the fulfilment of the company's objectives)	1. Support public companies in dealing with internal control requirements. 2. To provide a set of tools and guidelines that complement the internal control system scheme, achieving the organisation's objectives and protecting the organisation's assets	1. Maintenance of the Internal Control System 2. Review of the effectiveness of Internal Control. 3. Statement on the effectiveness of Internal Control. 4. Internal Audit	Increased likelihood of achieving objectives, long-term coverage, competitive advantages, lower capital costs, reduced time for emergencies
SOX—Art. 404	2002	United States	The issuer's senior management, the internal auditors, the independent audit firm	Financial report	Use of the internal control system principles set out in the COSO report or COBIT standard as a source of data on control procedures and control methods in the IT sector	1. The effectiveness of the financial reporting process. 2. The adequacy, completeness, and availability of information. 3. The functioning of information technologies. 4. Fraud prevention	1. Control of the environment. 2. Risk assessment. 3. Actions to be controlled. 4. Information and communication. 5. Follow-up	1. The assessment should include information on deficiencies in the internal control system. 2. The guide should not give a positive assessment of the internal control system in the presence of one or more of the deficiencies in functioning. 3. It is maintained for a certain period of time
MICIL (Latin American Integrated Internal Control Framework)	2003	Bolivia	Administration	Values-based approach and principles of ethical conduct of staff and organisations	Management tools	Establish a frame of reference for the needs and expectations of managers of private companies, public institutions, civil society organisations, and other stakeholders	1. Institutional working and control environment. 2. Risk assessment to achieve objectives. 3. Control activities to minimise risks. 4. Information and communication to promote transparency. 5. Continuous internal and regular external monitoring	Ensuring a control environment as a centrepiece, which promotes effective functioning at all levels of the organisation

Source: Prepared by the authors based on Rivas-Márquez (2011) and Laski (2017). Table 3 lists the different internal control models with their respective characteristics in terms of principles, target group, composition, and efficient results. It can be seen that, in general, the models have similarities in terms of their target group, which is management

Table 3 COSO versions

COSO I	COSO II	COSO III
Control environment Risk assessment Control activities Information and communication Monitoring	Control environment Target setting Identification of events Risk assessment Responding to risks Control activities Information and communication Monitoring	Control environment Risk assessment Control activities Information and communication Control and monitoring activities

Source: Estupiñan (2015)

Table 4 Component and principles of COSO III

Component	Control environment
Principles	1. Demonstrates commitment to integrity and ethical values 2. Exercises supervisory responsibility 3. It establishes structure, authority and responsibility 4. Demonstrates commitment to competition 5. It enforces accountability
Component	Risk assessment
Principles	6. Specify relevant objectives 7. Identify and analyse risks 8. Assesses the risk of fraud 9. Identifies and analyses important changes
Component	Control activities
Principles	10. Selects and develops control activities 11. Selects and develops general technology controls 12. It is implemented through policies and procedures 13. Use relevant information
Component	Information and communication
Principles	14. Communicates internally 15. Communicates externally
Component	Monitoring and supervision activities
Principles	16. Conducts ongoing and/or independent evaluations 17. Assesses and reports deficiencies

Source: (Estupiñan, 2015; COSO, 2013)

Specifically, the latest version of COSO differs from the others, and specifically from the first version, in that it includes seventeen principles that the management of any organisation should implement and is seen as the logical starting point for management, internal audit and external audit teams to begin to apply their approaches. The principles considered in each of the five components of COSO III are presented in Table 4.

In the case of the first component "Control Environment", the environment in which all organisational activities are carried out under the management of the administration is determined, influenced by both internal and external factors, such as the history of the entity, values, the market, and the competitive and regulatory environment. It also encompasses the rules, processes, and structures that form the basis for developing the organisation's internal control. This first component creates the discipline that supports the assessment of risk in meeting the entity's objectives, the performance of control activities, the use of information and communication systems, and the conduct of supervisory activities. In order to achieve an appropriate control environment, aspects such as organisational structure, division of labour and allocation of responsibilities, management style, and commitment must be taken into account. It can be noted that this first component influences and underpins the other components by providing discipline and structure. The second component, "Risk Assessment", identifies the potential risks associated with achieving the organisation's objectives by addressing internal and external risks through a dynamic and interactive assessment process, where mechanisms are put in place to identify, analyse, and mitigate these risks, enabling organisations to assess the risk of fraud and make significant changes to compete successfully, maintain a strong financial position and a positive public image. The third component, "Control Activities", establishes control actions through policies and procedures, achieving the objectives at acceptable levels. Similarly, within the component, relevant information is used to generate controls through a wide range of manual and automated activities, ensuring compliance with management instructions, and supporting the functioning of internal control. The fourth component, "Information and Communication", determines how the operational, administrative, and financial areas of the organisation identify, capture, and exchange information through a continuous and interactive process from outside to inside and vice versa, in order to respond to the needs and expectations of stakeholders. Such information, which must be of good quality and used appropriately, supports the functioning of internal control in the organisation and has to flow to internal and external stakeholders for corrective action. The fifth and final component, "Monitoring and Supervision Activities", seeks to incorporate the concept of continuous improvement, making the control system more flexible to react nimbly and adapt to circumstances. In this component, the organisation selects, develops, and carries out continuous and separate evaluations to determine whether the components of internal control are present and functioning. Once this information is gathered, internal control deficiencies are communicated in a timely manner to those responsible for taking corrective action, including management and the Steering Committee, as appropriate.

On the other hand, different models take the COSO model as a basis, seeking to adapt it to the country or to a specific group, as is the case with the SAC, CobiT, SAS software, and the SOX law. The COCO model, for its part, applies each of the COSO parameters but differs in the composition of the internal control system, applying four categories, broken down into 20 criteria, to obtain a simple and concise report, with COSO being distinguished by five components, in its recent version. Despite the existence of different laws, models, or reports in different countries, the COSO model continues to be the benchmark, making extensive use of the risk-based approach.

In terms of legislation, the Sarbanes-Oxley Act establishes the most far-reaching regulation in the US financial sector, addressing issues such as corporate governance, directors' liability, transparency, and other aspects of auditors' work. However, for several organisations the SAC, COSO, SAS55/78, and CobiT documents set the standards for internal control. Medina-López (2015) considers that the COSO Report includes the requirements on internal control required by the Sarbanes Oxley Act, by considering the reliability of financial information as one of the objectives, explicitly recommending the internal control framework to be followed in the evaluations and audits of companies, by providing guidelines for estimating the attributes of the control system.

Internal control has become a valuable strategic mechanism for companies to raise awareness of the importance of corporate social responsibility and business ethics (Husnaini & Basuki, 2020; Phornlaphatrachkorn & Na Kalasindhu, 2020; Chen et al., 2020; Tran, 2020). The evaluation of business control over financial reporting, improving operational efficiency and effectiveness, reliability, transparency and integrity of financial statements, usefulness and value of information, and compliance with laws, regulations, rules, and other related issues. Today, the assessment of internal control is a critical component of the overall audit process, required by auditing standards worldwide, and enables better performance and survival of companies in the long term.

3 Perspectives of Internal Control in Organisations

Internal control has become a subject analysed by many authors, with different opinions, most of them highlighting its importance and absolute necessity. Among the main debates in relation to internal control are the effectiveness of internal control in organisations, defining it as a comprehensive institutional arrangement involving different types of regulations and operating standards (Guo et al., 2015). Several studies consider internal control as a broad concept, conceiving it as a rigorous process that ensures the achievement of business objectives and manages potential risks (Gamage et al., 2014), according to a principle of self-control (Medina-López, 2015) and a moderating effect on the relationship between financial distress and earnings management (Ge & Mcvay, 2005; Järvinen & Myllymäki, 2016). Other research associates internal control problems with high cost of capital (Ashbaugh-Skaife et al., 2009; Kim et al., 2011), share value depreciation (Balsam et al., 2014; Hammersley et al., 2008), low quality of financial reporting (Skaife et al., 2009; Doyle et al., 2016), the auditor's effort (Raghunandan & Rama, 2006), decision making (Cheng et al., 2013), and the hiring of a chief financial officer and executive compensation (Hoitash et al., 2012; Li et al., 2010). For Ge and Mcvay (2005), the lack of internal control expertise often contributes to organisational accounting inefficiencies, although there is evidence that senior management is responsible for internal control and the implementation of equity incentives (Balsam et al., 2014; Dai & Song, 2018).

According to Medina-López (2015), internal control is an instrument for improving management. In this sense, it considers it essential to have objectives and actions in order to suppress risks in organisations, through identification, analysis, and categorisation; operational objectives; objectives related to financial reporting; and compliance objectives. For the COSO Report (1992), the objectives to be categorised within an organisation focus on: effectiveness and efficiency of operations, reliability of financial reporting, and compliance with applicable laws and regulations. On the other hand, in China, through the Ministry of Finance, they stipulated the Basic Regulations of Internal Control (2008) where they categorise internal control weaknesses into design defects and operational defects (designed but not properly implemented).

According to Mantilla (2005), internal control has three generations in line with the evolution of organisational structures and from an audit approach. The first generation was based on empirical actions aimed at accounting and administrative controls. The second generation was driven by the legal bias, attributing this tool to the public sector, leading to the distortion of the process. The third generation leads to efforts in quality derived from the positioning at the highest strategic and managerial levels, which made it possible to guarantee the efficiency of internal control to this day (Rivas-Márquez, 2011).

Under this umbrella, various reports have been developed in different geographical locations, branching out into areas, segments, and types of organisations in order to assess the key to internal control. A clear example is the annual report of information on the design and operation of internal controls, where the use of information to scrutinise managers is considered (Hammersley et al., 2008; Hermanson, 2000; Van de Poel & Vanstraelen, 2011). Chan et al. (2020) argue that internal control, as an integrated system, has a significant positive impact on innovation in firms. Similarly, quasi-SOX practices, introduced in China in 2008, have yielded positive results on the quality of reporting and do not generate side effects that damage the long-term value of companies (Hu et al., 2020). This law, commonly known as SOX China, enacts that listed organisations must disseminate management and audit reports on internal control, with the aim of helping companies to ensure the reliability of reporting, by means of objectives (legal compliance, asset security, financial reporting, operations, and strategies) set by the Chinese Ministry of Finance.

Nyakundi et al. (2014) find that internal control systems can reveal problems associated with lower revenues and explore links between earnings management and disclosure of material weaknesses and fraud. Authors such as Hanim et al. (2005) suggest that an effective internal control system is explicitly correlated with the organisation's success in meeting its target level of earnings.

Although the debate on the influence of internal control remains open, many countries have gone ahead and implemented the COSO Report. It is crucial to understand the potential consequences of applying such a model in different regulatory environments. Adequate internal controls within companies can lead to high quality financial reporting which, in turn, improves the quality of earnings.

4 Internal Control in Microfinance

The evolution of the microfinance industry increasingly emphasises the importance of mission fulfilment and sustainability of MFIs (Boss & Millone, 2015). However, existing tools to measure performance against planned goals may not be appropriate, according to the outreach (number of clients served and quality of products provided) and sustainability (generation of sufficient income to cover opportunity cost) of MFIs. There is still little research on the contribution of internal control in microfinance as a regulatory and normative tool to optimise resources and achieve efficient administrative and financial management in this industry. Although there are previous works that address the efficiency of MFIs (e.g., Gutiérrez-Nieto et al. (2007), Hermes et al. (2011), Haq et al. (2009), Bogan (2012) and Bayai and Ikhide (2016)), contributing greatly to the literature, there continues to be a dearth of research analysing the effects on internal control and the impact it has on financial variables in microfinance.

In addressing the relationship between internal control and financial distress in emerging markets, Chan and Hameed (2006) and Xiang et al. (2014) argue that financial distress varies across different capital markets, internal control standards, and management behaviours, due to historical, political, regulatory, cultural, and social differences. In the case of banks, which have remained in focus over the past decades (Cho & Chung, 2016) have been able to use internal control to accurately understand credit losses and adjust their financial statements with real information, demonstrating a close relationship between reserves and provisions set aside for potential credit losses of banks.

Authors such as Amudo and Inanga (2009), Ayagre et al. (2014), Gamage et al. (2014), Phan (2005), Phan (2007), Dung (2007), Dao and Le (2012), Nguyen (2015), Yakubu et al. (2017), Nguyen (2018), Shaman and Senan (2019), and Kumuthinidevi (2016) argue that the effectiveness of internal control in banking institutions through the factors of the COSO report has a positive effect on the performance and security of organisations, provided that the situation and characteristics of the country or countries to be analysed are taken into consideration. The study variables used in the research of Shaman and Senan (2019) focused on examining management effectiveness through surveys based on the five components of internal control (control environment, risk assessment, accounting information system and communication system, control activities, and self-monitoring), which have an impact on the effectiveness of internal control. The study concludes that banks in Saudi Arabia have a satisfactory internal control system. Sebiel (2008) and Wardiwiyono (2012) state that focusing on effective internal control allows for a reassessment of the participatory process in order to reduce operational risk and ensure sustainability, in line with the Committee of Sponsoring Organisations (COSO) benchmarks (Wardiwiyono, 2012).

Sultana and Haque (2011) conducted a critical evaluation of the internal control structures in six listed banks in Bangladesh, ensuring that the activities of these organisations are carried out in accordance with the stated procedures and objectives. The results of the study show that a large part of the study sample is successful in meeting the objectives of the control components. The case study by Pham et al. (2020) demonstrates that internal control of lending activities in commercial banks in Vietnam is essential to prevent the risk of asset loss in the bank's lending operations. According to Sulung (2017), the role of internal control system in Islamic microfinance cooperatives for micro and small enterprises plays an important role in managing credit risk in the three stages: ex ante (refinancing), financing, and ex post (co-financing), based on the COSO components, concluding that regular monitoring plays an important role in reducing the risk for loans. On the other hand, Ndiaye et al. (2019) find, through a multiple regression analysis, that all dimensions of internal control are positively and significantly associated with the four profitability indices of MFIs in Senegal.

Based on the above arguments, it can be noted that the internal control system is the cornerstone in organisations, especially in financial institutions, taking into account the impact on a nation's economy (Kumuthinidevi, 2016). Through internal control, efforts are made to prevent frauds that cause economic damage to the financial sector, thereby safeguarding the security of the financial and monetary system by creating stability and promoting the development of the countries (Ayagre et al., 2014).

5 Internal Control in Microfinance in Ecuador

Microfinance institutions are growing rapidly and reaching many households as well as small businesses. The development of these community-based financial institutions has been inspired by models that have emerged in other countries, such as the rural savings banks in Spain, the Credit Agricole in France, or the artisan banks in Italy. In Latin America, this model has been acquiring its own characteristics, focusing its strategy on deepening access to microfinance products where formal banking does not reach, providing financial services to the vulnerable population and seeking to efficiently serve the population at the bottom of the pyramid, especially in rural areas.

The experience in Ecuador shows that internal control is essential in the management of institutions in the popular and solidarity sector, allowing the inclusion of dependencies and actors of an organisation to ensure the fulfilment of its objectives in at least three categories: efficiency and effectiveness, reliability, and compliance with rules and regulations. According to Muhammad (2004) and Sulung (2017), internal control has benefits in terms of sustainability, applying prudent concepts in the delivery of funding in MFIs, effects that have already been demonstrated in conventional financial institutions (Wardiwiyono 2012; Ndiaye et al. 2019; Kule et al. 2020). However, the implementation of internal control systems for operational risk reduction in the popular and solidarity sector is both a challenge and an opportunity. Many MFIs are unaware of the benefits of internal control and how it can support their operations.

Aware of the leading role that this type of organisation is playing in Ecuador, the Superintendency of Popular and Solidarity Economy seeks to promote and strengthen the sector, providing it with the necessary instruments and mechanisms of protection, development, and control to promote efficient financial and non-financial services with a perspective that rescues cooperative principles and values and human and territorial development. In Ecuador, these organisations, known as popular and solidarity organisations, have emerged as the fourth largest economic sector in the country.

The Popular and Solidarity Economic Sector is made up of:

1. The popular and solidarity-based financial sector-SFPS, made up of:
   (a) Savings and credit cooperatives.
   (b) Central boxes.
   (c) Associative or solidarity-based institutions, community banks, and savings banks.
   (d) Ancillary services entities.,

(a) Savings and loan associations and mutual housing associations.

2. The Popular and Solidarity Economy-EPS, classified into:
   (a) Production cooperatives.
   (b) Consumer cooperatives.
   (c) Housing cooperatives.
   (d) Service cooperatives.
   (e) Productive partnerships.
   (f) Community organisations.

In the face of the unbridled growth of these institutions, the Superintendency of Popular and Solidarity Economy (SEPS) has established control guidelines defined in different legal bodies:

1. Organic Monetary and Financial Code (Código Orgánico Monetario y Financiero-COMYF).
2. Organic Law of Popular and Solidarity Economy—LOEPS.
3. Resolutions issued by the Monetary and Financial Policy and Regulation Board.
4. Resolutions issued by the Superintendency of Popular and Solidarity Economy.

Through the issuance of standards, efforts have been made to promote the internal control (administrative, financial, and accounting) of popular and solidarity economy organisations, as well as to strengthen risk management, regulate supervision, merger and liquidation processes, which have contributed to the prevention of money laundering and the financing of crimes. To date, 107 regulatory and control standards have been issued since 2013, 22 of which were developed in 2016.

Table 5 presents the regulations issued and issued by the Superintendency of Popular and Solidarity Economy, together with its legal body, to the financial sector.

Table 5 Standards issued by SEPS

Resolution	Standard	Date	Description
SEPS-IGPJ-2013-008	Rule on the use of electronic media keys by the Superintendence of HPS	15/02/2013	Use of electronic media keys duly signed by your legal representative
SEPS-IGT-IFPS-IGPJ-IR--IEN-2015-016	Standard for the imposition of sanctions in the popular and solidarity-based financial sector	11/03/2015	Definitions, subjects liable for sanctions, degree of sanctions
SEPS-IFMR-IGJ-2016-208	Procedure for the disposal of assets of financial and non-financial cooperatives in liquidation	16/09/2015	It details the procedure to be followed for the sale of the assets of cooperatives in liquidation
SEPS-IGT-IFMR-IGJ-DNN-2016-070	Regulation on the qualification, appointment, and responsibilities of temporary administrators and liquidators of entities in the popular and solidarity-based financial sector	28/03/2016	It establishes the requirements for the qualification of temporary administrators and liquidators of the Popular and Solidarity Financial Sector entities, as well as their responsibilities, fees, and obligations to the organisation
SEPS-IGT-ISF-ITICA-IGJ-2016-226	Single Chart of Accounts	31/10/2016	Defines the format for the presentation of the accounting record of administrative, economic, and social actions of HPS organisations
SEPS-IGT-IFMR-DNLQSNF-IGJ-2017-034	Amendment to Resolution No. SEPS-INEPS-IGPJ-2013-010 (Special Regulations on Interventions, Liquidations and Qualification of Specialists for Cooperatives)	24/03/2017	It includes two new obligations to be fulfilled by controllers or liquidators of cooperatives in the financial sector. At the same time, it modifies the calculation of fees for level 2 financial controllers of cooperatives
SEPS-IGT-IGJ-2018-003	Reform of the subject index of documents classified as confidential	17/01/2018	Contains amendments to Resolution No. SEPS-IENIGPJ-IFPS-INEPS-INEPS-IR-2015-008 of 2 March 2015
SEPS-IGT-IGJ-2018-008	Subject Index of Documents Classified as Restricted	16/02/2018	Lists the documents which, in accordance with legal provisions, are kept confidential from the general public
436-2018-F	Regulation for the establishment and registration of community banks and savings banks	19/01/2018	It establishes the requirements for the establishment and registration of community banks and savings banks

(continued)

Table 5 (continued)

Resolution	Standard	Date	Description
446-2018-F	Rule amending Section XIV that contains the "Financial services rule of the entities of the popular and solidarity financial sector", of Chapter XXXVI (popular and solidarity financial sector), of Book I (Monetary and Financial System), of the Codification of Monetary, Financial, Securities and Insurance Resolutions; issued by the Monetary and Financial Policy and Regulation Board	07/03/2018	Annexes 1, 2, and 3 of the "Financial services regulation of the entities of the popular and solidarity financial sector", related to the charges for basic, maximum, and differentiated financial services, are replaced
SEPS-IGT-ISF-IGJ-2018-0105	Control standard for the qualification and supervision of companies and organisations providing auxiliary services in the popular and solidarity financial sector	06/04/2018	Establishes the requirements to be met by auxiliary services companies and organisations in order to obtain the qualification of the Superintendence of Popular and Solidarity Economy
SEPS-IGT-ISF-IR-IGJ-2018-0150	Rule for the pre-authorisation of bond issuance and securitisation of credit unions	23/05/2018	This resolution establishes the requirements that credit unions in segments 1 and 2 must comply with in order to obtain from SEPS the approval resolution for the issuance of bonds or the positive criteria for securitisation
SEPS-IGT-SGE-IGJ-2018-016	Control standard for sending and receiving information and notifications	05/07/2018	It regulates the delivery of requests, writings, communications, and any type of information to the Superintendency of Popular and Solidarity Economy, through electronic means or channels, and the notifications of administrative actions and information requirements made or sent by this Control Body

Table 5 (continued)

Resolution	Standard	Date	Description
SEPS-IGT-IGJ-2018-017	Repeal of resolutions of the Superintendency of Popular and Solidarity Economy due to the entry into force of the Organic Administrative Code (COA)	06/07/2018	Repeals the resolutions:—Regulations for Handling Complaints. – Regulations for the exercise of Coactive Jurisdiction in the Superintendence of Popular and Solidarity Economy. – Regulations on Administrative Appeals of the Superintendency of Popular and Solidarity Economy. – First and Second General Provisions of the resolution "Rules for the Imposition of Sanctions in the popular and solidarity-based financial sector"
SEPS-IGT-IR-IGJ-2018-021	Reform of the "Control regulation for opening, transferring, and closing offices of savings and credit cooperatives, mutual savings, and credit associations for housing and central banks"	16/07/2018	Amends resolution No. SEPS-IGT-ITICAIGJ-2017-101 of 17 November 2017, related to outreach windows and public fund collection service
SEPS-IGT-IFPS-IEN-IGP-2015-087	Reformulation of the Single Chart of Accounts for the Deposit Insurance Trust Fund for the Popular and Solidarity Financial Sector	28/07/2018	Standardises a format for the accounting record of the operations of the Single Chart of Accounts of the Deposit Insurance Trust of the Popular and Solidarity Financial Sector
SEPS-ISFPS-INEPS-IGPJ-2015-155	Reformulation of the Standards for the Qualification of Auditors of SFPS and SNFPS Entities	28/07/2018	It sets out the procedure for convening the General Assembly in the event that the intervention of a co-operative is completed before the deadline
SEPS-IFMR-IGJ-2018-028	Summary liquidations of organisations subject to the control of the Superintendency of Popular and Solidarity Economy	03/08/2018	Determines the procedure for the summary liquidation of organisations that have no assets and have not carried out any economic activity or have not carried out any economic activity and have no assets
SEPS-IGT-IGJ-2018-030	Reform of the "Thematic Index of Documents Classified as Restricted"	13/08/2018	Repeals Article 4 of Resolution No. SEPS-IGTIGJ-2018-008 of 16 February 2018

(continued)

Table 5 (continued)

Resolution	Standard	Date	Description
SEPS-IGT-ISF-ITICAIGJ-2018-052	Amends the Annex to Resolution No. SEPS-IGTISF-ITICA-IGJ-2016-226 of 31 October 2016	03/09/2018	Modifies the Single Chart of Accounts for savings and credit cooperatives, the National Corporation of Popular and Solidarity Finance (CONAFIPS), and mutual savings and credit associations for housing
459-2018-F	Regulation amending Section XI (Regulation for the Prevention of Money Laundering and Financing of Crimes including Terrorism in the financial institutions of the EPS), Chapter XXXVI, Book I of the Codification of Monetary, Financial, Securities and Insurance Resolutions	28/09/2018	Amendments introduced by the amendments to the "General Regulations to the Organic Law on the Prevention, Detection and Eradication of Money Laundering and the Financing of Crime"
SEPS-IGT-IR-IGJ-2018-0259	Reformatory rule to Resolution No. SEPS-IGT-IRIGJ-2018-021 of 13 July 2018 "Control rule regarding physical and electronic security"	10/10/2018	It includes transitional provisions regarding the implementation of the standard due to the update of the segments carried out by the Superintendency in 2018
463-2018-F*	Includes Chapter LIII (Financial Users), in Title II (National Financial System), Book I (Monetary and Financial System) of the Codification of Monetary, Financial, Securities and Insurance Resolutions	26/10/2018	It regulates aspects related to debits or charges for non-financial services to members, customers, and users, provided by natural or legal persons outside the financial activity
SEPS-IGT-IR-IGJ-2018-0279	Control standard for the management of operational risk and legal risk in the entities of the popular and solidarity financial sector governed by the Superintendency of Popular and Solidarity Economy	26/11/2018	It regulates the management of operational risk and legal risk for an adequate comprehensive risk management, in order to minimise losses that may arise from events caused by failures or inadequacies of processes, people, information technology, and external events
470-2018-F	Regulation that determines the requirements and conditions for income tax exemption in the merger of entities in the popular and solidarity-based financial sector	30/11/2018	Applies to credit unions involved in merger processes

Table 5 (continued)

Resolution	Standard	Date	Description
SEPS-IGT-IR-IGJ-2018-0284	Reformatory rule to Resolution No. SEPS-IGTIR-IGJ-2018-0279 of 26 November 2018 containing the "Control rule for the management of operational risk and legal risk in the SFPS entities under the control of the SEPS"	13/12/2018	Replaces the definition of "Continuity Plan"
493-2018-F	Rule for the Constitution, Operation and Liquidation of the Trust established in article 312 of the Organic Monetary and Financial Code	28/12/2018	It regulates the entities of the national financial system that are subject to a compulsory liquidation process, which have assets, liabilities, equity, and other obligations that could not be liquidated once the term established in numeral 4 of article 307 of the Organic Monetary and Financial Code has expired
SEPS-IGT-IGS-IGJ-INGINT--DNRA-2020-021	Regulation of Administrative Appeals in the Superintendency of Popular and Solidarity Economy	28/09/2020	Resolves the procedure for hearing, substantiating, and resolving administrative appeals filed with the SEPS
SEPS-IGT-ISF-ITICA-IGJ-2016-225	Regulation issuing the Single Chart of Accounts for the Popular and Solidarity Financial Sector Liquidity Fund Trust	13/10/2020	Specifies a format for the Single Chart of Accounts for the purpose of keeping a record of the operations carried out by the Liquidity Fund of the Popular and Solidarity Financial Sector entities

Source: Own elaboration based on SEPS (2019)

Table 5 shows the resolutions issued to establish and strengthen a regulatory framework for the microfinance sector, promoting transparency and the provision of reliable and complete information from the organisations supervised by the technical body. In Ecuador, the gradual issuance of resolutions, from 2013 to the present, seeks to improve the microfinance sector and strengthen its regulatory framework, through the formulation of regulations, requirements, procedures, catalogues, sanctions, regulations, reforms, and modifications for operational and financial sustainability. It can also be seen that, during 2018, a large part of these resolutions was issued, achieving the sector's horizon to improve the internal control of the popular and solidarity-based financial sector. Resolution SEPS-IGT-IR-IGJ-2018-0279 establishes the controls to be carried out for the management of operational risk and legal risk in the five segments of the popular and solidarity financial sector.

Table 6 Control Standard for operational and legal risk management in the SFPS

Technology management structure			
Internal bodies	Segment 1 Central, mutual, and corporate savings banks	Segment 2	Segment 3
Information Technology Committee	X	X	N/A
Information Technology Unit	X	X	N/A
Head of Information Technology	N/A	N/A	X
Transitional provisions			
Process Management Manual	X	X	X
Operational Risk Manual	X	X	X
Register of identified risk events	X	X	
Contingency and continuity plans—ISO 22301 standard	X	X	N/A
Comprehensive process for supplier qualification and selection	X	X	X
Legal risk	X	X	X
Operational Risk			
Board of Directors	X	X	X
Integrated Risk Management Committee	X	X	X
The Unit or the risk manager	X	X	X
Internal and external auditors	X	X	X

Source: Own elaboration based on SEPS (2020)

Specifically, this resolution establishes compliance with information technology structures and management for segments 1, 2, and 3, corresponding to entities with the largest total assets, which are mutuals and savings and credit cooperatives that use policies, processes, procedures, and methodologies for their proper functioning, as shown in Table 6.

Table 6 shows the technology management structure, indicating the internal bodies that each segment must establish in order to comply with SEPS requirements. According to the table, the popular and solidarity financial sector in segments 1 and 2 are obliged to comply fully with the internal bodies, except for the IT manager. Segment 3 partially complies with these requirements.

With the new supervisory body, called SEPS, the cooperative sector began to be controlled in 2015, through Resolution No 038–2015, going from three to five segments according to the amount of total assets, which have monetary values in the accounts of members' contributions, assets, credit portfolio, and deposits. According to data issued by the Superintendency of Popular and Solidarity Economy (SEPS), detailed in Table 7, in April 2021 there were 518 entities, with $8,111,758 contribution certificates (member contributions), 67% of which are in segment 1. The gross loan portfolio of segments 1, 2, and 3 represents 68% of the assets of the popular and solidarity financial sector. With regard to the rate of change in the various accounts mentioned above, there was an increase of 5% in the contribution certificates, assets increased by 13%, the loan portfolio increased by 6%, and deposits increased by 15% year on year.

Table 7 Figures by segment of the Popular and Solidarity Financial Sector

Segments	Contribution certificates	Assets (USD Millions)	Credit portfolio (USD Millions)	Deposits (USD Millions)
Segment 1	5,433,708	14,721	10,084	11,978
Segment 2	1,343,500	2025	1568	1430
Segment 3	788,894	941	734	687
Segment 4	437,026	437	335	298
Segment 5	108,630	85	63	56
Total	8,111,758	18,209	12,784	14,449
Rate of change Feb 2020–Feb 2021	5%	13%	6%	15%

Source: (SEPS, 2021)

6 Conclusions

This chapter analyses internal control in the context of microfinance. It reviews different definitions of internal control, the perspectives of internal control in organisations, as well as the applications of internal control in financial sector institutions. Finally, the insertion of internal control in microfinance in Ecuador is explained.

Internal control arose as a response to corrupt and fraudulent acts in organisations of all kinds. Today, internal control is seen as a key element in the decision-making process in organisations, generating reliability of financial information through compliance with applicable laws and regulations and providing for effectiveness and efficiency of operations. The evolution in internal control thinking has come hand in hand with the growth of economic activity and the emergence of large business organisations, as a result of regulatory and competitive forces, creating reports, models, and laws with a broad conception of the global organisation. Despite the existence of various laws, models, or reports in different countries, the COSO model continues to be the benchmark as it makes extensive use of the risk-based approach, reflecting the internal control requirements in the financial sphere required by the Sarbanes Oxley Act. From a general perspective, adequate internal control in organisations leads to high quality financial reporting, better earnings, improved performance, and long-term stability.

References

Accountants, A. I. o. C. P. (1994). *Codification of statements on auditing standards*. Instituto Americano of Certified Public Accountants.

Accountants, A. I. o. C. P. (1996). *Codification of statements on auditing standards*. American Institute of Certified Public Accountants.

Amudo, A., & Inanga, E. (2009). Evaluation of internal control systems: A case study from Uganda. *International Research Journal of Finance and Economics, 27*, 125–144.

Ashbaugh-Skaife, H., Collins, D., Kinney, W. R., & La Fond, R. (2009). The effect of SOX internal control deficiencies on firm risk and cost of equity. *Journal of Accounting Research, 47*(1), 1–43.

Auditing, I. S. o. (1991). *Risk assessment and internal control*. International Federation of New York.

Ayagre, P., Gyamerah, I. A., & Naarctey. (2014). The effectiveness of internal control system of banks: The case of Ghanaian banks. *International Journal of Accounting and Financial Reporting, 4*(2), 377–389.

Balsam, S., Jiang, W., & Lu, B. (2014). Equity incentives and internal control weaknesses. *Contemporary Accounting Research, 31*, 178–201.

Bayai, L., & Ikhide, S. (2016). Financing and financial sustainability of microfinance institutions (MFIs): A conceptual view. *Bank and Bank Systems, 11*(2), 21–32.

Bogan, V. L. (2012). Capital structure and sustainability: An empirical study of microfinance institutions. *Review of Economics and Statistics, 94*(4), 1045–1058.

Boss, J. W., & Millone, M. (2015). Practice Ehat you preach: Microfinance business models and operational efficiency. *World Development, 70*, 28–42.

Chan, K., & Hameed, A. (2006). Stock price synchronicity and analyst coverage in emerging markets. *Journal of Financial Economics, 80*(1), 115–147.

Chan, K. C., Chen, Y., & Liu, B. (2020). The linear and non-linear effects of internal control and its five components on corporate innovation: Evidence from Chinese using the COSO framework. *European Accounting Review*.

Chen, X., Ma, Z., Shi, J., Tu, B., & Xu, S. (2020). Corporate social responsibility and unsecured debt: Evidence from China. *The Journal of Asian Finance, Economics and Business, 7*(11), 1–11.

Cheng, M., Dhaliwal, D., & Zhang, Y. (2013). Does investment efficiency improve after the disclosure of material weaknesses in internal control over financial reporting? *Journal of Accounting and Economics, 56*(1), 1–18.

Cho, M., & Chung, K.-H. (2016). The effect of commercial banks' internal control weaknesses on loan loss reserves and provisions. *Journal of Contemporary Accounting and Economics, 12*(1), 61–72.

CobiT, I. S. A. a. C. A. (1996). *Control objectives for information systems and related technology - CobiT*. s.l.: ISACA.

COSO, C. T. (1992). *Committee of Sponsoring Organizations of the Treadway – COSO*. Estados Unidos: Comisión Treadway.

COSO, C. o. S. O. o. t. T. (2013). *Internal control - Integrated framework*. Estados Unidos: Comisión Treadway.

Dai, I., & Song, D. (2018). The impact of mandatory design of performance targets of executive equity incentive contracts on corporate management performance. *China Industrial Economy, 4*, 117–136.

Dao, M., & Le, V. H. (2012). Internal control system associated with risk management at Vietnamese commercial banks in the current period. *Banking Magazine, 24*, 20–26.

Dashtbayaz, M. L., Salehi, M., & Safdel, T. (2019). The effect of internal controls on financial reporting quality in Iranian family firms. *Journal of Family Business Management, 9*(3), 254–270.

Doyle, J., Ge, W., & Mcvay, S. (2016). Determinants of weaknesses in internal control over financial reporting. *Journal of Accounting and Economics, 1–2*(193–223), 44.

Dung, V. (2007). Model of risk management organization in the bank. *Banking Magazine, 10*, 33–36.

Estupiñan, G. R. (2015). *Control interno y fraudes COSO I, II y III_Análisis de Informes con base a los siglos transaccionales*. 3era ed. Bogotá - Colombia: Ecoe Ediciones.

FCPA, C. d. l. E. U. (1977). Ley de Prácticas Corruptas en el Extranjero-FCPA, Congreso de los Esdados Unidos.

Gamage, C. T., Lock, K. L., & Fernando, A. A. (2014). A proposed research framework: Effectiveness of internal control system in state commercial banks in Sri Lanka. *International Journal of Scientific Research and Innovative Technology, 1*(5), 25–44.

Ge, W., & Mcvay, S. (2005). The disclosure of material weakness in internal control after the Sarbanes-Oxley Act. *Accounting Horizons, 19*(3), 137–158.

Guo, J., Huang, P., Zhang, Y., & Zhou, N. (2015). The effect of employee treatment policies on internal control weaknesses and financial restatements. *The Accounting Review, 91*(4), 1167–1194.

Gupta, P. K., & Sharma, S. (2023). Literature review on effect of microfinance institutions on poverty in South Asian countries and their sustainability. *International Journal of Emerging Markets, 18*(8), 1827–1845.

Gutiérrez-Nieto, B., Serrano-Cinca, C., & Mar-Molinero, C. (2007). Microfinance institutions and efficiency. *Omega, 35*(2), 131–142.

Hammersley, J., Myers, L., & Shakespeare, C. (2008). Market reactions to the disclosure oof internal control weaknesses and to the characteristics of those weaknesses under section 302 of the Sarbanes Oxley Act of 2002. *Review of Accounting Studies, 13*, 141–165.

Hanim, F., Haron, H., & Jantan, M. (2005). Internal audit practices and internal control systems. *Managerial Auditing Journal, 20*(8), 844–866.

Haq, M., Skully, M. T., & Pathan, S. (2009). *Efficiency of microfinance institutions: A data envelopment analysis* (Vol. 17, p. 63). Asia-Pacific Financial Markets.

Hermanson, H. M. (2000). An analysis of the demand for reporting on internal control. *Accounting Horizons, 14*(3), 325–341.

Hermes, N., Lensink, R., & Meesters, A. (2011). Outreach and efficiency of microfinance institutions. *World Development, 39*(6), 938–948.

Hoitash, R., Hoitash, U., & Johnstone, K. M. (2012). Internal control material weaknesses and CFO compensation. *Contemporary Accounting Research, 29*(3), 768–803.

Hu, J., Weng, Y.-C., & Wang, F. (2020). The effect of the internal control regulation on reporting quality. *Borsa Istanbul Review*, 2214–8450.

Husnaini, W., & Basuki, B. (2020). ASEAN corporate governance scorecard: Sustainability reporting and firm value. *Journal of Asian Finance Economics and Business, 7*(11), 315–326.

Järvinen, T., & Myllymäki, E.-R. (2016). Real earning management before and after reporting SOX 404 material weaknesses. *Accounting Horizons, 30*(1), 119–141.

Kendo, S., & Tchakounte, J. (2022). The drivers of the financial integration of microfinance institutions: Do financial development, agency costs and microfinance performance matter? *The Quarterly Review of Economics and Finance, 84*, 128–142.

Kim, J., Song, B., & Zhag, L. (2011). Internal control weakness and bank loan contracting: Evidence from SOX Section 404 disclosures. *The Accounting Review, 86*, 1157–1188.

Kule, B., Kamukama, N., & Kijjambu, N. (2020). Control environment and financial performance of savings and credit cooperatives (SACCOs) in Mid-Western Uganda. *Revista Internacional de Estrategias Empresariales, 5*(1), 15–26.

Kumuthinidevi, S. (2016). A study on effectiveness of the internal control system in the private banks of Trincomalee. *International Journal of Scientific and Publications, 6*(6), 600–612.

Laski, J. P. (2017). El control interno como estrategia de aprendizaje organizacional: El modelo COSO y sus alcances en América Latina. *Gestión y Estrategia, 34*(9), 9–24.

Li, C., Sun, L., & Ettredge, M. (2010). Financial executive qualifications, financial executive turnover, and adverse SOX 404 opinions. *Journal of Accounting & Economics, 50*(1), 93–110.

Lin, Y.-C., Wang, Y.-C., & Huang, H.-W. (2014). CEO characteristics and internal control quality. *Corporate Governance: An International Review, 22*(1), 24–42.

Mantilla, B. S. A. (2005). *Auditoría del Control Interno*, 4ta ed. Bogotá - Colombia: Ecoe Ediciones.

McMullen, D., Raghunandan, K., & Rama, D. V. (1996). Informes de control interno y problemas de informes financieros. *Asociación American de Contabilidad, 10*(4), 67.

Medina-López, P. (2015). *Análisis y aplicación del Modelo COSO de Control Interno en las áreas de Recursos Humanos de las organizaciones Sanitarias Públicas en Andalucía*. Universidad de Málaga.

Millichamp, A. (2000). *Auditing* (3rd ed.). Cengage Learning Emea.

Muhammad. (2004). *The fund management of Islamic Bank*. Ekonisia.

Ndiaye, G., Cheng, B., Azenga, V., & Juniter, K. (2019). The impact of internal control on the profitability of microfinance institutions in Senegal. *International Journal of Research in Business and Social Science, 8*(2), 41–51.

Nguyen, T. H. L. (2015). Lessons from the failure of the internal control system of commercial banks. *Auditing Science Journal, 3*.

Nguyen, P. (2018). Effectiveness of the internal control system in the private joint-stock commercial banks in Thai Nguyen Province, Vietnam. The 5th IBSM international conference on business. *Management and Accounting*, 766–780.

Nyakundi, D., Nyamita, M., & Tinega, T. (2014). Effect of internal control systems on financial performance of small and medium scale business Enterprises in Kisumu City, Kenya. *International Journal of Social Sciences and Entrepreneurship, 1*(11), 1–15.

Pham, Q., Thuy, H. X., Quyen, P. T. H., Truc, T. T. T., & Hien, N. T. D. (2020). Impact the internal control of the credit operations on the credit effectiveness of commercial banks: A case of HCMC and Dong Nai Province. *Academy of Strategic Management Journal, 19*(6), 1–11.

Phan, H. (2005). Internal inspection of commercial banks in the context of international economic integration. *Banking Magazine, 3*, 11–16.

Phan, V. (2007). Discuss the construction of an internal inspection and control system in commercial banks according to new requirements. *Banking Magazine, 8*, 23–26.

Phornlaphatrachkorn, K., & Na Kalasindhu, K. (2020). Internal control effectiveness and business survival: Evidence from Thai food businesses. *Journal of Asian Finance Economics and Business, 7*(12), 927–939.

Raghunandan, K., & Rama, D. V. (2006). SOX section 404 material weakness disclosures and audit fees. *Auditing A Journal of Practice & Theory, 25*(1), 99–114.

Rivas-Márquez, G. (2011). Modelos contemporáneos de control interno. *Fundamentos teóricos. Observatorio Laboral Revista Venezolana, 4*(8), 115–136.

SAC, I. o. I. A. (2002). *Sistemas de Control y Auditoría*. Instituto de Auditoría y Control de Sistemas.

SAS 78, I. A. d. C. P. C. (1995). *Statement on Auditing Standards*. s.l.: s.n.

Sebiel, H. (2008). Islamic microfinance in Indonesia: The challenge of institucional diversity, regulation, and supervision. *Journal of Social Issues in Southeast Asia, 23*(1), 86–103.

SEPS, S. d. E. P. y. S. (2019). *Informe de Rendición de Cuentas 2018*. Función de Transparencia y Control Social.

SEPS, S. d. E. P. y. S. (2020). *Superintendecia de Economía Popular y Solidaria*. Available at: https://apowerbi.com/view?r=eyJrIjoiZTA1ZTI3ZDMtYWI0My00ZjdlLWJmYTgtM2VkZWQ4ZTdiMDY0IiwidCI6ImMwNWUxMWU1LTcwNmMtNGNlZi1iYTVlLTE4ZWVkYmYxMDAzNyJ9

SEPS, S. d. E. P. y. S. (2021). *Actualidad y cifras*. SEPS.

Shaman, R., & Senan, N. (2019). A study on effectiveness of internal control system in selected banks in Saudi Arabia. *Asian Journal of Managerial Science, 8*(1), 41–47.

Skaife, H. A., Colins, D. W., Kinney, J. W. R., & Lafond, R. (2009). The effect of SOX internal control deficiencies on firm risk and cost of equity. *Journal of Accounting Research, 47*(1), 1–43.

SOX, U. C. (2002). *Ley Sarbanes-Oxley - SOX - Ley de Reforma de la Contabilidad Pública de Empresas y de Protección al Inversionista*. Inter-Affairs International Division.

Sultana, R., & Haque, M. E. (2011). Evaluation of internal control structure: Evidence from six listed banks in Bangladesh. *ASA University Review, 5*(1), 69–81.

Sulung, L. A. K. (2017). The role of internal control system in Islamic microfinance cooperatives for micro and small enterprises. *International Journal of Business Anthropology; Ocean Ridge, 7*(1), 113–136.

Tran, Q. T. L. T. T. & L. C. D. (2020). Effect of corporate governance on corporate social responsibility disclosure: Empirical evidence from Vietnamese commercial banks. *Journal of Asian Finance, Economics and Business, 7*(11), 327–333.

Van de Poel, K., & Vanstraelen, A. (2011). Management reporting on internal control and accruals quality: Insights from a "comply-or-explain" internal control regime. *Auditing A Journal of Practice & Theory, 30*(3), 181–209.

Wardiwiyono, S. (2012). Internal control system for Islamic micro financing: An exploratory study of Baitul Maal wat Tamwil in the City of Yogyakarta Indonesia. *International Journal of Islamic and Middle Eastern Finance and Management, 5*(4), 340–352.

Xiang, E., Tian, G., & Yang, F. (2014). Do mutual funds have information advantage? Evidence from seasoned equity offerings in China. *International Review of Financial Analysis, 31*, 70–79.

Yakubu, I., Adam, J., & Sumaila, M. (2017). The effectiveness of internal control system in safeguarding assets in the Ghanaian Nanking industry. *International Journal of Management and Commerce Innovations, 5*(1), 544–557.

Yu, S., & Neter, J. (1973). A stochastic model of the internal control system. *Journal of Accounting Research, 11*(2), 273–295.

Paola Martina Pucha Medina. Research Professor at the School of Business and Economics of Universidad del Pacífico. Financial Management Manager of the Business Consulting Group CAAPTES-Ecuador; Accredited Researcher by Senescyt (REG-INV-20-04346). Doctor in Legal and Business Sciences, Master in Management. Engineer in Finance. Dedicated from the business sector to contribute to the strengthening of the innovation ecosystem through work in national and international multidisciplinary teams. Additionally, she contributes in R+D+I processes, researching in lines related to Value and Risk Calculations in Investments; Quantitative Methods for Decision Making; Economics in Productive Sectors, among other areas, such as Corporate Social Responsibility (CSR) and Sustainable Finance.

Rebeca García-Ramos is Associate Professor of Finance in the Universidad de Cantabria (Spain) and Researcher of the Santander Financial Institute (SANFI). She is Graduate in Economics and Doctor of Business Administration by the University of Cantabria (UC), with a qualification of Distinction Cum Laude and International Mention. She has been visiting researcher of the Business School of the University of Essex (United Kingdom), the University of Oviedo (Spain), and the University of the Basque Country (Spain). Her researcher activity focuses on the field of Corporate Finance, Corporate Governance, CSR, Family Firms, and Gender Diversity, being author of several chapters in books and national and international prestigious scientific journals in her field. She has developed and coordinated several R+D reports about different economic issues requested by both public and private institutions. She is also referee of scientific journals in her field and has been part of various organizer and scientific committees of international conferences. Her research job has been awarded with several recognitions, as the "Jeff Rothstein Award for the Most Creative Paper", granted by the Family Firm Institute (FFI) and Hubler Family Business Consultants, or the "Research Award of the Section of Family Business" granted by the Spanish Scientific Association of Economy and Business Management, among others.

Belén Díaz Díaz holds a Ph.D. in Finance. She is Associate Professor of Finance at the University of Cantabria (Spain) and Academic Director at Santander Financial Institute (SANFI). Previously, she has been Vice-Dean of the Faculty of Economics and Business Administration and Director of Campus and Social Development at the University of Cantabria. She has been visiting researcher at the University of California in Berkeley, the London School of Economics, the University of Technology in Sydney, and at different universities in Mexico, Chile, Brazil, Argentina, and Morocco. Professor Díaz is author of several papers about CSR, Corporate Governance, banking and corporate finance in academic journals and books. The quality of her research was recognized with the "Sanchis Alcover Award", awarded by the Scientific Association of Economy and Management in 2006. Since 1996, she has written several reports and developed more than 50 R&D projects about different financial and economic issues commissioned by different public and private entities.

Index

B. Díaz Díaz et al. (eds.), *Building Global Societies Towards an ESG World*, CSR, Sustainability, Ethics & Governance,
https://doi.org/10.1007/978-3-031-56619-6

Printed by Printforce, the Netherlands